Lecture Notes in Computer Science 8084

Commenced Publication in 1973
Founding and Former Series Editors:
Gerhard Goos, Juris Hartmanis, and Jan van Leeuwen

Editorial Board

David Hutchison
  Lancaster University, UK
Takeo Kanade
  Carnegie Mellon University, Pittsburgh, PA, USA
Josef Kittler
  University of Surrey, Guildford, UK
Jon M. Kleinberg
  Cornell University, Ithaca, NY, USA
Alfred Kobsa
  University of California, Irvine, CA, USA
Friedemann Mattern
  ETH Zurich, Switzerland
John C. Mitchell
  Stanford University, CA, USA
Moni Naor
  Weizmann Institute of Science, Rehovot, Israel
Oscar Nierstrasz
  University of Bern, Switzerland
C. Pandu Rangan
  Indian Institute of Technology, Madras, India
Bernhard Steffen
  TU Dortmund University, Germany
Madhu Sudan
  Microsoft Research, Cambridge, MA, USA
Demetri Terzopoulos
  University of California, Los Angeles, CA, USA
Doug Tygar
  University of California, Berkeley, CA, USA
Gerhard Weikum
  Max Planck Institute for Informatics, Saarbruecken, Germany

Günther Ruhe   Yuanyuan Zhang (Eds.)

Search Based
Software Engineering

5th International Symposium, SSBSE 2013
St. Petersburg, Russia, August 24-26, 2013
Proceedings

 Springer

Volume Editors

Günther Ruhe
University of Calgary
2500 University Drive NW
Calgary, AB T2N 1N4, Canada
E-mail: ruhe@ucalgary.ca

Yuanyuan Zhang
University Colleage London
Department of Computer Science
Gower Street
WC1E 6BT London, UK
E-mail: yuanyuan.zhang@ucl.ac.uk

ISSN 0302-9743   e-ISSN 1611-3349
ISBN 978-3-642-39741-7   e-ISBN 978-3-642-39742-4
DOI 10.1007/978-3-642-39742-4
Springer Heidelberg Dordrecht London New York

Library of Congress Control Number: 2013943912

CR Subject Classification (1998): D.2, D.4, D.1, F.1-2, H.3

LNCS Sublibrary: SL 2 – Programming and Software Engineering

© Springer-Verlag Berlin Heidelberg 2013
This work is subject to copyright. All rights are reserved by the Publisher, whether the whole or part of
the material is concerned, specifically the rights of translation, reprinting, reuse of illustrations, recitation,
broadcasting, reproduction on microfilms or in any other physical way, and transmission or information
storage and retrieval, electronic adaptation, computer software, or by similar or dissimilar methodology
now known or hereafter developed. Exempted from this legal reservation are brief excerpts in connection
with reviews or scholarly analysis or material supplied specifically for the purpose of being entered and
executed on a computer system, for exclusive use by the purchaser of the work. Duplication of this publication
or parts thereof is permitted only under the provisions of the Copyright Law of the Publisher's location,
in its current version, and permission for use must always be obtained from Springer. Permissions for use
may be obtained through RightsLink at the Copyright Clearance Center. Violations are liable to prosecution
under the respective Copyright Law.
The use of general descriptive names, registered names, trademarks, service marks, etc. in this publication
does not imply, even in the absence of a specific statement, that such names are exempt from the relevant
protective laws and regulations and therefore free for general use.
While the advice and information in this book are believed to be true and accurate at the date of publication,
neither the authors nor the editors nor the publisher can accept any legal responsibility for any errors or
omissions that may be made. The publisher makes no warranty, express or implied, with respect to the
material contained herein.

Typesetting: Camera-ready by author, data conversion by Scientific Publishing Services, Chennai, India

Printed on acid-free paper

Springer is part of Springer Science+Business Media (www.springer.com)

Preface

Message from the SSBSE 2013 General Chair

It is my pleasure to welcome you to the proceedings of the 5th Symposium on Search-Based Software Engineering, SSBSE 2013, held in St. Petersburg, Russia, once the imperial capital of Russia. For the second time in the history of SSBSE, the symposium was co-located with the joint meeting of the European Software Engineering Conference and the ACM SIGSOFT Symposium on the Foundations of Software Engineering, ESEC/FSE. With work on search-based software engineering (SBSE) now becoming common in mainstream software engineering conferences like ESEC/FSE, SBSE offers an increasingly popular and exciting field to work in. The wide range of topics covered by SBSE is reflected in the strong collection of papers presented in this volume.

Many people contributed to the organization of this event and its proceedings, and so there are many people to thank. I am grateful to Bertrand Meyer, the General Chair of ESEC/FSE, and the ESEC/FSE Steering Committee for allowing us to co-locate with their prestigious event in St. Petersburg. Thanks in particular are due to Nadia Polikarpova and Lidia Perovskaya, who took care of the local arrangements and the interface between ESEC/FSE and SSBSE.

It was a pleasure to work with Yuanyuan Zhang and Guenther Ruhe, our Program Chairs. Many thanks for their hard work in managing the Program Committee, review process, and putting the program together. Thanks also go to Gregory Kapfhammer, who managed the Graduate Student Track with a record number of submissions. I would also like to thank Phil McMinn, who fearlessly accepted the challenge of setting up the new SSBSE challenge track. The SSBSE challenge is a wonderful opportunity to showcase the advances and achievements of our community, and will hopefully become an integral part of this series of events. I would like to thank the Program Committee, who supported all these tracks throughout a long and fragmented review process with their invaluable efforts in reviewing and commenting on the papers. I am very happy we were able to host two outstanding keynote speakers, Xin Yao and Westley Weimer, and David White with a tutorial. Finally, the program could not be formed without the work of the authors themselves, whom we thank for their high-quality work.

Thanks are also due to the Publicity Chairs, Shin Yoo, Kirsten Walcott-Justive, and Dongsum Kim. In particular I would like to thank Shin Yoo for managing our social networks on Twitter and Facebook, and maintaining our webpage, even from within airport taxis. Thanks to Fedor Tsarev, our Local Chair. I am grateful to Springer for publishing the proceedings of SSBSE. Thanks also to the Steering Committee, chaired by Mark Harman, and the General Chair of SSBSE 2012, Angelo Susi, who provided me with useful suggestions during the preparation of the event.

Finally, thanks are due to our sponsors, and to Tanja Vos for her support in securing industrial sponsorship. Thanks to UCL CREST, Google, Microsoft Research, Berner & Mattner, IBM, the FITTEST project, the RISCOSS project, and Softeam. Thanks also to Gillian Callaghan and Joanne Suter at the University of Sheffield, who assisted me in managing the finances of this event.

If you were not able to attend SSBSE 2013, I hope that you will enjoy reading the papers contained in this volume, and consider submitting a paper to SSBSE 2014.

June 2013   Gordon Fraser

Message from the SSBSE 2013 Program Chairs

On behalf of the SSBSE 2013 Program Committee, it is our pleasure to present these *Proceedings of the 5th International Symposium on Search-Based Software Engineering*. This year, the symposium was held in the beautiful and historic city of St. Petersburg, Russia. SSBSE 2013 continued the established tradition of bringing together the international SBSE community in an annual event to discuss and to celebrate the most recent results and progress in the field.

For the first time, SSBSE 2013 invited submissions to the SBSE Challenge Track. We challenged researchers to use their SBSE expertise and apply their existing tools by analyzing all or part of a software program from a selected list. We were happy to receive submissions from 156 authors coming from 24 different countries (Australia, Austria, Brazil, Canada, China, Czech Republic, Finland, France, Germany, India, Ireland, Luxembourg, New Zealand, Norway, Portugal, Russia, Spain, Sweden, Switzerland, The Netherlands, Tunisia, Turkey, UK and USA).

In all, 50 papers were submitted to the Research, Graduate Student and SBSE Challenge Tracks (39 to the Research Track - full and short papers, 4 to the SBSE Challenge Track, and 9 to the PhD Student Track). All submitted papers were reviewed by at least three experts in the field. After further discussions, 28 papers were accepted for presentation at the symposium. Fourteen submissions were accepted as full research papers and six were accepted as short papers. Six submissions were accepted as Graduate Student papers. In the SBSE Challenge Track, two papers were accepted.

We would like to thank all the members of the SSBSE 2013 Program Committee. Their continuing support was essential in improving the quality of accepted submissions and the resulting success of the conference. We also wish to especially thank the General Chair, Gordon Fraser, who managed the organization of every single aspect in order to make the conference special to all of us. We thank Gregory Kapfhammer, SSBSE 2013 Student Track Chair, for managing the submissions of the bright young minds who will be responsible for the future of the SBSE field. We also thank Phil McInn, who managed the challenge of attracting submissions and successfully running the new challenge track. Last, but certainly not least, we would like to thank Kornelia Streb for all her enthusiastic support and contribution in preparation of these proceedings.

Maintaining a successful tradition, SSBSE 2013 attendees had the opportunity to learn from experts both from the research fields of search as well as software engineering, in two outstanding keynotes and one tutorial talk. This year, we had the honor of receiving a keynote from Westley Weimer on "Advances in Automated Program Repair and a Call to Arms" and providing a survey on the recent success and momentum in the subfield of automated program repair. Furthermore, we had a keynote from Xin Yao, who talked about the state of the art in "Multi-objective Approaches to Search-Based Software Engineering." In addition, a tutorial was presented by David White on the emerging topic of "Cloud Computing and SBSE."

We would like to thank all the authors who submitted papers to SSBSE 2013, regardless of acceptance or rejection, and everyone who attended the conference. We hope that with these proceedings, anybody who did not have the chance to be in St. Petersburg will have the opportunity to feel the liveliness, growth and increasing impact of the SBSE community. Above all, we feel honored for the opportunity to serve as Program Chairs of SSBSE and we hope that everyone enjoyed the symposium!

June 2013   Guenther Ruhe
                                                            Yuanyuan Zhang

Conference Organization

General Chair

Gordon Fraser — University of Sheffield, UK

Program Chairs

Guenther Ruhe — University of Calgary, Canada
Yuanyuan Zhang — University College London, UK

Doctoral Symposium Chair

Gregory M. Kapfhammer — Allegheny College, USA

Program Committee

Enrique Alba	University of Málaga, Spain
Nadia Alshahwan	University of Luxembourg, Luxembourg
Giuliano Antoniol	Ecole Polytechnique de Montrèal, Canada
Andrea Arcuri	Simula Research Laboratory, Norway
Marcio Barros	Universidade Federal do Estado do Rio de Janeiro, Brazil
Leonardo Bottaci	University of Hull, UK
Francisco Chicano	University of Málaga, Spain
John Clark	University of York, UK
Mel Ó Cinnéide	University College Dublin, Ireland
Myra Cohen	University of Nebraska at Lincoln, USA
Massimiliano Di Penta	University of Sannio, Italy
Robert Feldt	University of Blekinge, Chalmers University of Technology, Sweden
Vahid Garousi	University of Calgary, Cadana
Mathew Hall	University of Sheffield, UK
Mark Harman	University College London, UK
Rob Hierons	Brunel University, UK
Colin Johnson	University of Kent, UK
Fitsum Meshesha Kifetew	University of Trento, Italy
Yvan Labiche	Carleton University, Canada
Kiran Lakhotia	University College London, UK
Spiros Mancoridis	Drexel University, USA
Phil McMinn	University of Sheffield, UK

Alan Millard	University of York, UK
Leandro Minku	University of Birmingham, UK
Pasqualina Potena	University of Bergamo, Italy
Simon Poulding	University of York, UK
Xiao Qu	ABB Corporate Research, USA
Marek Reformat	University of Alberta, USA
Marc Roper	University of Strathclyde, UK
Federica Sarro	University College London, UK
Jerffeson Souza	State University of Ceara, Brazil
Angelo Susi	Fondazione Bruno Kessler – IRST, Italy
Paolo Tonella	Fondazione Bruno Kessler – IRST, Italy
Silvia Vergilio	Universidade Federal do Paraná, Brazil
Tanja Vos	Universidad Politécnica de Valencia, Spain
Joachim Wegener	Berner and Mattner, Germany
Westley Weimer	University of Virginia, USA
David White	University of Glasgow, UK

Challenge Chair

Phil McMinn	University of Sheffield, UK

Publicity Committee

Shin Yoo	University College London, UK (Chair)
Kristen Walcott-Justice	University of Colorado/Colorado Spring, USA
Dongsun Kim	Hong Kong University of Science & Technology, Hong Kong

Local Chair

Fedor Tsarev	St. Petersburg State University of Information Technologies, Mechanics and Optics, Russia

Steering Committee

Mark Harman	UCL, UK
Andrea Arcuri	Simula, Norway
Myra Cohen	University of Nebraska Lincoln, USA
Massimiliano Di Penta	University of Sannio, Italy
Gordon Fraser	University of Sheffield, UK
Phil McMinn	University of Sheffield, UK
Mel Ó Cinnéide	University College Dublin, Ireland
Jerffeson Souza	Universidade Estadual do Ceara, Brazil
Joachim Wegener	Berner and Mattner, Germany

Sponsors

Table of Contents

Keynote Addresses

Advances in Automated Program Repair and a Call to Arms 1
Westley Weimer

Some Recent Work on Multi-objective Approaches to Search-Based
Software Engineering 4
Xin Yao

Tutorial

Cloud Computing and SBSE 16
David R. White

Full Papers

On the Application of the Multi-Evolutionary and Coupling-Based
Approach with Different Aspect-Class Integration Testing Strategies 19
Wesley Klewerton Guez Assunção, Thelma Elita Colanzi,
Silvia Regina Vergilio, and Aurora Pozo

An Experimental Study on Incremental Search-Based Software
Engineering 34
Márcio de Oliveira Barros

Competitive Coevolutionary Code-Smells Detection 50
Mohamed Boussaa, Wael Kessentini, Marouane Kessentini,
Slim Bechikh, and Soukeina Ben Chikha

A Multi-objective Genetic Algorithm to Rank State-Based Test
Cases 66
Lionel Briand, Yvan Labiche, and Kathy Chen

Validating Code-Level Behavior of Dynamic Adaptive Systems in the
Face of Uncertainty 81
Erik M. Fredericks, Andres J. Ramirez, and Betty H.C. Cheng

Model Refactoring Using Interactive Genetic Algorithm 96
Adnane Ghannem, Ghizlane El Boussaidi, and Marouane Kessentini

A Fine-Grained Parallel Multi-objective Test Case Prioritization
on GPU 111
Zheng Li, Yi Bian, Ruilian Zhao, and Jun Cheng

Search-Based Refactoring Detection Using Software Metrics
Variation   126
    Rim Mahouachi, Marouane Kessentini, and Mel Ó Cinnéide

Automated Model-in-the-Loop Testing of Continuous Controllers Using
Search   141
    Reza Matinnejad, Shiva Nejati, Lionel Briand,
    Thomas Bruckmann, and Claude Poull

Predicting Regression Test Failures Using Genetic Algorithm-Selected
Dynamic Performance Analysis Metrics   158
    Michael Mayo and Simon Spacey

A Recoverable Robust Approach for the Next Release Problem   172
    Matheus Henrique Esteves Paixão and Jerffeson Teixeira de Souza

A Systematic Review of Software Requirements Selection and
Prioritization Using SBSE Approaches   188
    Antônio Mauricio Pitangueira, Rita Suzana P. Maciel,
    Márcio de Oliveira Barros, and Aline Santos Andrade

Regression Testing for Model Transformations: A Multi-objective
Approach   209
    Jeffery Shelburg, Marouane Kessentini, and Daniel R. Tauritz

Provably Optimal and Human-Competitive Results in SBSE
for Spectrum Based Fault Localisation   224
    Xiaoyuan Xie, Fei-Ching Kuo, Tsong Yueh Chen, Shin Yoo, and
    Mark Harman

Short Papers

On the Synergy between Search-Based and Search-Driven Software
Engineering   239
    Colin Atkinson, Marcus Kessel, and Marcus Schumacher

Preference-Based Many-Objective Evolutionary Testing Generates
Harder Test Cases for Autonomous Agents   245
    Sabrine Kalboussi, Slim Bechikh, Marouane Kessentini, and
    Lamjed Ben Said

Efficient Subdomains for Random Testing   251
    Matthew Patrick, Rob Alexander, Manuel Oriol, and John A. Clark

Applying Genetic Improvement to MiniSAT   257
    Justyna Petke, William B. Langdon, and Mark Harman

Using Contracts to Guide the Search-Based Verification of Concurrent
Programs 263
    Christopher M. Poskitt and Simon Poulding

Planning Global Software Development Projects Using Genetic Algorithms 269
    *Sriharsha Vathsavayi, Outi Sievi-Korte, Kai Koskimies, and
    Kari Systä*

Challenge Track Papers

What Can a Big Program Teach Us about Optimization? 275
    Márcio de Oliveira Barros and Fábio de Almeida Farzat

eCrash: An Empirical Study on the Apache Ant Project 282
    *Ana Filipa Nogueira, José Carlos Bregieiro Ribeiro,
    Francisco Fernández de Vega, and Mário Alberto Zenha-Rela*

Graduate Track Papers

A Multi-objective Genetic Algorithm for Generating Test Suites from
Extended Finite State Machines 288
    Nesa Asoudeh and Yvan Labiche

An Approach to Test Set Generation for Pair-Wise Testing Using
Genetic Algorithms 294
    *Priti Bansal, Sangeeta Sabharwal, Shreya Malik,
    Vikhyat Arora, and Vineet Kumar*

Generation of Tests for Programming Challenge Tasks Using
Helper-Objectives 300
    Arina Buzdalova, Maxim Buzdalov, and Vladimir Parfenov

The Emergence of Useful Bias in Self-focusing Genetic Programming
for Software Optimisation 306
    Brendan Cody-Kenny and Stephen Barrett

Exploring Optimal Service Compositions in Highly Heterogeneous and
Dynamic Service-Based Systems 312
    *Dionysios Efstathiou, Peter McBurney, Steffen Zschaler, and
    Johann Bourcier*

Applying Search in an Automatic Contract-Based Testing Tool 318
    Alexey Kolesnichenko, Christopher M. Poskitt, and Bertrand Meyer

Author Index 325

Advances in Automated Program Repair and a Call to Arms

Westley Weimer

University of Virginia
weimer@virginia.edu

Abstract. In this keynote address I survey recent success and momentum in the subfield of automated program repair. I also encourage the search-based software engineering community to rise to various challenges and opportunities associated with test oracle generation, large-scale human studies, and reproducible research through benchmarks.

I discuss recent advances in *automated program repair*, focusing on the search-based GenProg technique but also presenting a broad overview of the subfield. I argue that while many automated repair techniques are "correct by construction" or otherwise produce only a single repair (e.g., AFix [13], Axis [17], Coker and Hafiz [4], Demsky and Rinard [7], Gopinath *et al.* [12], Jolt [2], Juzi [8], etc.), the majority can be categorized as "generate and validate" approaches that enumerate and test elements of a space of candidate repairs and are thus directly amenable to search-based software engineering and mutation testing insights (e.g., ARC [1], AutoFix-E [23], ARMOR [3], CASC [24], ClearView [21], Debroy and Wong [6], FINCH [20], PACHIKA [5], PAR [14], SemFix [18], Sidiroglou and Keromytis [22], etc.). I discuss challenges and advances such as scalability, test suite quality, and repair quality while attempting to convey the excitement surrounding a subfield that has grown so quickly in the last few years that it merited its own session at the 2013 International Conference on Software Engineering [3,4,14,18]. Time permitting, I provide a frank discussion of mistakes made and lessons learned with GenProg [15].

In the second part of the talk, I pose three challenges to the SBSE community. I argue for the importance of *human studies* in automated software engineering. I present and describe multiple "how to" examples of using crowdsourcing (e.g., Amazon's Mechanical Turk) and massive online education (MOOCs) to enable SBSE-related human studies [10,11]. I argue that we should leverage our great strength in testing to tackle the increasingly-critical problem of test *oracle generation* (e.g., [9]) — not just test data generation — and draw supportive analogies with the subfields of specification mining and invariant detection [16,19]. Finally, I challenge the SBSE community to facilitate reproducible research and scientific advancement through *benchmark* creation, and support the need for such efforts with statistics from previous accepted papers.

G. Ruhe and Y. Zhang (Eds.): SSBSE 2013, LNCS 8084, pp. 1–3, 2013.
© Springer-Verlag Berlin Heidelberg 2013

References

1. Bradbury, J.S., Jalbert, K.: Automatic repair of concurrency bugs. In: International Symposium on Search Based Software Engineering - Fast Abstracts, pp. 1–2 (September 2010)
2. Carbin, M., Misailovic, S., Kling, M., Rinard, M.C.: Detecting and escaping infinite loops with jolt. In: Mezini, M. (ed.) ECOOP 2011. LNCS, vol. 6813, pp. 609–633. Springer, Heidelberg (2011)
3. Carzaniga, A., Gorla, A., Mattavelli, A., Perino, N., Pezzè, M.: Automatic recovery from runtime failures. In: International Conference on Sofware Engineering (2013)
4. Coker, Z., Hafiz, M.: Program transformations to fix C integers. In: International Conference on Sofware Engineering (2013)
5. Dallmeier, V., Zeller, A., Meyer, B.: Generating fixes from object behavior anomalies. In: Automated Software Engineering, pp. 550–554 (2009)
6. Debroy, V., Wong, W.E.: Using mutation to automatically suggest fixes for faulty programs. In: International Conference on Software Testing, Verification, and Validation, pp. 65–74 (2010)
7. Demsky, B., Ernst, M.D., Guo, P.J., McCamant, S., Perkins, J.H., Rinard, M.C.: Inference and enforcement of data structure consistency specifications. In: International Symposium on Software Testing and Analysis (2006)
8. Elkarablieh, B., Khurshid, S.: Juzi: A tool for repairing complex data structures. In: International Conference on Software Engineering, pp. 855–858 (2008)
9. Fraser, G., Zeller, A.: Mutation-driven generation of unit tests and oracles. Transactions on Software Engineering 38(2), 278–292 (2012)
10. Fry, Z.P., Landau, B., Weimer, W.: A human study of patch maintainability. In: Heimdahl, M.P.E., Su, Z. (eds.) International Symposium on Software Testing and Analysis, pp. 177–187 (2012)
11. Fry, Z.P., Weimer, W.: A human study of fault localization accuracy. In: International Conference on Software Maintenance, pp. 1–10 (2010)
12. Gopinath, D., Malik, M.Z., Khurshid, S.: Specification-based program repair using SAT. In: Abdulla, P.A., Leino, K.R.M. (eds.) TACAS 2011. LNCS, vol. 6605, pp. 173–188. Springer, Heidelberg (2011)
13. Jin, G., Song, L., Zhang, W., Lu, S., Liblit, B.: Automated atomicity-violation fixing. In: Programming Language Design and Implementation (2011)
14. Kim, D., Nam, J., Song, J., Kim, S.: Automatic patch generation learned from human-written patches. In: International Conference on Sofware Engineering (2013)
15. Le Goues, C., Dewey-Vogt, M., Forrest, S., Weimer, W.: A systematic study of automated program repair: Fixing 55 out of 105 bugs for $8 each. In: International Conference on Software Engineering, pp. 3–13 (2012)
16. Le Goues, C., Weimer, W.: Measuring code quality to improve specification mining. IEEE Transactions on Software Engineering 38(1), 175–190 (2012)
17. Liu, P., Zhang, C.: Axis: Automatically fixing atomicity violations through solving control constraints. In: International Conference on Software Engineering, pp. 299–309 (2012)
18. Nguyen, H.D.T., Qi, D., Roychoudhury, A., Chandra, S.: SemFix: Program repair via semantic analysis. In: International Conference on Sofware Engineering, pp. 772–781 (2013)
19. Nguyen, T., Kapur, D., Weimer, W., Forrest, S.: Using dynamic analysis to discover polynomial and array invariants. In: International Conference on Software Engineering, pp. 683–693 (2012)

20. Orlov, M., Sipper, M.: Flight of the FINCH through the Java wilderness. Transactions on Evolutionary Computation 15(2), 166–192 (2011)
21. Perkins, J.H., Kim, S., Larsen, S., Amarasinghe, S., Bachrach, J., Carbin, M., Pacheco, C., Sherwood, F., Sidiroglou, S., Sullivan, G., Wong, W.-F., Zibin, Y., Ernst, M.D., Rinard, M.: Automatically patching errors in deployed software. In: Symposium on Operating Systems Principles (2009)
22. Sidiroglou, S., Keromytis, A.D.: Countering network worms through automatic patch generation. IEEE Security and Privacy 3(6), 41–49 (2005)
23. Wei, Y., Pei, Y., Furia, C.A., Silva, L.S., Buchholz, S., Meyer, B., Zeller, A.: Automated fixing of programs with contracts. In: International Symposium on Software Testing and Analysis, pp. 61–72 (2010)
24. Wilkerson, J.L., Tauritz, D.R., Bridges, J.M.: Multi-objective coevolutionary automated software correction. In: Genetic and Evolutionary Computation Conference, pp. 1229–1236 (2012)

Some Recent Work on Multi-objective Approaches to Search-Based Software Engineering

Xin Yao

CERCIA, School of Computer Science
University of Birmingham
Edgbaston, Birmingham B15 2TT, UK
x.yao@cs.bham.ac.uk
http://www.cs.bham.ac.uk/~xin

Abstract. Multi-objective algorithms have been used to solve difficult software engineering problems for a long time. This article summarises some selected recent work of applying latest meta-heuristic optimisation algorithms and machine learning algorithms to software engineering problems, including software module clustering, testing resource allocation in modular software system, protocol tuning, Java container testing, software project scheduling, software project effort estimation, and software defect prediction. References will be given, from which the details of such application of computational intelligence techniques to software engineering problems can be found.

1 Introduction

Although multi-objective algorithms has been applied to software engineering for many years, there has been a renewed interest in recent years due to the availability of more advanced algorithms and the increased challenges in software engineering that make many existing techniques for software engineering ineffective and/or inefficient. This paper reviews some selected work in recent years in computational intelligence techniques for software engineering, including software module clustering, testing resource allocation in modular software system, protocol tuning, Java container testing, software project scheduling, software project effort estimation, and software defect prediction. The key computational intelligence techniques used include multi-objective evolutionary optimisation, multi-objective ensemble learning and class imbalance learning.

In addition to existing work, this article will also introduce some speculative ideas of future applications of computational intelligence techniques in software engineering, including negative correlation for N-version programming and further development of co-evolution in software engineering.

G. Ruhe and Y. Zhang (Eds.): SSBSE 2013, LNCS 8084, pp. 4–15, 2013.
© Springer-Verlag Berlin Heidelberg 2013

2 Multi-objective Approach to Software Module Clustering

2.1 Software Module Clustering Problem

Software module clustering is the problem of automatically organizing software units into modules to improve the program structure [1]. A well-modularized software system is easier and cheaper to develop and maintain. A good module structure is regarded as one that has a high degree of cohesion and a low degree of coupling. Cohesion refers to the degree to which the elements of a module belong together. High cohesion is associated with several desirable traits of software including robustness, reliability, reusability, and understandability. Coupling or dependency is the degree to which each module relies on other modules.

Define Modularisation Factor, $MF(k)$, for cluster k as follows [1]:

$$MF = \begin{cases} 0 & \text{if } i = 0 \\ \frac{i}{i + \frac{1}{2}j} & \text{if } i > 0. \end{cases} \tag{1}$$

where i is the number of intra-edges and j is that of inter-edges. That is, j is the sum of edge weights for all edges that originate or terminate in cluster k. The reason for the occurrence of the term $j/2$ in the above equation (rather than merely j) is to split the penalty of the inter-edge across the two clusters that connected by that edge. If the module dependency graph (MDG) is unweighted, then the weights are set to 1.

Modularisation quality (MQ) has been used to evaluate the quality of module clustering results. The MQ can be calculated in terms of $MF(k)$ as [1]

$$MQ = \sum_{k=1}^{n} MF_k \tag{2}$$

where k is the number of clusters.

The software module system is represented using a directed graph called the Module Dependency Graph (MDG) [1]. The MDG contains modules (as nodes) and their relationships (as edges). Edges can be weighted to indicate a strength of relationship or unweighted, merely to indicate the presence of absence of a relationship.

Bunch [1] was the state-of-the-art tool for software module clustering. It used hill-climbing to maximise the MQ. Two improvements can be made to improve bunch: one is to use a better search algorithm algorithm than hill-climbing, and the other is to treat cohesion and coupling as separate objectives, rather than using MQ, which is a combination of the two.

2.2 Multi-objective Approaches to Software Module Clustering

In order to implement the above two improvements, a multi-objective approach to software module clustering was proposed [2]. In addition to cohesion and coupling, MQ was considered as a separate objective in order to facilitate the comparison between the new algorithm and Bunch, which used MQ. Because of the flexibility of the multi-objective framework, we can consider another objective where we want to maximise the number of modularised clusters. Two different multi-objective approaches are investigated. The first one is called the Maximizing Cluster Approach (MCA), which has the fifth objective for minimising the number of isolated clusters (i.e., clusters containing a single module only). The second one is the Equal-size Cluster Approach (ECA), which has the fifth objective for minimising the difference between the maximum and minimum number of modules in a cluster.

Because most existing algorithms were not designed to handle a large number of objectives [3], a two-archive algorithm for dealing with a larger number of objectives [4] was adopted in our study.

2.3 Research Questions

Five research questions were investigated through comprehensive experimental studies [2]:

1. How well does the two-archive multi-objective algorithm perform when compared against the Bunch approach using the MQ value as the assessment criterion?
   Somewhat surprisingly, ECA was never outperformed by the hill-climber, which was the state-of-the-art that specifically designed to optimise MQ. In particular, ECA outperformed the hill-climber for all weighted MDGs significantly.
2. How well do the two archive algorithm and the Bunch perform at optimizing cohesion and coupling separately?
   For both cohesion and coupling, in all but one of the problems studied, the ECA approach outperforms the hill-climbing approach with statistical significance. The remaining case has no statistically significant difference between ECA and Bunch.
3. How good is the Pareto front achieved by the two approaches?
   Our results provide strong evidence that ECA outperforms hill climbing for both weighted and unweighted cases.
4. What do the distributions of the sets of solutions produced by each algorithm look like?
   The resulting locations indicate that the three approaches produce solutions in different parts of the solution space. This indicates that no one solution should be preferred over the others for a complete explanation of the module clustering problem. While the results for the ECA multi-objective approach indicate that it performs very well in terms of MQ value, non-dominated solutions, cohesion and coupling, this does not mean that the other two approaches are not worthy of consideration, because the results suggest that they search different areas of the solution space.

5. What is the computational expense of executing each of the two approaches in terms of the number of fitness evaluations required?
   Hill climbing is at least two orders of magnitude faster. Whether the additional cost is justified by the superior results will depend upon the application domain. In many cases, re-modularization is an activity that is performed occasionally and for which software engineers may be prepared to wait for results if this additional waiting time produces significantly better results. Given the same amount of time, the hill-climber was still outperformed by ECA.

It is important to note that this work neither demonstrates nor implies any necessary association between quality of systems and the modularization produced by the approach used in this paper. Indeed, module quality may depend on many factors, which may include cohesion and coupling, but which is unlikely to be limited to merely these two factors. However, no matter what quality metrics might be, the multi-objective approach as proposed here would be equally useful.

3   Multi-objective Approach to Testing Resource Allocation in Modular Software Systems

A software system is typically comprised of a number of modules. Each module needs to be assigned appropriate testing resources before the testing phase. Hence, a natural question is how to allocate the testing resources to the modules so that the reliability of entire software system is maximized.

We formulated the optimal testing resource allocation problem (OTRAP) as two types of multi-objective problems [5], considering the reliability of the system and the testing cost as two separate objectives. NSGA-II was used to solve this two-objective problem.

The total testing resource consumed was also taken into account as the third objective. A Harmonic Distance Based Multi-Objective Evolutionary Algorithm (HaD-MOEA) was proposed and applied to the three-objective problem [5] because of the weakness of NSGA-II in dealing with the three objective problems.

Our multi-objective evolutionary algorithms (MOEAs) not only managed to achieve almost the same solution quality as that which can be attained by single-objective approaches, but also found simultaneously a set of alternative solutions. These solutions showed different trade-offs between the reliability of a system and the testing cost, and hence can facilitate informed planning of a testing phase.

When comparing NSGA-II and HaD-MOEA [5], both algorithms performed well on the bi-objective problems, while HaD-MOEA performed significantly better than NSGA-II on the tri-objective problems, for which the total testing resource expenditure is not determined in advance. The superiority of HaD-MOEA consistently holds for all four tested systems.

4   Protocol Tuning in Sensor Networks Using Multi-objective Evolutionary Algorithms

Protocol tuning can yield significant gains in energy efficiency and resource requirements, which is of particular importance for sensornet systems in which resource availability is severely restricted.

In our study [6], we first apply factorial design and statistical model fitting methods to reject insignificant factors and locate regions of the problem space containing near-optimal solutions by principled search. Then we apply the Strength Pareto Evolutionary Algorithm 2 and Two-Archive evolutionary algorithms to explore the problem space.

Our results showed that multi-objective evolutionary algorithms (MOEAs) can significantly outperform a simple factorial design experimental approach when tuning sensornet protocols against multiple objectives, producing higher quality solutions with lower experimental overhead. The two-archive algorithm outperformed the SPEA2 algorithm, at each generation and in the final evolved solution, for each protocol considered in this paper.

This work shows that MOEAs can be a vert effective approach to considering trade-offs between functional and non-functional requirements of a system and the trade-offs among different non-functional requirements. Multi-objective approaches enable us to incorporate different requirements easily It enables us to understand the trade-off between functional and non-functional requirements, as well as the trade-off among different non-functional requirements.

5   Multi-objective Ensemble Learning for Software Effort Estimation

Software effort estimation (SEE) can be formulated as a multi-objective learning problem, where different objectives correspond to different performance measures [7]. A multi-objective evolutionary algorithm (MOEA) is used to better understand the trade-off among different performance measures by creating SEE models through simultaneous optimisation of these measures. Such a multi-objective approach can learn robust SEE models, whose goodness does not change significantly when different performance measure was used. It also natural fits to ensemble learning, where the ensemble diversity is created by different individual learner using different performance measures. A good trade-off among different measures can be obtained by using an ensemble of MOEA solutions. This ensemble performs similarly or better than a model that does not consider these measures explicitly. Extensive experimental studies have been carried out to evaluate our multi-objective learning approach and compare it against existing work. In our work, we considered three performance measures, i.e., LSD, MMRE and PRED(25), although other measure can also be considered easily in the multi-objective learning framework. The MOEA used is HaD-MOEA [5]. The base learner considered is MLP. The results show clearly the advantages of the multi-objective approach over the existing work [7].

5.1 Online Learning Approach to Software Effort Estimation Using Cross-Company Data

Few work in SEE considered temporal information in learning the model, especially about concept drift. We have proposed a novel formulation of SEE as a online learning problem using cross-company data [8]. First, we learn a SEE model using the cross-company data. Then as individual in-company project data become available, the SEE model will be further learned online. Contrary to many previous studies, our research showed that cross-company data can be made useful and beneficial in learning in-company SEE models. Online learning with concept drifts played an important role.

6 Class Imbalance Learning for Software Defect Prediction

Software defect prediction (SDP) has often been formulated as a supervised learning problem without any special consideration of class imbalance. However, the class distribution for SDP is highly imbalanced, because defects are also a very small minority in comparison to correct software. Our recent work demonstrated that algorithms that incorporate class imbalance handling techniques can outperform those that do not in SDP [9].

We propose a dynamic version of AdaBoost.NC that adjusts its parameter automatically during training based on a performance criterion. AdaBoost.NC is an ensemble leanring algorithm that combines the advantages of boosting and negative correlation. The PROMISE data set was used in the experimental study.

Instead of treating SDP as a classification problem, wteher balanced or not, one can also rank software modules in order of defect-proneness because this is important to ensure that testing resources are allocated efficiently. Learning-to-rank algorithms can be used to learn such a rank directly, rather than trying to predict the number of defects in each module [10].

7 From SBSE to AISE

Artificial intelligence (AI) techniques have provided many inspirations for improving software engineering, both in terms of the engineering process as well as the software product. The application of AI techniques in software engineering is a well established research area that has been around for decades. There have been dedicated conferences, workshops, and journal special issues on applications of AI techniques to software engineering.

In recent years, there has been a renewed interest in this area, driven by the need to cope with increased software size and complexity and the advances in AI. Search-based software engineering [18] provided some examples of how difficult software engineering problems can be solved more effectively using search and optimisation algorithms.

It is interesting to note that search-based software engineering does not provide merely novel search and optimisation algorithms, such as evolutionary algorithms, to solve existing software engineering problems. It helps to promote rethinking and reformulation of classical software engineering problems in different ways. For example, explicit reformulation of some hard software engineering problems as true multi-objective problems, instead of using the traditional weighted sum approach, has led to both better solutions to the problems as well as richer information that can be provided to software engineers [19, 20]. Such information about trade-off among different objectives, i.e., competing criteria, can be very hard to obtained using classical approaches.

However, most work in search-based software engineering has been focused on increasing the efficiency of solving a software engineering problem, e.g., testing, requirement prioritisation, project scheduling/planning, etc. Much fewer work has been reported in the literature about AI techniques used in constructing and synthesizing actual software. Automatic programming has always been a dream for some people, but somehow not as popular as some other research topics.

The advances in evolutionary computation, especially in genetic programming [21], has re-ignited people's interest in automatic programming. For example, after the idea of automatic bug fixing was first proposed and demonstrated [11], industrial scale software has been tested using this approach and bugs fixed [22]. The continuous need to test and improve a software system can be modelled as a competitive co-evolutionary process [12], where the programs try to improve and gain a higher fitness by passing all the testing cases while all the testing cases will evolve to be more challenging to the programs. The fitness of a testing case is determined by its ability to fail programs. Such competitive co-evolution can create "arms race" between programs and testing cases, which help to improve the programs automatically. In fact, competitive co-evolution has been used in other engineering design domains with success.

In the rest of this article, we will describe briefly a few future research directions in combining AI with software engineering. Some research topics are related to better understanding of what we have been doing and how to advance the state-of-the-art based on the insight gained. Some other topics are more adventurous and long-term. Of course, these are not meant to be comprehensive. They reflect the biased and limited views of the author.

8   Fundamental Understanding of Algorithms and Problems

Many AI techniques have been applied to solve difficult software engineering problems with success. For example, many search and optimisation algorithms have been applied to software engineering [23]. In almost all such cases, only results from computational experiments were reported. Few analyses of the algorithms and the problems were offered. It was not always clear why a particular algorithm was used, whether a better one could be developed, which features of the algorithm make it a success, what software engineering problem characteristics were exploited by the algorithm, what is the relationship between algorithm features and problem characteristics. It is essential to have deep theoretical understanding of both algorithms and the problems in order to progress the research to a higher level than currently is.

Some recent work in understanding search algorithms has been on scalability, especially from computational time complexity's point of view [13]. If a search algorithm is used to solve a software engineering problem, how will the algorithm scale as the problem size increases? How do different features of an algorithms influence the algorithm's performance? While there have been experimental studies on such issues, more rigorous theoretical analyses are needed. In fact, theoretical analyses could reveal insights that are not easily obtainable using experimental studies. For example, a recent study [24] first showed rigorously that not only the interaction between mutation and selection in an evolutionary algorithm is important, the parameter settings (e.g., the mutation rate) can also drastically change the behaviour of an algorithm, from having a polynomial time to exponential time. Such theoretical results are important because it shows that operators should be designed and considered collectively, not in isolation, during the algorithm design process. Parameter settings may need more than just a few trial-and-error attempts.

The research in the theoretical analysis of search algorithms for software engineering problems is still at its initial stage with few results [14, 25]. Much more work is needed in this area.

A research topic that is inherently linked to the computational time complexity analysis of search algorithms is the analysis of software engineering problems. Unlike the classical analysis of computational time complexity, which considers the problem hardness independent of any algorithms, we are always very interested in the relationship between algorithms and problems so that we can gain insight into when to use which algorithms to solve what problems (or even problem instances). Fitness landscapes induced by an algorithm on a software engineering problem can be analysed to gain such insight. Although the results so far (e.g., [26]) are very preliminary, research in this direction holds much promise because any insight gained could potentially be very useful in guiding the design of new algorithms. Furthermore, one can use the information from the fitness landscape to guide search dynamically, which is one of our on-going research work [27].

9 Constructing Reliable Software Systems from Multiple Less Reliable Versions

Correctness and reliability have always been paramount in software engineering, just like in every other engineering fields. Nobody is interested in incorrect and unreliable software systems. Two major approaches, broadly speaking, in software engineering to software correctness and reliability are formal methods and empirical software testing. Formal methods try to prove the correctness of software mathematically, while testing tries to discover as many defects in the software as possible. Neither approach is perfect and neither scales well to large software systems.

Furthermore, almost all the existing approaches to enhancing software reliability assume prior knowledge of the environments in which the software will be used. While this is indeed the case for some applications, it is not true for some other applications where the environments in which the software will be used are unknown and contain uncertainty. A functionally correct software, which has been proven mathematically to be correct, may not be operating correctly in an uncertain environment because of unexpected memory space shortage or limited communications bandwidth. In addition to software correctness, there is an increasing need for software robustness, i.e., the ability of software to operate correctly in unseen environments.

We can learn from other engineering design domains where ensemble approaches have been used to design fault-tolerant circuits [15] and better machine learning systems [16]. The idea behind the ensemble approach to designing large and complex software systems is straightforward. Instead of trying to develop a monolithic system with an ever-increasing size and complexity, it seems to be more practical to develop a number of different software components/versions, as a whole they will perform the same functions as the monolithic system, but more reliably.

The ensemble idea actually appeared in very different domains in different forms. Not only is it popular within the machine learning community [16], it also has its incarnation in software engineering, i.e., in N-version programming [28–30], where "N-version programming is defined as the independent generation of $N \geq 2$ functionally equivalent programs from the same initial specification." It was proposed as an approach to software fault-tolerance. Many key issues were discussed then, including the need of redundancy in the software system and notions of design diversity and software distinctness [28–30]. One of the main hypothesis was that different versions were unlikely to have the same types of defects and hence created opportunities for the entire ensemble to be more reliable than any individual versions. However, N-version programming was criticised over the years, because independence among different software development teams can hardly be achieved [31].

What has changed since then? Why should we re-visit this old idea? There have been some recent developments in machine learning and evolutionary computation, which could help to move the old idea forward. First, instead of relying on human programming teams, it is now possible to produce programs or algorithms automatically through genetic programming, although for small scale programs for the time being. Second, we now understand much better what "diversity" and "distinctness" mean. There are various diversity measures [17, 32] that we can use and adapt for the software engineering domain. Third, we can do better than just maintaining independence among different versions by actively creating and promoting negative correlation [16] among different versions. We can learn from the initial success of using negative correlation in designing fault tolerant circuits and transfer such knowledge to software engineering. In the future, we will automatically generate N diverse versions of the software such that the integration of the N versions, e.g., the ensemble, will be more reliable than any individual versions. Lessons, and algorithms, from constructing diverse and accurate machine learning ensembles [33] can be learnt for the benefit of developing reliable software systems from multiple unreliable versions.

10   Concluding Remarks

This article covers two major parts. The first part reviews selected work related to search-based software engineering. The second part includes some speculations on possible future research directions, which go beyond search-based software engineering towards artificial intelligence inspired software engineering.

Acknowledgement. This work was supported by EPSRC DAASE project (No. EP/J017515/1) and a Royal Society Wolfson Research Merit Award.

References

1. Mancoridis, S., Mitchell, B.S., Chen, Y., Gansner, E.R.: Bunch: A clustering tool for the recovery and maintenance of software system structures. In: ICSM 1999: Proceedings of the IEEE International Conference on Software Maintenance, Washington, DC, USA, pp. 50–59. IEEE Computer Society (1999)
2. Praditwong, K., Harman, M., Yao, X.: Software module clustering as a multi-objective search problem. IEEE Transactions on Software Engineering 37, 264–282 (2011)
3. Khare, V.R., Yao, X., Deb, K.: Performance scaling of multi-objective evolutionary algorithms. In: Fonseca, C.M., Fleming, P.J., Zitzler, E., Deb, K., Thiele, L. (eds.) EMO 2003. LNCS, vol. 2632, pp. 376–390. Springer, Heidelberg (2003)
4. Praditwong, K., Yao, X.: A new multi-objective evolutionary optimisation algorithm: the two-archive algorithm. In: Proc. of the 2006 International Conference on Computational Intelligence and Security (CIS 2006), pp. 286–291. IEEE Press (2006)
5. Wang, Z., Tang, K., Yao, X.: Multi-objective approaches to optimal testing resource allocation in modular software systems. IEEE Transactions on Reliability 59, 563–575 (2010)
6. Tate, J., Woolford-Lim, B., Bate, I., Yao, X.: Evolutionary and principled search strategies for sensornet protocol optimisation. IEEE Trans. on Systems, Man, and Cybernetics, Part B 42(1), 163–180 (2012)
7. Minku, L.L., Yao, X.: Software effort estimation as a multi-objective learning problem. ACM Transactions on Software Engineering and Methodology (to appear, 2013)
8. Minku, L.L., Yao, X.: Can cross-company data improve performance in software effort estimation?. In: Proc. of the 2012 Conference on Predictive Models in Software Engineering (PROMISE 2012). ACM Press (2012), doi:10.1145/2365324.2365334
9. Wang, S., Yao, X.: Using class imbalance learning for software defect prediction. IEEE Transactions on Reliability 62(2), 434–443 (2013)

10. Yang, X., Tang, K., Yao, X.: A learning-to-rank algorithm for constructing defect prediction models. In: Yin, H., Costa, J.A.F., Barreto, G. (eds.) IDEAL 2012. LNCS, vol. 7435, pp. 167–175. Springer, Heidelberg (2012)

11. Arcuri, A., Yao, X.: A novel co-evolutionary approach to automatic software bug fixing. In: Proceedings of the 2008 IEEE Congress on Evolutionary Computation (CEC 2008), Piscataway, NJ, pp. 162–168. IEEE Press (2008)

12. Arcuri, A., Yao, X.: Coevolving programs and unit tests from their specification. In: Proc. of the 22nd IEEE/ACM International Conference on Automated Software Engineering (ASE 2007), New York, NY, pp. 397–400. ACM Press (2007)

13. Lehre, P.K., Yao, X.: Runtime analysis of search heuristics on software engineering problems. Frontiers of Computer Science in China 3, 64–72 (2009)

14. Arcuri, A., Lehre, P.K., Yao, X.: Theoretical runtime analyses of search algorithms on the test data generation for the triangle classification problem. In: Proceedings of the 2008 IEEE International Conference on Software Testing Verification and Validation Workshop (ICSTW 2008), pp. 161–169. IEEE Computer Society Press (2008)

15. Schnier, T., Yao, X.: Using negative correlation to evolve fault-tolerant circuits. In: Tyrrell, A.M., Haddow, P.C., Torresen, J. (eds.) ICES 2003. LNCS, vol. 2606, pp. 35–46. Springer, Heidelberg (2003)

16. Liu, Y., Yao, X.: Ensemble learning via negative correlation. Neural Networks 12, 1399–1404 (1999)

17. Brown, G., Wyatt, J.L., Harris, R., Yao, X.: Diversity creation methods: A survey and categorisation. Information Fusion 6, 5–20 (2005)

18. Harman, M., Jones, B.F.: Search-based software engineering. Information and Software Technology 43, 833–839 (2001)

19. Praditwong, K., Harman, M., Yao, X.: Software Module Clustering as a Multi-Objective Search Problem. IEEE Transactions on Software Engineering 37(2), 264–282 (2011)

20. Wang, Z., Tang, K., Yao, X.: Multi-objective Approaches to Optimal Testing Resource Allocation in Modular Software Systems. IEEE Transactions on Reliability 59(3), 563–575 (2010)

21. Cramer, N.L.: A Representation for the Adaptive Generation of Simple Sequential Programs. In: Grefenstette, J.J. (ed.) Proc. of ICGA 1985, pp. 183–187 (1985)

22. Weimer, W., Nguyen, T., Goues, C.L., Forrest, S.: Automatically Finding Patches Using Genetic Programming. In: Proc. of the 2009 International Conference on Software Engineering (ICSE), pp. 364–374 (2009)

23. Harman, M., Mansouri, A., Zhang, Y.: Search Based Software Engineering: Trends, Techniques and Applications. ACM Computing Surveys 45(1), Article 11 (2012)

24. Lehre, P.K., Yao, X.: On the Impact of Mutation-Selection Balance on the Runtime of Evolutionary Algorithms. IEEE Transactions on Evolutionary Computation 16(2), 225–241 (2012)

25. Lehre, P.K., Yao, X.: Crossover can be constructive when computing unique input-output sequences. Soft Computing 15(9), 1675–1687 (2011)

26. Lu, G., Li, J., Yao, X.: Fitness-Probability Cloud and a Measure of Problem Hardness for Evolutionary Algorithms. In: Proc. of the 11th European Conference on Evolutionary Computation in Combinatorial Optimization (EvoCOP 2011), pp. 108–117 (April 2011)

27. Lu, G., Li, J., Yao, X.: Embracing the new trend in SBSE with fitness-landscape based adaptive evolutionary algorithms. In: SSBSE 2012, pp. 25–30 (September 2012)

28. Avizienis, A.: Fault-tolerance and fault-intolerance: Complementary approaches to reliable computing. In: Proc. of 1975 Int. Conf. Reliable Software, pp. 458–464 (1975)

29. Avizienis, A., Chen, L.: On the implementation of N-version programming for software fault-tolerance during execution. In: Proc. of the First IEEE-CS Int. Computer Software and Application Conf (COMPSAC 1977), pp. 149–155 (November 1977)

30. Avizienis, A.: The N-Version Approach to Fault-Tolerant Software. IEEE Transactions on Software Engineering 11(12), 1491–1501 (1985)

31. Knight, J.C., Leveson, N.G.: An experimental evaluation of the assumption of independence in multiversion programming. IEEE Transactions on Software Engineering 12(1), 96–109 (1986)

32. Tang, E.K., Suganthan, P.N., Yao, X.: An Analysis of Diversity Measures. Machine Learning 65, 247–271 (2006)

33. Chandra, A., Yao, X.: Evolving hybrid ensembles of learning machines for better generalisation. Neurocomputing 69(7-9), 686–700 (2006)

Cloud Computing and SBSE

David R. White

School of Computing Science, University of Glasgow, Scotland, G12 8QQ
david.r.white@glasgow.ac.uk

Abstract. Global spend on Cloud Computing is estimated to be worth $131 billion and growing at annual rate of 19% [1]. It represents one of the most disruptive innovations within the computing industry, and offers great opportunities for researchers in Search Based Software Engineering (SBSE).

In the same way as the development of large scale electricity generation, the physical centralisation of computing resources that Cloud Computing involves provides opportunities for economies of scale [2]. Furthermore, it enables more extensive consolidation and optimisation of resource usage than previously possible: whereas in the past we have been resigned to the phenomenon of wasted spare cycles, the Cloud offers opportunities for large-scale consolidation, along with standardised measurement and control of resource consumption.

There are two key stakeholders within the Cloud Computing sector: providers, such as Amazon and Google, and clients, the consumers of Cloud services paying for infrastructure and other utilities by the hour. Both providers and clients are greatly concerned with solving optimisation problems that determine their resource usage, and ultimately their expenditure. Example resources include CPU time, physical RAM usage, storage consumption, and network bandwidth.

From the point of view of the provider, improving utilisation leads to greater return on capital investment – hence the emergence of over-subscription policies [3], where more resources are promised to clients than are physically provisioned. Similarly, clients wish to reduce their resource demands because there is a direct relationship between resource consumption and operating cost. The rise of Cloud Computing has in many cases made explicit the cost of computation that was previously considered only as depreciation of capital investment.

Example optimisation problems include: the configuration of servers, virtualisation, and operating systems to reduce storage and memory usage; transformation of software and architectures to adapt them to a Cloud platform; the intelligent placement of virtual machines to improve consolidation, reduce business risks and manage network usage; extensive, online and continuous testing to improve robustness; policy-level decisions such as management of scalability, demand modelling and spot market participation; and automated online software maintenance and improvement [4].

A relentless focus on efficiency offers researchers in SBSE the opportunity to make an important contribution. The field has an established record in solving similar optimisation problems within software engineering, and treating non-functional concerns as first class objectives.

G. Ruhe and Y. Zhang (Eds.): SSBSE 2013, LNCS 8084, pp. 16–18, 2013.
© Springer-Verlag Berlin Heidelberg 2013

The way in which software is deployed within Cloud systems also offers exciting possibilities for SBSE researchers, principally due to its centralised nature. Software is no longer deployed or versioned in the traditional manner, and this consequently enables dynamic, controlled and sometimes partial deployment of new code (a procedure known as "canarying" [5]). A key insight is that many different versions of software can be employed simultaneously, and that manipulation of this multifaceted distribution solves some of the problems traditionally faced by SBSE practitioners.

For example, consider recent work in bug fixing [6] [7]. One of the greatest challenges facing automatically and dynamically applying such work is ensuring that the existing semantics of a program are not disturbed in the process of correcting a bug. By running a form of N-Version programming on a Cloud platform, differences in behaviour caused by automated software repair could be rejected or reported.

Similarly, the extensive use of virtualisation improves the repeatability of execution. Technologies such as Xen [8] provide snapshotting, enabling a virtual machine to be paused, cloned and restarted (with some limitations). This lends itself to improving the robustness of automated repair and optimisation methods: we can rollback servers and examine hypothetical scenarios. Furthermore, due to the elasticity of the Cloud, we can quickly procure extra execution environments to test software on demand.

Applying traditional SBSE work to the Cloud will not be straightforward, and requires further development of both theory and implementation: many problems in the Cloud are real-time and dynamic; there are competing objectives and complex relationships between concerns; the problems faced and the software itself are distributed. One exciting example of how we may begin to adapt to this environment is You's proposed amortised optimisation [9].

The process of researching Cloud Computing is in itself a challenge, because the nature of the industry is secretive and closed. There is competitive advantage to be gained in proprietary technology, and as a result much detail of how deployed systems function is not available. Thus, we must occasionally re-invent the wheel and in some cases restrict ourselves to synthetic case studies or else recognise the limited reach we can have within certain subdomains.

More pressing is the concern about research evaluation: how can we evaluate our research ideas effectively? This problem is not limited to SBSE alone. There are parallels with difficulties carrying out networking research, and we may adopt that field's existing methods of modelling, simulation, testbed construction, and instrumentation. A recent and novel alternative is to construct a scale model, such that a low-cost system with similar logical properties to a commercial Cloud can be used for prototyping [10].

In summary, the rise of Cloud Computing provides great opportunities for SBSE research, both in terms of the problems that SBSE may be used to solve, and also the capabilities that Cloud Computing provides, which offer truly new methods of deploying SBSE techniques.

References

1. Columbus, L.: Gartner Predicts Infrastructure Services Will Accelerate Cloud Computing Growth. Forbes (February 19, 2013)
2. Carr, N.: The Big Switch: Rewiring the World, from Edison to Google. W.W. Norton & Company (2009)
3. Williams, D., Jamjoom, H., Liu, Y., Weatherspoon, H.: Overdriver: Handling Memory Overload in an Oversubscribed Cloud. SIGPLAN Not. 46(7), 205–216 (2011)
4. Harman, M., Lakhotia, K., Singer, J., White, D.R., Yoo, S.: Cloud Engineering is Search Based Software Engineering Too. Systems and Software (November 23, 2012) (to appear)
5. Barroso, L., Hölzle, U.: The Datacenter as a Computer. Morgan & Claypool Publishers (2009)
6. Le Goues, C., Nguyen, T., Forrest, S., Weimer, W.: GenProg: A Generic Method for Automatic Software Repair. IEEE Trans. Software Engineering 38(1), 54–72 (2012)
7. Arcuri, A., Yao, X.: A Novel Co-evolutionary Approach to Automatic Software Bug Fixing. In: Proceedings of the IEEE Congress on Evolutionary Computation, CEC 2008 (2008)
8. Barham, P., Dragovic, B., Fraser, K., Hand, S., Harris, T., Ho, A., Neugebauer, R., Pratt, I., Warfield, A.: Xen and the Art of Virtualization. SIGOPS Oper. Syst. Rev. 37(5), 164–177 (2003)
9. Yoo, S.: NIA^{3}CIN: Non-Invasive Autonomous and Amortised Adaptivity Code Injection. Technical Report RN/12/13, Department of Computer Science, University College London (2012)
10. Tso, F., White, D.R., Jouet, S., Singer, J., Pezaros, D.: The Glasgow Raspberry Pi Cloud: A Scale Model for Cloud Computing Infrastructures. In: International Workshop on Resource Management of Cloud Computing (to appear, 2013)

On the Application of the Multi-Evolutionary and Coupling-Based Approach with Different Aspect-Class Integration Testing Strategies

Wesley Klewerton Guez Assunção[1,2], Thelma Elita Colanzi[2],
Silvia Regina Vergilio[2], and Aurora Pozo[2,*]

[1] DInf - Federal University of Paraná, CP: 19081, CEP 81531-980, Curitiba, Brazil
[2] COINF - Technological Federal University of Paraná, CEP: 85902-490,
Toledo, Brazil
{wesleyk,thelmae,silvia,aurora}@inf.ufpr.br

Abstract. During the integration test of aspect-oriented software, it is necessary to determine an aspect-class integration and test order, associated to a minimal possible stubbing cost. To determine such optimal orders an approach based on multi-objective evolutionary algorithms was proposed. It generates a set of good orders with a balanced compromise among different measures and factors that may influence the stubbing process. However, in the literature there are different strategies proposed to aspect-class integration. For instance, the classes and aspects can be integrated in a combined strategy, or in an incremental way. The few works evaluating such strategies do not consider the multi-objective and coupling based approach. Given the importance of such approach to reduce testing efforts, in this work, we conduct an empirical study and present results from the application of the multi-objective approach with both mentioned strategies. The approach is implemented with four coupling measures and three evolutionary algorithms that are also evaluated: NSGA-II, SPEA2 and PAES. We observe that different strategies imply in different ways to explore the search space. Moreover, other results related to the practical use of both strategies are presented.

Keywords: Integration testing, aspect-oriented software, MOEAs.

1 Introduction

Testing aspect-oriented (AO) software is an active research area [1,6,16,25]. Several testing criteria have been proposed, as well as, testing tools have been developed exploring specific characteristics of the AO context, where new kind of faults and difficulties for testing are found. For example, some authors point out the importance of testing adequately existing dependencies between aspects and classes. To address this kind of test, existing works suggest different strategies. In the Incremental strategy [6,17,25,26] the classes are tested first, and after, the

---

* We would like to thank CNPq and Araucária Foundation for financial support.

G. Ruhe and Y. Zhang (Eds.): SSBSE 2013, LNCS 8084, pp. 19–33, 2013.
© Springer-Verlag Berlin Heidelberg 2013

aspects are integrated. This strategy presents some advantages such as easy implementation and fault localization. The Combined strategy generates sequences to test the interactions among classes and aspects in a combined way [21]. This strategy seems to be more practical since classes and aspects probably are tested together if both are under development.

Both strategies present points in favour and against. However to apply both it is necessary to establish an order of classes and aspects to be tested. The problem of determining such order, which minimizes the costs for stubs construction, is referred as CAITO (Class and Aspect Integration and Test Order) [8]. The costs are associated to the number of stubs and other factors related to different measures, to the test plans, and to the software development context.

Solutions to this problem are proposed based on a dependency graph, the extended ORD (Object Relation Diagram) [20]. In such graph the nodes represent either aspects or classes, and the edges represent the relationships between them. When dependency cycles exist in the graph, it is necessary to break the dependency and to construct a stub. There are evidences that is very common to find complex dependency cycles in Java programs [18]. In the AO context is very usual to find crosscutting concerns that are dependent of other crosscutting concerns, implying in dependency between aspects, and between classes and aspects [21]. To break the cycles and establish the test order, different approaches, from the object-oriented (OO) context, were adapted. The work of Ré et al. [20] uses the approach of Briand et al. [5] based on the Tarjan's algorithm. Other works use search-based algorithms [4]. Similarly to what happens in the OO context [22], most promising results were obtained with multi-objective algorithms [4]. These algorithms allow generation of more adequate solutions, evaluated according to Pareto's dominance concepts [19] and represent a good trade-off between objectives that can be in conflict.

In a previous work [8], we introduced a multi-objective and evolutionary coupling-based approach, named MECBA, to solve the CAITO problem. The approach treats the problem as a constrained combinatorial multi-objective optimization problem, where the goal is to find a test order set that satisfies constraints and optimizes different factors related to the stubbing process. The approach consists of some generic steps that include: the definition of a model to represent the dependency between classes and aspects, the quantification of the stubbing costs, and the optimization through multi-objective algorithms. At the end, a set of good solutions is produced and used by the testers according to the test goals and resources. However, the evaluation results reported in the AO context [4,8] were obtained with the Combined strategy, which integrates classes and aspects without any distinction among them.

Considering this fact, and following up on our previous work [8], in this paper we present results from MECBA evaluation with three evolutionary algorithms: NSGA-II, SPEA2 and PAES, and both strategies: Incremental and Combined. In the evaluation, we used the same systems and methodology adopted in our previous work [8] with the goal of answering the following questions:

- **RQ1.** How are the Incremental and Combined strategies results with respect to the stubbing process? It is important to know which strategy presents better solutions regarding costs related to the number of stubs and other factors. To evaluate costs, in our paper we consider four objectives (coupling measures) that consist on the number of: attributes, operations, types of return and types of operation parameters.
- **RQ2.** Does the kind of used evolutionary algorithm influence on the performance of the strategies? This question aims at investigating the performance of each integration strategy used with different kind of evolution strategies implemented by the three algorithms.
- **RQ3.** Does the selected strategy influence on the performance of the algorithms? This question aims at investigating the fact that some strategy can impose restrictions for the search space and maybe this influence in the results of the evolutionary algorithms.
- **RQ4.** How is the behaviour of each strategy to exploring the search space in the presence of four objectives? This question is derived from RQ3. It is expected that the Incremental strategy influences the exploitation on the search space due to its rule that integrates classes first and aspects later.

In our study context, both strategies achieve good results in order to make the integration test of aspect-oriented software less labour-intensive and expensive. The kind of evolutionary algorithm seems not to influence on the strategy performance, but we observed that the Incremental strategy explores the search space in a different way and finds the best results with PAES for one system.

The paper is organized as follows. Section 2 contains related work. Section 3 reviews the MECBA approach. Section 4 describes how the evaluation was conducted: systems, strategies and algorithms used. Section 5 presents and analyses the results, comparing the performance of algorithms and strategies, and answering our research questions. Section 6 concludes the paper.

2   Related Work

The use of the search-based multi-objective approaches to solve different testing problems is subject of some works found in the literature [15,24]. On the other hand, we observe works that studied the application of search-based techniques for AO testing, where in general the approaches are adapted from the OO context [8,13]. Among such works we can include that ones addressing the CAITO problem.

In the OO context the solution of the integration and test order is an active research area, subject of a recent survey [23]. Most promising approaches are based on search-based algorithms [3,22]. In the AO context, other relations and ways to combine the aspects are necessary. The work of Ceccato et al. [6] uses a strategy in which the classes are first tested without integrating aspects. After this, the aspects are integrated and tested with the classes, and, at the end, the classes are tested in the presence of the aspects. Solutions based on graphs were investigated by Ré et al. [20,21]. The authors propose an extended ORD to consider dependency relations between classes and aspects, and different graph-based strategies to perform the integration and test of AO software. They are: i) Combined: aspects and classes are integrated and tested together; ii) Incremental: first only classes are integrated and tested, and after the aspects; iii) Reverse: applies the reverse combined order; and iv) Random: applies a random selected order. As a result of the study, the Combined and Incremental strategies performed better than the other ones, producing a lower number of stubs. Due to this, only these strategies are being considered in our evaluation.

The use of evolutionary algorithms in the AO context is recent. Galvan et al. [11] introduced a simple and mono-objective GA that uses an aggregation of functions to the CAITO problem. This algorithm presented better solutions than the approach based on graphs and on the Tarjan's algorithm, proposed by Ré et al. After this, the multi-objective algorithms were successfully explored in the AO context using two objectives, number of attributes and operations [4] reaching better results than traditional and simple GA-based approaches. Motivated by this fact we introduced in a previous work [8] the MECBA approach to the CAITO problem. This approach, described in the next section, produces a set of good (non-dominated) solutions considering all the objectives.

The work of Ré et al. [21] provides some idea about the strategies performance. However, the strategies were only evaluated with a kind of algorithm and approach: the Tarjan's algorithm and Briand et al's approach [5]. Other limitations are: the strategies were applied to only one small system, with six classes and five aspects; and the different factors that may influence the stubbing costs were not considered, since the traditional approaches are very difficult to be adapted to consider such factors. In comparison with the traditional approaches, the evolutionary approaches do not have such limitation and present better results [4], but the strategy used in all evaluations [8] is always the Combined one. Considering this fact, a comparison of both strategies with the multi-objective approach using four coupling measures is the goal of the present paper. To do this, the Incremental approach was also implemented in the MECBA approach, subject of the next section.

3   The MECBA Approach

The MECBA approach includes a set of steps that produce artifacts and allows the use of different coupling measures for solving the CAITO problem through multi-objective evolutionary algorithms. It has the following steps: construction of the dependency model, definition of the cost model, multi-objective optimization, and selection of test orders. Next, we present how the steps were conducted in our study. The methodology adopted is similar to our previous work [8].

3.1   Construction of Dependency Model

This model specifies the kind of dependencies that should be considered. It can be obtained from a design model or from the source code. This last one generally provides more information and were used in our study. The model adopted is the extended ORD [20]. In the ORD the vertexes are classes, and the edges represent the dependencies between classes. In the extended ORD, the vertexes represent a module that can be both classes and aspects, and the following new relationships were proposed: Crosscutting Association: association generated by a pointcut with a class method or other advice; Use: is generated by a relation between advices and pointcuts, and between pointcuts; Association: occurs between objects involved in pointcuts; Intertype Declaration: occurs when there are intertype relationships between aspects and the base class; Inheritance: represents inheritance relationships among aspects or among classes and aspects.

As in other related works [20,21], we consider that Inheritance and Intertype declarations dependencies cannot be broken. This means that base modules must precede child modules in any test order. The dependencies that cannot be broken are an input for the algorithms, called dependency matrix. In the algorithms these constraints are checked during the generation of initial population and in the application of mutation and crossover operators. The treatment strategy involves a scan of the constraints from beginning to end of the chromosome, making sure that the precedence among the modules are not being broken.

3.2   Definition of the Cost Model

Our model is composed by a set of objectives to be minimized: these objectives are related to collected measures that serve as fitness functions. As mentioned before, several possible measures and factors can be used, such as coupling, cohesion and time constraints. We used the same coupling measures adopted by most related works [3,8,21]. They generally measure the dependencies between server and client modules. Considering that: (i) m_i and m_j are two coupled modules and m_i depends on m_j, (ii) modules are either classes or aspects, and (iii) the *operation* term represents class methods, aspect methods and aspect advices. The measures are defined as:

Attribute Coupling (A): number of attributes locally declared in m_j when references or pointers to instances of m_j appear in the argument list of some operations in m_i, as the type of their return value, in the list of attributes of m_i, or as local parameters of operations of m_i. It counts the number of attributes that would have to be handled in the stub if the dependency were broken.

Operation Coupling (O): number of operations locally declared in m_j which are invoked by operations of m_i. It counts the number of operations that would have to be emulated in the stub if the dependency were broken.

Number of distinct return types (R): number of distinct return types of the operations locally declared in m_j that are called by operations of m_i. Returns of type void are not counted as return type.

Number of distinct parameter types (P): number of distinct parameters of operations locally declared in m_j and called by operations of m_i. When there is overloading operations, the number of parameters is equal to the sum of all distinct parameter types among all implementations of each overloaded operation. The worst case is considered, represented by situations in which the coupling consists of calls to all implementation of a given operation.

The measures A and O are commonly used in related work. In the other hand, the measures R and P allow to consider different factors related directly to the stub complexity. Furthermore, O, R and P are interdependent.

3.3 Multi-Objective Optimization

This step is the application of the multi-objective evolutionary algorithm (MOEA). In our study we used three variants of GAs, which adopt different evolution and diversification methodologies. They are: NSGA-II (Non-dominated Sorting Genetic Algorithm) [9], SPEA2 (Strength Pareto Evolutionary Algorithm) [27] and PAES (Pareto Archived Evolution Strategy) [14]. Such MOEAs were chosen due to two main reasons. First, evolutionary algorithms have presented better performance, in the OO context, than other bio-inspired algorithms, such as PACO and MTabu [22]. Second, they implement different evolution strategies, and this help us to investigate the influence of the strategies in the search space.

For each generation NSGA-II sorts the individuals, from parent and offspring populations, considering the non-dominance relation, creating several fronts and, after the sorting, solutions with lower dominance are discarded. These fronts characterize the elitism strategy adopted by NSGA-II. This algorithm also uses a diversity operator (crowding distance) that sorts the individuals according to their distance from the neighbours of the border for each objective, in order to ensure greater spread of solutions.

SPEA2 maintains an external archive that stores non-dominated solutions in addition to its regular population. Some of them are selected for the evolutionary process. For each solution in the archive and in the population, a strength value is calculated, which is used as fitness of the individuals. The strength value of a solution i corresponds to the number j of individuals, belonging to the archive and to the population, dominated by i. The archive size s is fixed. When the number n of solutions exceeds s, a clustering algorithm is used to reduce n.

PAES works with a population concept that is different from other evolutionary algorithms strategies, since only one solution is maintained in each generation. The strategy to generate new individuals is to use only the mutation operator. As the algorithm works with only one solution for generation there is no possibility to use the crossover operator. Like in SPEA2, there is an external archive that is populated with the non-dominated solutions found along the evolutionary process. If the external archive size is exceeded, a diversity strategy is applied on the set of solutions in order to remove the similar solutions and to maintain wide the exploitation of a search space.

The implementation of those three algorithms used the same problem representation (chromosome). Since the CAITO problem is related to permutations of modules (classes and aspects), which form testing orders, the chromosome is represented by a vector of integers where each vector position corresponds to a module. The size of the chromosome is equal to the number of modules of each system. Thus, being each module represented by a number, an example of a valid solution for a problem with 5 modules is $(2, 4, 3, 1, 5)$. In this example, the first module to be tested and integrated is the module represented by number 2.

For both strategies (Combined and Incremental), the crossover operator follows the technique of Two Points Crossover, which swaps two genes inside two randomly selected points to form the children. The remaining genes are used to complete the solution, from left to right. There is no difference for crossover between the strategies. Despite of the division of classes and aspects, in the Incremental strategy implementation, the Two Points Crossover preserves the restriction. The technique Swap Mutation was used for the mutation operator. In the Incremental strategy if the randomly selected gene is a class, the gene to be swapped must be another class. In the other hand, if the gene is an aspect, it must be swapped by another aspect, in order to maintain the boundary between classes and aspects in the chromosome.

The use of crossover and mutation operators can generate test orders that break the precedence constraints between the modules. As mentioned, Inheritance and Intertype declarations dependencies cannot be broken. This means that base modules must precede child modules in any test order. The strategy adopted to deal with these constraints consists in to check the test order, and if an invalid solution is generated, the module that breaks the dependency constraint is placed at the end of the test order according to the module type, for instance, in the Incremental, if the module is a class, it must be placed at the end of the classes space; and analogously for aspects.

The fitness function (objectives) is calculated from five matrices, inputs to the algorithms, associated to (i) dependencies between modules; (ii) measure A; (iii) measure O; (iv) measure R; and (v) measure P. These measures are generally calculated during the software design, however it is difficult to obtain architectural design documentation of complex systems to conduct experiments. So, reverse engineering was performed to identify the existing dependencies between modules from programs code using the same parser adopted in our previous work [8]. Based on the dependency matrices, the precedence constraints are defined. The sum of the dependencies between the modules for each measure corresponds to an objective, and the goal is to minimize all objectives.

4 Evaluation Study Description

In order to answer the research questions we conduct an empirical study with four systems following the same methodology for the MOEAs application described in [8], now with the additional strategy - Incremental. The used systems are most complex systems than that ones used in related work, in terms of number of lines of code and dependencies (see their characteristics in Table 1).

We used the NSGA-II, SPEA2 and PAES versions available at jMetal [10] with the same parameters values adopted in our previous work [8], where an empirical

Table 1. Used Systems

System	LOC	# Classes	# Aspects	# Dependencies						
				I	U	As	It	PointCuts	Advices	Total
AJHotDraw	18586	290	31	234	1177	140	40	0	1	1592
AJHSQLDB	68550	276	15	107	960	271	0	0	0	1338
HealthWatcher	5479	95	22	64	290	34	3	1	7	399
Toll System	2496	53	24	24	109	46	4	0	5	188

parameters tuning was done [2]. Such values are: population size = 300; number of fitness evaluation = 60000; mutation rate = 0.02; crossover rate = 0.95; and archive size = 250 (required only by SPEA2 and PAES). The MOEAs executed the same number of fitness evaluations in order to analyse whether they produce similar solutions when they are restricted to the same resources. Each algorithm was executed 30 runs for each AO system. In each run, each MOEA found an approximation set of solutions named PF_{approx}. Furthermore, for each MOEA it is obtained a set, called PF_{known}, formed by all non-dominated solutions achieved in all runs. Considering that PF_{true} is not known, in our study, this set was obtained by the union of the non-dominated solutions from all PF_{approx} found by NSGA-II, SPEA2 and PAES according to [28]. PF_{approx}, PF_{known} and PF_{true} are necessary to calculate the quality indicators used to evaluate the results. The quality indicators are described below.

The most accepted indicator for performance assessment of multi-objective algorithms is the Hypervolume (HV) [28]. Comparing two PF_{approx} sets: whenever one PF_{approx} completely dominates another PF_{approx}, the HV of the former will be greater than the HV of the latter. The HV indicator calculates the volume in the region enclosed from the PF_{approx} to a reference point. A reference point is a point dominated by the solutions of all the PFs_{approx} found.

The Coverage (C) [28] indicator calculates the dominance between two sets of solutions. C provides a direct comparison of how many solutions achieved by an algorithm A are dominated by those achieved by an algorithm B. $C(PF_a, PF_b)$ represents a value between 0 e 1 according to how much the set PF_b is dominated by set PF_a. When dealing with many-objective optimization (four or more objective functions), then this measure will likely fail because the non-dominance probability among two solutions randomly drawn from the decision space rapidly goes to one as the number of objectives increases. Therefore, the coverage, here it is used as secondary indicator.

The third indicator, Euclidean Distance from the Ideal Solution (ED), it is not a quality indicator, instead, it is used as a measure to help the decision maker in his/her final decision, i.e., from all the solutions provided which one to select. ED is used to find the closest solution to the best objectives. An ideal solution has the minimum value of each objective, considering a minimization problem [7]. These minimum values are obtained from all PF_{true}'s solutions.

5   Results and Analysis

In this section the results are analysed considering the number of solutions found (test orders), the three indicators, solutions distribution on the search space, and number of stubs for classes and aspects. After that, we summarize our findings in order to answer our research questions.

Table 2 presents the number of solutions achieved by the MOEAs using each strategy. The number of solutions achieved in each strategy that belong to the set PF_{true} is presented in parentheses. The total number of solutions in PF_{true} is observed in the second and fifth columns. It is possible that the same solution was found by different algorithms or strategies.

Table 2. Number of Solutions

MOEA	AJHotDraw			AJHSQLDB		
	PF_{true}	Combined	Incremental	PF_{true}	Combined	Incremental
NSGA-II		95 (93)	122 (1)		244 (0)	205 (0)
PAES	106	68 (3)	77 (8)	393	428 (112)	318 (281)
SPEA2		76 (0)	188 (2)		317 (0)	172 (0)
	HealthWatcher			Toll System		
NSGA-II		1 (1)	1 (1)		1 (1)	1 (1)
PAES	1	1 (1)	1 (1)	1	1 (1)	1 (1)
SPEA2		1 (1)	1 (1)		1 (1)	1 (1)

Regarding to the system AJHotDraw, we can notice that the number of solutions found by all MOEAs is greater for the strategy Incremental. On the other hand, for AJHSQLDB, the MOEAs achieved the greatest number of solutions with the strategy Combined. For the systems HealthWatcher and Toll System we observe that the objectives are not interdependent, since only one solution was found. Taking into account AJHotDraw and AJHSQLDB, the greatest number of solutions found in PF_{known} does not imply in the quality of solutions, since there are cases in which lower number of solutions in PF_{known} represents greater number of solutions in PF_{true} considering the objectives, i.e., lower values for each objective, for instance, the solutions found by NSGA-II with Combined strategy for AJHotDraw. According to the results presented in Table 2, NSGA-II found more solutions in PF_{true} for AJHotDraw (93) whereas PAES achieved the greatest number for AJHSQLDB (281). For HealthWatcher and Toll System, all algorithms found the optimal solution for both strategies. Hence, they were not considered in the analysis hereafter.

Table 3 presents mean and standard deviation for HV indicator, considering the 30 runs of each MOEA. Friedman statistical test [12] was applied to assess the statistical difference among all MOEAs with both strategies. For all cases, the test did not point out difference, except for AJHSQLDB, where PAES is the best with any strategy, and NSGA-II and SPEA2 are equivalent. In this case, there is no statistical difference between PAES with Incremental or Combined strategy. For Health Watcher and Toll System, the test did not point out any significant difference considering this indicator.

Table 4 presents the comparison between both strategies using the Coverage indicator. Considering NSGA-II, the solutions found by Combined are better. For PAES, the solutions found by Incremental cover the most solutions found by Combined. And, for SPEA2, Combined was better for AJHotDraw and Incremental was better for AJHSQLDB.

Taking into account AJHotDraw and AJHSQLDB, Figures 1 and 2, respectively, allow analysing how the MOEAs explore the search space using each strategy. These pictures present the solutions distributed on the search space.

Table 3. Mean and Standard Deviation of Hypervolume

System	NSGA-II		PAES		SPEA2	
	Combined	Incremental	Combined	Incremental	Combined	Incremental
AJHotDraw	8.31E+06 (1.08E+06)	8.05E+06 (1.08E+06)	7.45E+06 (1.17E+06)	7.67E+06 (1.00E+06)	7.46E+06 (9.49E+05)	7.52E+06 (1.04E+06)
AJHSQLDB	2.09E+10 (8.04E+09)	2.06E+10 (7.42E+09)	4.62E+10 (4.53E+09)	4.61E+10 (5.58E+09)	1.81E+10 (5.96E+09)	1.57E+10 (6.70E+09)

Table 4. Coverage Indicator for the Strategies

MOEA	AJHotDraw		AJHSQLDB	
	C(Com,Inc)	C(Inc,Com)	C(Com,Inc)	C(Inc,Com)
NSGA-II	**0.991803**	0.0210526	**0.609756**	0.389344
PAES	0.311688	**0.485294**	0.116352	**0.738318**
SPEA2	**0.702128**	0.210526	0.0639535	**0.33123**

We grouped the measures that are more related in two pictures: (i) one with the measures (A,O), and (ii) another with the measures (O,R,P) in order to present them in three-dimensional graphics. Regarding the graphics presented in Figure 1 it is possible to observe that solutions achieved with the Incremental strategy are more spread on the search space. It seems that the restriction of the strategy enforces the MOEAs to explore other regions of search space, consequently increasing the number of solutions, and achieving as a result, the greatest number of solutions.

In Figure 2 we can notice that the Incremental strategy solutions form groups, they are restricted to certain areas of the search space. As observed in Table 2, the number of Combined strategy solutions, for AJHSQLDB, is greater than the solutions found for AJHotDraw, therefore for AJHSQLDB the restriction of Incremental seems to limit the search space, justifying the lowest number of solutions.

Table 5 presents the cost of solutions with the lowest Euclidean distance from the ideal solution. Based on such results we cannot state that some strategy is better. It is possible to observe that the best ED solutions, independently of the strategy, were achieved by NSGA-II and PAES, respectively for AJHotDraw and AJHSQLDB, as pointed by indicator HV (Table 3).

Table 5. Lowest ED's and Solutions Cost

System	Ideal Solution	Strategy	NSGA-II	PAES	SPEA2
AJHotDraw	(37,13,0,18)	Combined	17.492856 (45,17,1,33)	18.220867 (46,18,1,33)	21.610183 (52,17,1,33)
		Incremental	17.029386 (46,19,2,31)	18.275667 (44,18,2,34)	18.681542 (45,18,2,34)
AJHSQLDB	(1270,212, 89,136)	Combined	304.417477 (1428,403,172,292)	181.207064 (1335,329,140,247)	245.224387 (1441,337,139,249)
		Incremental	237.981092 (1374,369,160,263)	171.802212 (1334,322,143,238)	274.581500 (1459,367,157,241)

Table 6 presents the mean numbers of stubs, stubs for classes and stubs for aspects considering all solutions for each strategy and MOEA. Orders requiring aspect stubs were found only for AJHSQLDB, with NSGA-II and PAES when using the Combined strategy. This was expected since in the Incremental strategy, aspects are at the order end. Again we cannot point some strategy as the best, since a lower mean was not found by a single strategy. Among the MOEAs, NSGA-II with Combined strategy achieved the lowest mean number of stubs for AJHotDraw, and PAES with Incremental strategy, for AJHSQLDB.

In order to analyse the number of stubs required for each strategy when solutions with the same cost were found, we composed two sets with all MOEAs solutions: (i) one set with solutions of the Combined strategy; and (ii) another

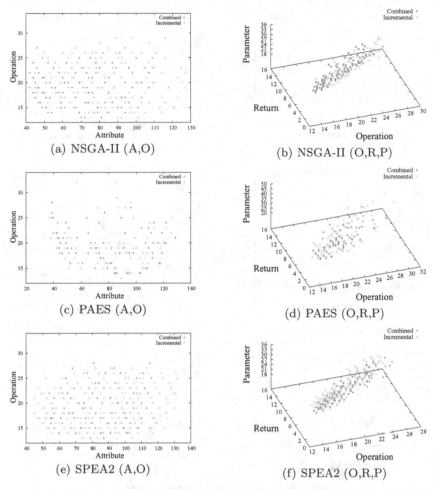

Fig. 1. Search Space of AJHotDraw

Table 6. Mean Number of Stubs for Classes and Aspects

Algorithm	Strategy	AJHotDraw				AJHSQLDB			
		# Sol.	Total	Class	Aspect	# Sol.	Total	Class	Aspect
NSGA-II	Combined	95	98.04	98.04	0	244	165.81	163.87	1.93
	Incremental	122	100.93	100.93	0	205	163.69	163.69	0
PAES	Combined	68	107.47	107.47	0	428	132.27	132.26	0.01
	Incremental	77	110.13	110.13	0	318	129.21	129.21	0
SPEA2	Combined	76	99.87	99.87	0	317	157.01	157.01	0
	Incremental	188	102.61	102.61	0	172	157.99	157.99	0

set with solutions of the Incremental strategy. From both sets we obtained the solutions with same cost. The solutions with the same cost were found only for AJHotDraw and they are presented in Table 7. In these cases, both strategies achieved solutions with the lowest number of stubs for classes and aspects, then none overcame the other at this point.

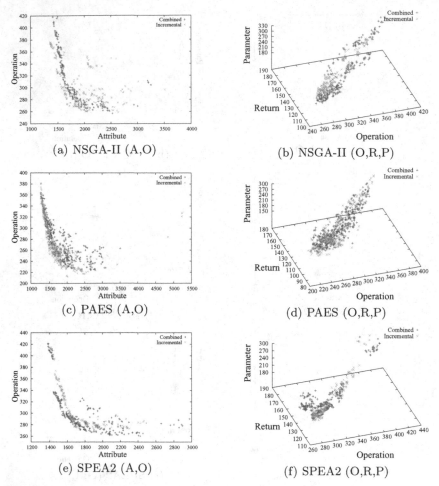

Fig. 2. Search Space of AJHSQLDB

Table 7. Number of Stubs for AJHotDraw Solutions with the Same Cost

Solution Cost	Combined			Incremental		
	Total	Class	Aspect	Total	Class	Aspect
(44,18,2,34)	**91**	**91**	0	99	99	0
(56,18,3,30)	101	101	0	**93**	**93**	**0**
(94,14,2,29)	**101**	**101**	0	116	116	0
(57,15,0,31)	101	101	0	**99**	**99**	**0**
(66,18,5,27)	100	100	0	**98**	**98**	**0**

Finally, aiming at answering our research questions, we summarize our findings as follows:

– **RQ1:** From the results we cannot point out one strategy as the best, since in all analysis about the stubbing process, considering all the four measures, both strategies achieved good solutions. Although, we use only four AO systems, what can be not significant to find particularities of each strategy.

- **RQ2:** During the experiment, we did not observe any influence of the algorithm used on the performance of the strategies. It seems that the characteristics of the program have an important role.
- **RQ3:** Independently of the adopted strategy, the behaviour of the MOEAs was the same. All MOEAs found the optimal solution for Toll System and HealthWatcher with both strategies. NSGA-II was the best MOEA for AJHotDraw and PAES was the best for AJHSQLDB. Similar results were obtained in the previous work [8] where only the Combined strategy was used. So, in the context of our exploratory study, the answer for this question is that the strategies do not influence on the MOEA performance.
- **RQ4:** When a lower number of solutions was achieved by Combined strategy, the restriction of Incremental seems to enforce the MOEAs to explore different areas of the search space (Figure 1). On the other hand, when the number of solutions found by Combined was greater, the restriction imposed by Incremental limits the solutions in certain areas of search space, so the solutions form groups (Figure 2). So, to answer the question, we can state that the strategy influences on the search space exploitation, however it does not represent significant difference in the stubbing process.

Besides the findings regarding the research questions, we observed that the performance of both strategies and algorithms is related to the systems characteristics under development and test. The low number of aspects in relation to the number of classes can explain why it was not necessary to develop stubs for aspects. Other possible explanation is on the kind of dependencies between aspects and classes. However, it was not possible to establish this kind of relation between system characteristics and strategy/algorithm. Other empirical studies are necessary involving a greater number of AO systems in order to identify such characteristics, that can be size, complexity, number of classes and aspects, number and types of dependency relations, number of dependency cycles, etc.

We observe in the experiment that the Combined strategy is able to generate some solutions obtained by the Incremental strategy. If they are good solutions it will be chosen anyway in the evolution process independently of the strategy adopted and can be selected by the tester in the last MECBA step. From this, we can state a guideline to choose a strategy. The Combined strategy may be chosen for any case, except in the presence of restrictions related to the software development requiring the integration of aspects after classes, when Incremental one should be applied. With respect to the algorithms if the systems are simple, any evolutionary algorithms can be selected. In more complex cases, PAES is the best choice among the MOEAs.

6 Conclusions

This work presented results from the application of the MECBA approach with two different integration strategies (Combined and Incremental) and three distinct MOEAs (NSGA-II, SPEA2 and PAES) with four objectives for solving the CAITO problem in four AO real systems.

We observe that both strategies achieve good orders to integrate and test AO systems independently of the used MOEA. We could not pointed out which strategy has the best performance with respect to the stubbing cost since they achieved similar results in all points that we analysed. However, we observed that the MOEA does not influence on the strategy performance, and Incremental strategy obliges the MOEAs to explore the search space in a different way. Hence, in the context of our study, we conclude that both strategies can be used with MECBA to solve efficiently the CAITO problem. NSGA-II and PAES have better results than SPEA2, so one of them can be adopted in further studies.

The main threat of our study is that the results are limited to the systems used and can not be generalized. So, to obtain better evidences about the integration strategies, it is interesting to perform a larger study involving other AO systems. Other points to be considered in further studies include the analysis of the aspects details, such as the dependencies between them and their complexity; the number of dependency cycles between modules; and the proportion of classes/aspects in the system. Such kind of analysis allow the identification of the most suitable situations to apply each strategy.

References

1. Alexander, R.T., Bieman, J.M., Andrews, A.A.: Towards the Systematic Testing of Aspect-Oriented Programs. Tech. rep., Colorado State University (2004)
2. Arcuri, A., Fraser, G.: On parameter tuning in search based software engineering. In: Cohen, M.B., Ó Cinnéide, M. (eds.) SSBSE 2011. LNCS, vol. 6956, pp. 33–47. Springer, Heidelberg (2011)
3. Assunção, W.K.G., Colanzi, T.E., Pozo, A., Vergilio, S.R.: Establishing integration test orders of classes with several coupling measures. In: 13th Genetic and Evolutionary Computation Conference (GECCO), pp. 1867–1874 (2011)
4. Assunção, W., Colanzi, T., Vergilio, S., Pozo, A.: Generating integration test orders for aspect-oriented software with multi-objective algorithms. RITA-Revista de Informática Teórica e Aplicada 20(2), 301–327 (2013)
5. Briand, L.C., Labiche, Y.: An investigation of graph-based class integration test order strategies. IEEE Trans. on Software Engineering 29(7), 594–607 (2003)
6. Ceccato, M., Tonella, P., Ricca, F.: Is AOP code easier or harder to test than OOP code. In: Workshop on Testing Aspect-Oriented Program, WTAOP (2005)
7. Cochrane, J., Zeleny, M.: Multiple Criteria Decision Making. University of South Carolina Press, Columbia (1973)
8. Colanzi, T.E., Assunção, W.K.G., Vergilio, S.R., Pozo, A.: Integration test of classes and aspects with a multi-evolutionary and coupling-based approach. In: Cohen, M.B., Ó Cinnéide, M. (eds.) SSBSE 2011. LNCS, vol. 6956, pp. 188–203. Springer, Heidelberg (2011)
9. Deb, K., Pratap, A., Agarwal, S., Meyarivan, T.: A fast and elitist multiobjective genetic algorithm: NSGA-II. IEEE Transactions on Evolutionary Computation 6(2), 182–197 (2002)
10. Durillo, J., Nebro, A., Alba, E.: The jMetal framework for multi-objective optimization: Design and architecture. In: IEEE Congress on Evolutionary Computation (CEC), Barcelona, Spain, pp. 4138–4325 (July 2010)

11. Galvan, R., Pozo, A., Vergilio, S.: Establishing Integration Test Orders for Aspect-Oriented Programs with an Evolutionary Strategy. In: Latinamerican Workshop on Aspect Oriented Software (2010)
12. Gárcia, S., Molina, D., Lozano, M., Herrera, F.: A study on the use of nonparametric tests for analyzing the evolutionary algorithms' behaviour: a case study on the CEC'2005 Special Session on Real Parameter Optimization. Journal of Heuristics 15(6), 617–644 (2009)
13. Harman, M., Islam, F., Xie, T., Wappler, S.: Automated test data generation for aspect-oriented programs. In: 8th ACM International Conference on Aspect-Oriented Software Development (AOSD), pp. 185–196. ACM (2009)
14. Knowles, J.D., Corne, D.W.: Approximating the nondominated front using the Pareto archived evolution strategy. Evol. Comput. 8, 149–172 (2000)
15. Lakhotia, K., Harman, M., McMinn, P.: A multi-objective approach to search-based test data generation. In: Annual Conference on Genetic and Evolutionary Computation (GECCO), pp. 1098–1105 (2007)
16. Lemos, O.A.L., Vincenzi, A.M.R., Maldonado, J.C., Masiero, P.C.: Control and data flow structural testing criteria for aspect-oriented programs. The Journal of Systems and Software 80, 862–882 (2007)
17. Massicotte, P., Badri, L., Badri, M.: Aspects-classes integration testing strategy: An incremental approach. In: Guelfi, N., Savidis, A. (eds.) RISE 2005. LNCS, vol. 3943, pp. 158–173. Springer, Heidelberg (2006)
18. Melton, H., Tempero, E.: An empirical study of cycles among classes in Java. Empirical Software Engineering 12, 389–415 (2007)
19. Pareto, V.: Manuel D'Economie Politique. Ams Press, Paris (1927)
20. Ré, R., Lemos, O.A.L., Masiero, P.C.: Minimizing stub creation during integration test of aspect-oriented programs. In: 3rd Workshop on Testing Aspect-Oriented Programs, Vancouver, British Columbia, Canada, pp. 1–6 (March 2007)
21. Ré, R., Masiero, P.C.: Integration testing of aspect-oriented programs: a characterization study to evaluate how to minimize the number of stubs. In: Brazilian Symposium on Software Engineering (SBES), pp. 411–426 (October 2007)
22. Vergilio, S.R., Pozo, A., Árias, J.C., Cabral, R.V., Nobre, T.: Multi-objective optimization algorithms applied to the class integration and test order problem. Software Tools for Technology Transfer 14, 461–475 (2012)
23. Wang, Z., Li, B., Wang, L., Li, Q.: A brief survey on automatic integration test order generation. In: Software Engineering and Knowledge Engineering Conference (SEKE), pp. 254–257 (2011)
24. Yoo, S., Harman, M.: Pareto Efficient Multi-Objective Test Case Selection. In: International Symposium on Software Testing and Analysis, pp. 140–150 (2007)
25. Zhao, J.: Data-flow based unit testing of aspect-oriented programs. In: 27th Conference on Computer Software and Applications, Washington, DC (2003)
26. Zhou, Y., Ziv, H., Richardson, D.J.: Towards a practical approach to test aspect-oriented software. In: Workshop on Testing Component-based Systems (TECOS), vol. 58, pp. 1–16 (2004)
27. Zitzler, E., Laumanns, M., Thiele, L.: SPEA2: Improving the Strength Pareto Evolutionary Algorithm. Tech. Rep. 103, Swiss Federal Institute of Technology (ETH) Zurich, CH-8092, Zurich, Switzerland (2001)
28. Zitzler, E., Thiele, L., Laumanns, M., Fonseca, C.M., da Fonseca, V.G.: Performance assessment of multiobjective optimizers: An analysis and review. IEEE Transactions on Evolutionary Computation 7, 117–132 (2003)

An Experimental Study on Incremental Search-Based Software Engineering

Márcio de Oliveira Barros

Post-graduate Information Systems Program – PPGI/UNIRIO
Av. Pasteur 458, Urca – Rio de Janeiro, RJ – Brazil
marcio.barros@uniriotec.br

Abstract. Since its inception, SBSE has supported many different software engineering activities, including some which aim on improving or correcting existing systems. In such cases, search results may propose changes to the organization of the systems. Extensive changes may be inconvenient for developers, who maintain a mental model about the state of the system and use this knowledge to be productive in their daily business. Thus, a balance between optimization objectives and their impact on system structure may be pursued. In this paper, we introduce *incremental search-based software engineering*, an extension to SBSE which suggests optimizing a system through a sequence of restricted search turns, each limited to a maximum number of changes, so that developers can become aware of these changes before a new turn is enacted. We report on a study addressing the cost of breaking a search into a sequence of restricted turns and conclude that, at least for the selected problem and instances, there is indeed huge penalty in doing so.

Keywords: incremental optimization, interactive optimization, Hill Climbing, software module clustering.

1   Introduction

In the course of twelve years since it was given a name, Search-based Software Engineering (SBSE) has been applied to many problems, including but not limited to testing [6, 14], requirement selection [3, 8], software design [7, 9, 10, 15], cost estimation [4, 11], project planning [2, 5], and process analysis [12, 13].

For many of these problems, heuristic search is performed when the software development project is in a planning stage. In such context, the solution found by the search algorithm eventually imparts new knowledge to the person or group responsible for making a decision regarding the problem. After a decision is made, the development team is given the task to put the solution to practice. For instance, consider the next release problem [3], which involves selecting a set of requirements to be implemented and deployed in a new version of a software product. Heuristic search supports the product manager in planning the features that will be added in the next release. The product manager may examine one or more search results, change them according to restrictions and assumptions which were not informed to the search

G. Ruhe and Y. Zhang (Eds.): SSBSE 2013, LNCS 8084, pp. 34–49, 2013.
© Springer-Verlag Berlin Heidelberg 2013

process, and create a release plan to be implemented by the team. Nevertheless, search results are taken into account before the development of the new release is started.

On the other hand, some problems addressed through SBSE approaches are related to scenarios in which a system already exists and heuristic search is applied to correct or improve the current state of that system. For instance, consider the problem of selecting a set of refactoring transformations to be applied to a software component in order to make it easier to reuse. In such a case, a version of the component already exists and the search process is applied to transform it into something better, according to the fitness functions driving the optimization. This is a typical SBSE application for maintenance purposes, which involves issues such as refactoring [16], software module clustering [9, 10], and design reorganization [15].

In scenarios related to the second group of problems there are developers who know about the state of the system before search results are applied. Such knowledge helps them in their daily job, pointing possible sources for a fault or parts of the design or source code which are related to a given feature. If the search comes out with a solution which is completely different from the current state of the system and this solution is put to practice, developers may find it difficult to work on the system because, despite the benefits brought by optimization, they might have to learn about its new organization. This may result in loss of quality, productivity, and ultimately resistance against using automated optimization approaches.

In this paper, we introduce the concept of *incremental search-based software engineering* (ISBSE) which takes into consideration the current state of a system and a maximum level of disturbance that can be applied to it without extensive loss of developer's knowledge (and the problems derived from this loss). ISBSE suggests applying automated search as a sequence of time-spaced small changes to a system, instead of a single, unrestricted and extensive change to its organization. By preserving the knowledge held by developers, adoption of heuristic search to support maintenance projects may increase. Moreover, due to its periodic interventions in the software development process, ISBSE may be a useful vehicle to collect information about human intention, as required by interactive search processes [10].

Despite of the advantages related to preserving developer's knowledge, there may be penalties associated with breaking an unrestricted search into smaller parts. We report on an experimental study that analyzed these potential losses on the context of the software clustering problem. We have observed that restricted optimization turns may lead the system to many local minima, proposing changes to the state of the system which are undone by further turns. The contributions of this paper include:

- Introducing the concept of incremental search-based software engineering, in the sense of breaking an unrestricted search into a sequence of restricted searches;
- Proposing an incremental approach to deal with the software module clustering problem in the context of software maintenance;
- The design, execution, and reporting of an experimental study that evaluated the penalties incurred in adopting ISBSE for the software module clustering problem.

This paper is organized into 6 sections. The first section conveys this introduction. Section 2 discusses the concepts underlying ISBSE. Section 3 proposes an ISBSE approach to software module clustering. Section 4 presents an experimental study on the penalties incurred by performing a sequence of restricted optimizations turns instead of an unrestricted search. Section 5 discusses the relation between ISBSE and interactive search-based optimization. Finally, Section 6 closes the report with our concluding remarks.

2   Incremental Search-Based Software Engineering

Search-based software engineering suggests reformulating Software Engineering problems as optimization problems and using search techniques to find (close to) optimal solutions for them. Incremental Search-based Software Engineering inherits this definition and adds a constraint requiring search techniques to be applied in a sequence of small steps, so that the solution proposed by each optimization turn does not substantially change the state of the system. This is a contrast to the "big bang" approach (suitable in a planning stage) in which extensive changes may be required to take the system from its current state to one representing the optimal solution. ISBSE takes a long term view on improvements to be garnered from optimization, each turn bringing the system closer to overall search objectives but also allowing developers to swiftly incorporate the suggested changes to their knowledge about the organization of the system. Optimization becomes integrated to the software development process, serving human developers with bits of insight while improving the system towards a better picture on regard of the selected fitness functions.

This "optimization with a human perspective" is strongly related with the maintenance of a mental model for the current state of the system [17, 25, 26]. Typically, software developers remember the structure of modules, classes, attributes, and methods for the parts of the system on which they have worked. They use this knowledge as leverage to perform their job, knowing in the large what parts of the software they have to change to add, modify, or correct a feature. If the system's structure is extensively disrupted, despite of the benefits brought by the new organization (such as more cohesion or less coupling), the short-term benefits of having the leverage provided by the mental model are gone and developers may require more time to perform their tasks and introduce more errors in the process. Thus, ISBSE accepts a smooth and potentially slow move towards long-term optimization goals in order to allow time for developers to become aware of the required changes to system structure.

Harman suggests that a problem must present two ingredients to be amenable to assessment through heuristic optimization [1]: a representation for the problem and a fitness function to drive the optimization process towards solutions which maximize expected benefits or minimize potential hazards. ISBSE adds two ingredients to these requirements: a representation for the current state of a system, using the same encoding selected for the problem, and a function which receives two search solutions, say A and B, and returns a set of transformations required to convert solution A into B. The first ingredient enables the representation of the current state of the system as a solution, while the second identifies changes that must be applied to a system to build a solution. The function allows calculating the cognitive distance (developer's perspective) between the state of the system and any solution produced by the search.

Suppose a problem having n fitness function, $f_1, ..., f_n$, each requiring a vector of parameters X representing a solution. Mono-objective SBSE approaches to this problem might be represented as $O(f_1,...,f_n) \rightarrow X$. Let this formulation be known as an unrestricted optimization, in the sense that no limits are imposed in the number of changes required to take a system from its current state to that suggested by solution X. Accept that there exists a function Δ, $\Delta(X, X') \rightarrow \{T\}$, where X and X' represent solutions and T represents an elementary transformation that converts a solution X_A to a solution X_B, so that $T(X_A) \rightarrow X_B$. Thus, $\{T\}$ is the list of transformations that converts solution X to solution X'. Then, an ISBSE approach to the same problem could be defined as a sequence of restricted optimizations $O_t(f_1, ..., f_n, X_0, X_{t-1}, \Delta, \alpha) \rightarrow X_t$, where $t > 0$, X_0 represents the current state of the system, X_t represents the result of an optimization turn O_t, and α represents the maximum number of changes acceptable in an optimization turn, that is, $|\Delta(X_{t-1}, X_t)| \leq \alpha$ for all $t > 0$.

Thus, besides creating the representation for the current state of the system and providing the transformation identification function, an analyst resorting to an ISBSE approach has to define the size of each optimization turn (step size, or α) and the frequency under which a new restricted optimization turn will be performed. Step size may influence the number of required restricted turns to achieve the same objective values produced by a single, unrestricted optimization. This relation is explored in the experimental study reported on Section 4.

There may be at least two ways to incrementally address a Software Engineering problem from a search perspective. The first alternative involves performing an unrestricted optimization to identify all transformations that should be applied to the system to attain the results presented by its solution. Afterwards, a sequence of optimization turns would be executed to select the best permutation in which these transformations should be applied, so that each turn would involve up to the maximum number of changes accepted by the analyst. This strategy is depicted in Algorithm 1.

$O_1(f_1,...,f_n, X_0, X_0, \Delta, \alpha)$:	$X_{target} = O(f_1,...,f_n)$
	$T_{target} = \Delta(X_0, X_{target})$
	$T_1 = $ Permutation Selection $(f_1,...,f_n, T_{target}, X_0, \alpha)$
	$T_{target} = T_{target} - T_1$
	return $T_1(X_0)$
$O_t(f_1,...,f_n, X_0, X_{t-1}, \Delta, \alpha)$:	If $T_{target} = \varnothing$ then stop
	$T_t = $ Permutation Selection $(f_1,...,f_n, T_{target}, X_{t-1}, \alpha)$
	$T_{target} = T_{target} - T_t$
	return $T_t(X_{t-1})$

Algorithm 1. – ISBSE through permutations of results selected by an unrestricted search

The second alternative involves performing a sequence of independent, restricted optimization turns considering the present state of the system at the start of each turn and a constraint on the number of changes to be applied to the solution. In such a case, the transformation identification function becomes part of the evaluation process, prohibiting solutions which involve more changes than the maximum number accepted by the analyst. This strategy is presented in Algorithm 2.

$$O_t(f_1,...,f_n, X_0, X_{t-1}, \Delta, \alpha): \quad loop$$
$$X_t = O(f_1,...,f_n)$$
$$T_t = \Delta(X_{t-1}, X_t)$$
$$until \mid T_t \mid \leq \alpha$$
$$return\ T_t(X_{t-1})$$

Algorithm 2. – ISBSE through a sequence of independent restricted searches

Each alternative has its own advantages and disadvantages. As each turn optimizes the solution bounded by the distance constraint, the second alternative may not walk a straight path from the current state of the system to the (close to) optimal state. Certain changes might be considered useful on a given optimization turn, just to be undone after a few more turns, as a large number of changes might take the system from local minima to states with better fitness. We call these changes *downturns*, as they may confuse developers, who might see the optimization process as a random walk, changing the system back and forth in unpredictable ways. Downturns, on the other hand, do not happen in the first alternative, since all transformations toward the best solution found by the unrestricted search are known beforehand.

Despite of downturns, we defend the adoption of the second alternative because it can incorporate changes made by developers into the optimization. Since useful software tends to be constantly changed to remain useful and it may take considerable time to perform the complete sequence of restricted optimization turns, it seems reasonable to accept that developers may change the system during this period and that those changes should be taken into account in the optimization. Also, as will be discussed on Section 5, the execution of several independent, restricted optimizations may allow capturing information about developer's intention and feeding these data into an interactive optimization process. Thus, in the next sections we present an application of ISBSE and experimentally evaluate the cost of downturns in this context.

3   An Application of ISBSE on Software Module Clustering

Software module clustering addresses the problem of finding a proper distribution for the modules representing domain concepts and computational constructs comprising a software system into larger, container-like structures. A good module distribution aids in identifying modules responsible for a given functionality [22], provides easier navigation among software parts [18] and enhances source code comprehension [21]. Therefore, it supports the development and maintenance of a software system.

A high-quality module distribution usually presents two characteristics: (i) modules pertaining to a given cluster depend on other modules from the same cluster to perform their duties; and (ii) modules pertaining to a given cluster do not depend on many external modules, that is, from other clusters, to perform their job. Thus, finding a good module distribution requires knowing which modules depend on one another in order to distribute them to clusters according to these dependencies. A module A depends on a module B if it requires some function, procedure, or definition declared in module B to perform its duties.

The software module clustering problem can be modeled as a graph partition problem which minimizes coupling (*inter-edges* or edges between different clusters) and maximizes cohesion (*intra-edges* or edges within a cluster). In a seminal work in the field, Mancoridis et al. [19] used a Hill Climbing search to find the best module distribution for a system. The search is guided by a fitness function called *modularization quality* (MQ), which looks for a balance between the number of intra- and inter-cluster edges, rewarding clusters with many internal dependencies and penalizing them for dependencies on other clusters.

Harman et al. [23] compare MQ with a second fitness function called EVM [24] regarding its robustness to the presence of noise in a set of dependencies. EVM is calculated as a sum of cluster scores and a given cluster' score is calculated as follows: starting from zero, for each pair of modules in the cluster the score is incremented if there is dependency between the modules; otherwise, it is decremented. EVM rewards modules which depend on other modules pertaining to the same cluster and penalizes those depending on modules from other clusters. When compared to a baseline module distribution, clusterings based on EVM were found to degrade more slowly in the presence of noise (random dependencies added to the original module dependency structure) than clusterings based on MQ. Barros [9] also found that the convergence of search processes based on EVM is faster than that based on MQ. Thus, EVM was used as the main fitness function for the software clustering problem throughout our experimental study and MQ was used as a surrogate measure.

Software clustering is a good candidate problem for introducing ISBSE. First and foremost, it is a maintenance problem, usually addressed for systems that already exist and, thus, there also exists developer memory on their current distribution of modules to clusters. Next, it presents the aspects that make it amenable for SBSE approaches: a large search space and quickly calculated fitness functions (MQ and EVM). The most frequently used strategy to encode solutions for this problem (see section 4.1) makes it simple to represent the current state of the system as a solution (first ISBSE requirement). Finally, the Hill Climbing search algorithm, which is frequently used to find solutions for the problem, can accommodate annotations on which modules are being moved from cluster to cluster as the search proceeds. Thus, one can modify the algorithm to record the set of transformations required to take an initial solution to the optimal state on each turn (second ISBSE requirement).

4   Empirical Design

This section conveys the design for an experimental study addressing the software module clustering problem through the tenets of ISBSE. This is a characterization study, in which we assess the number of restricted optimization turns required to take a problem instance (a software system) from its current state (a given distribution of modules to clusters) to the best solution found by an unrestricted optimization (another distribution of modules to clusters) and the number of downturns observed in the process. We do not compare different optimization techniques, but observe the relative loss incurred by performing a set of restricted optimization turns instead of an unrestricted, single optimization search.

4.1   Algorithm and Solution Encoding

The experiment used Hill Climbing searches to find solutions for the software clustering problem. Given a software system with N modules, an unrestricted search started by creating N clusters and assigning each module to a cluster according to the current state of the system. That is, modules located in the same cluster in the present system design occupied the same cluster in the initial solution. Thus, if the system had m < N clusters, N-m clusters remained empty (without modules) in the initial solution. A solution is represented as a vector with one entry per module, each entry containing an integer number in the [0, N-1] interval which indicates the cluster to which the related module is associated. Solution fitness was calculated, stored as the best solution found so far, and the main loop of the search followed.

The main loop attempted to find solutions with better fitness by iteratively moving a single module to a distinct cluster. The first module was selected and a move to any other cluster than the currently occupied one was evaluated. After all clusters had been evaluated for the first module, the search followed a similar procedure for the second one, the third, and so on. Whenever a solution with higher fitness was found, the new solution replaced the best known so far, and the main loop repeated its trials from the first module. If no movement could improve fitness, the search stopped. The search also stopped after a predefined budget of 2,000 times N^2 fitness evaluations was consumed, where N is the number of modules. The search approach was similar to the one followed Mancoridis et al. [19] and evaluation budget size was compatible with other works on the field [9, 20].

Restricted Hill Climbing searches representing the turns proposed by ISBSE were applied in sequence and followed the same search strategy described above, except for two differences: (a) while the first optimization turn used the current state of the system as starting solution, the following turns used the results of their preceding turn as starting point; and (b) after a predetermined number of module movements to distinct clusters were performed, the search was interrupted regardless of achieving a local maxima or consuming the available evaluation budget. Item (a) represented the sequence of improvements from an initial architecture to an improved one (on the perspective of the fitness function at hand), while item (b) enforced a maximum number of changes to be performed on each optimization turn.

4.2   Instances Used in the Experiment

The experiment was executed upon 32 real-world instances. We have selected open-source or free-software projects of distinct sizes, all developed in Java. We have also included a small IS developed for a Brazilian company in our instance pool (the SEEMP instance). Module dependency data was collected using the PF-CDA open-source static analysis tool. Table 1 presents the characteristics of the instances.

Table 1. Characteristics of the instances used in the experiment

Problem Instance	Modules	Clusters	Dependencies
jodamoney: Money type management library v0.6	26	2	102
jxlsreader: Library for reading Excel files v1.0	27	1	73
seemp: Small information system	31	9	61
apache_zip: File compression utility	36	2	86
udtjava: Native implementation for the UDT protocol v0.5	56	7	227
javaocr: Written text recognition library	59	13	155
servletapi: Java Servlets API v2.3	63	4	131
pfcda_base: Source code analisys software - model classes v1.1.1	67	8	197
forms: GUI form handling library v1.3.0	68	5	270
jscatterplot: Library for scatter-plot charts (part of JTreeview) v1.1.6	74	1	232
jfluid: Java profiler v1.7.0	82	4	315
jxlscore: Library to represent Excel files v1.0	83	10	330
jpassword96: Password management program - model classes v0.5	96	7	361
junit: Unit testing library v3.8.1	100	6	276
xmldom: Java XML DOM classes v1.0	119	9	209
tinytim: Topic Maps Engine v2.0	134	9	564
jkaryoscope: Library for karyoscope charts (part of JTreeview) v1.1.6	136	1	460
gae_core: Google App Engine core classes v2.5.1	140	22	375
javacc: Yacc implementation for Java v1.7	154	6	722
javageom: Java geometry library v0.11.0	172	21	1,445
jdendogram: Library for dendogram charts (part of JTreeview) v1.1.6	177	1	583
xmlapi: Java XML API v1.0	184	17	413
jmetal: Heuristic search algorithms library v3.1	190	46	1,137
dom4j: Alternative XML API for Java v1.5.2	195	16	930
pdf_renderer: Java PDF file renderer v0.2.1	199	10	629
jung_model: Jung Graph - model classes v2.0.1	207	21	603
jconsole: Java Console (part of JDK) v1.7.0	220	4	859
jung_visualization: Jung Graph - visualization classes v2.0.1	221	11	919
pfcda_swing: Source code analisys software - GUI classes v1.1.1	252	37	885
jpassword269: Password management program - complete v0.5	269	10	1,348
jml: Java MSN Messenger Library v1.0	270	15	1,745
notelab: Digital notebook for tablets v0.2.1	299	50	1,349

These instances were selected to cover a wide range of software products of different sizes, smoothly covering the space from small systems with less than 30 modules to mid-size systems with about 300 modules. For all further analysis, a module is a source code file, possibly conveying more than a single class. Since larger applications are usually divided into smaller deployment units, which can be independently subjected to the clustering process, we believe that the selected instances are representative of real systems. Finally, concentration on the Java language was due to the availability of an open-source static analysis tool.

4.3 Data Collection

For each instance we first collected the EVM value for the current distribution of modules to clusters (EVM_0), that is, the fitness of the solution as designed by the software development team. Then, we performed an unrestricted Hill Climbing search and computed the EVM value for the best solution found (EVM_C), as well as the number of module movements required to achieve this fitness (MOV_C) departing from the current distribution of modules to clusters.

Afterwards, we performed a sequence of restricted Hill Climbing searches, using 5 module movements as the maximum acceptable number of changes on each optimization turn (step size = 5). We recorded the number of turns (TRN_5) required to take the system from its initial state to a module distribution compatible with the EVM value found by the unrestricted search. We have also computed the number of downturns (DTN_5) incurred during the search, that is, the number of modules which were moved to a cluster A in a given turn, but then moved to a cluster B, A ≠ B, in a later turn.

The step size for the sequence of restricted optimizations was selected as a lower bound to the number of module movements which a development team could rememorize after each optimization turn. As this number is related to developers' short-term memory, we have used the 7±2 Miller number [27] as a reference and selected 5 as a lower bound to the number of movements. To determine how much this parameter affected our results, we performed similar sequences of restricted optimizations using 6, 7, 8, and 9 as step sizes. Thus, we produced and recorded the number of optimization turns (TRN_6 ... TRN_9) and downturns (DTN_6 ... DTN_9) on each scenario.

This experimental study aimed to determine if the nominal difference between EVM_0 and EVM_C or the number of module movements required by the unrestricted search (MOV_C) were correlated to instance size (number of modules) or complexity (number of dependencies). Similarly, we wanted to evaluate if the number of optimization turns or downturns were correlated to instance characteristics. Finally, we wanted to observe whether varying the step size would significantly change the number of required turns or downturns for our selected instances.

4.4   Analysis and Results

Table 2 presents the results collected from our experimental study for each instance listed in Table 1. The EVM_0 column presents the EVM value for the initial design of the referred instance (that is, the current state of the system). The EVM_C column presents the EVM found by the unrestricted Hill Climbing search. The MOV_C column conveys the number of module movements required to take the system from its present distribution of modules to clusters to the best distribution found by the unrestricted search. The TRN_5 column presents the number of restricted optimization turns, each with up to 5 module movements, required to achieve the same fitness of the unrestricted search. The DTN_5 column presents the number of downturns observed during the sequence of restricted optimizations. Columns TRN_X and DTN_X, where X varies from 6 to 9, represent similar values to TRN_5 and DTN_5 for step sizes 6, 7, 8, and 9, respectively. All numbers in Table 2 are deterministic, since all searches depart from the current solution and no random restart is enacted during the searches.

From Table 2 we observe that the difference between EVM_0 and EVM_C is quite large: it is 2,372 on average, strongly influenced by *jdendogram* (14,778), *jpassword* (8,970), and jkaryoscope (8,587). If these instances are suppressed, the average difference becomes 1,502. In relative terms, the average difference between the initial EVM and that found by the unrestricted search is more than 20 times larger than EVM_C (for no instance this difference is smaller than 170%). This is an interesting result because either all these programs have bad design or we (as a research community interested in the clustering problem) seem to be pursuing a different quality indicator than developers. To check whether the metric we have used would influence this result, we have performed a similar optimization procedure using MQ instead of EVM. The optimization with MQ fared better, producing an average nominal difference of 3.5 (max 14.91) and a percentile difference of 46% (max 100%).

Table 2. Results collected from unrestricted and restricted optimization turns. It can be observed that, even for small instances, a long sequence of restricted optimization turns is required to achieve the same results provided by an unrestricted optimization process.

Problem Instance	EVM_0	EVM_C	MOV_C	TRN_5	DTN_5	TRN_6	DTN_6	TRN_7	DTN_7	TRN_8	DTN_8	TRN_9	DTN_9
jodamoney	-33	28	14	6	10	4	5	4	8	3	6	2	3
jxlsreader	-205	26	25	8	11	6	9	5	6	5	8	4	6
seemp	-51	19	17	5	6	4	6	4	6	3	5	3	3
apache_zip	-302	29	34	12	24	10	21	8	15	7	19	6	17
udtjava	-126	65	33	12	22	10	19	8	13	7	17	6	11
javaocr	-28	39	29	8	7	7	7	6	9	5	6	4	7
servletapi	-338	49	59	21	41	19	49	14	34	12	35	10	27
pfcda_base	-410	45	58	20	39	18	44	13	26	12	30	10	29
forms	-412	77	56	18	32	15	28	11	19	11	26	9	20
jscatterplot	-2,355	58	73	26	54	20	44	17	46	14	37	12	32
Jfluid	-964	60	75	30	73	23	60	20	61	17	53	15	55
jxlscore	-200	81	62	22	44	19	45	16	42	13	38	11	32
jpassword96	-523	79	80	30	66	24	61	19	51	17	50	14	43
junit	-1,229	52	88	30	60	24	54	20	46	16	38	14	36
xmldom	-1,654	41	102	35	70	28	63	24	61	20	54	17	45
tinytim	-915	133	113	41	88	34	84	27	74	23	66	20	61
jkaryoscope	-8,484	103	135	48	101	38	89	31	79	27	79	24	74
gae_core	-929	65	97	34	68	26	52	22	50	17	37	14	28
javacc	-3,695	154	142	52	110	40	90	34	87	28	77	24	67
javageom	-295	359	118	44	92	35	83	29	79	25	71	22	69
jdendogram	-14,656	122	176	64	142	50	119	41	111	35	100	31	97
xmlapi	-1,841	98	151	53	107	41	90	35	87	30	86	26	74
jmetal	-470	170	124	44	86	34	72	28	65	25	63	22	63
dom4j	-1,851	180	167	59	123	49	120	40	104	35	107	30	97
pdf_renderer	-2,171	108	171	69	165	52	133	44	122	38	119	32	107
jung_model	-1,373	147	176	58	109	47	100	39	89	32	77	28	72
jconsole	-11,198	163	212	80	186	61	153	50	134	43	125	37	115
jung_visualization	-2,541	186	189	75	175	59	154	48	140	41	130	36	127
pfcda_swing	-674	215	175	60	116	46	94	39	87	32	76	29	78
jpassword269	-8,725	245	250	87	185	68	154	56	137	49	142	42	128
jml	-2,750	266	224	85	184	67	162	55	148	47	137	42	137
notelab	-788	251	198	59	92	48	82	39	65	34	70	29	59

We observe medium correlation between EVM_0 and the number of modules (-0.72) and the number of dependencies (-0.61). Throughout this paper, all correlations were calculated using the non-parametric Spearman rank-order coefficient and the R Statistics System, v2.15.3. We also observe strong correlation between EVM_C and the number of modules (+0.91) and the number of dependencies (+0.98). The same happens for the number of module movements on the unrestricted optimization, which is strongly correlated with both the number of modules (+0.98) and the number of dependencies (+0.90). Thus, we observe that the larger or the more complex the software system, the more module movements will be required to take the system from its present state to the module distribution found by the unrestricted optimization. The same results hold for MQ, though the unrestricted search with this metric required fewer module movements than the search using EVM for 31 out of 32 instances.

To assess the impact of running a sequence of restricted optimizations instead of a single, unrestricted search we must observe the TRN and DTN columns in Table 2.

The average number of restricted optimization turns required with a step size of five module movements is 40, while the average number of downturns is 84. These numbers are strongly correlated to the number of modules (+0.96 for TRN_5 and +0.93 for DTN_5) and dependencies (+0.89 for TRN_5 and +0.87 for DTN_5). If we take a large system, such as *jml*, 85 restricted turns would be required to take the system from its present state to the best EVM found by the unrestricted search. Moreover, 184 modules would be moved to a cluster in a turn just to be moved to another cluster later. To depict how large are these numbers, if an architect decided to perform one turn per week, it would take almost 20 months to fully optimize the system. Moreover, the unrestricted search requires 224 module movements, but a total of 408 movements would be required by restricted optimization due to the large number of downturns. Thus, we observe that there is significant cost in breaking the unrestricted search into small chunks, both in terms of the time required to reach the (close to) optimal state and the number of module movements that are later discarded.

These results present improvements if larger step sizes are acceptable. Table 3 shows the average TRN and DTN values for different step sizes. All results are strongly correlated with both the number of modules and dependencies. If we consider the *jml* instance with a step size of 9 movements, incremental optimization required 42 turns and incurred in 137 downturns to reach the effectiveness of the unrestricted search. Thus, it seems reasonable to use larger step sizes for large instances, possibly a fraction of their number of modules with a lower bound of 5 for small instances. Optimization with the MQ and a step size of 5 module movements confirms the pattern observed with EVM, but requires less restricted turns for 26 out of 32 instances (on average, EVM requires 6.4 times more turns) and produces less downturns in 24 out of 32 instances (on average, EVM produces 11.9 times more downturns).

Table 3. Average number of restricted optimization turns required to achieve the EVM value found by the unrestricted optimization and average number of downturns observed, according to step size

	TRN_5	DTN_5	TRN_6	DTN_6	TRN_7	DTN_7	TRN_8	DTN_8	TRN_9	DTN_9
Average value per instance	40	84	32	73	26	66	23	62	20	57

Figure 1 presents the evolution of EVM values over restricted optimization turns in an instance basis and using a step size of 5 module movements. The vertical axis of each chart represents EVM values, varying from EVM_0 (at the bottom) to EVM_C (at the top). The horizontal axis represents the number of optimization turns, from zero to TRN_5 for the related instance. We observe that some instances present super-linear growth in the first optimization turns (see *jxlsreader*), while others present a closer to linear behavior (see *javaocr*). Other instances also lag behind linear behavior on the first turns before increasing the pace towards EVM_C (see *xmldom*). Smaller step sizes may be considered for instances which present expressive improvements on their first turns, attaining gains from optimization while preserving developers' knowledge. On the other hand, larger step sizes may be considered for those instances which are reacting more slowly to the optimization process, fastening their evolution towards the best solution found by the unrestricted optimization process.

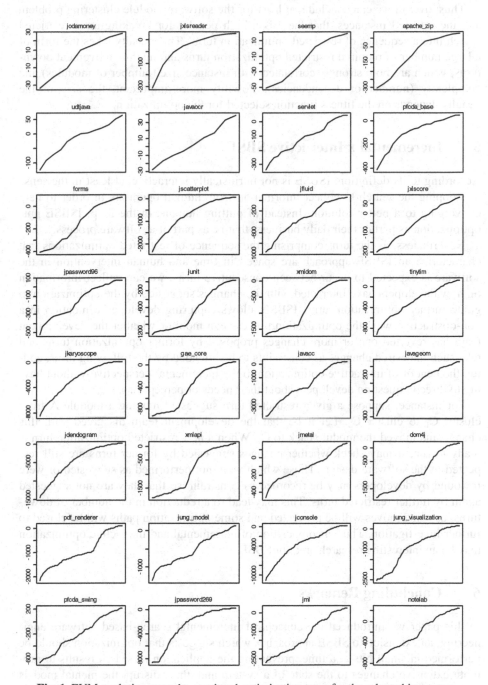

Fig. 1. EVM evolution over the restricted optimization turns for the selected instances

Thus, overall we can conclude, at least for the software module clustering problem and the selected instances, that there is a high penalty for breaking an unrestricted search into a sequence of restricted optimization turns. This penalty takes the form of a large number of required restricted optimization turns and module movement downturns, which are both strongly correlated with instance size (number of modules) and complexity (number of dependencies). Possibly more important, the size of the penalty depends on the fitness function selected for the optimization.

5   Incremental x Interactive SBSE

According to its definition, ISBSE is not intrinsically interactive, at least in the sense of stopping the search to collect information from human operators in order to help converging to a better solution. Instead of putting humans in the loop, ISBSE puts optimization as part of their daily business, that is, as part of a software process.

Nevertheless, as the turns comprising the sequence of restricted optimizations that characterize an ISBSE approach are spaced in time and human intervention in the software is expected to occur between consecutive turns, we can collect information on how developers have interacted with the changes suggested by the optimization to guide further optimization turns. ISBSE allows capturing developer's intention in a non-obstructive way: the optimization process can monitor whether the development team has reverted one or more changes proposed by former optimization turns and take such undesired changes as constraints to be attended by the following turns, adding the benefit of interactive optimization to the incremental perspective without having to directly question developers about their needs or perceptions.

For instance, suppose a given restricted turn suggested moving a module A from cluster C_1 to cluster C_2. Let it be that the development team disagreed with this change and moved the module back to C_1. When a new restricted optimization turn is ready to run, it may check whether changes suggested by former turns are still respected in the software design. Those which were not performed as suggested or were rewound by developers may be recorded as constraint so that they are not suggested again by further restricted turns. This may lead to a reduction in the number of downturns, as some moves will be prevented and some optimization paths will be closed to further investigation. Thus, a composition of incremental and interactive optimization may be an interesting research area for SBSE.

6   Concluding Remarks

In this paper we introduced the concept of incremental search-based software engineering, an extension to SBSE approaches which suggests that optimization should be performed in small bits at a time, preventing the application of search results to promote extensive changes to the state of a system and, thus, disrupt the mental models maintained by developers on regard of its structure. We have performed an experimental study to address potential losses in breaking large optimization processes into sequences of restricted optimization turns for the software clustering problem.

Results suggest that the penalty for breaking the search may be large, but it also depends on instance size, instance complexity, the number of changes accepted on each restricted optimization turn, and (most interestingly) on the fitness function driving the search. The experiment used a deterministic Hill Climbing search, but further work may explore stochastic search by shuffling the order in which modules are considered.

One of the most interesting results found during our research is the dependence between the size of penalties incurred by adopting a sequence of restricted optimization turns and the fitness function used to drive the search. Despite of being less resilient to noisy dependencies between modules, the MQ fitness function required less restricted optimization turns to achieve the same performance of an unrestricted search than the EVM function for 26 out of 32 instances. Moreover, MQ induced the search to significantly less downturns than EVM (almost 12 times less, on average). Thus, as it occurs with dynamic adaptive SBSE [28, 29], the adoption of ISBSE adds new requirements for fitness functions: a regular fitness landscape which allows a sequence of neighborhood-limited optimizations to follow a path as straight as possible to the one followed by an unrestricted search. Once again we see the two-fold relationship between SBSE and metrics [30], in which the first requires the latter to guide search processes but, at the same time, may help shaping new metrics as it prescribes new requirements and purposes for them. Further works may extend the present one to address this issue, as well as generalize and refine the terms used as part of ISBSE definition, such as turns, downturns, and restricted optimization.

Acknowledgements. The authors would like to express their gratitude to CNPq, the research agency that financially supported this project.

References

1. Harman, M.: The Current State and Future of Search Based Software Engineering. In: 29th International Conference on Software Engineering (ICSE 2007), Future of Software Engineering (FoSE), Minneapolis, USA, pp. 20–26 (May 2007)
2. Antoniol, G., Penta, M., Harman, M.: Search-based techniques applied to optimization of project planning for a massive maintenance project. In: 21st IEEE International Conference on Software Maintenance, Los Alamitos, California, USA, pp. 240–249 (2005)
3. Bagnall, A., Rayward-Smith, V., Whittley, I.: The next release problem. Information and Software Technology 43(14), 883–890 (2001)
4. Dolado, J.J.: A validation of the component-based method for software size estimation. IEEE Transactions on Software Engineering 26(10), 1006–1021 (2000)
5. Barreto, A., Barros, M., Werner, C.: Staffing a software project: A constraint satisfaction and optimization based approach. Computers and Operations Research (COR) focused issue on Search Based Software Engineeering 35(10), 3073–3089 (2008)
6. McMinn, P.: Search-based software test data generation: A survey. Software Testing, Verification and Reliability 14(2), 105–156 (2004)
7. Mitchell, B., Mancoridis, S.: On the automatic modularization of software systems using the bunch tool. IEEE Transactions on Software Engineering 32(3), 193–208 (2006)

8. Durillo, J.J., Zhang, Y., Alba, E., Nebro, A.J.: A Study of the Multi-objective Next Release Problem. In: Proceedings of the 1st Symposium on Search-based Software Engineering, Windsor, UK, pp. 49–58 (2009)
9. Barros, M.: An Analysis of the Effects of Composite Objectives in Multiobjective Software Module Clustering. In: Proceedings of the Genetic and Evolutionary Computation Conference (GECCO 2012), Philadelphia, USA (2012)
10. Bavota, G., Carnevale, F., De Lucia, A., Di Penta, M., Oliveto, R.: Putting the Developer in-the-loop: an Interactive GA for Software Re-Modularization. In: Proc. of the 4th Symposium on Search-based Software Engineering, Riva del Garda, Italy, pp. 75–89 (2012)
11. Ferrucci, F., Gravino, C., Sarro, F.: How Multi-Objective Genetic Programming is Effective for Software Development Effort Estimation? In: Proceedings of the 3rd Symposium for Search-based Software Engineering, Szeged, HU, pp. 274–275 (2011)
12. Francescomarino, C., Marchetto, A., Tonella, P.: Cluster-based modularization of processes recovered from web applications. Journal of Software: Evolution and Process 25(2), 113–138 (2013)
13. Magdaleno, A.: An optimization-based approach to software development process tailoring. In: Proc. of the 2nd Symposium for Search-based Software Engineering, Benevento, IT (2010)
14. Yoo, S., Harman, M.: Regression Testing, Minimisation, Selection and Prioritisation: A Survey. Software: Testing, Verification & Reliability 22(2), 67–120 (2012)
15. Bowman, M., Briand, L., Labiche, Y.: Solving the Class Responsibility Assignment Problem in Object-oriented Analysis with Multi-Objective Genetic Algorithms. IEEE Transactions on Software Engineering 36(6), 817–837 (2010)
16. O'Keeffe, M., Cinnéide, M.: Search-based Refactoring: An Empirical Study. Journal of Software Maintenance and Evolution: Research and Practice 20(5), 345–364 (2008)
17. Deligiannis, I., Shepperd, M., Roumeliotis, M., Stamelos, I.: An empirical investigation of an object-oriented design heuristic for maintainability. Journal of Systems and Software 65(2) (2003)
18. Gibbs, S., Tsichritzis, D., et al.: Class Management for Software Communities. Communications of the ACM 33(9), 90–103 (1990)
19. Mancoridis, S., Mitchell, B.S., Chen, Y., Gansner, E.R.: Bunch: A Clustering Tool for the Recovery and Maintenance of Software System Structures. In: Proceedings of the IEEE International Conference on Software Maintenance, pp. 50–59 (1999)
20. Praditwong, K., Harman, M., Yao, X.: Software Module Clustering as a Multiobjective Search Problem. IEEE Transactions on Software Engineering 37(2), 262–284 (2011)
21. Larman, C.: Applying UML and Patterns: An Introduction to Object-Oriented Analysis and the Unified Process. Prentice Hall, Upper Saddle River (2002)
22. Briand, L.C., Morasca, S., Basili, V.R.: Defining and Validating Measures for Object-based High-Level Design. IEEE Transactions on Software Engineering 25(5) (1999)
23. Harman, M., Swift, S., Mahdavi, K.: An Empirical Study of the Robustness of two Module Clustering Fitness Functions. In: Proceedings of the Genetic and Evolutionary Computing Conference (GECCO 2005), Washington, DC, USA (2005)
24. Tucker, A., Swift, S., Liu, X.: Grouping Multivariate Time Series via Correlation. IEEE Transactions on Systems, Man, & Cybernetics, B: Cybernetics 31(2), 235–245 (2001)
25. LaToza, T.D., Venolia, G., DeLine, R.: Maintaining Mental Models: A Study of Developer Work Habits. In: Proc. of the 28th International Conference on Software Engineering, Shangai, CH (2006)

26. Ko, A., DeLine, R., Venolia, G.: Information Needs in Collocated Software Development Teams. In: Proc. of the 29th International Conference on Software Engineering, EUA (2007)
27. Miller, G.A.: The magical number seven, plus or minus two: Some limits on our capacity for processing information. Psychological Review 63(2), 81–97 (1956)
28. Harman, M., Clark, J.A., Cinnédie, M.Ó.: Dynamic Adaptive Search Based Software Engineering Needs Fast Approximate Metrics. In: Proceedings of the 4th International Workshop on Emerging Trends in Software Metrics, San Francisco, USA (2013)
29. Harman, M., Burke, E., Clark, J.A., Yao, X.: Dynamic Adaptive Search Based Software Engineering. In: 6th IEEE International Symposium on Empirical Software Engineering and Measurement (ESEM 2012), Lund, Sweden, pp. 1–8 (2012)
30. Harman, M., Clark, J.A.: Metrics are fitness functions too. In: Proceedings of the 10th International Symposium on Software Metrics, pp. 58–69 (2004)

Competitive Coevolutionary Code-Smells Detection

Mohamed Boussaa[1], Wael Kessentini[1], Marouane Kessentini[1], Slim Bechikh[1,2],
and Soukeina Ben Chikha[2]

[1] CS, Missouri University of Science and Technology Missouri, USA
{bm217,marouanek,wa235,bechikhs}@mst.edu
[2] University of Tunis Tunis, Tunisia
soukeina.benchikha@insat.rnu.tn

Abstract. Software bad-smells, also called design anomalies, refer to design situations that may adversely affect the maintenance of software. Bad-smells are unlikely to cause failures directly, but may do it indirectly. In general, they make a system difficult to change, which may in turn introduce bugs. Although these bad practices are sometimes unavoidable, they should be in general fixed by the development teams and removed from their code base as early as possible. In this paper, we propose, for the first time, the use of competitive coevolutionary search to the code-smells detection problem. We believe that such approach to code-smells detection is attractive because it allows combining the generation of code-smell examples with the production of detection rules based on quality metrics. The main idea is to evolve two populations simultaneously where the first one generates a set of detection rules (combination of quality metrics) that maximizes the coverage of a base of code-smell examples and the second one maximizes the number of generated "artificial" code-smells that are not covered by solutions (detection rules) of the first population. The statistical analysis of the obtained results shows that our proposed approach is promising when compared to two single population-based metaheuristics on a variety of benchmarks.

1   Introduction

In general, object oriented software systems need to follow some traditional set of design principles such as data abstraction, encapsulation, and modularity [8]. However, some of these non-functional requirements can be violated by developers for many reasons like inexperience with object-oriented design principles, deadline stress, and much focus on only implementing main functionality.

As a consequence, there has been much research focusing on the study of bad design practices, also called code-smells, defects, anti-patterns or anomalies [8, 9, 11] in the literature. Although these bad practices are sometimes unavoidable, they should be in general prevented by the development teams and removed from their code base as early as possible. In fact, detecting and removing these code-smells help developers to easily understand source code [9]. In this work, we focus on the detection of code-smells.

G. Ruhe and Y. Zhang (Eds.): SSBSE 2013, LNCS 8084, pp. 50–65, 2013.
© Springer-Verlag Berlin Heidelberg 2013

The vast majority of existing work in code-smells detection relies on declarative rule specification [19, 20]. In these settings, rules are manually defined to identify the key symptoms that characterize a code-smell using combinations of mainly quantitative (metrics), structural, and/or lexical information. However, in an exhaustive scenario, the number of possible code-smells to manually characterize with rules can be large. For each code-smell, rules that are expressed in terms of metric combinations need substantial calibration efforts to find the right threshold value for each metric. Another important issue is that translating symptoms into rules is not obvious because there is no consensual symptom-based definition of code-smells [9]. When consensus exists, the same symptom could be associated to many code-smells types, which may compromise the precise identification of code-smell types. These difficulties explain a large portion of the high *false-positive* rates reported in existing research.

In this paper, we start from the observation that most of existing works related to the use of SBSE or machine learning techniques [12, 13] require a high number of code-smell examples (data) to provide efficient solutions that can be based on detection rules or classification algorithms. However, code-smells are not usually documented by developers (unlike bugs report). To this end, we introduce an alternative approach based on the use of a Competitive Co-Evolutionary Algorithm (*CCEA*) [2]. We believe that a *CCEA* approach to code-smells detection is attractive because it allows us to combine the generation of code-smell examples with the generation of detection rules based on quality metrics. We show how this combination can be formulated as two populations in a Competitive Co-evolutionary search. In *CCEA*, two populations of solutions evolve simultaneously with the fitness of each depending upon the current population of the other. The first population generates a set of detection rules (combination of quality metrics) that maximizes the coverage of a base of code-smell examples and simultaneously a second population tries to maximize the number of generated "artificial" code-smells that are not covered by solutions (detection rules) of the first population. The artificial code-smell examples are generated based on the notion of deviance from well-designed code fragments.

We implemented our *CCEA* approach and evaluated it on four systems [14, 15, 16, 17] using an existing benchmark [19, 13]. We report the results on the effectiveness and efficiency of our approach, compared to different existing single population-based approaches [12, 18]. The statistical analysis of our results indicates that the *CCEA* approach has great promise; *CCEA* significantly outperforms both random and single population-based approaches with an average of more than 80% of precision and recall based on an existing benchmark containing four large open source systems [14, 15, 16, 17].

The primary contributions of this paper can be summarized as follows: (1) the paper introduces a novel formulation of the code-smell's problem using Competitive Co-evolution and, to the best of our knowledge, this is the first paper in the literature to use competitive co-evolution to detect code-smells; (2) The paper reports the results of an empirical study with an implementation of our co-evolutionary approach, compared to existing single population approaches [12, 18]. The obtained results provide evidence to support the claim that competitive co-evolution is more efficient and effective than single population evolution.

The remainder of this paper is as follows: Section 2 presents the relevant background and the motivation for the presented work; Section 3 describes the search algorithm; an evaluation of the algorithm is explained and its results are discussed in Section 4; Section 5 is dedicated to related work. Finally, concluding remarks and future work are provided in Section 6.

2   Code-Smells Detection Overview

In this section, we first provide the necessary background of detecting code-smells and discuss the challenges and open problems that are addressed by our proposal.

2.1   Definitions

Code-smells, also called design anomalies or design defects, refer to design situations that adversely affect the software maintenance. As stated by [9], bad-smells are unlikely to cause failures directly, but may do it indirectly. In general, they make a system difficult to change, which may in turn introduce bugs. Different types of code-smells, presenting a variety of symptoms, have been studied in the intent of facilitating their detection [20] and suggesting improvement solutions. In [20], Beck defines 22 sets of symptoms of code smells. These include large classes, feature envy, long parameter lists, and lazy classes. Each code-smell type is accompanied by refactoring suggestions to remove it. Brown et al. [9] define another category of code-smells that are documented in the literature, and named anti-patterns. In our approach, we focus on the three following code-smell types: Blob: It is found in designs where one large class monopolizes the behavior of a system (or part of it), and the other classes primarily encapsulate data; Spaghetti Code: It is a code with a complex and tangled control structure; Functional Decomposition: It occurs when a class is designed with the intent of performing a single function. This is found in code produced by non-experienced object-oriented developers. We choose these code-smell types in our experiments because they are the most frequent and hard to detect and fix based on a recent empirical study [19, 13].

The code-smells' detection process consists in finding code fragments that violate structure or semantic properties such as the ones related to coupling and complexity. In this setting, internal attributes used to define these properties, are captured through software metrics and properties are expressed in terms of valid values for these metrics [21]. This follows a long tradition of using software metrics to evaluate the quality of the design including the detection of code-smells [11]. The most widely-used metrics are the ones defined by [21]. These metrics include Depth of Inheritance Tree, Weighted Methods per Class, Cohesion and Coupling Between Objects (CBO), etc. In this paper, we use variations of these metrics and adaptations of procedural ones as well, e.g., the number of lines of code in a class, number of lines of code in a method, number of attributes in a class, number of methods, lack of cohesion in methods, number of accessors, and number of private fields. We are using in this paper these metrics to generate code-smell examples and also detection rules.

2.2   Detection Issues

Overall, there is no general consensus on how to decide if a particular design fragment is a code-smell. In fact, deciding which classes are Blob candidates heavily depends on the interpretation of each analyst. In some contexts, an apparent violation of a design principle may be consensually accepted as normal practice. For example, a "Log" class responsible for maintaining a log of events in a program, used by a large number of classes, is a common and acceptable practice. However, from a strict code-smell definition, it can be considered as a class with an abnormally large coupling. Another issue is related to the definition of thresholds when dealing with quantitative information. For example, the Blob detection involves information such as class size. Although we can measure the size of a class, an appropriate threshold value is not trivial to define. A class considered large in a given program/community of users could be considered average in another.

Most of existing work related to the use of SBSE or machine learning techniques require a high number of code-smell examples to provide efficient solutions that can be based on detection rules or classification algorithms. However, code-smells are not usually documented by developers (not like bugs for example that are documented in bug reports). Thus, it is difficult to find these code-smell examples except in few open-source systems that are evaluated manually.

Finally, detecting dozens of code-smells occurrences in a system is not always helpful except if the list of code-smells is sorted by priority. In addition to the presence of false positives that may create a rejection reaction from development teams, the process of using the detected lists, understanding the code-smell candidates, selecting the true positives, and correcting them is long, expensive, and not always profitable. Thus, it is important to identify the type of code-smells when detecting them to help developers to prioritize the list of detected code-smells.

3   Competitive Coevolution for Code-Smells Detection

This section address the different issues described in Section 2 using *CCEA*. We first present an overview of the competitive coevolution algorithms and, subsequently, provide the details of our adaptation of *CCEA* to detect code-smells.

3.1   Approach Overview

3.1.1 Competitive Co-evolution Algorithms
The idea of *Co-evolutionary algorithms* (*CCEAs*) comes from the biological observation which shows that co-evolving some number of species defined as collections of phenotypically similar individuals is more realistic than simply evolving a population containing representatives of one species. Hence, instead of evolving a population (globally or spatially distributed) of similar individuals representing a global solution, it is more appropriate to co-evolve subpopulations of individuals representing specific parts of the global solution [1]. There are two types of co-evolution in the related literature: (1) *Cooperation* and (2) *Competition*.

Cooperation consists in subdividing the problem at hand into different sub-problems of smaller sizes than the original one and then solving it in a cooperative manner. In fact, each sub-population helps the others with the aim to solve the original problem. Competition consists in making solutions belonging to different species competing with each others with the goal to create *fitter* individuals in each species. Since we are interested in this paper in competitive co-evolution, we just detail, in what follows, *competitive CCEAs*. Differently to canonic EAs, in competitive CCEAs the population is subdivided into a pre-specified number of sub-populations (each denoting a species) where the fitness value of a particular individual depends on the fitness values of other individuals belonging to other sub-populations. The interaction in terms of fitness assignment could be seen as a *competition* between the individuals because an improvement of the fitness value of a particular individual leads to the degradation of the fitness value of some others. Such competition between different solutions belonging to different species allows not only guiding the search of each sub-population towards fitter individuals but also escaping from local optima [2]. Several competitive CCEAs have been demonstrated to be effective and efficient in solving different kinds of problems such as the sorting network problem [3] and the integrated manufacturing planning and scheduling one [4]. Within the SBSE community, there are three works using competitive CCEAs such as: (1) Wilkerson et al. [5] tackling the software correction problem, (2) Arcuri and Ya [6] handling the bug fixing problem and (3) Adamopoulos et al. [7] tackling the mutation testing problem. In this paper, we present the first adaptation of *CCEA* to detect code-smells.

3.1.2 Competitive Co-evolution-Based Code-Smells Detection

The concept of co-evolution is based on the idea that two populations are evolved in parallel with a specific designed genetic algorithm (GA) [2]. The main component of our proposal is the competitive co-evolutionary algorithm. This type of co-evolution is comparable to what happens between prey and predators. Preys are the potential solutions to the optimization problem, while the predators are individuals aiming to check the survival ability of prey. In general, faster prey escape predators easily, thus they have higher chance of generating offspring. This influences the predators, since they need to evolve as well to get faster if they need to survive.

As described in Figure 1, based on this metaphor two populations evolves in parallel to reach two objectives in a competitive way. The first population uses knowledge from code-smells' examples (input) to generate detection rules based on quality metrics (input). It takes as inputs a base (i.e. a set) of code smells' examples, and takes, as controlling parameters, a set of quality metrics [21] and generates as output a set of rules. The rule generation process chooses randomly, from the metrics provided list, a combination of quality metrics (and their threshold values) to detect a specific code-smell. Consequently, a solution is a set of rules that best detect the code-smells of the base of examples. For example, the following rule states that a class c having more than 10 attributes and more than 20 methods is considered as a blob smell: R1: IF NAD(c)$\geq$10 AND NMD(c)$\geq$20 Then Blob(c). In this exemplified sample rule, the number of attributes (NAD) and the number of methods (NMD) of a class correspond to two quality metrics that are used to detect a blob. The detection rules solutions are evaluated based on the coverage of the base of code-smell examples (input) and also the coverage of generated "artificial" code-smells by the second population. These two measures are to maximize by the population of detection rules solutions.

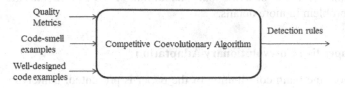

Fig. 1. Approach overview

The second population executed in parallel uses well-designed code examples to generate "artificial" code-smells based on the notion of deviation from a reference (well-designed) set of code fragments [18].The generation process of artificial code-smell examples is performed using a heuristic search that maximizes on one hand, the distance between generated code-smell examples and reference code examples and, on the other hand, minimizes the number of generated examples that are not detected by the first population (detection rules). The similarity function used is based on the distance (difference) between quality metrics [21].

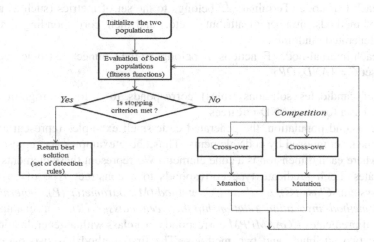

Fig. 2. Competitive co-evolutionary algorithm for code-smells detection

Figure 2 describe the overall process of CCEA for code-smells detection. The first step of the algorithm consists of generating randomly two populations. In our case, a first population generates detection rules from the list of metrics (input) and a second population generates "artificial" code-smell examples. Each population is evaluated using a fitness function. The first population maximizes the coverage of both: code-smells in the base of examples and generate "artificial" code-smell examples generated by the second population. The second population maximizes the number of generated code-smell examples that are not covered/detected by the first population and the distance with a reference (well-designed) set of code fragments. Then, change operators (selection, cross-over and mutation) are applied to generated new solutions (populations). The process is iterated until a termination criterion is met (e.g. number of iterations). Next we describe our adaptation of CCEA [2] to the test cases generation problem in more details.

3.2   Competitive Co-evolutionary Adaptation

In this section, the main contribution of the paper is presented, namely, a method for evolving test case models in parallel with mutation analysis using *CCEA*.

3.2.1 Solution Representations

For the first population that generated detection rules, a solution is composed of terminals and functions. After evaluating many parameters related to the code-smells detection problem, the terminal set and the function set are decided as follows. The terminals correspond to different quality metrics with their threshold values (constant values). The functions that can be used between these metrics are Union (OR) and Intersection (AND). More formally, each candidate solution S in this problem is a sequence of detection rules where each rule is represented by a binary tree such that:

(1)   each leaf-node (Terminal) L belongs to the set of metrics (such as number of methods, number of attributes, etc.) and their corresponding thresholds generated randomly.
(2)   each internal-node (Functions) N belongs to the Connective (logic operators) set $C = \{AND, OR\}$.

The set of candidates solutions (rules) corresponds to a logic program that is represented as a forest of AND-OR trees.

For the second population, the generated code-smell examples represent artificial code fragments composed by code elements. Thus, these examples are represented as a vector where each dimension is a code element. We represent these elements as sets of predicates. Each predicate type corresponds to a construct type of an object-oriented system: *Class (C), attribute (A), method (M), parameter (P), generalization (G), and method invocation relationship between classes (R).* For example, the sequence of predicates *CGAAMPPM* corresponds to a class with a generalization link, containing two attributes and two methods. The first method has two parameters. Predicates include details about the associated constructs (visibility, types, etc.). These details (thereafter called parameters) determine ways a code fragment can deviate from a notion of normality.

To generate initial populations, we start by defining the maximum tree/vector length (max number of metrics/code-elements per solution). The tree/vector length is proportional to the number of metrics/code-elements to use for code-smells detection. Sometimes, a high tree/vector length does not mean that the results are more precise. These parameters can be specified either by the user or chosen randomly.

3.2.2 Fitness Functions

The fitness function quantifies the quality of the proposed solutions (individuals). For the first population, to evaluate detection-rules solutions the fitness function is based on: (1) maximizing the coverage of the base of code-smell examples (input) and (2) maximizing the number of covered "artificial" code-smells generated by the second population executed in parallel. For the second population, executed in parallel, to evaluate generated code-smell examples the fitness function is based on: (1) a dissimilarity score, to maximize, between generated code-smells and different reference code fragments and (2) maximizing the number of generated code-smell examples un-covered by the solutions of the first population (detection rules). In the following, we detail these functions.

The objective function of the first population checks to maximize the number of detected code-smells in comparison to the expected ones in the base of examples (input) and the generated "artificial" code-smells by the second population. In this context, we define this objective function of a particular solution S, normalized in the range $[0,1]$ as follows:

$$Max\ f\_coverage(S) = r + \frac{\frac{\sum_{i=1}^{p} a_i(S)}{t} + \frac{\sum_{i=1}^{p} a_i(S)}{p}}{2}$$

where r is the minimum number (among all generated detection solutions) of detected "artificial" code-smells divided by the number of generated ones (precision), p is the number of detected code-smells after executing the solution (detection rules) on systems of the base of code-smell examples, t is the number of expected code-smells to detect in the base of examples and $a_i(S)$ is the ith component of S such that:

$$a_i(S) = \begin{cases} 1 \ \text{if the}\ i^{th}\ \text{detected code smell exists in the base of examples} \\ 0 \ \text{otherwise} \end{cases}$$

The second population should seek to optimize the following two objectives:

(1) Maximize the generality of the generated "artificial" code-smells by maximizing the similarity with the reference code examples;
(2) Maximize the number of un-covered "artificial" code-smells by the solutions of the first population (detection rules)

These two objectives define the cost function that evaluates the quality of a solution and, then guides the search. The cost of a solution D (set of generated code-smells) is evaluated as the average costs of the included code-smells. Formally, the fitness function to maximize is

$$\cos t(d_i) = Max(\sum_{j=1}^{w} \sum_{k=1}^{l} |M_k(d_i) - M_k(c_j)|) + z$$

where w is the number of code elements (e.g. classes) in the reference code (c), l is the number of metrics, M is a metric (such as number of methods, number of attributes, etc.) and z is the minimum number of artificial code-smells (among all solutions) un-covered by the solutions of the first population over the number of generated "artificial" code-smells.

3.2.3 Change Operators

Selection

In this work, we use an elitist scheme for both selection phases with the aim to: (1) exploit good genes of fittest solutions and (2) preserve the best individuals along the evolutionary process. The two selections schemes are described as follows. Concerning parent selection, once the population individuals are evaluated, we select the $|P|/2$ best individuals of the population P to fulfill the mating pool, which size is equal to $|P|/2$. This allows exploiting the past experience of the EA in discovering the best chromosomes' genes. Once this step is performed, we apply genetic operators (crossover and mutation) to produce the offspring population Q, which has the same size as P ($|P|=|Q|$). Since crossover and mutation are stochastic operators, some offspring individuals can be worse than some of P individuals. In order to ensure elitism, we merge both population P and Q into U ($|U|=|P|+|Q|=2|P|$), and then the population P for the next generation will be composed by the $|P|$ fittest individuals from U. By doing this, we ensure that we do not encourage the survival of a worse individual over a better one.

Mutation

For the first population, the mutation operator can be applied to a function node, or a terminal node. It starts by randomly selected a node in the tree. Then, if the selected node is a terminal (quality metric), it is replaced by another terminal (metric or another threshold value); if it is a function (AND-OR), it is replaced by a new function; and if tree mutation is to be carried out, the node and its subtree are replaced by a new randomly generated subtree.

For the second population, the mutation operator consists of randomly changing a predicate (code element) in the generated predicates.

Crossover

For the first population, two parent individuals are selected and a subtree is picked on each one. Then crossover swaps the nodes and their relative subtrees from one parent to the other. This operator must ensure the respect of the depth limits. The crossover operator can be applied with only parents having the same rules category (code-smell type to detect). Each child thus combines information from both parents. In any given generation, a variant will be the parent in at most one crossover operation.

For the second population, the crossover operator allows to create two offspring o1 and o2 from the two selected parents p_1 and p_2. It is defined as follows:

(1) A random position k, is selected in the predicate sequences.
(2) The first k elements of p_1 become the first k elements of o_1. Similarly, the first k elements of p_2 become the first k elements of o_2.
(3) The remaining elements of, respectively, p_1 and p_2 are added as second parts of, respectively, o_2 and o_1.

For instance, if $k = 3$ and $p_1 =$ CAMMPPP and $p_2 =$ CMPRMPP, then $o_1 =$ CAMRMPP and $o_2 =$ CMPMPPP.

4   Validation

In order to evaluate our approach for detecting code-smells using *CCEA*, we conducted a set of experiments based on four large open source systems [14] [15] [16] [17].

4.1   Research Questions and Objectives

The study was conducted to quantitatively assess the completeness and correctness of our code-smells detection approach when applied in real-world settings and to compare its performance with existing approaches [12] [18]. More specifically, we aimed at answering the following research questions (*RQ*):

- *RQ1:* To what extent can the proposed approach detect efficiently code-smells (in terms of correctness and completeness)?
- *RQ2:* To what extent does the competitive co-evolution approach performs better than the considered single-population ones?

To answer *RQ1*, we used an existing corpus [19] [13] containing an extensive study of code-smells on different open-source systems: (1) ArgoUML v0.26 [16], (2) Xerces v2.7 [15], (3) Ant-Apache v1.5 [14], and (4) Azureus v2.3.0.6 [17]. Our goal is to evaluate the correctness and the completeness of our *CCEA* code-smells detection approach. For *RQ2*, we compared our results to those produced, over 30 runs, by existing single-population approaches [12] [18]. Further details about our experimental setting are discussed in the next subsection.

4.2   Experimental Settings

Our study considers the extensive evolution of different open-source Java analyzed in the literature [13] [18] [19]. The corpus [19] [13] used includes Apache Ant [14], ArgoUML [16], Azureus [17] and Xerces-J [15]. Table 1 reports the size in terms of classes of the analyzed systems. The table also reports the number of code-smells identified manually in the different systems. More than 700 code-smells have been identified manually. Indeed, in [13] [18] [19], authors asked different groups of developers to analyze the libraries to tag instances of specific code-smells to validate their detection techniques. For replication purposes, they provided a corpus of describing instances of different code-smells that includes blob classes, spaghetti code, and functional decompositions. These represent different types of design risks. In our study, we verified the capacity of our approach to locate classes that correspond to instances of these code-smells.

We choose the above-mentioned open source systems because they are medium/large-sized open-source projects and were analyzed in the related work.

The initial versions of Apache Ant were known to be of poor quality, which has led to major revised versions. Xerces-J, ArgoUML, and Azureus have been actively developed over the past 10 years, and their design has not been responsible for a slowdown of their developments.

Table 1. The Systems Studied.

Systems	Number of classes	Number of code-smells
ArgoUML v0.26	1358	138
Xerces v2.7	991	82
Ant-Apache v1.5	1024	103
Azureus v2.3.0.6	1449	108

For the first population, one open source project is evaluated by using the remaining systems as a base of code-smells' examples to generate detection rules. For the second population, JHotdraw [22] was chosen as an example of reference code because it contains very few known code-smells. Thus, in our experiments, we used all the classes of JHotdraw as our example set of well-designed code.

When applying precision and recall in the context of our study, the precision denotes the fraction of correctly detected code-smells among the set of all detected code-smells. The recall indicates the fraction of correctly detected code-smells among the set of all manually identified code-smells (i.e., how many code-smells have not been missed).

We remove the system to evaluate from the base of code-smell examples when executing our *CCEA* algorithm then precision and recall scores are calculated automatically based on a comparison between the detected code-smells and expected ones. We compared our results with existing single-population approaches [12, 18]. We used precision and recall scores for all these comparisons over 51 runs. Since the used algorithms are meta-heuristics, they produce different results on every run when applied to the same problem instance. To cope with this stochastic nature, we used the Wilcoxon rank sum test [23] in the comparative study. For our experiment, we generated at each iteration up-to 150 "artificial" code-smells from deviation with JHotDraw (about a quarter of the number of reference examples) with a maximum size of 256 characters. We used the same parameter setting for *CCEA* and single-population algorithms [12, 18]. The population size is fixed to 100 and the number of generations to 1000. In this way, all algorithms perform 100000 evaluations. A maximum of 15 rules per solution and a set of 13 metrics are considered for the first population [21]. These standard parameters are widely used in the literature [2, 6, 7].

4.3   Results and Discussions

Tables 2 and 3 summarize our findings. Overall, as described in table 2, we were able to detect code-smells on the different systems with an average precision higher than 83%. For Xerces, and Ant-Apache, the precision is highest than other systems with more than 92%. This is can be explained by the fact that these systems are smaller than

others and contain lower number of code-smells to detect. For ArgoUML, the precision
is also high (around 90%) and most of detected code-smells are correct. This is
confirms that our *CCEA* precision results are independent from the size of the systems
to evaluate. For Azureus, the precision using CCEA is the lowest (71%) but still
acceptable. Azureus contains a high number of spaghetti-code that are difficult to
detect using metrics. For the same dataset, we can conclude that our CCEA approach
performs much better (with a 99% confidence level) than existing single-population
approaches (Genetic Programming and Artificial Immune Systems) [12, 18] on the
different systems since the median precision scores are much higher by using *CCEA*.
In fact, *CCEA* provides better results since both single-population approaches (GP and
AIS) are using only manually collected examples however CCEA has the strength to
generate also automatically code-smell examples during the optimization process. GP
and AIS requires high number of examples to achieve good detection results.

Table 2. Precision median values of CCEA, GP, and AIS over 30 independent simulation runs

	CCEA	GP [18]		AIS [12]	
Systems	Precision	Precision	*p-value*	Precision	*p-value*
Azureusv2.3.0.6	71	62	< 0.01	65	< 0.01
Argo UMLv0.26	91	81	< 0.01	77	< 0.01
Xercesv2.7	93	84	< 0.01	83	< 0.01
Ant-Apachev1.5	93	86	< 0.01	86	< 0.01

The same statistical analysis methodology is performed to compare the recall
median values. According to table 3, all median recall values of *GP/AIS* are
statistically different from the *CCEA* ones on almost problem instances. Thus, it is
clear that *CCEA* performs better than *GP* and *AIS*. The average recall score of *CCEA*
on the different systems is around 85% (better than precision). Azureus has the lowest
recall score with 74%. In fact, Azureus has the highest number of expected code-
smells. Single-population approaches (GP and AIS) provide also good results (an
average of 72%) but lower than CCEA ones. Overall, all the three code smell types are
detected with good precision and recall scores in the different systems since the
average precision and recall scores on the different systems is higher than 85%.

The reliability of the proposed approach requires an example set of good code and
code-smell examples. It can be argued that constituting such a set might require more
work than identifying and adapting code-smells detection rules. In our study, we
showed that by using JHotdraw directly, without any adaptation, the *CCEA* method can
be used out of the box and this will produce good detection results for the detection of
code-smells for the eight studied systems. In an industrial setting, we could expect a
company to start with JHotDraw, and gradually transform its set of good code
examples to include context-specific data. This might be essential if we consider that
different languages and software infrastructures have different best/worst practices.

Figures 2 shows that only code-smell examples extracted from three different open source systems can be used to obtain good precision and recall scores. In fact, since *CCEA* generates "artificial" code smell examples thus only few manually collected code-smells are required to achieve good detection results. This reduces the effort required by developers to inspect systems to produce code-smell examples.

Table 3. Recall median values of CCEA, GP, and AIS over 30 independent simulation runs

	CCEA	**GP [18]**		**AIS [12]**	
Systems	Recall	Recall	*p-value*	Recall	*p-value*
Azureus v2.3.0.6	74	62	< 0.01	66	< 0.01
ArgoUMLv 0.26	84	79	< 0.01	88	< 0.01
Xercesv2.7	88	83	< 0.01	86	< 0.01
Ant-Apachev1.5	92	80	< 0.01	84	< 0.01

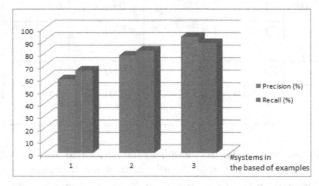

Fig. 3. The impact of number of systems in the base of examples on the detection results (Xerces)

Finally, all the algorithms under comparison were executed on machines with Intel Xeon 3 GHz processors and 8 GB RAM. We recall that all algorithms were run for 100 000 evaluations for all algorithms. This allows us to make fair comparisons in terms of CPU times. The average execution time for all the three algorithms over 30 runs is comparable with an average of 1h and 22 minutes for *CCEA*, 1h and 13 minutes for GP, and finally 1h and 4 minutes for AIS. We consider that this represents scalable results since code-smells detection algorithms are not used in real-time settings.

5   Related Work

In the literature, the first book that has been specially written for design smells was by Brown et al. [9] which provide broad-spectrum and large views on design smells, and antipatterns that aimed at a wide audience for academic community as well as in industry. Indeed, in [20], Fowler and Beck have described a list of design smells which may possibly exist on a program. They suggested that software maintainers should manually inspect the program to detect existing design smells. In addition, they specify particular refactorings for each code-smell type.

Moha et al. [19] described code-smell symptoms using a domain-specific-language (DSL) for their approach called DECOR. They proposed a consistent vocabulary and DSL to specify antipatterns based on the review of existing work on design code-smells found in the literature. Symptoms descriptions are later mapped to detection algorithms. Similarly, Munro [24] have proposed description and symptoms-based approach using a precise definition of bad smells from the informal descriptions given by the originators Fowler and Beck [20]. The characteristics of design code-smells have been used to systematically define a set of measurements and interpretation rules for a subset of design code-smells as a template form. This template consists of three main parts: (1) a code smell name, (2) a text-based description of its characteristics, and (3) heuristics for its detection. Marinescu [10] have proposed a mechanism called "detection strategy" for formulating metrics-based rules that capture deviations from good design principles and heuristics. Detection strategies allow to a maintainer to directly locate classes or methods affected by a particular design code-smell. As such, Marinescu has defined detection strategies for capturing around ten important flaws of object-oriented design found in the literature.

Our approach is inspired by contributions in the domain of Search-Based Software Engineering (SBSE) [25]. SBSE uses search-based approaches to solve optimization problems in software engineering. Once a software engineering task is framed as a search problem, many search algorithms can be applied to solve that problem. In [18], we have proposed another approach, based on search-based techniques, for the automatic detection of potential code-smells in code. The detection is based on the notion that the more code deviates from good practices, the more likely it is bad. In another work [12], we generated detection rules defined as combinations of metrics/thresholds that better conform to known instances of bad-smells (examples). Then, the correction solutions, a combination of refactoring operations, should minimize the number of bad-smells detected using the detection rules. Thus, our previous work treats the detection and correction as two different steps. In this work, we combine between our two previous work [12, 18] using CCEA to detect code-smells.Based on recent SBSE surveys [25], the use of parallel metaheuristic search is still very limited in software engineering. Indeed, there is no work that uses cooperative parallel metaheuristic search to detect code smells. This is the first adaptation of cooperative parallel metaheuristics to solve a software engineering problem. However, there is mainly three works that used *CCEA* for SBSE problems: Wilkerson et al. [5] tackling the software correction problem, Arcuri and Ya [6] handling the bug fixing problem and Adamopoulos et al. [7] tackling the mutation testing problem.

6   Conclusion

In this paper, we described a new search-based approach for code-smells detection. In our competitive co-evolutionary adaptation, two populations evolve simultaneously with the objective of each depending upon the current population of the other. The first population generates a set of detection rules that maximizes the coverage of code-smell examples and "artificial" code smells, and simultaneously a second population tries to maximize the number of "artificial" code-smells that cannot be detected by detection rules generated by the first population. We implemented our approach and evaluated it on four open-source systems. Promising results are obtained where precision and recall scores were higher than 80% on an existing benchmark [19] [13].

Future work should validate our approach with more open-source systems in order to conclude about the general applicability of our methodology. Also, in this paper, we only focused on only three types of code-smell. We are planning to extend the approach by automating the detection various other types.

References

1. Rosin, C.R., Belew, R.K.: New Methods for Competitive Coevolution. Evolutionary Computation 5(1), 1–29 (1997)
2. Stanley, K.O., Miikkulainen, R.: Competitive Coevolution through Evolutionary Complexification. Journal of Artificial Intelligence Research 21(1), 63–100 (2004)
3. Hillis, W.D.: Co-Evolving Parasites Improve Simulated Evolution as an Optimization Procedure. In: Langton, et al. (eds.) Artical Life II, pp. 313–324. Addison Wesley (1992)
4. Husbands, P.: Distributed Coevolutionary Genetic Algorithms for Multi-Criteria and Multi-Constraint Optimisation. In: Fogarty, T.C. (ed.) AISB-WS 1994. LNCS, vol. 865, pp. 150–165. Springer, Heidelberg (1994)
5. Wilkerson, J.L., Tauritz, D.R., Bridges, J.M.: Multi-objective Coevolutionary Automated Software Correction. In: GECCO 2012, pp. 1229–1236 (2012)
6. Arcuri, A., Yao, X.: Novel Co-evolutionary Approach to Automatic Software Bug Fixing. In: IEEE Congress on Evolutionary Computation, pp. 162–168 (2008)
7. Adamopoulos, K., Harman, M., Hierons, R.M.: How to Overcome the Equivalent Mutant Problem and Achieve Tailored Selective Mutation Using Co-Evolution. In: Deb, K., Tari, Z. (eds.) GECCO 2004. LNCS, vol. 3103, pp. 1338–1349. Springer, Heidelberg (2004)
8. Meyer, B.: Object Oriented Software Construction, 2nd edn. Prentice Hall, New Jersey (1997)
9. Brown, W.J., Malveau, R.C., Brown, W.H., Mowbray, T.J.: Anti Patterns: Refactoring Software, Architectures, and Projects in Crisis, 1st edn. John Wiley and Sons (March 1998)
10. Marinescu, R.: Detection strategies: metrics-based rules for detecting design flaws. In: Proceedings of the ICSM 2004, pp. 350–359 (2004)
11. Fenton, N., Pfleeger, S.L.: Software Metrics: A Rigorous and Practical Approach, 2nd edn. International Thomson Computer Press, London (1997)
12. Kessentini, M., Kessentini, W., Sahraoui, H., Boukadoum, M., Ouni, A.: Design Defects Detection and Correction by Example. In: 19th ICPC 2011, Canada, pp. 81–90 (2011)

13. Ouni, A., Kessentini, M., Sahraoui, H., Boukadoum, M.: Maintainability Defects Detection and Correction: A Multi-Objective Approach. In: Journal of Automated Software Engineering (JASE). Springer (2012)
14. http://ant.apache.org/
15. http://xerces.apache.org/xerces-j/
16. http://argouml.tigris.org/
17. http://sourceforge.net/projects/azureus/
18. Kessentini, M., Vaucher, S., Sahraoui, H.: Deviance from Perfection is a Better Criterion than Closeness to Evil when Identifying Risky Code. In: 25th IEEE/ACM ASE 2010 (2010)
19. Moha, N., Guéhéneuc, Y.-G., Duchien, L., Le Meur, A.-F.: DECOR: A Method for the Specification and Detection of Code and Design Smells. TSE 36, 20–36 (2010)
20. Fowler, M., Beck, K., Brant, J., Opdyke, W., Roberts, D.: Refactoring – Improving the Design of Existing Code, 1st edn. Addison-Wesley (1999)
21. Chidamber, S.R., Kemerer, C.F.: A metrics suite for object-oriented design. IEEE Trans. Softw. Eng. 20(6), 293–318 (1994)
22. http://www.jhotdraw.org/
23. Wilcoxon, F., Katti, S.K., Roberta, A.: Critical Values and Probability Levels for the Wilcoxon Rank Sum Test and the Wilcoxon Signed-rank Test. In: Selected Tables in Mathematical Statistics, vol. I, pp. 171–259. American Mathematical Society (1973)
24. Munro, M.J.: Product Metrics for Automatic Identification of "Bad Smell" Design Problems in Java Source-Code. In: 11th METRICS Symp. (2005)
25. Harman, M., Afshin Mansouri, S., Zhang, Y.: Search-based software engineering: Trends, techniques and applications. ACM Comput. Surv. 45, 61 pages (2012)

A Multi-objective Genetic Algorithm to Rank State-Based Test Cases

Lionel Briand[1], Yvan Labiche[2], and Kathy Chen[2]

[1] SnT Centre, University of Luxembourg, Luxembourg
lionel.briand@uni.lu
[2] Systems and Computer Engineering, Carleton University, Ottawa, Canada
labiche@sce.carleton.ca, kathy_h_chen@hotmail.com

Abstract. We propose a multi-objective genetic algorithm method to prioritize state-based test cases to achieve several competing objectives such as budget and coverage of data flow information, while hopefully detecting faults as early as possible when executing prioritized test cases. The experimental results indicate that our approach is useful and effective: prioritizations quickly achieve maximum data flow coverage and this results in early fault detection; prioritizations perform much better than random orders with much smaller variance.

Keywords: State-based testing, Prioritization, Multi-objective optimization, Genetic algorithm.

1   Introduction

The earlier defects are detected the better. During testing this can be achieved by prioritizing test case executions: test cases with higher (estimated) defect detection capabilities are executed earlier than others. Such a prioritization (or ranking) also allows one to stop test case execution when the budget dedicated to this activity is exhausted.

In this paper, we address the problem of ordering the execution of black-box test cases. Specifically, we rank state-based test cases derived according to the well-known transition tree method [1] as it has been shown to be a good compromise among available selection criteria [2] (e.g., all-transition pairs, all-transitions [3]). Prioritization is performed according to the data-flow the test cases cover in the test model since this relates to fault detection [4], and tester-defined constraints: goal to reach in terms of data-flow coverage and/or maximum budget (cost) of the execution of prioritized test cases. As a result, finding a ranking is a multi-objective optimization problem, which we solve with a multi-objective genetic algorithm. The solution is an optimal test sequence in the sense that it aims to find as many defects as possible as early as possible when executing prioritized test cases. We evaluate how optimal is approach on a data structure class that exhibits a state-based behavior.

Section 2 discusses related work. Section 3 describes our multi-objective genetic algorithm. Section 4 reports on a case study. Conclusions are drawn in Section 5.

G. Ruhe and Y. Zhang (Eds.): SSBSE 2013, LNCS 8084, pp. 66–80, 2013.
© Springer-Verlag Berlin Heidelberg 2013

2   Related Work

Our work relates to state-based testing, data-flow identification from operation contracts, and test case prioritization.

State-based testing consists in devising transition sequences to exercise different
elements of the state model, as stated by a selection criterion [3]. Several alternative
criteria exist [1, 3], including all transitions, all transition pairs, full predicates (an
adaptation of MC/DC to guards), and round-trip path (transition) tree. Binder's round-
trip path tree [1] adapts Chow's W method [5] to UML state machines, and has been
shown empirically to be a good compromise in terms of cost and effectiveness (at
detecting faults) between all transitions and all transition pairs (or full predicate) [2],
even though effectiveness depends on the way the tree has been built [6]. The reader
interested in more details on this criterion is referred to the above literature.

To ascertain the state reached by an implementation at the end of a test case execution and use that information in a test oracle, one can rely on the state invariant (when
the system state is observable, as in our case) or other characteristics of the state machine as in protocol conformance testing [5, 7].

One of the main challenges of state-based testing is the path feasibility problem,
that is, determining whether a transition sequence derived according to a selection
criterion is feasible (i.e., one can find test inputs for the sequence such that it executes). This problem, akin to the path sensitization problem in white-box testing [8],
is known to be un-decidable [9]. We assume test cases (i.e., transition sequences) are
feasible and we focus on prioritizing them.

Operation contracts include pre- and post-conditions. In UML, they can be expressed using the OCL [10]. Briand et al. [4] provided rules for identifying definitions
and uses of model elements from OCL operation contracts and transition guard conditions, and applied those rules to UML state machine diagrams. Then, they used
well-known criteria such as all-definitions and all-DU-paths to define test cases. One
important observation they made on three different case studies is that the set of DU-
paths equals the set of DU-pairs in the test model obtained when applying their strategy
(i.e., only one definition-clear path from the definition to the use for each DU-pair). It is
therefore sufficient to determine DU-pairs to cover DU-paths. This may not be the case
in general though, and only further studies will confirm (or not) this result. They also
noticed that the data flow analysis they propose can be used as an indicator of the defect
revealing power of a test suite. A general rule is that in a set of alternative transition
trees derived from a state machine diagram, the transition tree covering the most data
flow information (in the model) has a better capability to detect defects. Since the other
data-flow analysis methods for UML state machines were less complete (e.g., support
the UML notation to a lesser extent) [4], we adopted the rules defined by Briand et al.

Test case prioritization has received a lot of attention in two areas of software
testing [11]: ranking system level test cases, and prioritization during regression testing. In both cases the objective is to rank the test cases such that the most beneficial
ones (according to some criterion) are executed first. Criteria for prioritization are
varied, e.g., coverage (e.g., code, model element, requirements), priority, criticality.

Prioritization algorithms mostly employ greedy algorithms (e.g., [12]) or single objective meta-heuristic search (e.g., [13]). Harman concludes that test prioritization requires a multi-objective optimization [14]. To the best of our knowledge, there is no technique prioritizing state-based test cases using data flow information.

3   Genetic Algorithm

As advocated by Harman [14], we present below a multi-objective optimization (with four, possibly conflicting objectives), relying on a genetic algorithm, to produce a test order of transition tree paths [1] for state based testing, while accounting for several criteria (see below). The conflicting objectives place a partial ordering on the search space. GAs are well suited to this situation as they rely on a population of solutions: Individuals in the population can represent solutions that are close to an optimum and represent different tradeoffs among the various objectives.

For a given multi-objective problem, the Pareto (optimal) front refers to optimal trade-off solutions between the objectives. Because a GA works on a population of individual solutions it is possible to find many solutions in the Pareto optimal set, which thus present the many possible tradeoffs. Deciding which solution to select from that set is left with a decision maker, rather than the optimization algorithm. We have not explored ways to present the result of the optimization to a decision-maker.

We used SPEA2 [15] to implement our multi-objective GA. With SPEA2, a population P and an archive A evolve. During fitness assignment at iteration t, individuals in both P_t and A_t are evaluated. During selection, the non-dominated individuals of P_t and A_t (i.e., the interesting tradeoffs) are copied into archive A_{t+1}. SPEA2 has a clustering mechanism that removes some non-dominated solutions (that are too close to others) and therefore maintains the size of the archive constant while preserving diversity in the archive. Next, the genetic selection operator is applied on the individuals of A_{t+1} to fill a mating pool, and cross-over and mutation operators are applied to that pool to generate P_{t+1}. This continues until a number of generations is reached.

3.1   Chromosome Representation

Given our objective, a chromosome is a sequence of test cases. Since the data flow analysis method we use is based on data definitions and uses along transitions, we need to record the sequence of transitions in test cases forming the chromosome. (As transitions are uniquely identified, the chromosome also includes information about the sequence of states.) The chromosome is therefore made of genes and each gene is a test case (test path in the state machine). Chromosomes have the same number of genes (length) since the number of test paths in a test suite does not change, once set.

3.2   Objectives for Optimization: Cost, Data Flow, User-Defined Criteria

The **cost** of testing is related to time and resources needed to execute messages (events) in test cases [1]. There is no general way to quantify test design costs, set up costs, execution costs. The number of test cases has been used as a surrogate measure of cost. Since we have test cases (paths) of varying lengths, we instead assume test case cost to be proportional to the number of transitions triggered by the test case.

Following our previous work [4], we compute two different data flow coverage rates: $C_{allDefs}(tp)$, resp. $C_{allDU}(tp)$, is the number of definitions (resp. DU-pairs) covered by test path tp divided by the total number of definitions (resp. DU-pairs) that can be covered by the whole test suite. We also use similar, finer grained measures for individual transitions triggered in test paths: $C_{allDefs}(t)$ and $C_{allDU}(t)$ for transition t. (There may be definitions and DU-pairs in the model that are not covered by the whole test suite. These are not considered here.) In the rest of the paper, we simply write $C(tp)$ or $C(t)$ when the criterion is not relevant to the discussion.

In practice, in addition to the desire to obtain a ratio coverage to cost as high as possible, a user may want to achieve a **specific data flow coverage rate** or may have a **limited budget** to execute test cases, resulting in additional constraints to consider.

3.3   Fitness Functions

In general, a user would expect a good solution to the prioritization problem to increase cumulative coverage as fast as possible, so as to (hopefully) detect faults as early as possible, while keeping cost as low as possible. In addition, when there is a target coverage rate, we expect a good solution to reach that value as early as possible, and when a budget is provided, we expect a good solution to achieve a coverage rate as high as possible for that budget. We first discuss the fitness functions and then discuss the necessary change of budget and coverage objectives during optimization.

Four Fitness Functions. When a tester has a limited budget T (i.e., maximum allowed cost, which is smaller or equal to the total cost of the whole test suite) but needs to have enough confidence in the SUT by specifying a minimum coverage rate SC to achieve, the tester wants to (see illustration in Fig. 1):

- Maximize the sum of the cumulative coverage rates within the specified test cost, i.e., maximize $f_1(i) = \sum_{j=1}^{j=T} (T-j+1) * C(i,j)$; where $C(i,j)$ denotes the cumulative coverage rate at test cost j for chromosome i (i.e., up to transition j of chromosome i), i.e., $C(j)$ of chromosome i as we defined it earlier.
- Maximize the cumulative coverage rate at the specified budget, i.e., maximize $f_2(i) = C(i,T)$.

Objective SC may not be achievable given T, in which case the tester would still want to maximize coverage reached at T, that is (see illustration in Fig. 1):

- Minimize the area bounded by the solution's cumulative coverage rate curve, the y-axis and the straight (horizontal) line defined by SC, i.e., minimize

$f_3(i) = \sum_{j=1}^{j=\overline{T}-1} (T-j+1) * (SC - C(i,j))$, where $\overline{T} = l \,|\, C(i,l-1) < SC \wedge C(i,l) \geq SC$, the

first test cost l for which the cumulative coverage rate reaches or exceeds SC.

- Minimize the test cost to reach SC, i.e., minimize $f_4(i) = \overline{T}$.

$f_1(i)$ is an approximation of the area under the curve formed when plotting the cumulative coverage by test cost. An alternative can be to extrapolate the curve, for instance with 3rd degree splines, and compute the integral of the splines. We consider that our sum, though an approximation, would be a lower bound approximation (especially since the x-axis is split into equal segments of value one, as we assume the cost of a transition to be one) and would be more efficient (the GA will likely perform thousands of evaluations of this function).

Using these four objectives, the test engineer will possibly obtain alternative solutions to choose from: The solution that can achieve SC within T, the solution that can achieve SC with a smaller budget than T, the solution that maximize coverage (though smaller than the one targeted) within T.

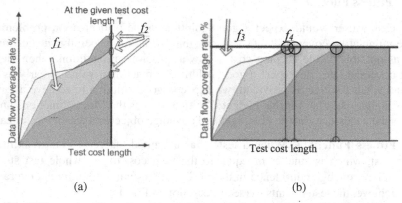

(a)   (b)

Fig. 1. Illustrating fitness functions $f_1(i)$ and $f_2(i)$ (part a), $f_3(i)$ and $f_4(i)$ (part b)

Reducing Specified Cost or Rate When Needed. If the tester-specified cost T is too large, all solutions in a population may reach SC before T as illustrated in Fig. 2. All solutions then have the same fitness value for f_2, i.e., 100%. The multi-objective optimization has one fewer objective since f_2 does not contribute any more. Since this suggests it is feasible to achieve SC at a lower cost than T, say for T', and the value of T' would likely be of interest to the tester, we suggest to change the maximum (user-specified) test cost T to a smaller value T' and let the optimization continue with T' instead of T: for instance T' can be set to the average value of test costs at which current solutions reach SC. We implemented this heuristic in our search algorithm.

In fact, we believe that it is not necessary to wait for all the retained solutions to reach SC within T to substitute T with T'. Our search algorithm allows the tester to choose a threshold S (e.g., 80) such that if S percent of the retained solutions reach SC within T then the heuristic discussed above is used. The rationale is to increase competition between individual solutions.

A similar heuristic is used to reduce the user-defined cumulative coverage SC when the value of SC is so high (and the specified test cost is so small) that no solution can reach SC within T: all solutions will get the same value for function f_4, which then does not contribute to the search any more. Our search algorithm automatically substitutes the user specified SC with SC' using the following heuristic: SC' is the average of cumulative coverage rates at T of all solutions in the set of retained solutions. Once again, the rationale is to encourage the competition between individual solutions by using all the fitness functions.

One question remains to be answered: When should SC be lowered to SC'? In particular, it is unlikely that any solution in the initial population will reach SC within T if we assume the initial population to be constructed randomly (which is often the case in optimizations), and this does not necessarily mean that SC is too high. We only want to substitute SC with SC' if no solution reaches SC within T after the search reaches a steady state, for example when the population average coverage rate at T does not improve by more than 3% over 50 generations. This is what we used in our GA, and we let the test engineer provide values for the number of generations to monitor for improvements (50 in the above example) and the minimum percentage of improvement in population average coverage rate (3 in the above example).

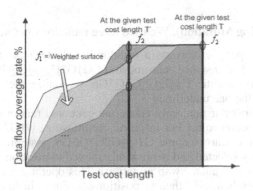

Fig. 2. Illustrating test cost update

3.4   Genetic Algorithm Operators

Crossover: Partially Matched Crossover [16]. Two crossing points are randomly picked for two parent chromosomes. The section between the two crossover points is called the matching section. The GA then swaps the matching sections in the two parents to form two children. This will (likely) result into duplicated genes in chromosomes: in our case, a test case appearing twice. A matching relationship is then identified to remove gene duplication, i.e., to identify how the duplicated genes before and after the matching section have to be changed. The matching relationship between two genes, one from the child chromosome (gc) in the matching section and one from the parent chromosome (gp), is defined as follows: gc matches gp if and only if gc and gp appear at the same place in the two chromosomes (i.e., at the same index in the sequences of genes). For each gene c outside of the matching section in a child chromosome, the GA identifies a gene c' in the matching section of that chromosome that is a duplicate of c (same gene but at a different position in the chromosome). If such a duplicate gene c' exists, the GA recursively applies the matching relationship to c' until the result is a gene that does not appear in the matching section of the chromosome. The result then replaces gene c in the child chromosome.

Consider the example of Fig. 3 with parent chromosomes Parent1 and Parent2 and matching section comprising genes 2 to 5. Swapping the matching sections results in the "proto" children 1 and 2. In proto child 1, genes A, B and I are duplicated. A at index 5 in proto child 1 matches F at index 5 in Parent1, and F at index 2 in proto child 1 matches C at index 2 in Parent 1. Therefore A at index 0 in proto child 1 is replaced by C to remove duplication. This is repeated for all the genes outside of the matching section. The result is child 1 and child 2.

Parent 1	A B C D E F G H I		
Parent 2	E D F I B A G H C		
Proto child 1	A B F I B A G H I	A->F->C, B->E	Child 1 C E F I B A G H D
Proto child 2	E D C D E F G H C	B->E, I->D	Child 2 B I C D E F G H A

Fig. 3. Crossover example

Mutation (Reordering Mutation). We used three mutation operators [17]:

- Inversion: This operator converts a (randomly selected) sub-sequence of genes into its inverse. For instance, chromosome G1G2G3G4G5G6 would be transformed into chromosome G1G2G5G4G3G6, assuming the randomly selected sub-sequence is the one underlined.
- Insertion: This operator randomly takes one gene and randomly moves it at any position in the chromosome. For instance, chromosome G1G2G3G4G5G6 would be transformed into chromosome G1G4G2G3G5G6, assuming the gene at position 3 is randomly selected and is randomly moved to position 1 (we start at 0).
- Reciprocal exchange (a.k.a. swap mutation): This operator randomly selects two genes and exchanges their positions. For instance, chromosome G1G2G3G4G5G6 would be transformed into chromosome G1G4G3G2G5G6, assuming genes at positions 1 and 3 are randomly selected.

3.5   Genetic Algorithm Parameters

The efficiency of a GA is highly dependent on a number of parameters, such as the population size, the archive size, the number of generations (as a stopping criterion), the crossover rate and the mutation rate. An inadequate selection of parameter values can lead to premature convergence or loss of good solutions.

A GA with a too small population may not adequately explore the search space while a GA with a too large population may take a long time to converge. Following Goldberg's work [16], De Jong applied a population size of 50 in a study for five optimizations [18]. Grefenstette [19] instead suggested a population size of 30. In other GA applications, a population size of 50 to 100 is widely used by many researchers (e.g., [20, 21]). But for a multi-objective GA, some authors tend to use a larger population size than for a traditional GA, and suggest a size of 30 to 80 for each objective (e.g., [22]). In our GA application, we use a population size of 50 for each objective, i.e., 200 in total.

In SPEA2, the size of the archive set determines how elitist the algorithm is. A small archive set will strengthen elitism, but the risk is that some (interesting) non-dominated solutions may not have room in the archive and may therefore not be kept by the GA. Archive sizes in the range [1/4, 4] of the population size are acceptable and perform well [22]. To keep computation time within reasonable bounds, we set the archive size to half the population size.

If the number of generations is too small, the evolution may stop although existing solutions may have a high probability of improving. If the number of generations is too large, the computation time may not be acceptable. Balancing budget and evolution, as studied in the literature where SPEA2 is used [23, 24], we used 500 generations for each trial execution of our GA.

The crossover rate is an important factor as well. A moderate crossover rate is able to achieve a good balance between exploration in the whole search space and exploitation of a specific area in the search space. Consistent with some studies that observe a crossover rate in the range [0.45, 0.95] performs well [25], we set it to 0.7.

The mutation rate also affects the performance of the genetic algorithm (e.g., [16, 19, 22]). We selected the widely used GA mutation rate of 0.01 [19, 23, 26].

4 Case Study

4.1 Design

We first generated a transition tree test suite. We then applied the multi-objective GA to generate test case sequences. We tried different values for user inputs (cost T, coverage SC) to study their impact on trends in coverage and mutation rates. (We tried several executions of the GA for each configuration to account for its stochastic nature. We observed similar results and only discuss results for one execution of each configuration.) Then we seeded mutants into the source code of the case study system and executed GA-evolved test case sequences to obtain their mutant detection capability. As a baseline of comparison, we generated random orders of test case sequences and determined their mutant detection capability. Finally, we compared the data flow coverage rate and the mutant detection capability of the different orders to verify whether the GA-evolved test case sequences detect these mutants earlier, and whether with a user-specified test cost, the GA-evolved sequences detect more mutants.

Our case study aims to answer the three following research questions: Can the data flow information derived at the model level help testers identify interesting (data flow coverage, fault detection) test cases prioritizations (Q1)? Do the GA-evolved test case sequences detect defects in source code earlier than randomly ordered test case sequences, or detect more defects within a limited budget (Q2)? What is the variation (standard deviation) in defect detection of GA-evolved test case sequences (using data flow information at the model level), and how does it compare with the variation in defect detection of random test case sequences (Q3)?

Random Test Case Sequences. As a baseline of comparison with SPEA2 solutions, we generated the same number of random test case sequences as the size of the SPEA2 archive set at the end of an SPEA2 evolution. In addition, since GA ordered non-dominated solutions entail the same cost, we ensured the generated random test case sequences matched that cost.

Criteria to Compare Test Case Sequences. To answer the research questions, we compare data flow coverage and mutant detection rates. Because at the end of each GA execution we obtain a set of non-dominated solutions, we compare the average rate of the whole set with the average rate of a set of randomly ordered test case sequences.

Comparing Data Flow. With N test case sequences, the data flow coverage rate at each test cost i on average is: $DF(i) = \frac{1}{N} \sum_{k=1}^{N} C(k,i)$.

Comparing Mutation Rate. The average of the percentage of faults detected (APFD) metric [12], and its APFDc extension ("cost-cognizant APFD") that accounts for varying test case costs and varying faults severities [27] were defined for comparing test case prioritizations during regression testing. Since solutions returned by our GA executions may not have the same number of test cases, we cannot use APFD (APFDc). We therefore defined our own metric.

Let m(k,i) be the mutation rate of test case sequence k at test cost i, i.e., the number of detected mutants up to the i-th test cost divided by the number of all known detectable mutants. With N test case sequences, the mutation rate at each test cost on average is $M(i) = \frac{1}{N} \sum_{k=1}^{N} m(k,i)$. We then compare the set of mutation rate M(i) from the GA-evolved sequences with the set of mutation rate M(i) from a set of random sequences.

User-Defined Inputs (Cost and Coverage). In our GA application, a tester has to define a goal in terms of minimum data-flow coverage and maximum cost. Since 100% coverage can be too expensive and empirical results indicate 90% is a reasonable target (e.g., [2, 28]), we selected data flow coverage rates of 90% and 80% (both for all-definitions and all-DU pairs) as inputs.

With respect to budget (cost) input, since our GA can provide a reduced test cost, which satisfies data flow coverage requirements, we set the cost to 80% and 90% of the total cost of the full test suite because we want to reduce test costs in proportion to the specified data flow coverage rates (which we set to 80% and 90%). To complement the study of the impact of a specified test cost, we then use test cost values a bit larger and smaller than the one discovered by the GA. For example, if with user input data (T=90%, SC=90%) our GA reduces test cost T to T'=45 (i.e., a cost of 45 is sufficient to reach SC), we then try the optimization again twice, with pairs of input data (T=50%, SC=90%) and (T=40%, SC=90%). In the former case, we expect our GA application to return similar results as with input (T=90%, SC=90%). Since these results might be very similar to the initial inputs, we will not report all detailed results. In the latter case, we expect our GA application to present solutions that can reach a cumulative coverage SC' (smaller than SC) for test cost $T=40\%$ and we will discuss them when presenting results.

Mutation Operators. We used MuJava [29], using all its mutation operators (method-level and class-level), to automatically generate mutants for our case study since this is a well-accepted procedure to study effectiveness of test techniques [30]. We do not discuss further the list of mutation operators we used because of lack of space and since MuJava automatically decides which operators it could use on our case study.

Since we prioritize the test cases in an existing test suite, the best mutation rate of the prioritizations is the one of that initial test suite. Since this test suite may not kill all mutants created by MuJava, we only consider the mutants killed by the initial test suite when comparing the mutation rate of prioritizations.

There is significant variation in terms of detection rates across faults/mutants: mutants that are only killed by less than 1.5% of the initial test cases are considered to be "very hard to kill" whereas mutants that are killed by 1.5% to 5% of the test cases are considered to be "hard to kill" [30]. In our case study, 4.9% of the mutants are hard to kill whereas 0.7% of the mutants are very hard to kill.

The OrderedSet Case Study. The case study is a data structure that implements a set of integer values and has the capability to resize itself when more room is required to add elements. We chose this case study since it has a complex state-based behaviour (because of the resizing capability), even though it is small in size, and events triggering inputs have parameters (the elements to add/remove to/from the set). The case study is 232 LOC (24 methods), the test suite to prioritize has 165 test cases, including 916 triggered transitions. The test cases exercise 152 definitions and 619 DU pairs in the model. MuJava created 575 mutants. The test case average mutation rate is 27.1%.

Although it represents a typical case where a state machine is used to model behavior (a complex data structure) the case study system is admittedly small. However, this kind of complex data structure is usually modeled using state machines in UML-based development [31]. Additionally, it is very uncommon in practice to model subsystems or entire systems using state machines, as this is far too complex in realistic cases. So we believe our case study is representative of a large set of situations.

4.2   Results

Following the procedure described earlier, with 80% and 90% data flow coverage rates (SC) and 80% and 90% of total costs (T), we analyzed the coverage and mutation rates of GA-evolved sequences (all the sequences from the Pareto front are considered) and random sequences. Fig. 3 (a) shows example results for definition coverage and specific values for SC and T, but other results for DU-pairs (Fig. 4) and other values of SC and T show similar trends. We can clearly see that GA-evolved sequences increase their data flow coverage rates quicker than random sequences, which is the intended behaviour, except for the initial part of the sequence (as further discussed below), and reach SC with lower test cost than T. The random sequences also show much higher variation than GA-evolved sequences. Though Fig. 3 (a) plots, for each cost value, the minimum, maximum and average definition coverage value for the set of GA-evolved and random test sequences, the maximum value for the latter does not represent an actual sequence of test cases. In contrast, since there is very little variation in the GA-evolved curves (they overlap), these are a close approximation of the coverage rate of each GA-evolved sequence.

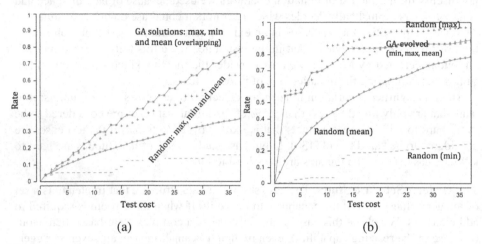

Fig. 4. Coverage vs. cost (a), mutation rate vs. cost (b) when comparing GA-evolved sequences (optimizing for definitions) and random sequences, both with SC=80%, T=80%

To explain why in the initial part of the sequence the GA-evolved sequences do not perform better than random ones, recall objective function $f_1(i)$. If the value of $C(i, j)$, the cumulative coverage rate at test cost j for chromosome i, is small and gene j appears early in the sequence (j is small), it does not contribute much though it has a large $(T-j+1)$ factor value, and therefore the coverage curve grows slowly and is similar to the random average. This happens in particular if the total amount of data flow elements to cover is very large. If test cases are not extremely long, their cumulative coverage rates are all small. This is the case here: the test model shows 619 DU-pairs, and each of the 165 test cases, with a maximum of 18 transitions, therefore covers a small portion of those data flow elements. Since the GA optimized according to DU-pairs coverage, it then takes a few test cases to see differences with random sequences. This trend is more pronounced with DU pairs (Fig. 4) than definitions (Fig. 3) because there are always many more DU-pairs than definitions to cover.

Since our GA application shortens T to T' (the average test cost where the GA-evolved sequences reach SC), we use T' in a second set of GA runs. A larger value than T' is first used to verify whether our GA application consistently shortens T to T' if T is large enough to satisfy SC. A smaller value than T' is also used to verify our GA application will present a new SC' and tell the user that the cost budget is not enough to satisfy SC but the user could expect SC' within T'. Although we do not further discuss these results due to space constraints, we confirm that when the new T

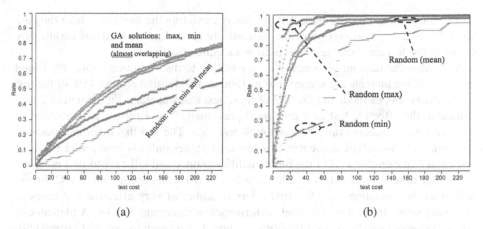

(a)   (b)

Fig. 5. Coverage vs. cost (a), mutation rate vs. cost (b) when comparing GA-evolved sequences (optimizing for DU-pairs) and random sequences, both with SC=80%, T=80%

values are larger than T' our GA application again shortens them to values around T' (+/- 3% of T' due to random variations). Results with reduced T values lead to curves similar to those presented earlier, except that the achieved coverage is lower.

With respect to mutation rate, it appears that the all-definitions criterion performs better (mutation rates) than all-DU pairs: the all-definitions curve is consistently above the random average (Fig. 3 (b)) whereas this is not the case for all-DU pairs (Fig. 4 (b)), especially early during the sequence. All-definitions results for specific SC and T values are presented in Fig. 3 (b), where the GA-evolved sequences detect 80% of the mutants at (approx.) cost values 15 and 20, under different GA runs with different initial cost inputs. On average, random sequences do not reach a 80% mutation rate by cost value 35. After that, the curve in Fig. 3 (b) then enters a plateau, though the coverage continues to slightly increase. This plateau is a consequence of (i) the way the test suite, i.e., the transition tree is built, and (ii) the way data flow information is identified from the tree. When building the transition tree [1], if a transition has a guard condition that is a disjunction, a branch is added to the tree for each truth value combination that is sufficient to make the guard true. Each added branch in the tree therefore contains uses of the same model variables. In GA-evolved sequences for all-definitions, after test cost value 20, we observe that all states and triggering events in the state machine diagram are covered. By cost value 15 (or 20 depending on the run), however, only a subset of the uses have been covered. Since it is sufficient to exercise once some methods to kill a large proportion of mutants, we therefore reach a mutation rate slightly above 80% by cost value 15 (or 20). The plateau corresponds to the coverage of additional uses due to branch exercising additional combinations of truth values to make guards true. Since the corresponding methods have already been covered, this does not increase much the mutation rate, thus explaining the plateau.

The early sharp increase of mutation rate is due to a very effective test case which kills around 54% of the mutants by covering eight definitions and seven du-pairs with cost 2. Since many mutants are killed by simply executing the methods where they are seeded, and a large proportion of the mutants are seeded in the methods (in)directly called in this test case, that test case becomes a quite effective test case.

We notice the random sequences do very well in terms of mutation rate. We found that 42% of the mutants are seeded into method union(), that around 45% of the test cases invoke this method, and that 2/3 of those test cases exercise the system in a way similar to the effective test case discussed previously. These form a powerful set of test cases, with mutation rates between 40% and 55%. The fact that random sequences are close to GA-evolved sequences (for low cost values only) is therefore a result of test cases that exercise a lot of the functionalities at once and kill easy to find mutants.

Similar observations can be made from Fig. 4 (b) when optimizing for DU-pairs and observing mutation rate. We find a large number of very effective test cases to randomly select from, thus the good performance of the random order. A plateau can also be observed for the GA-evolved orders, though at a much higher cost (around 60) than when optimizing for definitions.

5   Conclusion

In this paper, we presented a solution to the problem of ordering the execution of black-box test cases derived from state machines, and proposed a heuristic search technique for obtaining test case sequences maximizing chances of early fault detection. Specifically, we rank state-based test cases derived according to the transition tree method according to the amount of data-flow the test cases cover in the test model. Prioritization aims to achieve maximum data flow coverage as soon as possible, while accounting for user-defined criteria such as maximum testing budget or minimum data flow coverage. As a result we propose a multi-objective optimization with four different objective functions. We dedicated a fair amount of the paper to the design of our GA and our case study to facilitate replications and comparisons.

We evaluated our approach on one case study that exhibits a state-based behaviour: a complex data structure class. Results indeed show that our optimization leads to test case sequences that have a sharp increase in data flow coverage early, which is the desired behaviour, and that this translates into early fault detection, with much less variance, when compared to randomly generated sequences. Data is available for two other case studies that confirm these results, which could not be included here.

Another lesson we have learnt regarding multi-objective optimization, though we did not have room to elaborate on this in the paper, is the likely presence of deceptive attractors in the search space [32]. In our optimization, a deceptive attractor is a subsequence in the chromosome that will lead to a local optimum rather than a global optimum. We identified that, in our solution, the presence of deceptive attractors is likely a by-product of the genetic algorithm we used (i.e., SPEA2) since it relies on the phenotype to maintain diversity in solutions, while optimization should also rely on the genotype to maintain diversity. We did not try to change the implementation of the well-known, multi-objective optimization algorithm (SPEA2) we used to solve this problem, and leave this to future work.

Future work should include the following: Using a greedy algorithm which takes into account a single metric being optimized, such as coverage rate, to produce prioritizations is another baseline of comparison that can be considered; Studying the impact of the ease of detection of mutants on results (e.g., easy to kill mutants, i.e., those killed by 90% of the test cases for instance could be removed from the analysis).

References

1. Binder, R.V.: Testing Object-Oriented Systems - Models, Patterns, and Tools. Addison-Wesley (1999)
2. Briand, L.C., Labiche, Y., Wang, Y.: Using Simulation to Empirically Investigate Test Coverage Criteria. In: IEEE/ACM International Conference on Software Engineering, pp. 86–95 (2004)
3. Ammann, P., Offutt, A.J.: Introduction to Software Testing. Cambridge University Press (2008)
4. Briand, L.C., Labiche, Y., Lin, Q.: Improving the Coverage Criteria of UML State Machines Using Data Flow Analysis. Software Testing, Verification and Reliability 20, 177–207 (2010)
5. Chow, T.S.: Testing Software Design Modeled by Finite-State Machines. IEEE Transactions on Software Engineering SE-4, 178–187 (1978)
6. Khalil, M., Labiche, Y.: On the Round Trip Path Testing Strategy. In: IEEE International Symposium on Software Reliability Engineering, pp. 388–397 (2010)
7. Lee, D., Yannakakis, M.: Principles and Methods of Testing Finite State Machines - A Survey. Proceedings of the IEEE 84, 1090–1123 (1996)
8. Beizer, B.: Software Testing Techniques. Van Nostrand Reinhold, New York (1990)
9. Kalaji, A.S., Hierons, R., Swift, S.: An integrated search-based approach for automatic testing from extended finite state machine (EFSM) models. Information and Software Technology 53, 1297–1318 (2011)
10. Warmer, J., Kleppe, A.: The Object Constraint Language. Addison Wesley (2003)
11. Yoo, S., Harman, M.: Regression testing minimization, selection and prioritization: a survey. Software Testing, Verification and Reliability 22, 67–120 (2012)
12. Rothermel, G., Untch, R.H., Chu, C., Harrold, M.J.: Prioritizing test cases for regression testing. IEEE Transactions on Software Engineering 27, 929–948 (2001)
13. Li, Z., Harman, M., Hierons, R.: Search Algorithms for Regression Test Case Prioritization. IEEE Transactions on Software Engineering 33, 225–237 (2007)
14. Harman, M.: Making the Case for MORTO: Multi Objective Regression Test Optimization. In: IEEE International Conference on Software Testing, Verification and Validation Workshops, pp. 111–114 (2011)
15. Zitzler, E., Laumanss, M., Thiele, L.: SPEA2: Improving the Strength Pareto Evolutionary Algorithm. Technical Report, Swiss Federal Institute of Technology, Computer Engineering and Networks Laboratory (2001)
16. Goldberg, D.E.: Genetic Algorithms in Search, Optimization & Machine Learning. Addison Wesley (1989)
17. Affenzeller, M., Winkler, S., Wagner, S., Beham, A.: Genetic Algorithms and Genetic Progrmming-Modern concetps and practical applications. CRC Press (2009)
18. De Jong, K.A.: Learning with Genetic Algorithms: An Overview. Machine Learning 3, 121–138 (1988)

19. Grefenstette, J.J.: Optimization of control parameters for genetic algorithms. IEEE Transactions on Systems, Man and Cybernetics 16, 122–128 (1986)
20. Pargas, R.P., Harrold, M.J., Peck, R.: Test-Data Generation Using Genetic Algorithms. Software Testing, Verification and Reliability 9, 263–282 (1999)
21. Tiwari, A., Vergidis, K., Majeed, B.: Evolutionary Multiobjective Optimization of Business Processes. In: IEEE Congress on Evolutionary Computation, pp. 3091–3097 (2006)
22. Laumanns, M., Zitzler, E., Thiele, L.: On The Effects of Archiving, Elitism, an Density Based Selection in Evolutionary Multi-objective Optimization. In: Zitzler, E., Deb, K., Thiele, L., Coello Coello, C.A., Corne, D.W. (eds.) EMO 2001. LNCS, vol. 1993, pp. 181–196. Springer, Heidelberg (2001)
23. Zitzler, E., Thiele, L.: Multiobjective Evolutionary Algorithms: A Comparative Case Study and the Strength Pareto Approach. IEEE Transactions on Evolutionary Computation 3 (1999)
24. Rivas-Dávalos, F., Irving, M.R.: An Approach Based on the Strength Pareto Evolutionary Algorithm 2 for Power Distribution System Planning. In: Coello Coello, C.A., Hernández Aguirre, A., Zitzler, E. (eds.) EMO 2005. LNCS, vol. 3410, pp. 707–720. Springer, Heidelberg (2005)
25. Haupt, R.L., Haupt, S.E.: Practical Genetic Algorithms. Wiley-Interscience (1998)
26. Bui, L.T., Essam, D., Abbass, H.A., Green, D.: Performance analysis of evolutionary multi-objective optimization algorithms in noisy environment. In: Asia Pacific Symposium on Intelligent and Evolutionary Systems, pp. 29–39 (2004)
27. Elbaum, S., Malishevsky, A.G., Rothermel, G.: Incorporating varying test costs and fault severities into test case prioritization. In: ACM/IEEE International Conference on Software Engineering, pp. 329–338 (2001)
28. Hutchins, M., Froster, H., Goradia, T., Ostrand, T.: Experiments on the Effectiveness of Dataflow- and Controlflow-Based Test Adequacy Criteria. In: ACM/IEEE International Conference on Software Engineering, pp. 191–200 (1994)
29. Ma, Y.-S., Offutt, A.J., Kwon, Y.-R.: MuJava: A Mutation System for Java. In: ACM/IEEE International Conference on Software Engineering, pp. 827–830 (2006)
30. Andrews, J.H., Briand, L.C., Labiche, Y., Namin, A.S.: Using Mutation Analysis for Assessing and Comparing Testing Coverage Criteria. IEEE Transactions on Software Engineering 32, 608–624 (2006)
31. Gomaa, H.: Designing Concurrent, Distributed, and Real-Time Applications with UML. Addison Wesley (2000)
32. Kargupta, H., Deb, K., Goldberg, D.E.: Ordering genetic algorithms and deception. In: Parallel Problem Solving from Nature, pp. 47–56 (1992)

Validating Code-Level Behavior of Dynamic Adaptive Systems in the Face of Uncertainty

Erik M. Fredericks, Andres J. Ramirez, and Betty H.C. Cheng

Michigan State University, East Lansing, Michigan 48824-1226, USA
{freder99,ramir105,chengb}@cse.msu.edu

Abstract. A dynamically adaptive system (DAS) self-reconfigures at run time in order to handle adverse combinations of system and environmental conditions. Techniques are needed to make DASs more resilient to system and environmental uncertainty. Furthermore, automated support to validate that a DAS provides acceptable behavior even through reconfigurations are essential to address assurance concerns. This paper introduces FENRIR, an evolutionary computation-based approach to address these challenges. By explicitly searching for diverse and interesting operational contexts and examining the resulting execution traces generated by a DAS as it reconfigures in response to adverse conditions, FENRIR can discover undesirable behaviors triggered by unexpected environmental conditions at design time, which can be used to revise the system appropriately. We illustrate FENRIR by applying it to a dynamically adaptive remote data mirroring network that must efficiently diffuse data even in the face of adverse network conditions.

Keywords: search-based software engineering, novelty search, genetic algorithm, software assurance.

1 Introduction

A dynamically adaptive system (DAS) can self-reconfigure at run time by triggering adaptive logic to switch between configurations in order to continually satisfy its requirements even as its operating context changes. For example, a hand-held device may need to dynamically upload an error-correction communication protocol if the network is lossy or noisy. Despite this self-reconfiguration capability, a DAS may encounter operational contexts of which it was not explicitly designed to handle. If the DAS encounters such an operational context, then it is possible that it will no longer satisfy its requirements as well as exhibit other possibly undesirable behaviors at run time. This paper presents FENRIR, a design-time approach for automatically exploring how a broad range of combinations of system and environmental conditions impact the behavior of a DAS and its ability to satisfy its requirements.

In general, it is difficult to identify *all* possible operating contexts that a DAS may encounter during execution [7,6,18,28]. While design-time techniques have

G. Ruhe and Y. Zhang (Eds.): SSBSE 2013, LNCS 8084, pp. 81–95, 2013.
© Springer-Verlag Berlin Heidelberg 2013

been developed for testing a DAS [4,20,21,22,24,25,31], these are typically restricted to evaluating requirements satisfaction within specific operational contexts and do not always consider code-level behaviors. Researchers have also applied search-based heuristics, including evolutionary algorithms, to efficiently generate conditions that can cause failures in a system under test to provide code coverage [2,15,16]. Automated techniques are needed to make a DAS more resilient to different operational contexts as well as validate that it provides acceptable behavior even through reconfigurations.

This paper introduces FENRIR,[1] an evolutionary computation-based approach that explores how varying operational contexts affect a DAS at the code level at run time. In particular, FENRIR searches for combinations of system and environmental parameters that exercise a DAS's self-reconfiguration capabilities, possibly in unanticipated ways. Tracing the execution path of a DAS can provide insights into its behavior, including the conditions that triggered an adaptation, the adaptation path itself, and the functional behavior exhibited by the DAS after the adaptation. At design time, an adaptation engineer can analyze the resulting execution traces to identify possible bug fixes within the DAS code, as well as optimizations to improve the run-time self-adaptation capabilities of the DAS.

FENRIR leverages novelty search [17], an evolutionary computation technique, to explicitly search for diverse DAS execution traces. Specifically, FENRIR uses novelty search to guide the generation of diverse DAS operational contexts comprising combinations of system and environmental conditions that produce previously unexamined DAS execution traces. Since we do not know in advance which combinations of environmental conditions will adversely affect system behavior, we cannot define an explicit fitness function for generating the operational contexts. Instead, we opt for *diverse* operational contexts with the intent of considering a representative set of "all" operational contexts. FENRIR then executes the DAS under these differing operational contexts in order to evaluate their effects upon the DAS's execution trace. As part of its search for novel execution traces, FENRIR analyzes and compares the traces to determine which operational contexts generate the most diverse behaviors within the DAS.

We demonstrate FENRIR by applying it to an industry-provided problem, management of a remote data mirroring (RDM) network [12,13]. An RDM network must replicate and distribute data to all mirrors within the network as links fail and messages are dropped or delayed. Experimental results demonstrate that FENRIR provides a significantly greater coverage of execution paths than can be found with randomized testing. The remainder of this paper is as follows. Section 2 provides background information on RDMs, evolutionary algorithms, and execution tracing. Section 3 describes the implementation of FENRIR with an RDM network as a motivating example. Following, Section 4 presents our experimental results, and then Section 5 discusses related work. Lastly, Section 6 summarizes our findings and presents future directions.

---

[1] In Norse mythology, Fenrir is the son of Loki, god of mischief.

2   Background

In addition to overviewing the key enabling technologies used in this work, this section also overviews the remote data mirroring application.

2.1   Remote Data Mirroring

Remote data mirroring (RDM) [12,13] is a data protection technique that can maintain data availability and prevent loss by storing data copies, or replicates, in physically remote locations. An RDM is configurable in terms of its network topology as well as the method and timing of data distribution among data mirrors. Network topology may be configured as a minimum spanning tree or redundant topology. Two key data distribution methods are used. *Synchronous* distribution automatically distributes each modification to all other nodes, and *asynchronous* distribution batches modifications in order to combine edits made to the data. Asynchronous propagation provides better network performance, however it also has weaker data protection as batched data could be lost when a data mirror fails. In our case, an RDM network is modeled as a DAS to dynamically manage reconfiguration of network topology and data distribution.

2.2   Genetic Algorithms

A genetic algorithm (GA) [11] is a stochastic search-based technique grounded in Darwinian evolution that leverages natural selection to efficiently find solutions for complex problems. GAs represent a solution as a population, or collection, of genomes that encode candidate solutions. A fitness function evaluates the quality of each individual genome within the population in order to guide the search process towards an optimal solution. New genomes are produced through crossover and mutation operators. In particular, crossover exchanges portions of existing genomes and mutation randomly modifies a genome. The best performing individuals are retained at the end of each iteration, or generation, via the selection operator. These operations are repeated until a viable solution is found or the maximum number of generations is reached.

Novelty search [17] is another type of genetic algorithm that explicitly searches for unique solutions in order to avoid becoming caught in local optima. Novelty search replaces the fitness function in a traditional genetic algorithm with a novelty function that uses a distance metric, such as Euclidean distance [3], to determine the distance between a candidate solution and its k-nearest solutions. Furthermore, a solution may be added to a novelty archive in order to track areas of the space of all possible solutions that have been already thoroughly explored.

2.3   Execution Tracing

Following the execution path of a software system can provide insights into system behavior at run time, as it may behave differently than intended due to uncertainty within its operating context. Tracing system execution has been applied to various aspects of software analysis, from understanding the behavior of distributed systems [19] to identifying interactions between the software and hardware of superscalar processors [23]. An execution trace can be generated by introducing logging statements. Many different approaches to software logging exist [34], however for this paper we consider a subset of *branch coverage* [10] as our metric for tracing execution paths. Branch coverage follows all possible paths that a program may take during execution, such as method invocations, `if-else`, or `try-catch` blocks.

3   Approach

FENRIR is a design-time assurance technique for exploring possible execution paths that a DAS may take in response to changing environmental and system contexts. Conceptually, we consider a DAS (see Figure 1) to comprise a collection of target (non-adaptive) configurations, TC_i, connected by adaptive logic, A_{ij}, that moves execution from one target configuration (TC_i) to another (TC_j) [35]. Therefore, the functional logic of the system (i.e., requirements) is implemented by the target configurations, where each target configuration may differ in how it implements the requirements (e.g., different performance requirements), and how it may handle specific environmental conditions.

FENRIR starts with instrumented code for both the adaptive logic and functional logic for a DAS. Then the set of operating contexts that can trigger DAS self-reconfigurations are generated using novelty search, in order to provide a diverse and representative set of environmental and system contexts that the DAS may encounter during execution. These operating contexts are based on different combinations of identified sources of uncertainty that may affect the DAS at run time, where the combinations may be unintuitive, but feasible, and therefore not anticipated by a human developer. Next, the instrumented DAS is executed for different operational contexts, where each operational context will have a corresponding execution trace that reflects the execution path of a DAS as it self-reconfigures and executes its target configurations. This trace provides information necessary to fully realize the complexity inherent within the DAS as it executes and performs self-reconfigurations.

Figure 2 provides an overview of a DAS that has been instrumented with logging statements. The instrumented DAS is split into two parts: Configuration and Adaptation Manager. The Configuration refers to the collection of target configurations connected by the adaptive logic as shown in Figure 1, and the Adaptation Manager comprises a monitoring, decision logic, and reconfiguration engine to manage the self-adaptation capabilities for the DAS. Together, these two parts make up the system that can reconfigure itself at run time in order to handle uncertainties within its operating context.

Logging statements are then inserted into both the Configuration and Adaptation Manager to provide an engineer with information regarding the target configuration state, conditions that trigger adaptations, and steps taken during

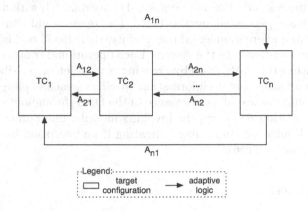

Fig. 1. DAS comprising a collection of target configurations TC_i connected by adaptation logic A_{ij}

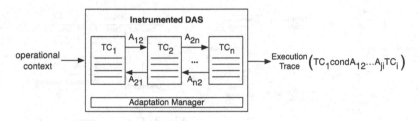

Fig. 2. Overview of an instrumented DAS

self-reconfiguration at each time step throughout execution. Furthermore, the instrumented DAS requires an operational context to specify the sources of environmental and system uncertainty, as previously identified by the domain engineer. The DAS generates a trace that represents the execution path for a given set of environmental conditions.

The remainder of this section describes how FENRIR generates novel execution traces. First, we present an overview of FENRIR and state its assumptions, required inputs, and expected outputs. We then discuss each step in the FENRIR process.

3.1 Assumptions, Inputs, and Outputs

FENRIR requires instrumented executable code for a DAS to exercise the adaptive logic and functional logic triggered by different operational contexts. In particular, the instrumented code within the DAS should provide a measure of *branch coverage* in order to properly report the various execution paths that a DAS may traverse. Furthermore, the logging statements should monitor possible exceptions or error conditions that may arise.

FENRIR produces a collection of operational contexts, each with a corresponding execution trace generated by the DAS. The operational contexts specify sources of system and environmental uncertainty, their likelihood of occurrence, and their impact or severity to the system. Each operational context may trigger adaptations within the DAS, thereby creating a vast set of possible execution paths. Execution traces contain information specific to each explored path, providing insights into the overall performance of the DAS throughout execution. In particular, information regarding the invoking module, line number, a description of intended behavior, and a flag indicating if an exception has occurred is provided for further analysis.

3.2   Fenrir Process

The data flow diagram (DFD) in Figure 3 provides a process overview for using FENRIR. Each step is described next in detail.

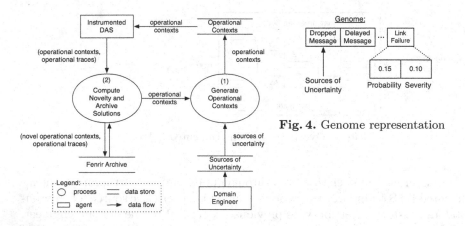

Fig. 4. Genome representation

Fig. 3. DFD diagram of Fenrir process

(1) **Generate Operational Contexts.** FENRIR uses novelty search [17], an evolutionary computation-based technique, to generate operational contexts that specify the sources of environmental and system uncertainty. Operational contexts are represented as genomes within a population. Each genome comprises a vector of genes of length n, where n defines the number of environmental and system sources of uncertainty. Each gene defines the likelihood and impact of occurrence for each source. Figure 4 illustrates a sample genome used by FENRIR to configure sources of uncertainty. For instance, the displayed genome has a parameter for a network link failure that has a 15% chance of occurrence, and, at most, 10% of all network links within the RDM network can fail at any given time step. Each generated operational context is then applied to an instrumented

DAS, resulting in an execution trace. Both the operational context and execution trace are provided as inputs to the novelty value calculation, as is described in the following subsection.

Novelty search is similar in approach to genetic algorithms [11], however it differs in the search objective. Novelty search aims to create a set of diverse solutions that are representative of the solution space, whereas a genetic algorithm searches instead for an optimal solution. The novelty search process is constrained by a set of parameters that govern how new solutions are created. These include *population size, crossover* and *mutation rates,* a *termination criterion,* and a *novelty threshold value.* Population size determines the number of genomes created per generation, and a starting population is randomly generated that specifies different sources of uncertainty based on the system and environmental conditions. The crossover and mutation rates define the number of new genomes that may be created through recombination and random modifications, respectively. The termination criterion defines the number of generations that the novelty search algorithm will run before termination, and the novelty threshold provides a baseline value for inclusion of a solution within the novelty archive. New genomes are created in each subsequent generation via the crossover and mutation operators. Crossover creates new genomes by swapping genes between two candidate genomes, and mutation produces a new genome by randomly mutating a gene within the original candidate.

(2) Compute Novelty and Archive Solutions. FENRIR calculates a novelty value for each solution within a population by first constructing a weighted call graph (WCG) [1] from each corresponding execution trace then calculating the difference against every other solution within the novelty archive in a pair-wise fashion. The WCG is an extension to a program call graph [27] and is represented as a directed graph, with nodes populated by unique identifiers corresponding to each logging statement, directed edges symbolizing execution order, and weights representing execution frequency. Figures 5(a) and 5(b) present an example of a WCG with corresponding example code, respectively, where each node represents a statement from the execution trace, and each edge label represents the execution frequency (i.e., weight).

The novelty value is computed by calculating the differences in nodes and edges between two WCGs, as shown in Equation 1, and then applying a Manhattan distance metric [3] to measure the distance between each WCG, as shown in Equation 2. Any novelty value that exceeds the novelty archive threshold, or is within the top 10% of all novelty values, is then added to the novelty archive at the end of each generation.

$$dist(\mu_i, \mu_j) = len(\{v \in g_i\} \oplus \{v \in g_j\}) + len(\{e \in g_i\} \oplus \{e \in g_j\})) \qquad (1)$$

$$p(\overline{\mu}, k) = \frac{1}{k} \sum_{i=1}^{k} dist(\mu_i, \mu_j) \qquad (2)$$

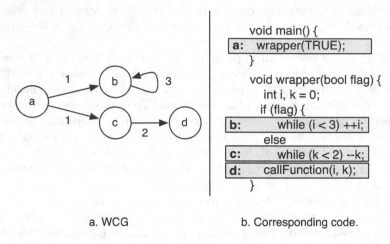

a. WCG   b. Corresponding code.

Fig. 5. WCG Example

Upon completion, FENRIR returns a set of operational contexts, each with their corresponding execution trace stored in the novelty archive. Together, these outputs provide insight into the behavior of the DAS throughout execution, including triggers to self-reconfigurations, parameters for each target configuration, raised exceptions, and unwanted or unnecessary adaptations. Unnecessary adaptations refer to adaptations that may occur as the DAS transitions back and forth between target configurations before finally settling on a new target configuration to handle the current operating context. Unacceptable behaviors may then be corrected through bug fixes, augmentation of target configurations, or by introducing satisfaction methods such as RELAX [6,33] that tolerate flexibility in DAS requirements.

4   Experimental Results

This section describes our experimental setup and discusses the experimental results found from applying FENRIR to an RDM application.

4.1   Experimental Setup

For this work, we implemented an RDM network as a completely connected graph. Each node represents an RDM and each edge represents a network link. Our network was configured to comprise 25 RDMs and 300 network links that may be activated and used to transfer data between RDMs. Logging statements comprise a unique identifier, module information such as function name, line number, and a custom description, and are inserted into the RDM source code to properly generate an execution trace. The RDM was executed for 150 time steps, with 20 data items randomly inserted into varying RDMs that were then responsible for distribution of those data items to all other RDMs. Furthermore, the novelty search algorithm was configured to run for 15 generations with a population size of 20 individual solutions per generation. The crossover, mutation, and novelty threshold rates were set to 25%, 50%, and 10%, respectively.

Environmental uncertainties, such as dropped messages or unpredictable network link failures, can be applied to the RDM network throughout a given execution. The RDM network may then self-adapt in response to these adverse conditions in order to properly continue its execution. A self-adaptation results in a target system configuration and series of reconfiguration steps that enables a safe transition of the RDM network from the current configuration to target configuration. This adaptation may include updates to the underlying network topology, such as changing to a minimum spanning tree, or updating network propagation parameters, such as moving from synchronous to asynchronous propagation.

In order to validate our approach, we compared and evaluated the resulting execution traces produced by FENRIR with the novelty metric previously introduced in Equations 1 and 2. To demonstrate the effectiveness of novelty search, we compared FENRIR execution traces with those generated for random operational contexts. We compared FENRIR results to random testing since we could not define an explicit fitness function because we do not know *a priori* which operational contexts adversely impact the system. As such, FENRIR provides a means for us to consider a representative set of all possible operational contexts. For statistical purposes, we conducted 50 trials of each experiment and, where applicable, plotted or reported the mean values with corresponding error bars or deviations.

4.2   DAS Execution in an Uncertain Environment

For this experiment, we define the null hypothesis H_0 to state that there is no difference between execution traces generated by configurations produced by novelty and those created by random search. We further define the alternate hypothesis H_1 to state that there is a difference between execution traces generated from novelty search (FENRIR) and random search.

Figure 6 presents two box plots with the novelty distances obtained by the novelty archive generated by FENRIR and a randomized search algorithm. As this plot demonstrates, FENRIR generated execution traces that achieved statistically significant higher novelty values than those generated by a randomized search algorithm ($p < 0.001$, Welch Two Sample t-test). This plot also demonstrates that FENRIR discovered execution traces with negative kurtosis, thereby suggesting that the distribution of operational contexts were skewed towards larger novelty values. These results enable us to reject our null hypothesis, H_0. Furthermore, these results enable us to accept our alternate hypothesis, H_1, as novelty search discovered a significantly larger number of unique DAS execution paths when compared to the randomized search algorithm. Figure 6 also demonstrates that the solutions generated by FENRIR provide a better representation of the solution space with fewer operational contexts, as the FENRIR box plot contains novelty

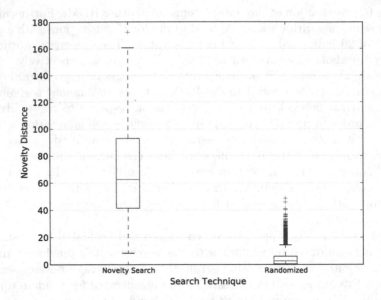

Fig. 6. Novelty distance comparison between novelty and random search

values from 30 solutions, and the randomized search box plot contains novelty values from 300 solutions. As such, using FENRIR enables a DAS developer to assess behavior assurance of a DAS in uncertain environments more efficiently, both in terms of computation time and information to be analyzed.

Figure 7 presents two separate RDM network execution paths that were generated by novelty search, with each represented as a WCG. Each node represents a unique logging point and each directed edge represents a sequential execution from one node to the next. The weight on each edge indicates the frequency that the statement was executed. For instance, in Figure 7(a), the weight on the edge between Nodes (g) and (h) shows that Node (g) was executed 28 times and then Node (h) was executed once. Further analysis of the execution trace indicates that the RDM network consisted of 28 data mirrors. Visual inspection of Figures 7(a) and 7(b) indicates that FENRIR is able to find execution paths that vary greatly in both structure and in frequency of executed instructions. The large variance in structure helps us to better understand the complexity of the DAS behavior in response to different operational contexts. Furthermore, the diversity of execution traces can be used to focus our efforts in revising the functional and/or adaptive logic in order to reduce complexity, optimize configurations, or repair erroneous behavior and code.

Threats to Validity. This research was a proof of concept study to determine the feasibility of using execution trace data for a DAS to determine what evolutionary computation-generated system and system and environmental conditions warrant dynamic adaptation. We applied our technique to a problem that was provided by industrial collaborators. Threats to validity include whether this

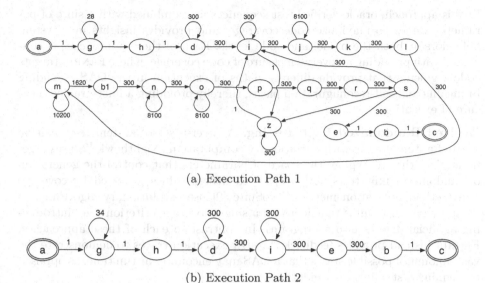

(a) Execution Path 1

(b) Execution Path 2

Fig. 7. Unique execution paths

technique will achieve similar results with other DAS implementations and other problem domains. Furthermore, as an optimization to maintain trace files that are manageable in size, we focused on coverage points rather than providing full branching code coverage. As such, exploration of additional code coverage may be necessary to provide extended information on the generated execution paths.

5   Related Work

This section presents related work on approaches for providing code coverage, evolving randomized unit test data, automated methods for testing distributed systems, and automatically exploring how uncertainty affects requirements.

Code Coverage. Assurance of a system can be augmented by providing a measure of code coverage testing. Chen *et al.* [5] proposed code coverage as an approach for enhancing the reliability measurements of software systems during testing. A software system may successfully pass all test cases in a testing suite and yet can still have latent errors. Augmenting traditional testing with code coverage analysis can improve testing reliability. Furthermore, instrumenting software to provide code coverage can be a non-trivial task, incurring extra time and overhead. Tikir and Hollingsworth [32] have introduced an approach that can dynamically insert and remove logging calls in a codebase. Moreover, optimizations to traditional logging techniques were introduced in order to reduce both the number of instrumentation points and program slowdown. Finally, automated code coverage, as well as automated model coverage, can be provided via gray-box testing [14]. Gray-box testing can be provided through a combination of white-box parameterized unit testing and black-box model-based testing.

In this approach, oracle-verified test sequences are combined with a suite of parameter values to maximize code coverage, and provides insights into system behaviors at both the model and code levels. Each of these approaches is concerned with providing an overall measure of code coverage, where FENRIR targets code segments that provide differing paths of execution in the DAS, including branching and self-reconfiguration paths, thereby providing a finer-grained measure of execution.

Evolved Randomized Unit Testing. A diverse set of system tests can be created automatically with evolutionary computation. Nighthawk [2] uses a genetic algorithm to explore the space of parameters that control the generation of randomized unit tests with respect to fitness values provided by coverage and method invocation metrics. EvoSuite [9] uses evolutionary algorithms to create whole test suites that focus on a single coverage criterion (i.e., introducing artificial defects into a program). In contrast to each of these approaches, FENRIR instead provides feedback through execution traces to demonstrate the vast amount of possible states that a DAS may encounter at run time, as opposed to defining test suites for validation.

Automated Testing of Distributed Systems. Distributed systems comprise asynchronous processes that can also send and receive data asynchronously, and as a result can contain a large number of possible execution paths. Sen and Agha [30] have proposed the use of *concolic* execution, or simultaneous concrete and symbolic execution, in order to determine a partial order of events incurred in an execution path. Concolic execution was proven to efficiently and exhaustively explore unique execution paths in a distributed system. Furthermore, automated fault injection can explore and evaluate fault tolerance to ensure that a distributed system continually satisfies its requirements specification [8] and ensures system dependability [29]. Conversely, FENRIR explores how a system can handle faults by studying its reaction to varying operational contexts, rather than by direct injection of faults into the system.

Automatically Exploring Uncertainty in Requirements. Ramirez *et al.* [26] introduced Loki, an approach for creating novel system and environmental conditions that can affect DAS behavior, and in doing so uncover unexpected or latent errors within a DAS's *requirements specification*. FENRIR extends Loki by exploring uncertainty at the code level in an effort to distinguish how a DAS will react in uncertain situations and attempt to uncover errors made in the *implementation* of a DAS.

6   Conclusion

In this paper we presented FENRIR, an approach that applies novelty search at design time to automatically generate operational contexts that can affect a DAS during execution at the code level. Specifically, FENRIR introduces logging statements to trace a DAS's execution path and then uses the distance between execution paths to measure the level of novelty between operational contexts.

By creating a set of configurations that more extensively exercise a DAS, it is possible to identify undesirable behaviors or inconsistencies between requirements and system implementation. We demonstrated the use of FENRIR on an RDM network that was responsible for replicating data across a network. This network was subjected to uncertainty in the form of random link failures and dropped or delayed messages. Experimental results from this case study established that FENRIR was able to successfully generate more unique execution paths with a smaller set of execution traces than purely random search. Future directions for FENRIR will extend the technique and apply it to additional applications. We are investigating different distance metrics for novelty search as well as other evolutionary strategies to generate unique execution traces.

Acknowledgements. We gratefully acknowledge conceptual and implementation contributions from Jared M. Moore.

This work has been supported in part by NSF grants CCF-0854931, CCF-0750787, CCF-0820220, DBI-0939454, Army Research Office grant W911NF-08-1-0495, and Ford Motor Company. Any opinions, findings, and conclusions or recommendations expressed in this material are those of the author(s) and do not necessarily reflect the views of the National Science Foundation, Army, Ford, or other research sponsors.

References

1. Ahn, S.-Y., Kang, S., Baik, J., Choi, H.-J.: A weighted call graph approach for finding relevant components in source code. In: 10th ACIS International Conference on Software Engineering, Artificial Intelligences, Networking and Parallel/Distributed Computing, SNPD 2009, pp. 539–544 (2009)
2. Andrews, J.H., Menzies, T., Li, F.C.H.: Genetic algorithms for randomized unit testing. IEEE Transactions on Software Engineering 37(1), 80–94 (2011)
3. Black, P.E.: Dictionary of Algorithms and Data Structures. U.S. National Institute of Standards and Technology (May 2006)
4. Camara, J., de Lemos, R.: Evaluation of resilience in self-adaptive systems using probabilistic model-checking. In: Software Engineering for Adaptive and Self-Managing Systems, pp. 53–62 (June 2012)
5. Chen, M.-H., Lyu, M.R., Wong, E.: Effect of code coverage on software reliability measurement. IEEE Transactions on Reliability 50(2), 165–170 (2001)
6. Cheng, B.H.C., Sawyer, P., Bencomo, N., Whittle, J.: A goal-based modeling approach to develop requirements of an adaptive system with environmental uncertainty. In: Schürr, A., Selic, B. (eds.) MODELS 2009. LNCS, vol. 5795, pp. 468–483. Springer, Heidelberg (2009)
7. Cheng, B.H.C, De Lemos, R., Giese, H., Inverardi, P., Magee, J., Andersson, J., Becker, B., Bencomo, N., Brun, Y., Cukic, B., et al.: Software engineering for self-adaptive systems: A research roadmap. Springer (2009)
8. Dawson, S., Jahanian, F., Mitton, T., Tung, T.-L.: Testing of fault-tolerant and real-time distributed systems via protocol fault injection. In: Proceedings of Annual Symposium on Fault Tolerant Computing, pp. 404–414. IEEE (1996)

9. Fraser, G., Arcuri, A.: Evosuite: automatic test suite generation for object-oriented software. In: Proceedings of the 19th ACM SIGSOFT Symposium and the 13th European Conference on Foundations of Software Engineering, ESEC/FSE 2011, Szeged, Hungary, pp. 416–419. ACM (2011)

10. Gupta, R., Mathur, A.P., Soffa, M.L.: Generating test data for branch coverage. In: Proceedings of the 15th IEEE International Conference on Automated Software Engineering (ASE 2000), pp. 219–227 (2000)

11. Holland, J.H.: Adaptation in Natural and Artificial Systems. MIT Press, Cambridge (1992)

12. Ji, M., Veitch, A., Wilkes, J.: Seneca: Remote mirroring done write. In: USENIX 2003 Annual Technical Conference, Berkeley, CA, USA, pp. 253–268. USENIX Association (June 2003)

13. Keeton, K., Santos, C., Beyer, D., Chase, J., Wilkes, J.: Designing for disasters. In: Proceedings of the 3rd USENIX Conference on File and Storage Technologies, Berkeley, CA, USA, pp. 59–62. USENIX Association (2004)

14. Kicillof, N., Grieskamp, W., Tillmann, N., Braberman, V.: Achieving both model and code coverage with automated gray-box testing. In: Proceedings of the 3rd International Workshop on Advances in Model-Based Testing, pp. 1–11. ACM (2007)

15. Lajolo, M., Lavagno, L., Rebaudengo, M.: Automatic test bench generation for simulation-based validation. In: Proceedings of the Eighth International Workshop on Hardware/Software Codesign, San Diego, California, United States, pp. 136–140. ACM (2000)

16. Ledru, Y., Petrenko, A., Boroday, S.: Using string distances for test case prioritisation. In: Proceedings of the 2009 IEEE/ACM International Conference on Automated Software Engineering, ASE 2009, Auckland, New Zealand, pp. 510–514. IEEE Computer Society (November 2009)

17. Lehman, J., Stanley, K.O.: Exploiting open-endedness to solve problems through the search for novelty. In: Proceedings of the Eleventh International Conference on Artificial Life (ALIFE XI), Cambridge, MA, USA. MIT Press (2008)

18. McKinley, P.K., Sadjadi, S.M., Kasten, E.P., Cheng, B.H.C.: Composing adaptive software. Computer 37(7), 56–64 (2004)

19. Moc, J., Carr, D.A.: Understanding distributed systems via execution trace data. In: Proceedings of the 9th International Workshop on Program Comprehension (IWPC 2001), pp. 60–67. IEEE (2001)

20. Nguyen, C.D., Perini, A., Tonella, P., Kessler, F.B., Tonella P.: Automated continuous testing of multiagent systems. In: Fifth European Workshop on Multi-Agent Systems, EUMAS (2007)

21. Nguyen, C.D., Perini, A., Tonella, P., Miles, S., Harman, M., Luck, M.: Evolutionary testing of autonomous software agents. In: Proceedings of the Eighth International Conference on Autonomous Agents and Multiagent Systems, Budapest, Hungary, pp. 521–528. International Foundation for Autonomous Agents and Multiagent Systems (May 2009)

22. Nguyen, D.C., Perini, A., Tonella, P.: A goal-oriented software testing methodology. In: Luck, M., Padgham, L. (eds.) AOSE 2007. LNCS, vol. 4951, pp. 58–72. Springer, Heidelberg (2008)

23. Ramírez, A., Larriba-Pey, J.-L., Navarro, C., Torrellas, J., Valero, M.: Software trace cache. In: Proceedings of the 13th International Conference on Supercomputing, pp. 119–126. ACM (1999)

24. Ramirez, A.J., Cheng, B.H.C.: Verifying and analyzing adaptive logic through uml state models. In: Proceedings of the 2008 IEEE International Conference on Software Testing, Verification, and Validation, Lillehammer, Norway, pp. 529–532 (April 2008)
25. Ramirez, A.J., Fredericks, E.M., Jensen, A.C., Cheng, B.H.C.: Automatically relaxing a goal model to cope with uncertainty. In: Fraser, G., Teixeira de Souza, J. (eds.) SSBSE 2012. LNCS, vol. 7515, pp. 198–212. Springer, Heidelberg (2012)
26. Ramirez, A.J., Jensen, A.C., Cheng, B.H.C., Knoester, D.B.: Automatically exploring how uncertainty impacts behavior of dynamically adaptive systems. In: Proceedings of the 2011 International Conference on Automatic Software Engineering, ASE 2011, Lawrence, Kansas, USA (November 2011)
27. Ryder, B.G.: Constructing the call graph of a program. IEEE Transactions on Software Engineering SE-5(3), 216–226 (1979)
28. Sawyer, P., Bencomo, N., Letier, E., Finkelstein, A.: Requirements-aware systems: A research agenda for re self-adaptive systems. In: Proceedings of the 18th IEEE International Requirements Engineering Conference, Sydney, Australia, pp. 95–103 (September 2010)
29. Segall, Z., Vrsalovic, D., Siewiorek, D., Yaskin, D., Kownacki, J., Barton, J., Dancey, R., Robinson, A., Lin, T.: Fiat-fault injection based automated testing environment. In: Eighteenth International Symposium on Fault-Tolerant Computing, FTCS-18, Digest of Papers, pp. 102–107. IEEE (1988)
30. Sen, K., Agha, G.: Automated systematic testing of open distributed programs. In: Baresi, L., Heckel, R. (eds.) FASE 2006. LNCS, vol. 3922, pp. 339–356. Springer, Heidelberg (2006)
31. Stott, D.T., Floering, B., Burke, D., Kalbarczpk, Z., Iyer, R.K.: Nftape: a framework for assessing dependability in distributed systems with lightweight fault injectors. In: Computer Performance and Dependability Symposium, pp. 91–100 (2000)
32. Tikir, M.M., Hollingsworth, J.K.: Efficient instrumentation for code coverage testing. ACM SIGSOFT Software Engineering Notes 27, 86–96 (2002)
33. Whittle, J., Sawyer, P., Bencomo, N., Cheng, B.H.C., Bruel, J.-M.: RELAX: Incorporating uncertainty into the specification of self-adaptive systems. In: Proceedings of the 17th International Requirements Engineering Conference (RE 2009), Atlanta, Georgia, USA, pp. 79–88 (September 2009)
34. Yuan, D., Park, S., Zhou, Y.: Characterizing logging practices in open-source software. In: Proceedings of the 2012 International Conference on Software Engineering, ICSE 2012, Piscataway, NJ, USA, pp. 102–112. IEEE Press (2012)
35. Zhang, J., Cheng, B.H.C.: Model-based development of dynamically adaptive software. In: Proceedings of the 28th International Conference on Software engineering, ICSE 2006, Shanghai, China, pp. 371–380. ACM (2006)

Model Refactoring Using Interactive Genetic Algorithm

Adnane Ghannem[1], Ghizlane El Boussaidi[1], and Marouane Kessentini[2]

[1] École de Technologie Supérieure, Montréal, Canada
adnane.ghannem.1@ens.etsmtl.ca, ghizlane.Elboussaidi@etsmtl.ca
[2] Missouri University of Science and Technology, Rolla, MO, USA
marouanek@mst.edu

Abstract. Refactoring aims at improving the quality of design while preserving its semantic. Providing an automatic support for refactoring is a challenging problem. This problem can be considered as an optimization problem where the goal is to find appropriate refactoring suggestions using a set of refactoring examples. However, some of the refactorings proposed using this approach do not necessarily make sense depending on the context and the semantic of the system under analysis. This paper proposes an approach that tackles this problem by adapting the Interactive Genetic Algorithm (IGA) which enables to interact with users and integrate their feedbacks into a classic GA. The proposed algorithm uses a fitness function that combines the structural similarity between the analyzed design model and models from a base of examples, and the designers' ratings of the refactorings proposed during execution of the classic GA. Experimentation with the approach yielded interesting and promising results.

Keywords: Software maintenance, Interactive Genetic Algorithm, Model refactoring, Refactoring by example.

1   Introduction

Software maintenance is considered the most expensive activity in the software system lifecycle [1]. Maintenance tasks can be seen as incremental modifications to a software system that aim to add or adjust some functionality or to correct some design flaws. However, as the time goes by, the system's conceptual integrity erodes and its quality degrades; this deterioration is known in the literature as the software decay problem [2]. A common and widely used technique to cope with this problem is to continuously restructure the software system to improve its structure and design. The process of restructuring object oriented systems is commonly called refactoring [3]. According to Fowler [2], refactoring is the disciplined process of cleaning up code to improve the software structure while preserving its external behavior. Many researchers have been working on providing support for refactoring operations (e.g., [4], [2], and [5]). Existing tools provide different environments to manually or automatically apply refactoring operations to correct, for example, code smells. Indeed, existing work has, for the most part, focused on refactorings at the source code level. Actually, the rise of the model-driven engineering (MDE) approach increased the interest and

G. Ruhe and Y. Zhang (Eds.): SSBSE 2013, LNCS 8084, pp. 96–110, 2013.
© Springer-Verlag Berlin Heidelberg 2013

the needs for tools supporting refactoring at the model-level. In MDE, abstract models are successively refined into more concrete models, and a model refactoring tool will be of great value within this context.

The search-based refactoring approaches proved their effectiveness to propose refactorings to improve the model's design quality. They adapted some of the known heuristics methods (e.g. Simulated annealing, Hill_climbing) as proposed in [6-8] and Genetic Algorithms as in [9]. These approaches relied, for the most part, on a combination of quality metrics to formulate their optimization goal (i.e., the fitness function). A major problem founded in these approaches is that the quality metrics consider only the structural properties of the system under study; the semantic properties of the system are not considered. In this context, Mens and Tourwé [3] argue that most of the refactoring tools cannot offer a full-automatic support because part of the necessary knowledge– especially those related to the semantics– for performing the refactoring remains implicit in designers' heads. Indeed, recognizing opportunities of model refactoring remains a challenging issue that is related to the model marking process within the context of MDE which is a notoriously difficult problem that requires design knowledge and expertise [10].

To take into account the semantics of the software system, we propose a model refactoring approach based on an Interactive Genetic Algorithm (IGAs) [11]. Two types of knowledge are considered in this approach. The first one comes from the examples of refactorings. For this purpose, we hypothesize that the knowledge required to propose appropriate refactorings for a given object-oriented model may be inferred from other existing models' refactorings when there is some structural similarities between these models and the given model. From this perspective, the refactoring is seen as an optimization problem that is solved using a Genetic Algorithm (GA). The second type of knowledge comes from the designer's knowledge. For this purpose, the designer is involved in the optimization process by continuously interacting with the GA algorithm; this enables to adjust the results of the GA progressively exploiting the designer's feedback. Hence the proposed approach (MOREX+I: MOdel REfactoring by eXample plus Interaction) relies on a set of refactoring examples and designer's feedbacks to propose sequences of refactorings. MOREX+I takes as input an initial model, a base of examples of refactored models and a list of metrics calculated on both the initial model and the models in the base of examples, and it generates as output a solution to the refactoring problem. In this paper, we focus on UML class diagrams. In this case, a solution is defined as a sequence of refactorings that maximize as much as possible the similarity between the initial and revised class diagrams (i.e., the class diagrams in the base of examples) while considering designer's feedbacks.

The primary contributions of the paper are 3-fold: 1) We introduce a model refactoring approach based on the use of examples. The approach combines implicitly the detection and the correction of design defects at the model-level by proposing a sequence of refactorings that must be applied on a given model. 2) We use the IGA to allow the integration of feedbacks provided by designers upon solutions produced during the GA evolution. 3) We report the results of an evaluation of our approach.

The paper is organized as follows. Section 2 is dedicated to the background where we introduce some basic concepts and the related work. The overall approach is described in Section 3. Section 4 reports on the experimental settings and results, while Section 5 concludes the paper and outlines some future directions to our work.

2   Background

2.1   Class Diagrams Refactorings and Quality Metrics

Model refactoring is a controlled technique for improving the design (e.g., class diagrams) of an existing model. It involves applying a series of small refactoring operations to improve the design quality of the model while preserving its behavior. Many refactorings were proposed and codified in the literature (see e.g., [2]). In our approach, we consider a subset of the 72 refactorings defined in [2]; i.e., only those refactorings that can be applied to UML class diagrams. Indeed, some of the refactorings in [2] may be applied on design models (e.g. *Move_Method, Rename_method, Move_Attribute, Extract_Class* etc.) while others cannot be (e.g. *Extract_Method, Inline_Method, Replace_Temp_With_Query* etc.). In our approach we considered a list of twelve refactorings (e.g. *Extract_class, Push_down_method, Pull_up_method,* etc.) based on [2]. The choice of these refactorings was mainly based on two factors: 1) they apply at the class diagram-level; and 2) they can be link to a set of model metrics (i.e., metrics which are impacted when applying these refactorings).

Metrics provide useful information that help assessing the level of conformance of a software system to a desired quality [12]. Metrics can also help detecting some similarities between software systems. The most widely used metrics for class diagrams are the ones defined by Genero et al. [13]. In the context of our approach, we used a list of sixteen metrics (e.g. *Number of attributes: NA, Number of methods: NMeth, Number of dependencies: NDep*, etc.) including the eleven metrics defined in [13] to which we have added a set of simple metrics (e.g., *number of private methods in a class, number of public methods in a class*). All these metrics are related to the class entity which is the main entity in a class diagram.

2.2   Interactive Genetic Algorithm (IGA)

Heuristic search are serving to promote discovery or learning [14]. There is a variety of methods which support the heuristic search as hill_climbing [15], genetic algorithms (GA) [16], etc. GA is a powerful heuristic search optimization method inspired by the Darwinian theory of evolution [17]. The basic idea behind GA is to explore the search space by making a population of candidate solutions, also called individuals, evolve toward a "good" solution of a specific problem. Each individual (i.e., a solution) of the population is evaluated by a fitness function that determines a quantitative measure of its ability to solve the target problem. Exploration of the search space is achieved by selecting individuals (in the current population) that have the best fitness values and evolving them by using genetic operators, such as crossover and mutation. The crossover operator insures generation of new children, or offspring, based on parent individuals while the mutation operator is applied to modify some randomly selected nodes in a single individual. The mutation operator introduces diversity into the population and allows escaping local optima found during the search. Once selection, mutation and crossover have been applied according to given probabilities, individuals of the newly created generation are evaluated using the fitness function. This process is repeated iteratively, until a stopping criterion is met. This criterion usually corresponds to a fixed number of generations.

Interactive GA (IGAs) [18] combines a genetic algorithm with the interaction with the user so that he can assign a fitness to each individual. This way IGA integrates the user's knowledge during the regular evolution process of GA. For this reason, IGA can be used to solve problems that cannot be easily solved by GA [19]. A variety of application domains of IGA include development of fashion design systems [19], music composition systems [20], software re-modularization [21] and some other IGAs' applications in other fields [11]. One of the key elements in IGAs is the management of the number of interactions with the user and the way an individual is evaluated by the user.

2.3   Related Work

Model refactoring is still at a relatively young stage of development compared to the work that has been done on source-code refactoring. Most of existing approaches for automating refactoring activities at the model-level are based on rules that can be expressed as assertions (i.e., invariants, pre-and post-conditions) [22, 23], or graph transformations targeting refactoring operations in general [24, 25] or design patterns' applications in particular (e.g., [26]). In [22] invariants are used to detect some parts of the model that require refactoring and the refactorings are expressed using declarative rules. However, a complete specification of refactorings requires an important number of rules and the refactoring rules must be complete, consistent, non-redundant and correct. In [26] refactoring rules are used to specify design patterns' applications. In this context, design problems solved by these patterns are represented using models and the refactoring rules transform these models according to the solutions proposed by the patterns. However, not all design problems are representable using models. Finally an issue that is common to most of these approaches is the problem of sequencing and composing refactoring rules. This is related to the control of rules' applications within rule-based transformational approaches in general.

Our approach is inspired by contributions in search-based software engineering (SBSE) (e.g. [6, 7, 9, 27, 28]). Techniques based on SBSE are a good alternative to tackle many of the above mentioned issues [9]. For example, a heuristic-based approach is presented in [6, 7, 27] in which various software metrics are used as indicators for the need of a certain refactoring. In [27], a genetic algorithm is used to suggest refactorings to improve the class structure of a system. The algorithm uses a fitness function that relies on a set of existing object oriented metrics. Harman and Tratt [6] propose to use the Pareto optimality concept to improve search-based refactoring approaches when the evaluation function is based on a weighted sum of metrics. Both the approaches in [27] and [6] were limited to the Move Method refactoring operation. In [7], the authors present a comparative study of four heuristic search techniques applied to the refactoring problem. The fitness function used in this study was based on a set of 11 metrics. The results of the experiments on five open-source systems showed that hill-climbing performs better than the other algorithms. In [28], the authors proposed an automated refactoring approach that uses genetic programming (GP) to support the composition of refactorings that introduce design patterns. The fitness function used to evaluate the applied refactorings relies on the same set of metrics as in [12] and a bonus value given for the presence of design patterns in the refactored design. Our approach can be seen as linked to this approach as we aim at proposing a combination of refactorings that must be applied to a design model. Our approach was inspired by the work in [21] where the authors apply an Interactive Genetic Algorithm to the re-modularization problem which can be seen as a specific subtype of the refactoring problem. Our work is also related to the approach in [29] where the authors apply an SBSE approach to model transformations. However this approach focuses on general model transformations while our focus is on refactorings which are commonly codified transformations that aim at correcting design defaults.

To conclude, most of the approaches that tackled the refactoring as an optimization problem by the use of some heuristics suppose, to some extent, that a refactoring operation is appropriate when it optimizes the fitness function (FF). Most of these approaches defined their FF as a combination of quality metrics to approximate the quality of a model. However, refactoring operations are design transformations which are context-sensitive. To be appropriately used, they require some knowledge of the system to be refactored. Indeed, the fact that the values of some metrics were improved after some refactorings does not necessarily mean or ensure that these refactorings make sense. This observation is at the origin of the work described in this paper as described in the next section.

3   Heuristic Search Using Interactive Genetic Algorithm

3.1   Interactive Genetic Algorithm Adaptation

The approach proposed in this paper exploits examples of model refactorings, a heuristic search technique and the designer's feedback to automatically suggest sequences of refactorings that can be applied on a given model (i.e., a UML class diagram). A high-level view of our adaptation of IGA to the model refactoring problem is given in Fig. 1. The algorithm takes as input a set of quality metrics, a set of model refactoring examples, a percentage value corresponding to the percentage of a population of solutions that the designer is willing to evaluate, the maximum number of iterations for the algorithm and the number of interactions with the designer. First, the algorithm runs classic GA (line 2) for a number of iterations (i.e., the maximum number of iterations divided by the number of interactions). Then a percentage of solutions from the current population is selected (line 3). In lines 4 to 7, we get designers' feedbacks for each refactoring in each selected solution and we update their fitness function. We generate a new population (p+1) of individuals (line 8) by iteratively selecting pairs of parent individuals from population p and applying the crossover operator to them; each pair of parent individuals produces two children (solutions). We include both the parent and child variants in the new population. Then we apply the mutation operator, with a probability score, for both parent and child to ensure the solution diversity; this produces the population for the next generation. The algorithm terminates when the maximum iteration number is reached, and returns the best set of refactorings' sequences (i.e., best solutions from all iterations).

```
Input: Set of quality metrics
Input: Set of model refactoring examples
Input: Percentage (P%)
Input: MaxNbrIterations
Input: NbrOfInteractions
Output: A sequence of refactorings
1: for i = 1 . . . NbrOfInteractions do
2:   Evolve GA for NbrIterations
3:   Select P% of best solutions from the current population.
4:   for-each selected solution do
5:     Ask the designer whether each refactoring within
       the selected solution makes sense.
6:     Update the FF of the selected solution to integrate
       the feedback.
7:   end for-each
8:   Create a new GA population using the updated solutions
9: end for
10: Continue (non-interactive) GA evolution until it converges
    or it reaches maxNbrIterations
```

Fig. 1. High-level pseudo-code for IGA adaptation to our problem

In the following subsections we present the details of the regular GA adaptation to the problem of generating refactoring sequences and how we collect the designers' feedbacks and integrate it in the fitness function computation.

3.2 Representing an Individual and Generating the Initial Population

An individual (i.e., a candidate solution) is a set of blocks. The upper part of Fig. 2 shows an individual with three blocks. The first part of the block contains the class (e.g. Order) chosen from the initial model (model under analysis) called CIM, the second part contains the class (e.g Person) from the base of examples that was matched to CIM called CBE, and finally the third part contains a list of refactorings (e.g. *Pull_Up_Method(calc_taxes(), LineOrder, Orde)*) which is a subset of the refactorings that were applied to CBE (in its subsequent versions) and that can be applied to CIM. In our approach, classes from the model (CIMs) and the base of examples (CBEs) are represented using predicates that describe their attributes, methods and relationships. In addition, the representation of a CBE class includes a list of refactorings that were applied to this class in a subsequent version of the system's model to which CBE belongs. The subset of a CBE subsequent refactorings that are applicable to a CIM class constitutes the third part of the block having CIM as its first part and

CBE as its second part. Hence, the selection of the refactorings to be considered in a block is subjected to some constraints to avoid conflicts and incoherence errors. For example, if we have a *Move_attribute* refactoring operation in the CBE class and the CIM class doesn't contain any attribute, then this refactoring operation is discarded as we cannot apply it to the CIM class.

Hence the individual represents a sequence of refactoring operations to apply and the classes of the initial model on which they apply. The bottom part of Fig. 2 shows the fragments of an initial model before and after the refactorings proposed by the individual (at the top of the figure) were applied.

Order	LineOrder	Product
Person	Teacher	Agency
Pull_Up_Method(calc_taxes(), LineOrder, Order)	**Rename_Attribute**(tax, taxStatus)	**Move_Attribute**(quantity, Product, LineOrder)

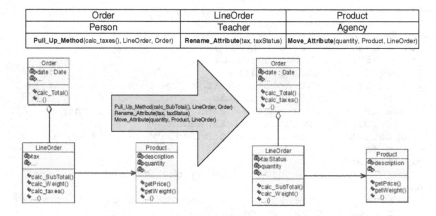

Fig. 2. Individual representation

To generate an initial population, we start by defining the maximum individual size. This parameter can be specified either by the user or randomly. Thus, the individuals have different sizes. Then, for each individual we randomly assign: 1) a set of classes from the initial model that is under analysis and their matched classes from the base of examples, and 2) a set of refactorings that we can possibly apply on the initial model class among the refactorings proposed from the base of examples class.

3.3   Genetic Operators

Selection: To select the individuals that will undergo the crossover and mutation operators, we used the stochastic universal sampling (SUS) [17], in which the probability of selection of an individual is directly proportional to its relative fitness in the population. For each iteration, we use SUS to select 50% of individuals from population p for the new population p+1. These (population_size/2) selected individuals will "give birth" to another (population_size/2) new individuals using crossover operator.

Crossover: For each crossover, two individuals are selected by applying the *SUS* selection [17]. Even though individuals are selected, the crossover happens only with a certain probability. The crossover operator allows creating two offspring *p'1* and *p'2* from the two selected parents *p1* and *p2* as follows: A random position, *k*, is selected. The first *k* refactorings of *p1* become the first *k* elements of *p'2*. Similarly, the first *k* refactorings of *p2* become the first *k* refactorings of *p'1*. The rest of refactorings (from position k+1 until the end of the sequence) in each parent *p1* and *p2* are kept. For instance, Fig. 3 illustrates the crossover operator applied to two individuals (parents) *p1* and *p2* where the position *k* takes the value 2.

Mutation: The mutation operator consists of randomly changing one or more elements in the solution. Hence, given a selected individual, the mutation operator first randomly selects some refactorings among the refactoring sequence proposed by the individual. Then the selected refactorings are replaced by other refactorings. Fig. 4 illustrates the effect of a mutation on an individual.

$K = 2$

P1:	Order	LineOrder	Product
	Person	Teacher	Agency
	Pull_Up_Method(calc_taxes(), LineOrder, Order)	Rename_Attribute(tax, taxStatus)	Move_Attribute(quantity, Product, LineOrder)

P2:	School	Pilot	
	Course	Student	
	Add_parameter(version : String)	Move_Attribute(typePlane, Pilot, Plane)	

P'1:	School	Pilot	Product
	Course	Student	Agency
	Add_parameter(version : String)	Move_Attribute(typePlane, Pilot, Plane)	Move_Attribute(quantity, Product, LineOrder)

P'2:	Order	LineOrder	
	Person	Teacher	
	Pull_Up_Method(calc_taxes(), LineOrder, Order)	Rename_Attribute(tax, taxStatus)	

Fig. 3. Crossover operator

Order	LineOrder	Product
Person	Teacher	Agency
Pull_Up_Method(calc_taxes(), LinePrder, Order)	Rename_Attribute(tax, taxStatus)	Move_Attribute(quantity, Product, LineOrder)

↓

Order	LineOrder	Product
Person	Student	Agency
Pull_Up_Method(calc_taxes(), LinePrder, Order)	Rename_Method(calc_SubTotal, calc_TotalLine)	Move_Attribute(quantity, Product, LineOrder)

Fig. 4. Mutation operator

3.4   Evaluating an Individual within the Classic GA

The quality of an individual is proportional to the quality of the refactoring operations composing it. In fact, the execution of these refactorings modifies various model fragments; the quality of a solution is determined with respect to the expected refactored model. However, our goal is to find a way to infer correct refactorings using the knowledge that has been accumulated through refactorings of other models of past projects and feedbacks given by designers. Specifically, we want to exploit the similarities between the actual model and other models to infer the sequence of refactorings that we must apply. Our intuition is that a candidate solution that displays a high similarity between the classes of the model and those chosen from the examples base should give the best sequence of refactorings. Hence, the fitness function aims to maximize the similarity between the classes of the model in comparison to the revised ones in the base of examples. In this context, we introduce first a similarity measure between two classes denoted by *Similarity* and defined by formula 1 and 2.

$$Similarity\ (CMI, CBE) = \frac{1}{m}\sum_{i=1}^{m} Sim(CMI_i, CBE_i) \tag{1}$$

$$Sim\ (CMI_i, CBE_i) = \begin{cases} 1 & if\ CMI_i = CBE_i \\ 0 & if\ CMI_i = 0\ or\ CBE_i = 0 \\ \frac{CMI_i}{CBE_i} & if\ CMI_i < CBE_i \\ \frac{CBE_i}{CMI_i} & if\ CBE_i < CMI_i \end{cases} \tag{2}$$

Where m is the number of metrics considered in this project. CIM_i is the ith metric value of the class CIM in the initial model while CBE_i is the ith metric value of the class CBE in the base of examples. Using the similarity between classes, we define the fitness function of a solution, normalized in the range [0, 1], as:

$$f = \frac{1}{n}\sum_{j=1}^{n} Similarity(CMI_{Bj}, CBE_{Bj}) \tag{3}$$

Where n is the number of blocks in the solution and CMI_{Bj} and CBE_{Bj} are the classes composing the first two parts of the jth block of the solution. To illustrate how the fitness function is computed, we consider a system containing two classes as shown in Table 1 and a base of examples containing two classes shown in Table 2. In this example we use six metrics and these metrics are given for each class in the model in Table 1 and each class of the base of examples in Table 2.

Table 1. Classes from the initial model and their metrics values

CMI	NPvA	NPbA	NPbMeth	NPvMeth	NAss	NGen
LineOrder	4	1	3	1	1	1
Product	2	2	6	0	1	0

Table 2. Classes from the base of examples and their metrics values

CBE	NPvA	NPbA	NPbMeth	NPvMeth	NAss	NGen
Student	2	1	3	0	3	0
Plane	5	1	4	0	1	0

Consider an individual/solution I_1 composed by two blocks (*LineOrder/Student* and *Product/Plane*). The fitness function of I_1 is calculated as follows:

$$f_{I_1} = \frac{1}{12}\left[\left(\frac{2}{4}+1+1+0+\frac{1}{3}+0\right)+\left(\frac{2}{5}+\frac{1}{2}+\frac{4}{6}+0+1+0\right)\right] = 0{,}45$$

3.5   Collecting and Integrating the Feedbacks from Designers

Model refactoring is a design operation that is context-sensitive. In addition, depending on the semantics of the system under analysis and the system's evolution as foreseen by different designers, a refactoring proposed by the classic GA can be considered as mandatory by a designer and as acceptable by another. Even if a sequence of refactorings optimizes the fitness function (as defined in the previous section), that does not ensure that these refactorings conform to and preserve the semantics of the system. Consequently, we use Interactive GA (IGA) to partly tackle this problem by interacting with designers and getting their feedbacks on a number of the proposed refactoring sequences. To do so, we adopted a five level scale to rate the proposed refactorings; i.e., we distinguish five types of rating that a designer can assign to a proposed refactoring. The meaning and the value of each type of rating are as follows:

- Critical (value = 1): it is mandatory to apply the proposed refactoring;
- Desirable (value = 0.8): it is useful to apply the refactoring to enhance some aspect of the model but it's not mandatory;
- Neutral (value = 0.5): the refactoring is applicable but the designer does not see it as necessary or desirable;
- Undesirable (value = 0.3): the refactoring is applicable but it is not useful and could alter the semantics of the system;
- Inappropriate (value = 0): the refactoring should not be applied because it breaks the semantics of the system.

As described in section 3.1., during the execution of IGA, the designer is asked to rate a percentage of the best solutions found by the classic GA after a defined number of iterations. For each of the selected solutions, the designer assigns a rating for each refactoring included in the solution. Depending on the values entered by the designer, we re-evaluate the global fitness function of the solution as follows. For each block of the solution, we compute the block rating as an average of the ratings of the refactorings in the block. Then we compute the overall designer's rating as an average of all blocks ratings. Finally, the new fitness function of the solution is computed as an average of its old fitness function and the overall designer's rating. The new values of the fitness functions of the selected solutions are injected back into the IGA process to form a new population of individuals.

4   Experiments

The goal of the experiment is to evaluate the efficiency of our approach for the generation of the refactorings' sequences. In particular the experiment aimed at answering the following research questions:

- **RQ1:** To what extent can the interactive approach generate correct refactorings' sequences?
- **RQ2:** What types of refactorings are correctly suggested?

To answer these questions we implemented and tested the approach on open source projects. In particular, to answer RQ1, we used an existing corpus of known models refactorings to evaluate the precision and recall of our approach, and to answer RQ2, we investigated the type of refactorings that were suggested by our tool. In this section, we present the experimental setup and discuss the results of this experiment.

4.1   Supporting Tool and Experimental Setup

We implemented our approach as a plugin within the Eclipse™ development environment. Fig. 5 shows a screenshot of the model refactoring plugin perspective. This plugin takes as input a base of examples of refactored models and an initial model to refactor. The user specifies the population size, the number of iterations, the individual size, the number of mutations, the number of interactions, and the percentage of the solutions shown in each interaction. It generates as output an optimal sequence of refactorings to be applied on the analyzed system.

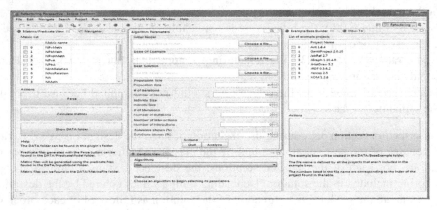

Fig. 5. Model Refactoring Plugin

To build the base of examples, we used the Ref-Finder tool [43] to collect the refactoring that were applied on six Java open source projects (Ant, JabRef, JGraphx, JHotDraw, JRDF, and Xom). Ref-Finder helps retrieving the refactorings that a system has undergone by comparing different versions of the system. We manually validated the refactorings returned by Ref-finder before including them in the base of examples. To answer the research questions reported above, we analyzed two open-source Java projects in our experiment. We have chosen these open source projects because they are medium-sized open-source projects and they have been actively developed over the past 10 years. The participants in the experiment were three Ph.D students enrolled in Software Engineering and all of them are familiar with the two analyzed systems and have a strong background in object-oriented refactoring.

4.2   Results and Discussions

To assess the accuracy of the approach, we compute the precision and recall of our IGA algorithm when applied to the two projects under analysis. In the context of our study, the precision denotes the fraction of correctly proposed refactorings among the set of all proposed refactorings. The recall indicates the fraction of correctly proposed refactorings among the set of all actually applied refactorings in the subsequent versions of the analyzed projects. To assess the validity of the proposed refactorings, we compare them to those returned by Ref-Finder when applied to the two projects and their subsequent versions. The precision and recall results might vary depending on the refactorings used, which are randomly generated, though guided by a meta-heuristic. Fig. 6 and Fig. 7 show the results of 23 executions of our approach on Xerces and GanttProject, respectively. Each of these figures displays the precision and the recall values for each execution.

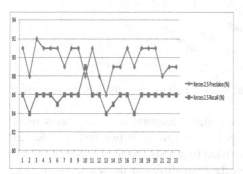

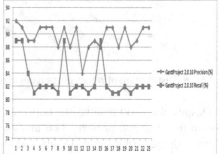

Fig. 6. Multiple execution results for Xerces

Fig. 7. Multiple Execution results for GanttProject

Generally, the average precision and recall (around 88%) allows us to positively answer our first research question RQ1 and conclude that the results obtained by our approach are very encouraging. The precision in the two projects under analysis (on average 90% of all executions) proves that a big number of the refactorings proposed by our approach were indeed applied to the system's model in its subsequent version (i.e., the proposed refactorings match, in most cases, those returned by Ref-Finder when applied on the system's model and its subsequent version). To ensure that our results are relatively stable, we compared the results of the multiple executions (23) of the approach on the two analyzed projects shown in Fig. 6 and Fig. 7. The precision and recall scores are approximately the same for different executions in the two considered projects. We also compared the sequences of refactorings returned by different executions of our algorithm on the same project. We found that when a class (from the model under analysis) is part of two different returned sequences, the refactoring operations proposed for this class within these sequences are similar. We consequently conclude that our approach is stable.

Our experiment through the interactions with designers allowed us to answer the second research question RQ2 by inferring the types of refactorings they recognized as good refactorings. Fig. 8 shows that 82% of the the *Move_method* and *Pull_up_method* refactorings proposed during the executions are recognized as good refactoring versus only 70% of the *Rename_method* refactorings. We noticed also, that only 9 of 12 refactorings used in the approach are considered in this analysis. This may result from the quality of the base of examples or from the random factor which characterizes genetic algorithm. We made a further analysis to understand the causes of such results. We found out that through the interactions, the designers have to recognize the meaningless refactorings and penalize them by assigning them a 0 as a rating value; this has significantly reduced the number of these types of refactorings in the optimal solution.

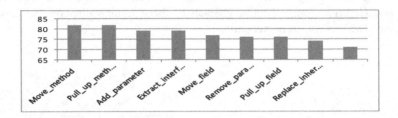

Fig. 8. Distribution of refactorings recognized as correct refactorings through intercations

Despite the good results, we noticed a very slight decrease in recall versus precision in the analyzed projects. Our analysis pointed out towards two factors. The first factor is the project domain. In this study we tried to propose refactorings using a base of examples which contains different projects from different domains. We noticed that some projects focus on some types of refactorings compared to others (i.e., some projects in the base of examples has a big frequency of «*pull_up_Attribute*» and «*pull_up_method*»). The second factor is the number and types of refactorings considered in this experimentation. Indeed, we noticed that some refactorings (e.g., «*pull_up_method*», «*pull_up_Attribute*», «*add_parameter*») are located correctly in our approach. We have no certainty that these factors can improve the results but we consider analyzing them as a future work to further clarify many issues.

4.3   Threats to Validity

We have some points that we consider as threats to the generalization of our approach. The most important one is the use of the Ref_finder Tool to build the base of examples and at the same time we compare the results obtained by our algorithm to those given by Ref_finder. Other threats can be related to the IGAs parameters setting. Although we applied the approach on two systems, further experimentation is needed. Also, the reliability of the proposed approach requires an example set of applied refactoring on different systems. It can be argued that constituting such a set might require more work than these examples. In our study, we showed that by using some open source projects, the approach can be used out of the box and will produce good refactoring results for the studied systems. In an industrial setting, we could expect a company to start with some few open source projects, and gradually enrich its refactoring examples to include context-specific data. This is essential if we consider that different languages and software infrastructures have different best/worst practices. Finally, since we viewed the model refactorings' generation problem as a combinatorial problem addressed with heuristic search, it is important to contrast the results with the execution time. We executed the plugin on a standard desktop computer (i7 CPU running at 2.67 GHz with 8GB of RAM). The number of interactions was set to 50. The execution time for refactorings' generation with a number of iterations (stopping criteria) fixed to 1000 was less than seventy minutes. This indicates that our approach is reasonably scalable from the performance standpoint.

5   Conclusion and Future Work

In this article, we presented a new approach that aims to suggest appropriate sequences of refactorings that can be applied on a given design model and in particular on a UML class diagram. To do so, we adapted Interactive Genetic Algorithms (IGAs) to build an algorithm which exploits both existing model refactoring examples and the designer's knowledge during the search process for opportunities of model refactorings. We implemented the approach as a plugin integrated within the Eclipse platform and we performed multiple executions of the approach on two open source projects. The results of our experiment have shown that the approach is stable regarding its correctness, completeness and the type and number of the proposed refactorings per class. IGA has significantly reduced the number of meaningless refactorings in the optimal solutions for these executions. While the results of the approach are very promising, we plan to extend it in different ways. One issue that we want to address as a future work is related to the base of examples. In the future we want to extend our base of examples to include more refactoring operations. We also want to study and analyze the impact of using domain-specific examples on the quality of the proposed sequences of refactorings. Actually, we kept the random aspect that characterizes genetic algorithms even in the choice of the projects used in the base of examples without prioritizing one or more specific projects on others to correct the one under analysis. Finally, we want to apply the approach on other open source projects and further analyze the type of refactorings that are correctly suggested.

References

1. Lientz, B.P., Swanson, E.B., Tompkins, G.E.: Characteristics of application software maintenance. Commun. ACM 21(6), 466–471 (1978)
2. Fowler, M.: Refactoring: Improving the Design of Existing Code. Addison-Wesley (1999)
3. Mens, T., Tourwé, T.: A Survey of Software Refactoring. IEEE Trans. Softw. Eng. 30(2), 126–139 (2004)
4. Opdyke, W.F.: Refactoring: A Program Restructuring Aid in Designing Object-Oriented Application Frameworks, U. Illinois at Urbana-Champaign (1992)
5. Moha, N.: DECOR: Détection et correction des défauts dans les systèmes orientés objet, p. 157. UdeM & USTdeLille, Montréal (2008)
6. Harman, M., Tratt, L.: Pareto optimal search based refactoring at the design level. In: Proceedings of the 9th Annual GECCO 2007, pp. 1106–1113. ACM, London (2007)
7. O'Keeffe, M.: Search-based refactoring: an empirical study. J. Softw. Maint. Evol. 20(5), 345–364 (2008)

8. O'Keeffe, M., Cinneide, M.O.: Search-based software maintenance. In: CSMR (2006)
9. Kessentini, M., Sahraoui, H.A., Boukadoum, M.: Model Transformation as an Optimization Problem. In: Czarnecki, K., Ober, I., Bruel, J.-M., Uhl, A., Völter, M. (eds.) MODELS 2008. LNCS, vol. 5301, pp. 159–173. Springer, Heidelberg (2008)
10. El-Boussaidi, G., Mili, H.: Detecting Patterns of Poor Design Solutions Using Constraint Propagation. In: Czarnecki, K., Ober, I., Bruel, J.-M., Uhl, A., Völter, M. (eds.) MODELS 2008. LNCS, vol. 5301, pp. 189–203. Springer, Heidelberg (2008)
11. Takagi, H.: Interactive evolutionary computation: fusion of the capabilities of EC optimization and human evaluation. Proceedings of the IEEE 89(9), 1275–1296 (2001)
12. Fenton, N.E., Pfleeger, A.S.L.: Software Metrics: A Rigorous and Practical Approach, 2nd edn., p. 656. PWS Pub., Boston (1998)
13. Genero, M., Piattini, M., Calero, C.: Empirical validation of class diagram metrics. In: Proceedings of the International Symposium on ESE (2002)
14. Pearl, J.: Heuristics: intelligent search strategies for computer problem solving, p. 382. Addison-Wesley Longman Publishing Co., Inc. (1984)
15. Mitchell, M.: An Introduction to Genetic Algorithms, p. 209. MIT Press (1998)
16. Goldberg, D.E.: Genetic Algorithms in Search, Optimization and Machine Learning, p. 372. Addison-Wesley Longman Publishing Co., Inc. (1989)
17. Koza, J.R.: Genetic programming: on the programming of computers by means of natural selection, p. 680. MIT Press (1992)
18. Dawkins, R.: The BlindWatchmaker, 1st edn., p. 358. Longman, Essex (1986)
19. Kim, H.S., Cho, S.B.: Application of interactive genetic algorithm to fashion design. In: Engineering Applications of Artificial Intelligence (2000)
20. Chen, Y.-P.: Interactive music composition with the CFE framework. SIGEVOlution 2(1), 9–16 (2007)
21. Bavota, G., Carnevale, F., De Lucia, A., Di Penta, M., Oliveto, R.: Putting the developer in-the-loop: an interactive GA for software re-modularization. In: Fraser, G., Teixeira de Souza, J. (eds.) SSBSE 2012. LNCS, vol. 7515, pp. 75–89. Springer, Heidelberg (2012)
22. Van Der Straeten, R., Jonckers, V., Mens, T.: A formal approach to model refactoring and model refinement. J. SoSyM 6(2), 139–162 (2007)
23. Van Kempen, M., et al.: Towards proving preservation of behaviour of refactoring of UML models. In: Proceedings of the annual SAICSIT 2005, pp. 252–259. White River, South Africa (2005)
24. Mens, T., Taentzer, G., Runge, O.: Analysing refactoring dependencies using graph transformation. J. SoSyM 6(3), 269–285 (2007)
25. Biermann, E.: EMF model transformation based on graph transformation: formal foundation and tool environment. In: Ehrig, H., Rensink, A., Rozenberg, G., Schürr, A. (eds.) ICGT 2010. LNCS, vol. 6372, pp. 381–383. Springer, Heidelberg (2010)
26. El Boussaidi, G., Mili, H.: Understanding design patterns — what is the problem? Software: Practice and Experience (2011)
27. Seng, O., Stammel, J., Burkhart, D.: Search-based determination of refactorings for improving the class structure of object-oriented systems. In: Proc. of the 8th Annual GECCO 2006, pp. 1909–1916. ACM, Seattle (2006)
28. Jensen, A.C., Cheng, B.H.C.: On the use of genetic programming for automated refactoring and the introduction of design patterns. In: Proc. of the 12th Annual GECCO 2010, pp. 1341–1348. ACM, Portland (2010)
29. Kessentini, M., et al.: Search-based model transformation by example. J. SoSyM 11(2), 209–226 (2012)

A Fine-Grained Parallel Multi-objective Test Case Prioritization on GPU

Zheng Li[1], Yi Bian[1], Ruilian Zhao[1], and Jun Cheng[2]

[1] Department of Computer Science
Beijing University of Chemical Technology
Beijing 100029, P.R. China
[2] Chongqing Institute of Green and Intelligent Technology
Chinese Academy of Sciences
Chongqing 401122, P.R. China

Abstract. Multi-Objective Evolutionary Algorithms (MOEAs) have been widely used to address regression test optimization problems, including test case selection and test suite minimization. GPU-based parallel MOEAs are proposed to increase execution efficiency to fulfill the industrial demands. When using binary representation in MOEAs, the fitness evaluation can be transformed a parallel matrix multiplication that is implemented on GPU easily and more efficiently. Such GPU-based parallel MOEAs may achieve higher level of speed-up for test case prioritization because the computation load of fitness evaluation in test case prioritization is more than that in test case selection or test suite minimization. However, the non-applicability of binary representation in the test case prioritization results in the challenge of parallel fitness evaluation on GPU. In this paper, we present a GPU-based parallel fitness evaluation and three novel parallel crossover computation schemes based on ordinal and sequential representations, which form a fine-grained parallel framework for multi-objective test case prioritization. The empirical studies based on eight benchmarks and one open source program show a maximum of 120x speed-up achieved.

Keywords: Test Case Prioritization, Mulit-Objective Optimization, NSGA-II, GPU, CUDA.

1 Introduction

Test suite optimization has been widely used to reduce the cost of regression testing [1], in which test case prioritization [2] is a technique that sorts test cases order so that those test cases with the highest priority, according to some test adequacy criteria, can run as soon as possible. Many related studies have been proposed in literature [3,4,5,6]. One dimension of the research is to consider test case prioritization as a search problem [7], where search based optimization algorithms are used to find optimal solution with respect to a certain adequacy criterion. Li et al. [7] compared the effectiveness of several search algorithms on test case prioritization, but just for single objective optimization. However, test

G. Ruhe and Y. Zhang (Eds.): SSBSE 2013, LNCS 8084, pp. 111–125, 2013.
© Springer-Verlag Berlin Heidelberg 2013

case prioritization can address a wide variety of objectives in regression testing. Such test case prioritization becomes a multi-objective optimization problem.

Over the past few decades, a number of different EAs were suggested to solve multi-objective optimization problems, including Zitzler and Thiele's SPEA [8], Knowles and Corne's Pareto-archived PAES [9], and Rudolph's elitist GA [10]. Deb et al. proposed a fast multi-objective genetic algorithm (NSGA-II) [11], which enabled much better spread of solutions and better convergence close to the truly optimal set for most optimization problems. NSGA-II has also been widely used in search based software engineering (SBSE), such as regression test case selection [12] and requirements management [13].

Since EAs work with a population of solutions, they have classified as "embarrassingly parallel" because of their scalability in parallel fitness evaluations [14]. Recently, GPU computing has been recognized as a powerful way to achieve high-performance on long-running scientific applications [15]. Consequently EAs on GPU have attracted a growing interest and a lot of research work on GPU have been proposed: genetic algorithm [16], hybrid of genetic algorithm and local search [17], island model evolutionary algorithm [15]. Yoo et al. [14] applied GPU-based MOEAs to multi-objective test suite minimization, in which the fitness computation was transformed into a matrix multiplication that can be implemented on GPU easily and more efficiently.

This paper focuses on the GPU-based parallelism for multi-objective test case prioritization. The motivation is that the fitness evaluation in test case prioritization is much more complex than that in test case selection or test suite minimization, as test case prioritization is to re-order test suite that all test cases have to be involved in fitness evaluation. Such parallel computation can be more scalable. However, the challenge comes from chromosome representation, where the binary coding, which is used in test case selection and test suite minimization, cannot be used in test case prioritization. Consequently the technique proposed by Yoo et al. [14] would not be able to be adapted into test case prioritization.

We present a new GPU-based parallel fitness evaluation algorithm for test case prioritization, namely the coarse-grained GPU-based parallel framework. Furthermore, we propose parallel crossover computation schemes for ordinal and sequential coding, namely the fine-grained parallel framework. The primary contributions of this paper are as follows:

1. The paper firstly proposes three types of GPU-based parallel crossover schemes using ordinal representation and sequential representations in EAs. Experimental results show that the best scheme achieves up to 14x times speed-up than that of CPU-based.
2. This paper presents a fine-grained parallel framework for multi-objective test case prioritization using graphic processing units, where both fitness evaluation and crossover computation are implemented on GPU.
3. Empirical studies based on eight benchmark subjects and one large open source program are implemented, of which a maximum of dramatic speed-up over 120x are achieved, and the results also suggest that it will get increase more as the program size increased.

The rest of this paper is organized as follows. Section 2 presents backgrounds of multi-objective test case prioritization and GPU-based evolutionary computation. Section 3 describes the details of how to parallel multi-objective test case prioritization on GPU through different parallel schemes of genetic operations. The empirical study and corresponding results analysis are described in section 4 and Section 5. Section 6 discusses related work and Section 7 is the conclusion.

2 Backgrounds

2.1 Multi-objective Test Case Prioritization

The purpose of test case prioritization is to increase the likelihood that if the test cases are used for regression testing in the given ordering, they will be much closer to meet some objectives than they would if they are executed in some other ordering [2]. Various prioritization criteria are often applied to a test suite in reality. The multi-objective test case prioritization is defined as follows:

Definition 1 (Multi-objective Test Case Prioritization). Given: *a test suite, T, the set of permutations of T, PT; a vector of M objective functions, f_i, $i = 1, 2, \ldots, M$.*

Problem: *to find $T' \subset PT$ such that T' is a Pareto-optimal permutation set with respect to the objective functions, f_i, $i = 1, 2, \ldots, M$.*

Here, the objective functions are the mathematical descriptions of the concerned prioritization criteria. Pareto-optimal is a notion from economics with a broad range of applications in engineering, which means that given a set of alternative allocations and a set of individuals, allocation A is an improvement over allocation B, without making any other worse off.

2.2 Parallel Multi-Objective Evolutionary Algorithms

Scalability problem is one of the main barrier to widely use of evolutionary algorithms in Software Engineering [14]. A simple engineering problem may cost several hours or even months by using MOEAs due to the huge scale of population size and large number of iterations. The request for greater MOEA efficiency has integrated MOEAs and parallel processing to yield parallel MOEAs. In order to parallelize MOEAs, researchers were aware of intuitively executed either several MOEAs on different processors or distributing an MOEA population among multi-processors in a natural manner [18]. Three major parallel paradigms are implemented on CPU in the current MOEA literature, and they are Master-slave, Island and Diffusion models. The master-slave model MOEAs [19,20] are based on the idea that the computational bottleneck in MOEAs is fitness evaluation, so objective function evaluations are distributed among several slave processors while a master processor manages the entire process. The island model MOEAs [21] are based on the phenomenon of natural populations relatively isolated from each other. The straightforward implementation runs a number of

MOEA populations independently, which are trying to obtain the Pareto optimal solutions and migrations that take place between sub-populations according to a certain rate.

2.3 GPU Computing

Over the past several decades, the major architectures exploited for parallelism are distributed, clustered and multi-core, whereas General-purpose computing on graphics processing units (GPGPU) is a huge shift of paradigm in parallel computing in recent years. GPU has evolved into a highly parallel, multi-threaded, multi-core processor with tremendous computational horsepower and very high memory bandwidth. For example, NVIDIA GeForce GTX480 (the graphic card used for this research), based on the Fermi architecture, which provides 168GFlops peak double-precision arithmetic rate and 177.4GB/s memory bandwidth, is faster compared to the CPU. In general, the growth rate of the GPU's computational capabilities significantly outpaces the often-quoted Moore's Law as applied to traditional microprocessors [22]. Regarding the logical organization of GPU, a thread on GPU can be seen as an element of the data to be processed and threads are organized into so called thread blocks. A kernel is executed by multiple thread blocks and blocks can be organized into one-dimensional or two-dimensional grid.

3 Parallel NSGA-II Framework on CPU+GPU Architecture

NSGA-II is one of the most well known MOEAs, in which fitness evaluation is a task with a high frequency and large data size computation. In traditional implementations of NSGA-II, binary representation is often used to represent individuals, and accomplishes the genetic operations in a bit-wise way for each generation. However, this representation is no longer suitable in multi-objective test case prioritization, because an order of test cases cannot be transformed into a binary string. This, in hence, may lead to another issue that the principle of the genetic operations in other representations is different from that in binary representation, as well as in the parallel schemes. In this section we consider the ordinal and sequential representations and present a coarse-grained framework with only parallel fitness evolution on GPU and a fine-grained framework with additional parallel crossover computation on GPU.

Figure 1 presents the parallel framework on CPU+GPU architecture. The task distribution is clearly defined: CPU manages the entire NSGA-II evolution process except fitness evaluation and crossover which are paralleled on GPU.

3.1 Coarse-Grained Parallel Framework on GPU

Although NSGA-II adds elitism to the simple evolution, fitness evaluation is still the most time-consuming part. Fortunately, the parallel feature of fitness evaluation is more intuitive than any other parts of the algorithm. During fitness

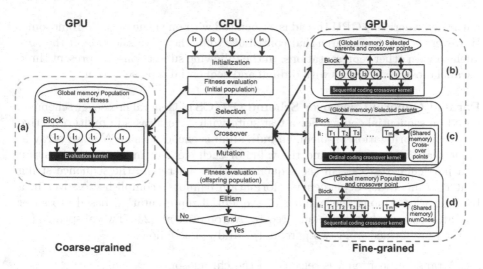

Fig. 1. The parallel NSGA-II framework on CPU+GPU architecture, in which (a) is the coarse-grained GPU-based parallel, where fitness evaluation is implemented on GPU; (b), (c), (d) are three types of fine-grained GPU-based parallel, where crossover computation is implemented on GPU

evaluation, multiple individuals in a population can be seen as multiple data, while the calculation of fitness for these individuals is regarded to be single instruction. This Single Instruction Multiple Data (SIMD) architecture facilitates the massive data-parallelism of GPGPU computing and results in higher performance.

Figure 1(a) illustrates the parallel fitness evaluation scheme (PFES) on GPU. CPU sends a number of individuals to GPU where the kernel function of fitness evaluation is executed and then the evaluation results return back to CPU. Since there is no dependence among individuals at the population level, fitness evaluations can simultaneously run on each individual without latency. However, at the individual level, fitness evaluation needs to traverse each gene according to their positions. The parallelism is therefore restricted by the order relationship among genes. Therefore, the parallelism of PFES is only on the population level. The GPU computing resource can be divided as follows: one GPU thread is associated with one individual and the number of GPU threads equals to population size. This is so called a "coarse-grained" scheme.

However, depending on population size and the number of iterations, the data transmission between CPU and GPU will become more frequent, which may cause a performance decrease and thus directly influences the accelerating effect of PFES.

3.2 Fine-Gained Parallel Framework on GPU

This section focuses on fine-grained strategy with three parallel crossover schemes. With binary representation, it is easy to divide the GPU computing resource naturally, where one GPU thread is associated with one gene of the chromosome. However there is no research that contribute to further discussion about the parallelism with other representations. In the following subsections, we present three parallel crossover schemes with ordinal and sequential representations.

Parallel General Crossover Scheme (PGCS). General crossover scheme is based on sequential coding. For a test suite with N test cases in multi-objective test case prioritization problem, an individual is encoded as an N-sized array in sequential representation, and the value of each element indicates the position of a particular test case in the sequence string. Therefore, the sequence string that contains order dependency information cannot accomplish crossover in a bit-wise way. Among the number of sequential representation based crossover operators, we apply the one adopted by Antoniol et al. [23]. Two offsprings (o_1 and o_2) are formed from two parents (p_1 and p_2) as follows:

1. A random position k is selected in the chromosome.
2. The first k elements of p_1 become the first k elements of o_1.
3. The last $N - k$ elements of o_1 are the sequence of the $N - k$ elements which remain when the k elements selected from p_1 are removed from p_2.
4. o_2 is obtained similarly, composed of the first $N - k$ elements of p_2 and the remaining elements of p_1 (when the first $N - k$ elements of p_2 are removed).

In order to execute crossover computation on GPU, all individuals and crossover points are transmitted to GPU global memory where two chromosomes are assigned to one GPU thread, and then generate two offspring. Figure 1(b) gives an illustration of two particular parents executing the general crossover in one GPU thread, where $I_1,I_2...I_i$ and I_j are all individuals stored in GPU global memory. The kernel function takes input array of selected parents and crossover points from global memory, and generates the same number of offspring in the global memory.

Although this parallel scheme is simple and easy to implement, it doesn't fully utilize the parallel capability of GPU. The computational task of each thread in this scheme is too heavy and GPU only allocates *popsize*/2 (*popsize* denotes the number of the individuals in a population) threads, so the speed-up may not be very high due to the poor degree of parallelism.

Parallel Ordinal Crossover Scheme (POCS). Besides the sequential representation of individuals, some other representations are also suggested, in which the research on ordinal representation is one of the essential branches. The main idea is to enable a sequential representation to do a bit-wise crossover that used in binary representation. It eliminates the order dependency of each element in sequential representation by transformation, and then binary representation based crossover operation can be reused.

Ordinal representation is firstly proposed for Travelling Salesman Problem [24], in which it refers to represent a travelling path by using an order list that is composed by all cities. For a travelling path, each city in the path gets a gene representation according to its position in the order list, then all city genes that are connected become the representation of the travelling path. Meanwhile, in multi-objective test case prioritization problem, we can get the ordinal string of each individual in the same way. For instance, if the order list is $C = (1, 2, 3, 4, 5, 6, 7, 8, 9)$, and one sequence string of the test cases is $1 - 2 - 4 - 3 - 8 - 5 - 9 - 6 - 7$, according to the above mentioned, this sequence string is converted to the ordinal string $l = (112141311)$.

Hence, this parallel crossover scheme is to associate one individual with one GPU thread block, and each thread is associated with one element in an ordinal string. From this point, the degree of parallelism is higher than PGCS. An illustration of two selected parents is doing ordinal crossover in one GPU block is shown in Figure 1(c). It can be clearly seen that I_i is an individual in global memory, and T_i is a test case of I_i. We implemented the ordinal crossover in a kernel function: the inputs of this kernel are the selected parents I_i and an array of crossover points, while the outputs are the generated offsprings. Individuals are represented as ordinal strings, each T_i in parent string would know its right position in offspring string after simultaneously comparing the crossover points with the gene's position in the parent string. Since one thread block represents an individual, the corresponding crossover points are stored in shared memory, so that all threads in a block can access the crossover points at the same time and in a faster way.

Even if this scheme improves the efficiency of the parallelism, there still exists two limitations :

1. The transformation between ordinal string and sequence string can become frequent and thus leads to a considerable performance decrease;
2. The maximum size of test suite, which depends on the number of threads, is constrained by the graphic card.

Parallel Scan Crossover Scheme (PSCS). Regarding the sequential representation based crossover, the output position of each element to be written in offspring should have been known before implementing crossover. It depends on, in other words, what the other threads output if one thread is associated with one element. This parallel crossover scheme is to use *Scan* operation (or the all-prefix-sums operation), which is one of the simplest and most useful parallel algorithms to build blocks. The operation is defined as follows [25]:

Definition 2 (Scan operation). *Scan operation takes a binary associative operator with identity I, and an ordered set of n elements*

$$[a_0, a_1, \ldots, a_n - 1],$$

and returns the order set

$$[I, a_0, (a_0 \oplus a_1), \ldots, (a_0 \oplus a_1 \oplus \ldots \oplus a_{n-2})](exclusive)$$

$$[a_0, (a_0 \oplus a_1), \ldots, (a_0 \oplus a_1 \oplus \ldots \oplus a_{n-1})](inclusive)$$

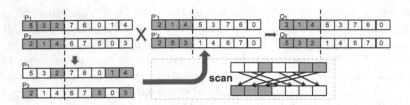

Fig. 2. An example of sequential representation based crossover using scan operation

Scan operation has a variety of applications in many fields. The partition parallel pattern, which is widely used in radix sort, building trees and cell-list etc, is one of its basic implementations. *Scan* operation can parallelly merge the same type of elements and give the new locations of the elements. Figure 2 illustrates how the scan operation can be used in sequential representation based single point crossover. As shown in the dot box of Figure 2, scan operation can move a number of marked elements forward to the front in a chromosome. For two chromosomes P_1 and P_2 with decided crossover point, all elements before the crossover point of P_1 are marked in P_2, and vice verse. Then scan operation is applied to the two marked chromosomes and P_1' and P_2' are generated. Finally the crossover operation is applied between P_1 and P_2', where all elements before the cross point of P_2' are replace by the elements at the same position of P_1, and the offspring O_2 is produced. Similarly, P_2 and P_1' would produce O_1.

4   Experimentation

4.1   Research Questions

The following two research questions motivated this study:

RQ1 What are effectiveness of three types crossover parallel schemes?

RQ2 What are the speed-up achieved by using fine-grained parallel framework over the original CPU-based framework for multi-objective test case prioritization problem?

4.2   Subjects

In the empirical study, there are a variety of subjects including eight benchmarks from the Software-artifact Infrastructure Repository (SIR)[1] and an open source program of *V8*[2]. *V8* is an open source JavaScript engine which is written in C++ and used by Google Chrome. In the experiment a core code file, named "objects.cc", of *V8* is selected. Table 1 provides the size of subjects in terms of source lines of code (SLOC) and the size of test case pool.

---

[1] http://sir.unl.edu/
[2] http://code.google.com/p/v8/

Table 1. Subjects and the corresponding test pool size

Subject	SLOC	Test Pool Size
printtokens	209	4130
printtokens2	198	4115
schedule	129	2650
schedule2	135	2710
replace	273	5542
tcas	73	1608
flex	3406	1472
space	3813	13550
V8	11876	9287

4.3 Experiment Implementation

The multi-objective test case prioritization is the target of this paper. Harman [26] presented several examples of regression test objectives that incorporated into Multi-objective Regression Test Optimization (MORTO) approaches. Such objectives are categorized into two types, those to be maximized (called 'value') and those to be minimized (called 'cost'). In this study, we instantiate the objectives with statement coverage as a measure of test adequacy ('value') and execution time as a measure of cost, because these have been widely studied from the outset and natural candidates for a MORTO. The Average Percent of Statement Coverage(APSC) and Effect Execute Time(EET) are defined as following:

$$APSC = 1 - \frac{TS_1 + TS_2 + ... + TS_M}{NM} + \frac{1}{2N} \tag{1}$$

$$EET = \sum_{i=0}^{N'} ET_i \tag{2}$$

Where T is a test suite containing N test cases, S is statements of the software under test, TS_i means the first test case covering the statement i, N' is the number of test case which firstly achieves the biggest coverage rate, and ET_i is the time consuming of test case i in this generation.

In order to measure the effect of multi-object criteria to the test case prioritization, NSGA-II[11], which is one of the most popular Pareto dominance based multi-objective evolutionary algorithms(MOEAs), is used in the experiments. NSGA-II algorithm is configured with the parameters as follows:

– Population size: 256
– Test suite size: 256
– Maximum number of generation: 250
– Selection: *roulette selection*
– Mutation: *simple inversion mutation* [24]
– Probability of crossover and mutation: 0.9 and $1/n$ (n is the test suite size)
– Independent execution times: 30

Because of the limit of the shared memory on GPU, the population size and test suite size is set to 256.

All configurations have been evaluated on a machine with Intel Core i5-2300 CPU (2.80GHz clock speed and 4GB memory), and a NVIDIA GeForce GTX 480 graphic card (15 multiprocessors), running on Windows 7 64bit.

4.4   Evaluation

The object of the following experiments is to evaluate the impact of the GPU version of parallel schemes in terms of efficiency. So execution time and speed-up rate have been reported to compare with the CPU version. Execution time of each step of NSGA-II for each generation is recorded by using system clock. Speed-up is calculated by dividing the time that the corresponding part of the CPU version took with the time that the GPU version of parallel schemes took.

5   Results

This section mainly answers the two research questions proposed in section 4.1. Section 5.1 presents the speed-up results of fitness with general crossover on GPU and the coarse-grained of parallel schemes, section 5.2 compares the three types of GPU-based parallel crossover schemes of fine-grained strategy.

5.1   Speed-Up of Parallel Crossover Schemes

In order to address RQ1, the experiment compares the three types of GPU-based parallel crossover schemes in term of average execution time of each crossover computation.

Subjects	T_{CPU}	T_{PGCS}	T_{POCS}	T_{PSCS}
printtokens	0.1571	0.0644	0.0376	0.0113
printtokens2	0.1513	0.0746	0.0375	0.0107
replace	0.1590	0.0703	0.0372	0.0108
schedule	0.1567	0.0841	0.0372	0.0108
schedule2	0.1594	0.0625	0.0373	0.0108
tcas	0.1565	0.0820	0.0373	0.0110
flex	0.1584	0.0717	0.0396	0.0118
space	0.1582	0.0648	0.0370	0.0109
v8	0.1566	0.0784	0.0397	0.0109

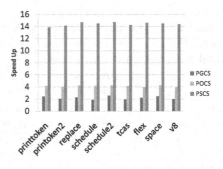

Fig. 3. The average execution time of crossover (in seconds) and speed-up results of three different parallel algorithm

In Figure 3 we can see the details of execution time with CPU approach and fine-grained approach and the speed up rate. The first column is the execution time on CPU and other columns are fine-grained approach execution time with speed-up rate. Compared with the serial execution result, the speed-up of PGCS is more than almost 2x times in the programs, the POCS is more than 4x times, and the PSCS is the best, nearly 14x times than the serial execution result. The most important is that all the speed-up rate is all stable in different scale of the programs, because the crossover speed-up rate is only related to number of test case which we used in experiment. The PGCS parallel scheme is simple and easy to implement, but it doesn't fully use the parallel capability of GPU that only *popsize*/2 threads are allocated. In POCS scheme, since one thread block represents an individual, the corresponding crossover points are stored in shared memory which different block has its own shared memory and every thread can visit it more quick than global memory, so all the threads in a block can access the crossover point at the same time and in a faster way. But compared with sequence string, transformation from an ordinal string may become frequent and thus may lead a considerable performance decrease. The PSCS scheme would be better than POCS because genes do not need to compare with the crossover point, and no data dependence during the whole process, so the speed-up of PSCS is the best in the three schemes.

Table 2. The standard deviation σ for three types of crossover parallel schemes.(in seconds)

Subjects	σ_{PGCS}	σ_{POCS}	σ_{PSCS}
printtokens	13.946×10^{-3}	0.870×10^{-3}	0.200×10^{-3}
printtokens2	12.359×10^{-3}	0.338×10^{-3}	0.238×10^{-3}
replace	17.331×10^{-3}	0.247×10^{-3}	0.290×10^{-3}
schedule	15.889×10^{-3}	0.324×10^{-3}	0.268×10^{-3}
schedule2	14.566×10^{-3}	0.298×10^{-3}	0.304×10^{-3}
tcas	16.874×10^{-3}	0.305×10^{-3}	0.258×10^{-3}
flex	12.213×10^{-3}	0.231×10^{-3}	0.210×10^{-3}
space	12.450×10^{-3}	0.234×10^{-3}	0.245×10^{-3}
V8	14.576×10^{-3}	0.256×10^{-3}	0.256×10^{-3}

Table 2 presents the standard deviation of the three parallel crossover schemes for all the subjects, the results show that PGCS has much bigger standard deviation than the other two. This indicates that the accelerated effectiveness of PGCS is less stable. The reason for this result is that there is one GPU thread responsible for the crossover of a couple of individuals in PGCS, so the execution time of each GPU thread is associated with the complexity of the crossover algorithm that has been chosen(Antoniol's single point crossover [27] was used in this experiment). The complexity of Antoniol's algorithm is $O(x(n - x))$, where x is crossover position and n is the length of the chromosome. Because x is randomly generated, so the complexity changes are effected only by x. Thus the execution time of each GPU thread is unstable and the overall execution time of PGCS is also unstable.

5.2   Speed-Up of Fine-Grained Parallel Framework

In the previous section, we empirically compared three types of crossover schemes, in which the scan-based crossover scheme achieves the largest speed-ups and the lowest standard deviation. In this section, we combine the parallel fitness evaluation and scan-based parallel crossover computation together, to investigate the whole speed-up achieved.

Figure 4 presents the table with data of execution time of each generation of NSGA-II on CPU and GPU, and the figure of the speed-up. The table shows that GPU execution speed-up effect is very different between different programs. About $V8$ program, the speed-up rate of parallel execution is more than 100x than serial execution results and $tcas$ also has more than 2x speed-up. It may because we use C with CUDA run-time API in the parallel execution code, we can have more obvious speed-up effect. The former six programs are less than 300 lines code, and their speed-up rates are all less than 10x times. Compared with these programs, other three programs are all large scale programs, and their speed-up rates are all more than 90x times, specially the speed-up rate of $V8$, the biggest program, is also having the largest speed up.

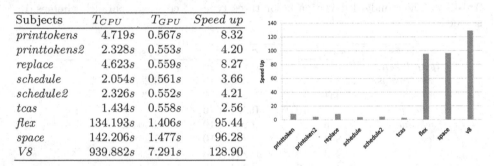

Subjects	T_{CPU}	T_{GPU}	Speed up
printtokens	4.719s	0.567s	8.32
printtokens2	2.328s	0.553s	4.20
replace	4.623s	0.559s	8.27
schedule	2.054s	0.561s	3.66
schedule2	2.326s	0.552s	4.21
tcas	1.434s	0.558s	2.56
flex	134.193s	1.406s	95.44
space	142.206s	1.477s	96.28
V8	939.882s	7.291s	128.90

Fig. 4. The average execution time of each generation on CPU and on GPU using fine-grained parallel framework and the speed-up

6   Related Work

Test case prioritization had been considered as a single-objective optimization problem [7]. Yoo and Harman [12] introduced the Multi-Objective Evolutionary Algorithm(MOEA) to test case selection and test suite minimization. For test case prioritization, Islam et al. [28] applied MOEA to prioritize test cases based on latent semantic indexing on multi-objects of code coverage and requirement coverage information.

Parallel execution of MOEAs had been suggested and investigated as a solution to the efficiency problem suffered by, in which the study of GPU based parallel MOEAs is a new orientation proposed recently.

Because of GPU based parallel computing mechanism and fast float-point operation, it has shown great advantages in scientific computing fields, and achieved many successful applications. Kromer et al. [29] implemented Genetic Algorithm (GA) on GPU for clustering problem, where the fitness function of computing the distance between pins and objects is parallelly implemented on GPU and an large speed-up is achieved. Zhou and Tan [30] presented a GPU based parallel Particle Swarm Optimization (PSO) algorithm. To further improve the speed-up, dual or multi GPU graphics card was introduced in the architecture. Qin et al. [31] presented an improved differential evolution with multi-kernel function on GPU platform.

GPU-based MOEAs are first introduced to multi-objective optimization on regression testing by Yoo et al. [14], where NSGA-II is implemented with openCL on GPU to multi-objective test suite minimization problem. In this study, only binary representation is considered and the fitness computation is turned into a matrix multiplication that can be implemented on GPU easily and more efficiently. This paper focuses on test case prioritization where binary representation is not suitable, so sequential coding and ordinal coding are used in NSGA-II instead. Further to implement fitness evaluation on GPU, we proposed three types of parallel crossover schemes in which the scan-based parallel crossover is the first applied in sequential representation.

7   Conclusion and Future Work

This paper presents a highly efficient GPU-based parallel fitness evaluation scheme and three novel parallel crossover computation schemes in the NSGA-II based multi-objective test case prioritization. It is the first exploration for the parallelism of genetic operations, and the empirical results based on eight benchmarks and one open source subject show that the speed-up rates of at least 2x to 10x times. The results also show that the proposed combination of parallel fitness evaluation and crossover computation can achieve a speed-up of over 100x times compared to CPU based, and the larger the scale of program under test, the higher speed-up rate of GPU achieves.

For future work, we will evaluate the proposed parallel schemes for more large real-world applications to prove their availability. Moreover, GPU-based implementations of other MOEAs will be attempted.

Acknowledgements. This research work is supported in part by National Natural Science Foundation of China No.61170082 and No.61073035 and by Program for New Century Excellent Talents in University NCET-12-0757.

References

1. Yoo, S., Harman, M.: Regression testing minimization, selection and prioritization: a survey. Software Testing, Verification and Reliability 22(2), 67–120 (2012)
2. Rothermel, G., Untch, R.H., Chu, C., Harrold, M.J.: Test case prioritization: An empirical study. In: Proceedings of the IEEE International Conference on Software Maintenance, Los Alamitos, California, USA, pp. 179–188. IEEE Computer Society Press (1999)

3. Rothermel, G., Untch, R., Chu, C., Harrold, M.J.: Prioritizing test cases for regression testing. IEEE Transactions on Software Engineering 27(10), 929–948 (2001)
4. Elbaum, S., Malishevsky, A., Rothermel, G.: Test case prioritization: a family of empirical studies. IEEE Transactions on Software Engineering 28(2), 159–182 (2002)
5. Wong, W.E., Horgan, J.R., London, S., Bellcore, H.A.: A study of effective regression testing in practice. In: Proceedings of the Eighth International Symposium on Software Reliability Engineering (ISSRE 1997), vol. 264. IEEE Computer Society (1997)
6. Kim, J.M., Porter, A.: A history-based test prioritization technique for regression testing in resource constrained environments. In: Proceedings of the 24th International Conference on Software Engineering, ICSE 2002, pp. 119–129 (2002)
7. Li, Z., Harman, M., Hierons, R.: Meta-heuristic search algorithms for regression test case prioritization. IEEE Transactions on Software Engineering 33(4), 225–237 (2007)
8. Zitzler, E.: Evolutionary algorithms for multiobjective optimization: Methods and applications, vol. 63. Shaker, Ithaca (1999)
9. Knowles, J., Corne, D.: The pareto archived evolution strategy: a new baseline algorithm for pareto multiobjective optimisation. In: Proceedings of the 1999 Congress on Evolutionary Computation, CEC 1999, vol. 1, p. 105 (1999)
10. Rudolph, G.: Evolutionary search under partially ordered fitness sets. HT014601767 (2001)
11. Deb, K., Pratap, A., Agarwal, S., Meyarivan, T.: A fast and elitist multiobjective genetic algorithm: NSGA-II. IEEE Transactions on Evolutionary Computation 6(2), 182–197 (2002)
12. Yoo, S., Harman, M.: Pareto efficient multi-objective test case selection. In: International Symposium on Software Testing and Analysis (ISSTA 2007), London, United Kingdom, pp. 140–150. Association for Computer Machinery (July 2007)
13. Zhang, Y., Harman, M., Lim, S.L.: Empirical evaluation of search based requirements interaction management. Information and Software Technology 55(1), 126–152 (2013)
14. Yoo, S., Harman, M., Ur, S.: Highly scalable multi objective test suite minimisation using graphics cards. In: Cohen, M.B., Ó Cinnéide, M. (eds.) SSBSE 2011. LNCS, vol. 6956, pp. 219–236. Springer, Heidelberg (2011)
15. Luong, T.V., Melab, N., Talbi, E.G.: GPU-based island model for evolutionary algorithms. In: Proceedings of the 12th Annual Conference on Genetic and Evolutionary Computation, GECCO 2010. ACM, New York (2010)
16. Tsutsui, S., Fujimoto, N.: Solving quadratic assignment problems by genetic algorithms with GPU computation: a case study. In: GECCO, vol. 9, pp. 2523–2530 (2009)
17. Munawar, A., Wahib, M., Munetomo, M., Akama, K.: Hybrid of genetic algorithm and local search to solve MAX-SAT problem using nVidia CUDA framework. Genetic Programming and Evolvable Machines 10(4), 391–415 (2009)
18. Veldhuizen, D.A.V., Lamont, G.B.: Multiobjective evolutionary algorithms: Analyzing the state-of-the-art. Evolutionary Computation 8(2), 125–147 (2000)
19. Cantu-Paz, E.: Designing efficient master-slave parallel genetic algorithms (1997)
20. Makinen, R., Neittaanmaki, P., Periaux, J., Sefrioui, M., Toivanen, J.: Parallel genetic solution for multiobjective mdo. In: Parallel Computational Fluid Dynamics: Algorithms and Results Using Advanced Computers, pp. 352–359 (1997)

21. Horii, H., Miki, M., Koizumi, T., Tsujiuchi, N.: Asynchronous migration of island parallel ga for multi-objective optimization problem. In: Asia-Pacific Conference on Simulated Evolution and Learning, vol. 1, pp. 86–90 (2002)
22. Owens, J.D., Luebke, D., Govindaraju, N., Harris, M., Krger, J., Lefohn, A.E., Purcell, T.J.: A survey of general-purpose computation on graphics hardware. Computer Graphics Forum 26(1), 80–113 (2007)
23. Antoniol, G., Penta, M.D., Harman, M.: Search-based techniques applied to optimization of project planning for a massive maintenance project. In: 21st IEEE International Conference on Software Maintenance, Los Alamitos, California, USA, pp. 240–249. IEEE Computer Society Press (2005)
24. Larraaga, P., Kuijpers, C., Murga, R., Inza, I., Dizdarevic, S.: Genetic algorithms for the travelling salesman problem: A review of representations and operators. Artificial Intelligence Review 13(2), 129–170 (1999)
25. Harris, M., Sengupta, S., Owens, J.D.: Parallel prefix sum (scan) with CUDA. GPU Gems 3(39), 851–876 (2007)
26. Harman, M.: Making the case for morto: Multi objective regression test optimization. In: 2011 IEEE Fourth International Conference on Software Testing, Verification and Validation Workshops (ICSTW), pp. 111–114 (2011)
27. Antoniol, G., Di Penta, M., Harman, M.: A robust search-based approach to project management in the presence of abandonment, rework, error and uncertainty. In: Proceedings of the 10th International Symposium on Software Metrics, pp. 172–183 (2004)
28. Islam, M.M., Marchetto, A., Susi, A., Scanniello, G.: A multi-objective technique to prioritize test cases based on latent semantic indexing. In: Proceedings of the 2012 16th European Conference on Software Maintenance and Reengineering, CSMR 2012, Washington, DC, pp. 21–30. IEEE Computer Society (2012)
29. Kromer, P., Platos, J., Snasel, V.: Genetic algorithm for clustering accelerated by the CUDA platform. In: 2012 IEEE International Conference on Systems, Man, and Cybernetics (SMC), pp. 1005–1010 (2012)
30. Zhou, Y., Tan, Y.: GPU-based parallel particle swarm optimization. In: IEEE Congress on Evolutionary Computation, CEC 2009, pp. 1493–1500 (2009)
31. Qin, A.K., Raimondo, F., Forbes, F., Ong, Y.S.: An improved CUDA-based implementation of differential evolution on GPU. In: Proceedings of the Fourteenth International Conference on Genetic and Evolutionary Computation Conference, GECCO 2012, pp. 991–998. ACM, New York (2012)

Search-Based Refactoring Detection Using Software Metrics Variation

Rim Mahouachi[1], Marouane Kessentini[1], and Mel Ó Cinnéide[2]

[1] CS, Missouri University of Science and Technology, Missouri, USA
{rimmah,marouanek}@mst.edu
[2] School of CS and Informatics, University College Dublin, Ireland
mel.ocinneide@ucd.ie

Abstract. Software is frequently refactored to improve its design, either as part of an agile development process or as part of a major design overhaul. In either case, it is very useful to determine what refactorings have recently taken place in order to comprehend better the software and its development trajectory. To this end, we have developed an approach to automate the detection of source code refactorings using structural information extracted from the source code. Our approach takes as input a list of possible refactorings, a set of structural metrics and the initial and revised versions of the source code. It generates as output a sequence of detected changes expressed as refactorings. This refactoring sequence is determined by a search-based process that minimizes the metrics variation between the revised version of the software and the version yielded by the application of the refactoring sequence to the initial version of the software. We use both global and local heuristic search algorithms to explore the space of possible solutions. In applying our approach to several versions of four open source projects we find the average Precision and Recall to be over 90%, thus confirming the effectiveness of our detection approach.

Keywords: Search-based software engineering, refactoring, software metrics.

1 Introduction

Software systems are frequently refined and restructured for many reasons such as bug-fixing or source code modification to accommodate requirement changes. To perform these activities, one of the most widely used techniques is refactoring which improves design structure while preserving external behavior [6]. Many techniques to support refactoring have been proposed in the literature [9][10][16][18]. The majority of these techniques enable the application of manual or automated refactoring to fix design problems, e.g., bad smells [10].

A related but distinct problem arises when a software developer is faced with a version of an application that has been recently refactored. They may wish to comprehend what changes have occurred since the previous version, or the changes may require that other parts of the software be changed as well [2]. It would be very useful for them to know what refactorings have been applied to the previous version of the

G. Ruhe and Y. Zhang (Eds.): SSBSE 2013, LNCS 8084, pp. 126–140, 2013.
© Springer-Verlag Berlin Heidelberg 2013

software to create the current, revised version. In addition, the detection of changes between different code versions can be used for regression testing. We address this problem in this paper, by using a stochastic search through the space of possible refactorings, using the metrics profile of the revised software to guide the search. The approach proposed in this paper is best suited to the *root canal refactoring* scenario where the software has undergone significant refactoring, rather than the *floss refactoring* scenario where refactorings are interspersed with changes to functionality [26].

A number of existing approaches attempt to detect changes between two software versions by identifying the specific refactoring operations that lead from the initial program to the revised version. We distinguish between two categories in this existing work: the first category [3][4][5] detects only atomic differences (elementary refactorings), while the second category [18] is also able to detect complex differences (composite refactorings). Our approach can be classified in the second category. In general, existing approaches attempt to detect differences between software versions using the pre- and post-conditions that are specified for each refactoring. In this case, the specified pre- and post-conditions are compared with the changes that are detected by comparing the source and revised code. It may be relatively easy to detect explicit refactoring operations using pre- and post-conditions by performing code matching, however complex refactorings that represent a composition of atomic operations are far more difficult to detect. In addition to this problem, the number of possible changes between initial and revised software versions can be very large, so calculating pre- and post-conditions for these possible changes is likely to be a very onerous task.

To overcome the above-mentioned limitations, we propose to consider the detection of refactorings between software versions as an optimization problem using structural metrics. Our approach takes as input a complete set of refactoring types and a set of software metrics, and generates as output a list of detected changes expressed as refactorings. In this case, a solution is defined as the sequence of refactoring operations that minimizes the metrics variation between the revised version of the software and the version yielded by the application of the refactoring sequence to the initial version of the software. Due to the large number of possible refactoring combinations, an enumerative approach is infeasible, so a heuristic method is used to explore the space of possible solutions. To this end, we adapt and use a genetic algorithm [12] to perform a global heuristic search. The list of refactorings generated can be used by software engineers in a practical context to understand how the software has evolved since its previous revision.

The primary contributions of the paper can be summarized as follows: (1) we introduce a novel refactoring detection approach using structural measures. Our proposal does not require an expert to write conditions for each possible combination of refactorings. Indeed, we identify hidden (implicit) refactorings that are difficult to detect by other means. (2) We report the results of an evaluation of our approach; we used four large open-source systems that have an extensive evolution history [23]. These systems were analyzed manually to find the applied refactorings between different versions. (3) We report the comparison results of our approach as applied using a genetic algorithm, random search, simulated annealing [13] and our previous work [18] over 30 runs.

The remainder of this paper is organized as follows. Section 2 is dedicated to the problem statement, while Section 3 describes the details of our approach. Section 4 explains the experimental method, the results of which are discussed in Section 5. Section 6 introduces related work, and the paper concludes with Section 7.

2   Problem Statement

In this section, we start by providing the definitions of important concepts used in our proposal. Following this, we detail the challenges that are addressed by our approach.

2.1   Background: Software Metrics and Refactoring

In general, internal attributes are captured through software metrics and higher-level properties are expressed in terms of valid values for these metrics [27]. In this paper, we use a number of metrics including Depth of Inheritance Tree (DIT), Weighted Methods per Class (WMC) and Coupling Between Objects (CBO). We also use variations of the following metrics: the number of lines of code in a class (LOCCLASS), number of lines of code in a method (LOCMETHOD), number of attributes in a class (NAD), number of methods (NMD), lack of cohesion in methods (LCOM5), number of accessors (NACC), and number of private fields (NPRIVFIELD).

Refactoring is the standard technique used in practice to improve the design of software either as part of radical restructuring or as a component of an agile development methodology. The best-known catalog of software refactorings is that of Fowler et al. [6], which include refactorings such as *push down field*: moves a field from some class to those subclasses that require it, *add parameter*: adds a new parameter to a method, *move method*: moves a method from one class to another. In our work, we make use of a subset of Fowler's refactorings.

2.2   Challenges

Several notable techniques have been proposed to detect the changes applied to source code by either recording the changes directly as they are applied by a developer, or by analyzing two versions of a model and computing the differences between them. Although change recording produces a very precise change log efficiently, this technique is often not applicable in practice because a tight integration with the editor is necessary. Existing model comparison tools are capable of detecting atomic changes only. However, the composition of these atomic changes can lead to complex refactoring that cannot be detected using such comparison tools [14]. Only a few approaches have been proposed that address also the detection of high-level changes [18]. These approaches search for change patterns of pre-defined high-level operations among the atomic changes obtained from model comparison tools and, if a change pattern of a high-level operation is found, the pre- and post-conditions of the respective operation are evaluated before an occurrence of the operation is reported. A detailed case study of such an approach revealed that good results can be achieved as long as there are no overlapping sequences of systematic operations; that is, operations are applied in a sequence, whereas one operation is necessary before a subsequent operation can be applied. Moreover, in several scenarios the subsequent operations render the post-conditions of the preceding operations invalid such that current approaches are not able to detect the operations correctly. However, overlapping sequences of systematic operations occur quite frequently, and the problem of finding the appropriate sequence in which to apply a given set of refactorings has been addressed [17]. Moreover, the graph-comparison approaches [18] cannot detect, on average, all changes. In fact, this problem has the same complexity as the graph isomorphism problem, which is NP-hard. In particular, we can find a generated model/code and an expected model that look different (contain different model/code elements) but have the same meaning (semantics).

To address these challenges, we describe in the next section how to consider the detection of refactorings between different software versions as an optimization problem using structural metrics.

3   Refactoring Detection by Studying Metrics Variation

This section shows how the above-mentioned issues can be addressed and describes the principles that underlie the proposed method for detecting refactorings from structural information. Therefore, we first present an overview of the search-based algorithm employed and subsequently provide the details of the approach and our adaptation of a genetic algorithm to detect refactorings.

3.1   Overview

The general structure of our approach is introduced in Fig. 1. The approach takes as input the initial and revised source code, a set quality metrics and a complete set of refactoring types. The approach generates a set of refactorings that represents the evolution from the initial source code to the revised one. An Eclipse plug-in [25] is used to calculate metrics values from the revised code version and the new version obtained after applying the proposed solution (refactoring sequence). The process of detecting refactorings can be viewed as the mechanism that finds the best way to combine refactoring operations of the input set of refactoring types, in order to minimize the dissimilarity between the metrics value of the revised code and the code that results from applying the detected refactorings.

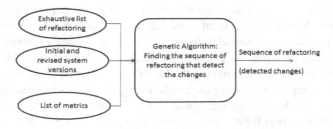

Fig. 1. Overview

Due to the large number of possible refactoring solutions, we consider the detection of refactoring between different software versions as an optimization problem. The algorithm explores a huge search space. In fact, the search space is determined not only by the number of possible refactoring combinations, but also by the order in which they are applied. To explore this huge search space, we use a global search by the use of a Genetic Algorithm (GA). This algorithm and its adaptation to the refactoring problem are described in the next section.

3.2 Genetic Algorithm Adaptation

This section describes how a Genetic Algorithm (GA) is adapted to detect refactorings using software metrics variation.

3.2.1 Genetic Algorithm

Genetic algorithms (GA) are a heuristic search optimization method inspired by the Darwinian theory of evolution [12]. The basic idea is to explore the search space by creating a population of candidate solutions, also called individuals, and evolve them towards an optimal solution of a specific problem. In GA, a solution can be represented as a vector. Each dimension of this vector contains symbols that are appropriate for the target problem. Each individual of the population is evaluated by a fitness function that determines a quantitative measure of its ability to solve the target problem. The exploration of the search space is achieved by evolution of candidate solutions using selection and genetic operators, such as crossover and mutation. Once selection, mutation and crossover have been applied according to given probabilities, individuals of the newly created generation are evaluated using the fitness function. This process is repeated iteratively, until a stopping criterion is met.

3.2.2 Adaptation

A high level view of our GA approach to the refactoring detection problem using structural information is described in this section. The algorithm takes as input two versions of the same object-oriented system, a set of structural metrics and a complete set of refactoring types; and generates as output a solution, which corresponds to a sequence of refactoring operations that minimize the dissimilarity in the metrics variation between the revised code and the new code version (after applying the refactoring sequence to the initial code).

The algorithm starts by extracting the structural information (metrics measure) from the expected code version. Then it constructs an initial population of solutions (refactorings combination), generated randomly using a set of refactorings and evaluates them. The next step includes the main GA loop, which explores the search space. During each iteration, we evaluate the quality of each solution (individual) in the population, and the solution having the best fitness is saved. A new code version is obtained after applying the proposed refactoring operations (solution). Then the algorithm calculates the new metrics value of the obtained code. The next step compares (dissimilarity score) between the expected metrics value and those obtained in the new code. We generate a new population of solutions using the crossover operator to the selected solutions; each pair of parent solutions produces two children (new solutions). We include the parent and child variants in the population and then apply the mutation operator to each variant; this produces the population for the next generation. An invalid child can simply be replaced by a new one randomly. The algorithm terminates when it achieves the termination criterion (maximum iteration number), and returns the best refactoring sequence found. The following three subsections describe more precisely our adaption of GA to the refactorings detection problem.

3.2.2.1 Solution Representation

We consider the potential solution as a vector of refactoring operations. Figure 2 shows an example where the solution represents a sequence of refactoring operations to be applied. The order of application of the refactorings corresponds to their order in the table (dimension number). The execution of these refactorings must conform to certain semantics and postconditions (to avoid conflicts and incoherence semantic errors). For example, we cannot remove a method from a class that was already moved to another class, thus the preconditions of each refactoring have to be fulfilled before its execution. If the preconditions are not met, we partially regenerate the solution randomly.

For instance, the solution represented in Figure 2 comprises two dimensions corresponding to two refactoring operations to apply in an initial version (V1). In fact, the two refactorings are Push Feature that is applied to the reference description and Unfold Class that is applied to the class Description. After applying the proposed refactorings we obtain a new model that will be compared with the expected revised model using a fitness function.

To generate an initial population, we start by defining the maximum vector length including the number of refactorings. These parameters can be specified either by the

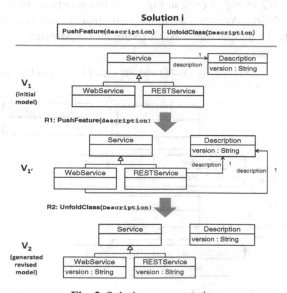

Fig. 2. Solution representation

user or chosen randomly. Thus, the individuals have different vector length (structure). Then, for each individual we randomly assign one refactoring, with its parameters, to each dimension.

3.2.2.2 Fitness Function

Solutions are evaluated using a fitness function that determines their efficiency. This function is based on a metrics variation (dissimilarity score) to minimize between the new code version (after applying proposed refactorings) and the revised version of the software.

After applying a generated solution (proposed refactorings) to the initial code version V1, the fitness function calculates the difference between the metrics value on the two code versions (V1 and the expected revised version). Fitness function can be formulated as follows:

$$\text{Fitness\_function} = \sum_{i=1}^{n}\sum_{j=1}^{m}\left|ve_i(e_j)-ve'_i(e_j)\right|$$

Where:

- n: maximum number of code elements (classes) between the two versions
- m: number of quality metrics
- $ve_i(e_j)$ = value of metric$_i$ for the class e_j in the expected revised version V2
- $ve'_j(e_j)$ = value of metric$_j$ for the class e_j in the new version V'1 (after applying the solution on the initial version V1)

Some metrics have been normalized to [0, 1] since otherwise the fitness function could be dominated by a single metric. To illustrate the fitness function, we consider the example shown in Fig. 3. The model V2 of Fig. 3 is considered as the expected revised model and V2 of Fig. 2 (V'2 in Fig. 3) as the generated model after applying the refactoring solution. We use as input two quality metrics: metric$_1$ = NOM (Number Of Methods) and metric$_2$ = NOA (Number Of Attributes). Thus, the fitness function in this case is:

$$\left(\left(\left|0-0\right|+\left|0-0\right|\right)+\left(\left|0-0\right|+\left|0-1\right|\right)+\left(\left|0-0\right|+\left|1-1\right|\right)+\left(\left|0-0\right|+\left|1-1\right|\right)\right)=1$$

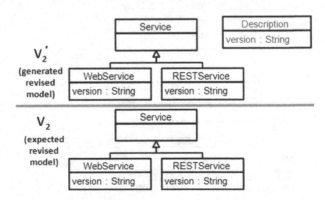

Fig. 3. Comparison between expected and revised versions

3.2.2.3 Change Operators

Selection. To select the individuals that will undergo the crossover and mutation operators, we use Stochastic Universal Sampling (SUS) [12], in which the probability of selection of an individual is directly proportional to its relative fitness in the population. SUS is a random selection algorithm that gives higher probability of selection to the fittest solutions, while still giving a chance to every solution.

Crossover. For each crossover, two individuals are selected by applying SUS selection. Even though individuals are selected, the crossover happens only with a certain probability.

The crossover operator allows creating two offspring P_1' and P_2' from the two selected parents P_1 and P_2. It is defined as follows. A random position k is selected. The first k refactorings of P_1 become the first k elements of P_1'. Similarly, the first k refactorings of P_2 become the first k refactorings of P_2'.

Fig. 4 shows an example of the crossover process. In this example, P_1 and P_2 are combined to generate two new solutions. The right sub-vector of P_1 is combined with the left sub-vector of P_2 to form the first child, and the right sub-vector of P_2 is combined with the left sub-vector of P_1 to form the second child. In Fig. 4, the position k takes the value 1. The second refactoring of P_1 becomes the second element of P_2. Similarly, the second refactoring of P_2 become the second refactorings of P_1.

Mutation. The mutation operator consists of randomly changing one or more dimensions (refactoring) in the solution (vector). Given a selected individual, the mutation operator first randomly selects some dimensions in the vector representation of the individual. Then the selected dimensions are replaced by other refactorings. Furthermore, the mutation can only modify the parameters of some dimensions without changing the type of the refactoring involved.

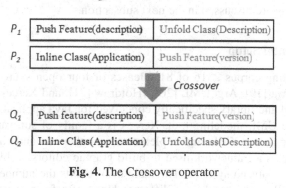

Fig. 4. The Crossover operator

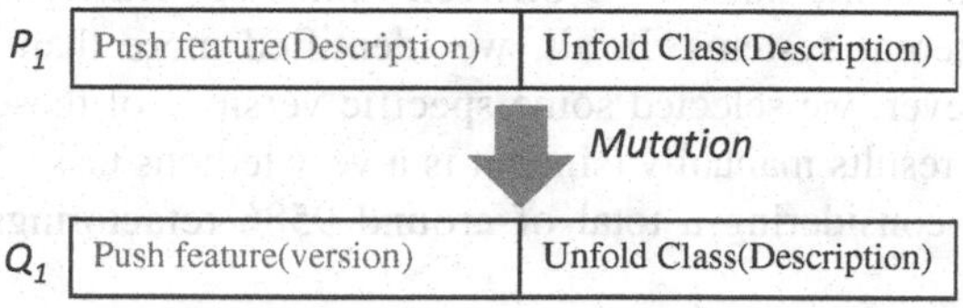

Fig. 5. The Mutation operators

Fig. 5 illustrates the effect of a mutation that replaced the dimension number one *Push Feature (description)* by *Push Feature (version)*.

4   Evaluation

In order to evaluate the feasibility of our approach for detecting refactorings, we conducted an experiment based on different versions of real-world large open source systems [19][20][21][22]. We start by presenting our research questions. Then, we describe and discuss the obtained results.

4.1   Goals and Objectives

The study was conducted to quantitatively assess the completeness and correctness of our approach when applied to a real-world scenario and to compare its performance with existing approaches. More specifically, we aimed at answering the following research questions RQ1) To what extent can the proposed approach detect changes between different code versions (in terms of correctness and completeness)? RQ2) What types of changes (refactorings) does it detect correctly? RQ3) How does the performance of the GA compare with that of random search and local search (simulated annealing 13)?

To answer RQ1, we used an existing corpus [23][16] containing an extensive evolution of four large open source systems to evaluate the correctness and completeness of our approach. To answer RQ2, we investigated the type of changes that were found. For the remaining question RQ3, we compared our GA results to those produced by random search and simulated annealing (SA). Further details about our experiments setting are discussed in the next subsection.

4.2   Experimental Setup

We used an existing corpus 2316 of 81 releases of four open source Java projects, namely Apache Ant [19], ArgoUML [20], JHotdraw [21], and Xerces-J [22]. Apache Ant is a build tool and library specifically conceived for Java applications. ArgoUML is an open source UML modeling tool. Xerces is a family of software packages for parsing and manipulating XML, and implements a number of standard APIs for XML parsing. JHotdraw is a framework used to build graphic editors. Table I reports characteristics of the analyzed systems. The table also reports the number of refactoring operations (as well as the number of different kinds of refactorings) identified manually for the different systems. In all, we identified more than 16000 refactoring applications. However, we selected some specific versions of these open source system to analyze the results manually (since it is a very tedious task). Thus, as described in table I, we are considering a total of around 9586 refactorings applied between different versions.

We choose Xerces-J, JHotDraw, ArgoUML, and Apache Ant because they are medium-sized open-source projects and were analyzed in related work. The initial versions of GMF and Apache Ant are known to be of poor quality, which has led to major revised versions. Xerces-J, ArgoUML, and JHotDraw have been actively developed over the past 10 years, and their design has not been responsible for a slowdown of their developments.

For this experiment, Ref-Finder [5] was used in [23] to automatically detect refactoring operations of 34 different types on 72 releases of the different open source systems. From the refactorings detected by Ref-Finder, 9586 refactorings have been manually validated as correct refactorings. In total, 34 different types of refactoring operations have been applied. The evolution of the different versions provides a relatively large set of revisions. In total, the evolution of the considered versions comprises 81 revisions that involved at least one refactoring operation. Overall, 9586 refactoring operations have been applied, whereas one transition between two revisions contains on average 116 refactorings. Most of the commits comprise between 1 and 29 refactorings. Table 1 describes the number of expected refactorings to be detected by our approach on the different code versions. These operations cover 34 refactoring types (e.g. move method, move feature, etc.). Finally, we used a set of 18 quality metrics that are available on an existing Eclipse plug-in [25].

Table 1. The Systems Studied

System	Number of expected refactoring	Classes (min, max)
Apache Ant	1094	87, 1191
ArgoUML	1967	777, 1519
JHotdraw	1884	291, 603
Xerces-J	4641	181, 776

To assess the accuracy of our approach, we compute the standard Information Retrieval measures of Precision and Recall. In the context of our study, Precision denotes the fraction of correctly detected refactoring operations among the set of all detected operations. Recall indicates the fraction of correctly detected refactoring operations among the set of all expected refactorings (i.e., how many operations have not been missed). In general, Precision denotes the probability that a detected operation is correct while Recall is the probability that an actually applied operation is detected. Thus, both values may range from 0 to 1, whereas a higher value is better than a lower one. The quality of our results was measured by two methods: Automatic Correctness (AC) and Manual Correctness (MC). Automatic correctness consists of comparing the detected changes to the reference/expected ones, operation-by-operation using Precision (AP) and Recall (AR). AC method has the advantage of being automatic and objective. However, since different refactoring combinations exist that describe the same evolution (different changes but same new code version), AC could reject a good solution because it yields different refactoring operations from reference/expected ones. To account for those situations, we also use MC, which involves manually evaluating the detected changes, here again operation-by-operation. In addition, we compared the performance of random search and simulated annealing, using AC scores for these comparisons.

4.3   Results and Discussions

Table 2 summarizes our results over 30 runs. Our approach detects 9387 refactoring operations. Overall, we were able to find 8912 refactoring operations correctly among all 9586 operations (i.e., Recall of 93%), whereas fewer than 600 operations have been incorrectly detected, which leads to a Precision of around 92%. It is worth noting that the evolution history of these four open source systems is very different. As the studied evolution of the remaining systems covers a time period of ten years, they have a large number of refactorings to be detected. However, our proposal performs well on the large evolutions of these systems. For Apache, most of the detected changes are correct with 96% and 94% respectively for Precision and Recall. For ArgoUML and JHotDraw, they have approximately the same number of refactorings to detect and our approach detected most of them with an average Precision of 98% and average Recall of 95%. Xerces-J is the larger system that we studied with more than 4646 refactoring applied over 10 years and our proposal succeeds in detecting almost all of them with a Precision and Recall of more than 91%. Thus, overall we can conclude that using our approach we could identify most of the applied operations correctly with an average of 92% of Precision and 94% of Recall. We noticed also that our technique does not have a bias towards the types of refactoring since most of them were detected (RQ2).

With regards to manual correctness (MC), the Precision and Recall scores for all the four open source systems were improved since we found interesting refactoring alternatives that deviate from the reference ones proposed by the developers/experts. In addition, we found that the sequence of applying the refactoring is sometimes different between generated refactoring and reference ones. We found that sometimes a different sequence can reduce the number of refactorings required. Another observation is that the Precision and Recall scores depend on the number of changes. When the number of changes increases then Precision and Recall decrease. However, we still have acceptable scores even when a large number of changes has occurred.

Table 2. Average Detection Results

Model	AP: Precision	AR: Recall	MP:Precision	MR: Recall
Apache Ant	1033/1073= 96%	1033/1094 = 94%	1037/1073 = 96%	1037/1094 = 95%
ArgoUML	1874/1904 = 98%	1874/1967 = 95%	1877/1904 = 98%	1877/1967 = 95%
JHot-Draw	1769/1874 = 94%	1769/1884 = 93%	1791/1874 = 95%	1791/1884 = 94%
Xerces-J	4236/4536 = 93%	4236/4641 = 91%	4247/4536 = 93%	4247/4641 = 91%

Fig. 4 illustrates the comparison between the results obtained using GA, random search and simulated annealing (SA). The detection results for SA were also acceptable. Especially, with the smaller system (ApacheAnt) the Precision is better using SA than GA. In fact, GA is a global search that gives good results when the search space is large. For this reason, GA performs well with large systems. However, compared to GA, SA takes a lot of time to converge to an optimal solution as it requires many more iterations. In our experiments, we used the same number of iterations as a termination criterion (10000 iterations). In addition, to ensure the stability of the results during the comparison we calculated an average of Precision and Recall over 30 runs. Finally, the random search did not perform well on all the systems due to the huge search space to explore.

The correlation between the number of used metrics and the Recall and Precision values is analyzed in Figure 5 based on the data gathered in our study. More precisely, we calculate the Precision and Recall for different versions of the larger system Xerces-J. We conclude that the Precision and Recall depends on the number of metrics employed. When the number of metrics decreases then the Precision and Recall decrease. For example, the Recall/Precision decreases from 90% to 62% when the number of metrics decreases from 18 to 8. However, number of metrics used on our experiments can be considered as reasonable.

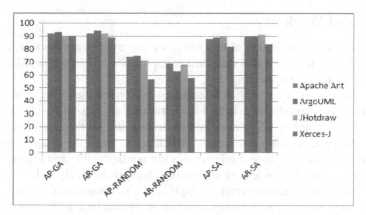

Fig. 6. Comparison between GA, SA and Random Search (average Precision and Recall over 30 runs)

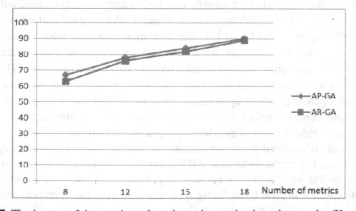

Fig. 7. The impact of the number of used metrics on the detection results (Xerces-J)

Finally, it is important to contrast the results with the execution time. The execution time for finding the optimal refactoring solution with a fixed number of 10000 iterations (stopping criteria) was less than 30 minutes on the larger open source system (Xerces-J). This indicates that our approach is reasonably scalable from the performance standpoint.

Our proposal has some limitations that we will address in our future work. The major challenge in this work lies in the assumption made in section 3.2.1.2, that each class in the original source maps to one class in the revised version. Sometimes after radical refactoring it becomes very difficult to understand/detect the changes with a high precision score. One possibility is to explore the use of semantic measures in order to find a suitable matching between the names of classes. Another challenge that is not addressed, in this work, is conflict and dependency in the refactoring sequence. This only appears experimentally when a large number of refactorings are applied to a small number of classes. We will address this problem in our future work by finding the best sequence that minimizes the number of conflicts.

5   Related Work

With respect to the contribution of this work, we survey existing work in the area of refactoring detection and we also state further applications of search-based techniques in the field of software engineering.

The easiest way to detect applied refactorings is to track their execution in the development environment directly. Refactoring tracking is realized by [1] in programming environments and by [2] in modeling environments. All these approaches highly depend on the development environment, which has to track the refactorings as they are applied. Furthermore, manual refactorings are not detectable and refactorings that have in fact been made obsolete by successive changes are likely to be wrongly detected. In contrast to refactoring tracking approaches, state-based refactoring detection mechanisms aim to reveal refactorings a posteriori on the base of the two successive versions of a software artifact. Several approaches are tailored to detect refactorings in program code. For instance, Dig et al. [2] propose an approach to detect applied refactorings in Java code. They first perform a fast syntactic analysis and, subsequently, a semantic analysis in which operational aspects like method call graphs are also considered. Weissgerber and Diehl [3] take a similar approach where after a preprocessing and a syntactical analysis have been conducted, conditions indicating the application of a refactoring are evaluated. Recent work by Kim et al. [4][5] on the Ref-Finder tool involves an approach for refactoring detection that improves on several issues left open in previous approaches. In particular, the Ref-Finder tool is capable of detecting complex refactorings that comprise a set of atomic refactorings by using logic-based rules executed by a logic programming engine.

Our approach is inspired by contributions in Search-Based Software Engineering (SBSE) [24]. As the name indicates, SBSE uses a search-based approach to solve optimization problems in software engineering. Once a software engineering task is framed as a search problem, by defining it in terms of solution representation, fitness function and solution change operators, there are many search algorithms that can be applied to solve that problem. To the best of our knowledge, the idea of detecting refactorings from structural information using search-based techniques was not studied before. However, several other works are proposed to find refactoring opportunities using search-based techniques [15, 16, 18]. We proposed a search-based approach to detect changes between different model versions by comparing them [18]. However, the comparison between two model versions is a difficult task. In fact, this problem has the same complexity as the graph isomorphism problem, which is NP-hard. In particular, we can find a generated model and an expected model that look different (i.e., contain different model elements) but have the same semantics. Moreover, in [18] detected refactorings are related only to the model level. In the work of O'Keeffe and Ó Cinnéide [15], software design improvement is treated as an optimization problem. The authors use a combination of 12 metrics to measure the improvements achieved when sequences of simple refactorings are applied, such as moving methods between classes. The goal of the optimization is to refactor a program to a revised version that has improved quality based of a set of software metrics. Another application of this approach by Ó Cinnéide et al. [16] uses search-based refactoring to assess software metrics and explore relationships between them.

6   Conclusion

In this paper we introduce a novel, search-based approach to software refactoring detection between an initial software version and a refactored software version. Our approach is based on representing a proposed solution as a sequence of refactorings, and evaluating this solution in terms of its metrics profile as compared with the metrics profile of the refactored software version. Framing the problem in this manner enables us to use a Genetic Algorithm to evolve better solutions whose metric profiles more closely match that of the refactored software version. Our key hypothesis is that as the metric profiles converge, so too will the evolved refactoring sequence converge to the actual refactoring sequence that was originally applied to generate the refactored version from the initial version.

We evaluated our approach on four real-world, open source software applications involving a total of 81 different versions and a total of 9,586 refactorings (as verified manually). Experiments show the Precision of our approach to be 92% and the Recall 93%, which provide strong evidence of the validity of our approach. As part of future work, we will investigate situations where no direct mapping exists between the elements of the initial software version and the refactored version, study the effects various metrics have on the quality of refactoring sequences obtained and attempt to classify the detected model changes as risky or not in terms of quality improvement.

References

1. Robbes, R.: Mining a Change-Based Software Repository. In: Proceedings of MSR 2007, pp. 15–23. IEEE Computer Society (2007)
2. Dig, D., Comertoglu, C., Marinov, D., Johnson, R.: Automated Detection of Refactorings in Evolving Components. In: Thomas, D. (ed.) ECOOP 2006. LNCS, vol. 4067, pp. 404–428. Springer, Heidelberg (2006)
3. Weissgerber, P., Diehl, S.: Identifying Refactorings from Source-Code Changes. In: Proceedings of ASE 2006, pp. 231–240. IEEE (2006)

4. Kim, M., Notkin, D., Grossman, D., Wilson Jr., G.: Identifying and Summarizing Systematic Code Changes via Rule Inference. TSE: IEEE Transactions on Software Engineering, 45–62 (2013)
5. Prete, K., Rachatasumrit, N., Sudan, N., Kim, M.: Template-based reconstruction of complex refactorings. In: ICSM 2010, pp. 1–10 (2010)
6. Fowler, M., Beck, K., Brant, J., Opdyke, W., Roberts, D.: Refactoring – Improving the Design of Existing Code, 1st edn. Addison-Wesley (June 1999)
7. Liu, H., Yang, L., Niu, Z., Ma, Z., Shao, W.: Facilitating software refactoring with appropriate resolution order of bad smells. In: Proc. of the ESEC/FSE 2009, pp. 265–268 (2009)
8. Harman, M., Tratt, L.: Pareto optimal search based refactoring at the design level. In: Proceedings of the Genetic and Evolutionary Computation Conference (GECCO 2007), pp. 1106–1113 (2007)
9. Seng, O., Stammel, J., Burkhart, D.: Search-based determination of refactorings for improving the class structure of object-oriented systems. In: GECCO 2006, pp. 1909–1916 (2006)
10. Du Bois, B., Demeyer, S., Verelst, J.: Refactoring—Improving Coupling and Cohesion of Existing Code. In: Proc. 11th Working Conf. Reverse Eng., pp. 144–151 (2004)
11. Mens, T., Tourwé, T.: A Survey of Software Refactoring. IEEE Trans. Software Eng. 30(2), 126–139 (2004)
12. Koza, J.R.: Genetic Programming: On the Programming of Computers by Means of Natural Selection. MIT Press, Cambridge (1992)
13. Kirkpatrick, S., Gelatt Jr., C.D., Vecchi, M.P.: Optimization by simulated annealing. Sciences 220(4598), 671–680 (1983)
14. Langer, P.: Adaptable Model Versioning based on Model Transformation By Demonstration, PhD Thesis, Vienna University of Technology (2011)
15. O'Keeffe, M., Cinnéide, M.Ó.: Search-based Refactoring for Software Maintenance. Journal of Systems and Software 81(4), 502–516
16. Ó Cinnéide, M., Tratt, L., Harman, M., Counsell, S., Hemati Moghadam, I.: Experimental assessment of software metrics using automated refactoring. In: Proceedings of the International Symposium on Empirical Software Engineering and Measurement (Septembrer 2012)
17. Hemati Moghadam, I., Cinnéide, M.Ó.: Automated refactoring using design differencing. In: Proc. of European Conference on Software Maintenance and Reengineering, Szeged (March 2012)
18. Fadhel, A.B., Kessentini, M., Langer, P., Wimmer, M.: Search-based detection of high-level model changes. In: ICSM 2012, pp. 212–221 (2012)
19. http://www.eclipse.org/gmf http://www.eclipse.org/gmf;
20. http://argouml.tigris.org
21. http://www.jhotdraw.org
22. http://xerces.apache.org
23. Bavota, G., De Carluccio, B., De Lucia, A., Di Penta, M., Oliveto, R., Strollo, O.: When does a Refactoring Induce Bugs? An Empirical Study. In: Proceedings of the WCRE 2012, IEEE Press (2012)
24. Harman, M., Afshin Mansouri, S., Zhang, Y.: Search-based software engineering: Trends, techniques and applications. ACM Comput. Surv. 45(1), 11 (2012)
25. http://metrics.sourceforge.net
26. Murphy-Hill, E., Parnin, C., Black, A.P.: How We Refactor, and How We Know It. IEEE Transactions on Software Engineering (2011)
27. Briand, L.C., Wüst, J., Daly, J.W., Victor Porter, D.: A Comprehensive Empirical Validation of Design Measures for Object-Oriented Systems. In: IEEE METRICS 1998, pp. 246–257 (1998)

Automated Model-in-the-Loop Testing of Continuous Controllers Using Search

Reza Matinnejad[1], Shiva Nejati[1], Lionel Briand[1], Thomas Bruckmann[2], and Claude Poull[2]

[1] SnT Center,
University of Luxembourg, Luxembourg
{reza.matinnejad,shiva.nejati,lionel.briand}@uni.lu
[2] Delphi Automotive Systems Luxembourg
{thomas.bruckmann,claude.poull}@delphi.com

Abstract. The number and the complexity of software components embedded in today's vehicles is rapidly increasing. A large group of these components monitor and control the operating conditions of physical devices (e.g., components controlling engines, brakes, and airbags). These controllers are known as *continuous controllers*. In this paper, we study testing of continuous controllers at the Model-in-Loop (MiL) level where both the controller and the environment are represented by models and connected in a closed feedback loop system. We identify a set of common requirements characterizing the desired behavior of continuous controllers, and develop a search-based technique to automatically generate test cases for these requirements. We evaluated our approach by applying it to a real automotive air compressor module. Our experience shows that our approach automatically generates several test cases for which the MiL level simulations indicate potential violations of the system requirements. Further, not only do our approach generates better test cases faster than random test case generation, but we also achieve better results than test scenarios devised by domain experts.

1 Introduction

Modern vehicles are increasingly equipped with Electronic Control Units (ECUs). The amount and the complexity of software embedded in the ECUs of today's vehicles is rapidly increasing. To ensure the high quality of software and software-based functions on ECUs, the automotive and ECU manufacturers have to rely on effective techniques for verification and validation of their software systems. A large group of automotive software functions require to monitor and control the operating conditions of physical components. Examples are functions controlling engines, brakes, seatbelts, and airbags. These controllers are widely studied in the control theory domain as *continuous controllers* [1,2] where the focus has been to *optimize* their design for a specific platform or a specific hardware configuration [3,4]. Yet a complementary and important problem, of how to systematically and automatically *test* controllers to ensure their correctness and safety, has received almost no attention in the control engineering research [1].

In this paper, we concentrate on the problem of automatic and systematic test case generation for continuous controllers. The principal challenges when analyzing such

G. Ruhe and Y. Zhang (Eds.): SSBSE 2013, LNCS 8084, pp. 141–157, 2013.
© Springer-Verlag Berlin Heidelberg 2013

controllers stem from their continuous interactions with the physical environment, usually through feedback loops where the environment impacts computations and vice versa. We study the testing of controllers at an early stage where both the controller and the environment are represented by models and connected in a closed feedback loop process. In model-based approaches to embedded software design, this level is referred to as *Model-in-the-Loop (MiL)* testing.

Testing continuous aspects of control systems is challenging and is not yet supported by existing tools and techniques [4,1,3]. There is a large body of research on testing *mixed* discrete-continuous behaviors of embedded software systems where the system under test is represented using state machines, hybrid automata, hybrid petri nets, etc [5,6,7]. These techniques, however, are not amenable to testing *purely* continuous controllers described in terms of mathematical models, and in particular, differential equations. A number of commercial verification and testing tools have been developed, aiming to generate test cases for MATLAB/Simulink models, namely the Simulink Design Verifier software [8], and Reactis Tester [9]. Currently, these tools handle only combinatorial and logical blocks of the MATLAB/Simulink models, and fail to generate test cases that specifically evaluate continuous blocks (e.g., integrators) [1].

Contributions. In this paper, we propose a search-based approach to automate generation of MiL level test cases for continuous controllers. We identify a set of common requirements characterizing the desired behavior of such controllers. We develop a search-based technique to generate stress test cases attempting to violate these requirements by combining *explorative* and *exploitative* search algorithms [10]. Specifically, we first apply a purely explorative random search to evaluate a number of input signals distributed across the search space. Combining the domain experts' knowledge and random search results, we select a number of regions that are more likely to lead to requirement violations in practice. We then start from the worst case input signals found during exploration, and apply an exploitative *single-state* search [10] to the selected regions to identify test cases for the controller requirements. Our search algorithms rely on *objective* functions created by formalizing the controller requirements. We evaluated our approach by applying it to an automotive air compressor module. Our experiments show that our approach automatically generates several test cases for which the MiL level simulations indicate potential errors in the controller or the environment models. Furthermore, the resulting test cases had not been previously found by manual testing based on domain expertise. Our industry partner is interested to investigate these test cases further by evaluating them in a more realistic setting (e.g., by testing them on their *Hardware-in-the-Loop (HiL)* platform). In addition, our approach computes test cases better and faster than a random test case generation strategy.

2   MiL Testing of Continuous Controllers: Practice and Challenges

Control system development involves building of control software (controllers) to interact with mechatronic systems usually referred to as plants or environment [2]. An example of such controllers is shown in Figure 1. These controllers are commonly used in many domains such as manufacturing, robotics, and automotive. Model-based development of control systems is typically carried out in three major levels described below. The models created through these levels become increasingly more similar to real controllers, while verification and testing of these models become successively more complex and expensive.

Model-in-the-Loop (MiL): At this level, a model for the controller and a model for the plant are created in the same notation and connected in the same diagram. In many sectors and in particular in the automotive domain, these models are created in MAT-LAB/Simulink. The MiL simulation and testing is performed entirely in a virtual environment and without any need to any physical component. The focus of MiL testing is to verify the control algorithm, and to ensure that the interactions between the controller and the plant do not violate the system requirements.

Software-in-the-Loop (SiL): At this level, the controller model is converted to code (either autocoded or manually). This often includes the conversion of floating point data types into fixed-point values as well as addition of hardware-specific libraries. The testing at the SiL-level is still performed in a virtual and simulated environment like MiL, but the focus is on controller code which can run on the target platform. Further, in contrast to verifying the algorithms, SiL testing aims to ensure correctness of floating point to fixed-point conversion and the conformance of code to control models (particularly in the case of manual coding).

Hardware-in-the-Loop (HiL): At this level, the controller software is fully installed into the final control system (e.g., in our case, the controller software is installed on the ECUs). The plant is either a real piece of hardware, or is some software that runs on a real-time computer with physical signal simulation to lead the controller into believing that it is being used on a real plant. The main objective of HiL is to verify the integration of hardware and software in a more realistic environment. HiL testing is the closest to reality, but is also the most expensive and slowest among the three testing levels.

In this paper, among the above three levels, we focus on the MiL level testing. MiL testing is the primary level intended for verification of the control algorithms logic and ensuring the satisfaction of their requirements. Development and testing at this level is considerably fast as the engineers can quickly modify the control model and immediately test the system. Furthermore, MiL testing is entirely performed in a virtual environment, enabling execution of a large number of test cases in a small amount of time. Finally, the MiL level test cases can later be used at SiL and HiL levels either directly or after some adaptations.

Currently, in most companies, MiL level testing of controllers is limited to running the controller-plant Simulink model (e.g., Figure 1) for a small number of simulations, and manually inspecting the results of individual simulations. The simulations are often selected based on the engineers' domain knowledge and experience, but in a rather ad hoc way. Such simulations are useful for checking the overall sanity of the control algorithms, but cannot be taken as a substitute for MiL testing. Manual simulations fail to find erroneous scenarios that the engineers might not be aware of a priori. Identifying such scenarios later during SiL/HiL is much more difficult and expensive than during MiL testing. Also, manual simulation is by definition limited in scale and scope.

Our goal is to develop an automated MiL testing technique to verify controller-plant systems. To do so, we formalize the properties of continuous controllers regarding the functional, performance, and safety aspects. We develop an automated test case generation approach to evaluate controllers with respect to these properties. In our work, the test inputs are signals, and the test outputs are measured over the simulation diagrams generated by MATLAB/Simulink plant models. The simulations are discretized where the controller output is sampled at a rate of a few milliseconds. To generate test cases, we combine two search algorithms: (1) An explorative random search that allows us to achieve high diversity of test inputs in the space, and to identify the most critical regions that need to be explored further. (2) An exploitative search that enables us to focus our search and compute worst case scenarios in the identified critical regions.

3   Background on Continuous Controllers

Figure 1 shows an overview of a controller-plant model at the MiL level. Both the controller and the plant are captured as models and linked via virtual connections. We refer to the input of the controller-plant system as *desired* or *reference* value. For example, the desired value may represent the location we want a robot to move to, the speed we require an engine to reach, or the position we need a valve to arrive at.The *system output* or the *actual* value represents the actual state/position/speed of the hardware components in the plant. The actual value is expected to reach the desired value over a certain time limit, making the *Error*, i.e., the difference between the actual and desired values, eventually zero. The task of the controller is to eliminate the error by manipulating the plant to obtain the desired effect on the system output.

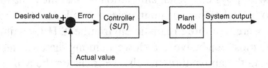

Fig. 1. MiL level Controller-Plant Model

The overall objective of the controller in Figure 1 may sound simple. In reality, however, the design of such controllers requires calculating proper corrective actions for the controller to stabilize the system within a certain time limit, and further, to guarantee that the hardware components will eventually reach the desired state without oscillating too much around it and without any damage. Controllers design is typically captured via complex differential equations known as *proportional-integral-derivative (PID)* [2]. For example, Figure 2(a) represents an example output diagram for a typical controller. As shown in the figure, the actual value starts at an initial value (here zero), and gradually moves to reach and stabilize at a value close to the desired value. To ensure that a controller design is satisfactory, engineers perform simulations, and analyze the output simulation diagram with respect to a number of requirements. After careful investigations, we identified the following requirements for controllers:

Liveness (functional): The controller shall guarantee that the actual value will reach and stabilize at the desired value within x seconds. This is to ensure that the controller indeed satisfies its main functional requirement.

Smoothness (safety): The actual value shall not change abruptly when it is close to the desired one. That is, the difference between the actual and desired values shall not exceed w, once the difference has already reached v for the first time. This is to ensure that the controller does not damage any physical devices by sharply changing the actual value when the error is small.

Responsiveness (performance): The difference between the actual and desired values shall be at most y within z seconds, ensuring the controller responds within a time limit.

The above three generic requirements are illustrated on a typical controller output diagram in Figure 2 where the parameters x, v, w, y, and z are represented. As shown in the figure, given specific controller requirements with concrete parameters and given an output diagram of a controller under test, we can determine whether that particular controller output satisfies the given requirements.

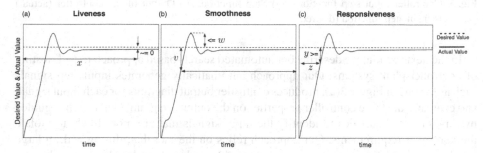

Fig. 2. The controller requirements illustrated on the controller output: (a) Liveness, (b) Smoothness, and (c) Responsiveness

Having discussed the controller requirements and outputs, we now describe how we generate input test values for a given controller. Typically, controllers have a large number of configuration parameters that affect their behaviors. For the configuration parameters, we use a value assignment commonly used for HiL testing, and focus on two essential controller inputs in our MiL testing approach: (1) the initial actual value, and (2) the desired value. Among these two inputs, the desired value can be easily manipulated externally. However, since the controller is a closed loop system, it is not generally possible to start the system from an arbitrary initial state. In other words, the initial actual state depends on the plant model and cannot be manipulated externally. For the same reason, in output simulation diagrams (e.g., Figure 2), it is often assumed that the controller starts from an initial value of zero. However, assuming that the system always starts from zero is like testing a cruise controller only for positive car speed increases, and missing a whole range of speed decreasing scenarios.

To eliminate this restriction, we provide two consecutive signals for the desired value of the controller (see Figure 3(a)): The first one sets the controller at the *initial* desired value, and the second signal moves the controller to the *final* desired value. We refer to these input signals as *step functions* or *step signals*. The lengths of the two signals in a step signal are equal (see Figure 3(a)), and should be sufficiently long to give the controller enough time to stabilize at each of the initial and final desired values. Figure 3(b) shows an example of a controller output diagram for the input step function in Figure 3(a). The three controller properties can be evaluated on the actual output diagram in Figure 3(b) in a similar way as that shown in Figure 2.

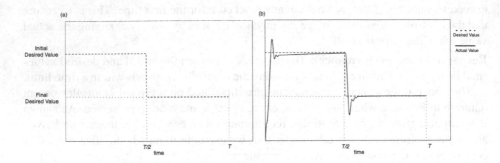

Fig. 3. Controller input step functions: (a) Step function. (b) Output of the controller (actual) given the input step function (desired).

In the next section, we describe our automated search-based approach to MiL testing of controller-plant systems. Our approach automatically generates input step signals such as the one in Figure 3(a), produces controller output diagrams for each input signal, and evaluates the three controller properties on the output diagram. Our search is guided by a number of heuristics to identify the input signals that are more likely to violate the controller requirements. Our approach relies on the fact that, during MiL, a large number of simulations can be generated quickly and without breaking any physical devices. Using this characteristic, we propose to replace the existing manual MiL testing with our search-based automated approach that enables the evaluation of a large number of output simulation diagrams and the identification of critical controller input values.

4 Search-Based Automated Controller MiL Testing

In this section, we describe our search-based algorithm for automating MiL testing of controllers. We first describe the search elements and discuss how we formulate controller testing as a search problem in Section 4.1. We, then, show how we combine search algorithms to guide and automate MiL testing of controllers in Section 4.2.

4.1 Search Elements

Given a controller-plant model and a set of controller properties, our search algorithms, irrespective of their heuristics, perform the following common tasks: (1) They generate input signals to the controller, i.e., step function in Figure 3(a). (2) They receive the output, i.e., Actual in Figure 3(b), from the model, and evaluate the output against the controller properties formalizing requirements. Below, we first formalize the controller input and output, and define the search space for our problem. We then formalize the three objective functions to evaluate the properties over the controller output.

Controller input and output: Let $\mathcal{T} = \{0, \ldots, T\}$ be a set of time points during which we observe the controller behavior, and let min and max be the minimum and maximum values for the Actual and Desired attributes in Figure 1. In our work, since input is assumed to be a step function, the observation time T is chosen to be long enough so that the controller can reach and stabilize at two different Desired positions successively (e.g., see Figure 3(b)). Note that Actual and Desired are of the same type and bounded within the same range, denoted by [min...max]. As discussed in Section 3, the test inputs are step functions representing the Desired values (e.g. Figure 3(a)). We define an input step function in our approach to be a function Desired : $\mathcal{T} \to \{$min,...,max$\}$ such that there exist a pair Initial Desired and Final Desired of values in [min...max] that satisfy the following conditions:

$\forall t \cdot 0 \leq t < \frac{T}{2} \Rightarrow$ Desired$(t) =$ Initial Desired $\wedge$
$\forall t \cdot \frac{T}{2} \leq t < T \Rightarrow$ Desired$(t) =$ Final Desired

We define the controller output, i.e., Actual, to be a function Actual : $\mathcal{T} \to \{$min,...,max$\}$ that is produced by the given controller-plant model, e.g., in MATLAB/Simulink environment.

Search Space: The search space in our problem is the set of all possible input functions, i.e., the Desired function. Each Desired function is characterized by the pair Initial Desired and Final Desired values. In control system development, it is common to use floating-point data types at MiL level. Therefore, the search space in our work is the set of all pairs of floating point values for Initial Desired and Final Desired within the [min...max] range.

Objective Functions: Our goal is to guide the search to identify input functions in the search space that are more likely to break the properties discussed in Section 3. To do so, we create three objective functions corresponding to the three controller properties.

- **Liveness:** Let x be the liveness property parameter in Section 3. We define the liveness objective function O_L as: $max_{x+\frac{T}{2}<t\leq T}\{|$Desired$(t) -$ Actual$(t)|\}$
  I.e., O_L is the max of the difference between Desired and Actual after time $x + \frac{T}{2}$.

- **Smoothness**: Let v be the smoothness property parameter in Section 3. Let $tc \in \mathcal{T}$ be such that $tc > \frac{T}{2}$ and

  $|$Desired$(tc) -$ Actual$(tc)| \leq v \wedge$
  $\forall t \cdot \frac{T}{2} \leq t < tc \Rightarrow |$Desired$(t) -$ Actual$(t)| > v$

  That is, tc is the first point in time after $\frac{T}{2}$ where the difference between Actual and Final Desired values has reached v. We then define the smoothness objective function O_S as: $max_{tc<t\leq T}\{|$Desired$(t) -$ Actual$(t)|\}$
  That is, O_S is the maximum difference between Desired and Actual after tc.

- **Responsiveness**: Let y be the responsiveness parameter in Section 3. We define the responsiveness objective function O_R to be equal to tr such that $tr \in \mathcal{T}$ and $tr > \frac{T}{2}$ and

  $|$Desired$(tr) -$ Actual$(tr)| \leq y \wedge$
  $\forall t \cdot \frac{T}{2} \leq t < tr \Rightarrow |$Desired$(t) -$ Actual$(t)| > y$

  That is, O_R is the first point in time after $\frac{T}{2}$ where the difference between Actual and Final Desired values has reached y.

We did not use w from the smoothness and z from the responsiveness properties in definitions of O_S and O_R. These parameters determine pass/fail conditions for test cases, and are not required to guide the search. Further, w and z depend on the specific hardware characteristics and vary from customer to customer. Hence, they are not known at the MiL level. Specifically, we define O_S to measure the maximum overshoot rather than to determine whether an overshoot exceeds w, or not. Similarly, we define O_R to measure the actual response time without comparing it with z.

The three above objective functions are heuristics and provide numerical approximations of the controller properties, allowing us to compare different test inputs. The higher the objective function value, the more likely it is that the test input violates the requirement corresponding to that objective function. We use these objective functions in our search algorithms discussed in the next section.

4.2 Search Algorithms

Figure 4 shows an overview of our automated MiL testing approach. In the first step, we receive a controller-plant model (e.g., in MATLAB/Simulink) and a set of objective functions obtained from requirements. We divide the input search space into a set of regions, and assign to each region a value indicating the evaluation of a given input objective function on that region based on random search (Exploration). We refer to the result as a *HeatMap* diagram [11]. Based on domain expert knowledge, we select some of the regions that are more likely to include critical and realistic errors. In the second step, we focus our search on the selected regions and employ a single-state heuristic search to identify within those regions the worst-case scenarios to test the controller.

Fig. 4. An overview of our automated approach to MiL testing of continuous controllers

In the first step of our approach in Figure 4, we apply a random (unguided) search to the entire search space. The search explores diverse test inputs to provide an unbiased estimate of the average objective function values at different regions of the search space. In the second step, we apply a heuristic single-state search to a selection of regions in order to find worst-case scenarios that may violate the controller properties.

Figure 5(a) shows the random search algorithm used in the first step. The algorithm takes as input a controller-plant model M and an objective function O, and produces a HeatMap diagram (e.g., see Figure 5(b)). Briefly, the algorithm divides the search space S of M into a number of equal regions. It then generates a random point p in S in line 4. The dimensions of p characterize an input step function `Desired` which is given to M as input in line 6. The model M is executed in Matlab/Simulink to generate the `Actual` output. The objective function O is then computed based on the `Desired` and `Actual` functions. The tuple (p, o) where o is the value of the objective function at p is added to P. The algorithm stops when the number of generated points in each region is at least N. Finding an appropriate value for N is a trade off between accuracy and efficiency. Since executing M is relatively expensive, it is not efficient to generate many points (large N). Likewise, a small number of points in each region is unlikely to give

(a)   (b)

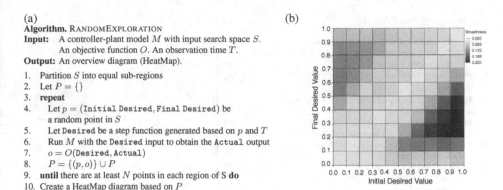

Algorithm. RANDOMEXPLORATION
Input: A controller-plant model M with input search space S.
　　　　An objective function O. An observation time T.
Output: An overview diagram (HeatMap).

1.　Partition S into equal sub-regions
2.　Let $P = \{\}$
3.　**repeat**
4.　　Let $p = (\text{Initial Desired}, \text{Final Desired})$ be
　　　a random point in S
5.　　Let Desired be a step function generated based on p and T
6.　　Run M with the Desired input to obtain the Actual output
7.　　$o = O(\text{Desired}, \text{Actual})$
8.　　$P = \{(p, o)\} \cup P$
9.　**until** there are at least N points in each region of S **do**
10.　Create a HeatMap diagram based on P

Fig. 5. The first step of our approach in Figure 4: (a) The exploration algorithm. (b) An example HeatMap diagram produced by the algorithm in (a).

us an accurate estimate of the average objective function for that region. In Section 5, we discuss how we select a value for N for our controller case study.

The output of the algorithm in Figure 5(a) is a set P of (p, o) tuples where p is a point and o is the objective function value for p. We visualize the set P via HeatMap diagrams [11] where the axes are the initial and final desired values. In HeatMaps, each region is assigned the average value of the values of the points within that region. The intervals of the region values are then mapped into different shades, generating a shaded diagrams such as the one in Figure 5(b). In our work, we generate three HeatMap diagrams corresponding to the three objective functions O_L, O_S and O_R (see Section 4.1). We run the algorithm once, but we compute O_L, O_S and O_R separately for each point.

The HeatMap diagrams generated in the first step are reviewed by domain experts.They select a set of regions that are more likely to include realistic and critical inputs. For example, the diagram in Figure 5(b) is generated based on an air compressor controller model evaluated for the smoothness objective function O_S. This controller compresses the air by moving a flap between its open position (indicated by 0) and its closed position (indicated by 1.0). There are about 10 to 12 dark regions, i.e., the regions with the highest O_S values in Figure 5(b). These regions have initial flap positions between 0.4 to 1.0 and final flap positions between 0.5 and 1.0. Among these regions, the domain expert chooses to focus on the regions with the initial value between 0.8 and 1.0. This is because, in practice, there is more probability of damage when a closed (or a nearly closed) flap is being moved.

Figure 6(a) presents our single-state search algorithm for the second step of the procedure in Figure 4. The single-state search starts with the point with the worst (highest) objective function value among those computed by the random search in Figure 5(a). It then iteratively generates new points by tweaking the current point (line 8) and evaluates the given objective function on the points. Finally, it reports the point with the worst (highest) objective function value. In contrast to random search, the single-state search is guided by an objective function and performs a tweak operation. The design of the tweak is very important and affects the effectiveness of the search. In our work,

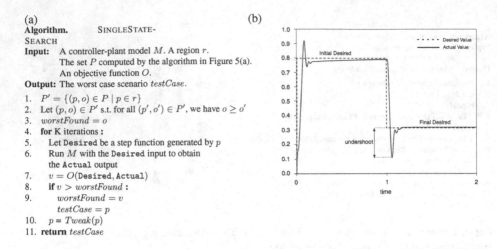

(a)
Algorithm.   SINGLESTATE-
SEARCH
Input: A controller-plant model M. A region r.
        The set P computed by the algorithm in Figure 5(a).
        An objective function O.
Output: The worst case scenario $testCase$.

1. $P' = \{(p, o) \in P \mid p \in r\}$
2. Let $(p, o) \in P'$ s.t. for all $(p', o') \in P'$, we have $o \geq o'$
3. $worstFound = o$
4. **for** K iterations :
5.   Let Desired be a step function generated by p
6.   Run M with the Desired input to obtain
        the Actual output
7. $v = O(\text{Desired}, \text{Actual})$
8.   **if** $v > worstFound$:
9. $worstFound = v$
            $testCase = p$
10. $p = Tweak(p)$
11. **return** $testCase$

Fig. 6. The second step of our approach in Figure 4: (a) The single-state search algorithm. (b) An example output diagram produced by the algorithm in (a)

we use the $(1+1)$EA tweak operator [10]. Specifically, at each iteration, we shift p in the space by adding values x' and y' to the dimensions of p. The x' and y' values are selected from a normal distribution with mean $\mu = 0$ and variance σ^2. The value of σ enables us to control the degree of exploration vs. exploitation in the search. With a low σ, $(1+1)$EA becomes highly exploitative allowing to reach an optimum fast. But for a noisy landscape, we need a more explorative $(1+1)$EA with a high σ [10]. We discuss in Section 5 how we select σ. Since the search is driven by the objective function, we have to run the search three times separately for O_L, O_S and O_R.

Figure 6(b) shows the worst case scenario computed by our algorithm for the smoothness objective function applied to an air compressor controller. As shown in the figure, the controller has an undershoot around 0.2 when it moves from an initial desired value of 0.8 and is about to stabilize at a final desired value of 0.3.

5   Evaluation

To empirically evaluate our approach, we performed several experiments reported in this section. The experiments are designed to answer the following research questions:

RQ1: In practice, do the HeatMap diagrams help determine a list of critical regions?
RQ2: Does our single-state search algorithm effectively and efficiently identify worst-case scenarios within a region?
RQ3: Can we use the information in the HeatMap diagrams to explain the performance of the single-state search in the second step?

Setup. To perform the experiment, we applied our approach in Figure 4 to a case study from our industry partner. Our case study is a **S**upercharger **B**ypass *Flap* **P**osition *Control (SBPC)* module. SBPC is an air compressor blowing into a turbo-compressor to increase the air pressure, and consequently the engine torque at low engine speeds. The SBPC module includes a controller component that determines the position of a mechanical flap. In SBPC, the desired and actual values in Figure 1 represent the desired and actual positions of the flap, respectively. The flap position is a float value bounded within $[0...1]$ (open when 0 and closed when 1.0). The SBPC module is implemented and simulated in Matlab/Simulink. Its Simulink model has 21 input and 42 output variables, among which the flap position is the main controller output. It is a complex and hierarchical function with 34 sub-components decomposed into 6 abstraction levels. On average, each sub-component has 21 Simulink blocks and 4 MATLAB function blocks. We set the simulation time (the observation time) to 2 sec, i.e., $T = 2s$. The controller property parameters were given as follows: $x = 0.9s$, $y = 0.03$, and $v = 0.05$.

We ran the experiment on Amazon micro instance machines which is equal to two Amazon EC2 compute units. Each EC2 compute unit has a CPU capacity of a 1.0-1.2 GHz 2007 Xeon processor. A single 2-sec simulation of the SBPC Simulink model (e.g., Figure 6(b)) takes about 31 sec on the Amazon machine.

RQ1. A HeatMap diagram is effective if it has the following properties: (1) The region shades are stable and do not change on different runs of the exploration algorithm. (2) The regions are not so fine grained that it leads to generating too many points during exploration. (3) The regions are not too coarse grained such that the points generated within one region have drastically different objective function values.

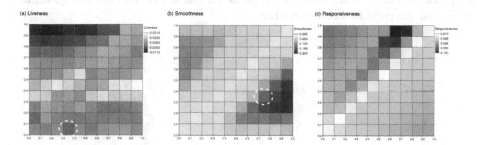

Fig. 7. HeatMap diagrams generated for our case study for the Liveness (a), Smoothness (b) and Responsiveness (c) requirements

For the SBPC module, the search space S is the set of all points with float dimensions in the $[0..1] \times [0..1]$ square. We decided to generate around 1000 points in S during the exploration step. We divided up S into 100 equal squares with 0.1×0.1 dimensions, and let $N = 10$, i.e., at least 10 points are simulated in each region during exploration. The exploration algorithm takes on average about 8.5 hours on an Amazon machine and can therefore be run overnight.

We executed our exploration algorithm three times for SBPC and for each of our three objective functions. For each function, the region shades remained completely unchanged across the three different runs. In all the resulting HeatMap diagrams, the points in the same region have close objective function values. On average, the variance over the objective function values for an individual region was about 0.001. Hence, we concluded that $N = 10$ is suitable for our case study.

The resulting HeatMap diagrams, shown in Figure 7, were presented to our industry partner. They found the diagrams visually appealing and useful. They noted that the diagrams, in addition to enabling the identification of critical regions, can be used in the following ways: (1) They can gain confidence about the controller behaviors over the light shaded regions of the diagrams. (2) The diagrams enable them to investigate potential anomalies in the controller behavior. Specifically, since controllers have continuous behaviors, we expect a smooth shade change over the search space going from clear to dark. A sharp contrast such as a dark region neighboring a light-shaded region may potentially indicate an abnormal behavior that needs to be further investigated.

RQ2. For the second step of our approach in Figure 4, we opt for a single-state search method in contrast to a population search such as Genetic Algorithms (GA) [10]. In our work, a single computation of the fitness function takes a long time ($31s$), and hence, fitness computation for a set of points (a population) would be very inefficient. We implemented the *Tweak* statement in the algorithm in Figure 6(a) using the (1+1) EA heuristic [10] by letting $\sigma = 0.01$. Given $\sigma = 0.01$ and a point located at the center of a 0.1×0.1 region, the result of the tweak stays inside the region with a probability around 99%. Obviously, this probability decreases when the point moves closer to the corners. In our search, we discard the points that are generated outside of the regions, and never generate simulations for them. In addition, for $\sigma = 0.01$, the (1+1) EA search tends to converge to a point not far from the search starting point. This is because with the probability of 70%, the result of the tweak for this search does not change neither dimension of a point further than 0.01.

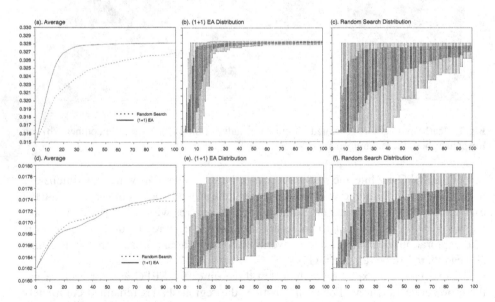

Fig. 8. Comparing (1+1) EA and random search average and distribution values for two representative HeatMap regions: (a)-(c) Diagrams related to the region specified by dashed white circle in Figure 7(b). (d)-(f) Diagrams related to the region specified by dashed white circle in Figure 7(a).

We applied (1+1)EA to 11 different regions of the HeatMap diagrams in Figure 7 that were selected by our domain experts among the regions with the highest objective function average values. Among these, three were chosen for Liveness, four for Smoothness and four for Responsiveness. As shown in Figure 6(a), for each region, we start the search from the worst point found in that region during the exploration step. This enables us to reuse the existing search result from the first step. Each time we run (1+1)EA for 100 iterations, i.e., $K = 100$. This is because the search has always reached a plateau after 100 iterations in our experiments. On average, both (1+1)EA and random search took about around one hour to run for 100 iterations.

We identified 11 worst case scenarios. Figure 6(b) shows the simulation for one of these scenarios concerning smoothness. The simulations for all 11 regions indicate potential violations of the controller requirements that might be due to errors in the controller or plant models. To precisely identify the sources of violations and to take the right course of action, our industry partner plans to apply the resulting scenarios at the HiL testing level. In our work, we could identify better results than test scenarios devised by domain experts. For example, Figure 6(b) shows an undershoot scenario around 0.2 for the SBPC controller. The maximum identified undershoot/overshoot for this controller by manual testing was around 0.05. Similarly, for the responsiveness property, we found a scenario in which it takes $200ms$ for the actual value to get close enough to the desired value while the maximum corresponding value in manual testing was around $50ms$.

Note that in all the 11 regions, the results of the single-state search (step 2 in Figure 4) showed improvements over the scenarios identified by pure exploration (step 1 in Figure 4). On average, the results of the single-state search showed a 12% increase for liveness, a 35% increase for smoothness, and a 18% increase for responsiveness compared to the result of the exploration algorithm.

Random search within each selected region was used as a baseline to evaluate the efficiency and effectiveness of (1+1)EA in finding worst-case scenarios. In order to account for randomness in these algorithms, each of them was run for 50 rounds. We used 22 concurrent Amazon machines to run random search and (1+1)EA for 11 regions. The comparison results for two representative HeatMap regions are shown in Figure 8. Figures 8(a)-(c) are related to the HeatMap region specified in Figure 7(b), and Figures 8(d)-(f) are related to that in Figure 7(a). Figures 8(a) and (d) compare the average objective function values for 50 different runs of (1+1)EA and random search over 100 iterations, and Figures 8(b) and (e) (resp. (c) and (f)) show the distributions of the objective function values for (1+1)EA (resp. random search) over 100 iterations using box plots. To avoid clutter, we removed the outliers from the box plots.

Note that the computation time for a single (1+1)EA iteration and a single random search iteration are both almost equal to the computation time for an objective function, i.e., $31s$. Hence, the horizontal axis of the diagrams in Figure 8 shows the number of iterations instead of the computation time. In addition, we start both random search and (1+1)EA from the same initial point, i.e., the worst case from the exploration step.

Overall in all the regions, (1+1)EA eventually reaches its plateau at a value higher than the random search plateau value. Further, (1+1)EA is more deterministic than random, i.e., the distribution of (1+1)EA has a smaller variance than that of random search, especially when reaching the plateau (see Figure 8). In some regions (e.g., Figure 8(d)), however, random reaches its plateau slightly faster than (1+1)EA, while in some other regions (e.g. Figure 8(a)), (1+1)EA is faster. We will discuss the relationship between the region landscape and the performance of (1+1)EA in **RQ3**.

RQ3. We drew the landscape for the 11 regions in our experiment. For example, Figure 9 shows the landscape for two selected regions in Figures 7(a) and 7(b). Specifically, Figure 9(a) shows the landscape for the region in Figure 7(b) where (1+1)EA is faster than random, and Figure 9(b) shows the landscape for the region in Figure 7(a) where (1+1)EA is slower than random search.

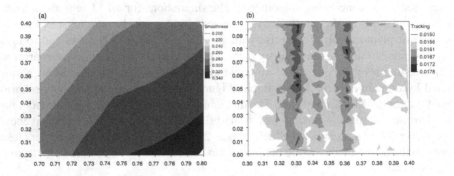

Fig. 9. Diagrams representing the landscape for two representative HeatMap regions: (a) Landscape for the region in Figure 7(b). (b) Landscape for the region in Figure 7(a).

Our observations show that the regions surrounded mostly by dark shaded regions typically have a clear gradient between the initial point of the search and the worst case point (see e.g., Figure 9(a)). However, dark regions located in a generally light shaded area have a noisier shape with several local optimum (see e.g., Figure 9(b)). It is known that for regions like Figure 9(a), exploitative search works best, while for those like Figure 9(b), explorative search is most suitable [10]. This is confirmed in our work where for Figure 9(a), our exploitative search, i.e., (1+1)EA with $\sigma = 0.01$, is faster and more effective than random search, whereas for Figure 9(b), our search is slower than random search. We applied a more explorative version of (1+1)EA where we let $\sigma = 0.03$ to the region in Figure 9(b). The result (Figure 10) shows that the more explorative (1+1)EA is now both faster and more effective than random search. We conjecture that, from the HeatMap diagrams, we can predict which search algorithm to use for the single-state search step. Specifically, for dark regions surrounded by dark shaded areas, we suggest an exploitative (1+1)EA (e.g., $\sigma = 0.01$), while for dark regions located in light shaded areas, we recommend a more explorative (1+1)EA (e.g., $\sigma = 0.03$).

6   Related Work

Testing continuous control systems presents a number of challenges, and is not yet supported by existing tools and techniques [4,1,3]. The modeling languages that have been

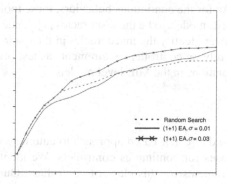

Fig. 10. Comparing average values for (1+1) EA with $\sigma = 0.01$, (1+1) EA with $\sigma = 0.03$, and random search for the region in Figure 7(a)

developed to capture embedded software systems mostly deal with discrete-event or mixed discrete-continuous systems [5,1,7]. Examples of these languages include timed automata [12], hybrid automata [6], and Stateflow [13]. Automated reasoning tools built for these languages largely rely on formal methods, e.g., model checking [4]. Formal methods are more amenable to verification of logical and state-based behaviors such as invariance and reachability properties. Further, their scalability to large and realistic systems is still unknown. In our work, we focused on pure continuous systems, and evaluated our work on a representative industrial case study.

Search-based techniques have been previously applied to discrete event embedded systems in the context of model-based testing [14]. The main prerequisite in these approaches, e.g [15], is that the system or its environment has to be modeled in UML or its extensions. While being a modeling standard, UML has been rarely used in control system development. In our work, we apply our search to Matlab/Simulink models that are actually developed by our industry partner as part of their development process. Furthermore, our approach is not specifically tied to any particular modeling language, and can be applied to any executable controller-plant model.

Continuous controllers have been widely studied in the control theory domain where the focus has been to optimize their design for a specific platform or a specific hardware configuration [3,4]. There has been some approaches to automated signal analysis where simulation outputs are verified against customized *boolean* properties implemented via Matlab blocks [16]. In our work, we automatically evaluate *quantitative* objective functions over controller outputs. In addition, the signal analysis method in [16] does neither address systematic testing, nor does it include identification and formalization of the requirements.

Finally, a number of commercial verification and testing tools have been developed, aiming to generate test cases for MATLAB/Simulink models, namely the Simulink Design Verifier software [8], and Reactis Tester [9]. To evaluate requirements using these tools, the MATLAB/Simulink models need to be augmented with boolean assertions. The existing assertion checking mechanism, however, handles combinatorial and logical blocks only, and fails to evaluate the continuous MATLAB/Simulink blocks (e.g., integrator blocks) [1]. As for the continuous behaviors, these tools follow a methodology that considers the MiL models to be the test oracles [1]. Under this assumption, the MiL level testing can never identify the inaccuracies in the controller-plant models. In our work, however, we rely on controller requirements as test oracles, and are able to identify requirement violations in the MiL level models.

7   Conclusions

In this paper, we proposed a search-based approach to automate generation of Model-in-the-loop level test cases for continuous controllers. We identified and formalized a set of common requirements for this class of controllers. Our proposed technique relies on a combination of explorative and exploitative search algorithms. We evaluated our approach by applying it to an automotive air compressor module. Our experiments showed that our approach automatically generates several test cases that had not been previously found by manual testing based on domain expertise. The test cases indicate potential violations of the requirements at the MiL level, and our industry partner is interested in investigating them further by evaluating the test cases at the Hardware-in-the-loop level. In addition, we demonstrated the effectiveness and efficiency of our search strategy by showing that our approach computes better test cases and is faster than a pure random test case generation strategy.

In future, we plan to perform more case studies with various controllers and from different domains to demonstrate generalizability and scalability of our work. In addition, we are interested to experiment with various search methods and improve our results by tuning and combining them. Finally, in collaboration with our industry partner, we plan to expand upon our current MiL testing results and investigate the identified test cases at the HiL level.

References

1. Skruch, P., Panel, M., Kowalczyk, B.: Model-Based Testing in Embedded Automotive Systems, 1st edn. CRC Press (2011)
2. Nise, N.S.: Control Systems Engineering, 4th edn. John-Wiely Sons (2004)
3. Lee, E., Seshia, S.: Introduction to Embedded Systems: A Cyber-Physical Systems Approach (2010), http://leeseshia.org
4. Henzinger, T., Sifakis, J.: The embedded systems design challenge. In: Misra, J., Nipkow, T., Sekerinski, E. (eds.) FM 2006. LNCS, vol. 4085, pp. 1–15. Springer, Heidelberg (2006)
5. Pretschner, A., Broy, M., Krüger, I., Stauner, T.: Software engineering for automotive systems: A roadmap. In: FOSE, pp. 55–71 (2007)
6. Henzinger, T.: The theory of hybrid automata. In: LICS, pp. 278–292 (1996)
7. Stauner, T.: Properties of hybrid systems-a computer science perspective. Formal Methods in System Design 24(3), 223–259 (2004)
8. Inc., T.M.: Simulink, http://www.mathworks.nl/products/simulink
9. Inc. Reactive Systems,
http://www.reactive-systems.com/
simulink-testing-validation.html
10. Luke, S.: Essentials of Metaheuristics. Lulu (2009),
http://cs.gmu.edu/~sean/book/metaheuristics/

11. Grinstein, G., Trutschl, M., Cvek, U.: High-dimensional visualizations. In: 7th Workshop on Data Mining Conference KDD Workshop, pp. 7–19 (2001)
12. Alur, R.: Timed automata. In: Halbwachs, N., Peled, D.A. (eds.) CAV 1999. LNCS, vol. 1633, pp. 8–22. Springer, Heidelberg (1999)
13. Sahbani, A., Pascal, J.: Simulation of hyibrd systems using stateflow. In: ESM, pp. 271–275 (2000)
14. Neto, A.C.D., Subramanyan, R., Vieira, M., Travassos, G.H.: A survey on model-based testing approaches: A systematic review. In: ASE, pp. 31–36 (2007)
15. Iqbal, M.Z., Arcuri, A., Briand, L.: Combining search-based and adaptive random testing strategies for environment model-based testing of real-time embedded systems. In: SBSE (2012)
16. Zander-Nowicka, J.: Model-based Testing of Real-Time Embedded Systems in the Automotive Domain. PhD thesis, Elektrotechnik und Informatik der Technischen Universitat, Berlin (2009)

Predicting Regression Test Failures Using Genetic Algorithm-Selected Dynamic Performance Analysis Metrics

Michael Mayo and Simon Spacey

Waikato University, Hamilton, New Zealand
{mmayo,sspacey}@waikato.ac.nz
http://cs.waikato.ac.nz/

Abstract. A novel framework for predicting regression test failures is proposed. The basic principle embodied in the framework is to use performance analysis tools to capture the runtime behaviour of a program as it executes each test in a regression suite. The performance information is then used to build a dynamically predictive model of test outcomes. Our framework is evaluated using a genetic algorithm for dynamic metric selection in combination with state-of-the-art machine learning classifiers. We show that if a program is modified and some tests subsequently fail, then it is possible to predict with considerable accuracy which of the remaining tests will also fail which can be used to help prioritise tests in time constrained testing environments.

Keywords: regression testing, test failure prediction, program analysis, machine learning, genetic metric selection.

1 Introduction

Regression testing is a software engineering activity in which a suite of tests covering the expected behaviour of a software system are executed to verify a system's integrity after modification. As new features are added to a system, regression tests are re-run and outputs compared against expected results to ensure new feature code and system changes have not introduced bugs into old feature sets.

Ideally, we would like to run all regression tests as part of the normal development process when each new feature is committed. However, regression testing the large number of tests required to cover (an ever expanding) previous feature set can take considerable time. For example, the regression test suite [14, 15] used in Section 4 of this work takes approximately 12 hours to execute fully in our environment which makes on-line regression testing difficult.

Recently authors concerned with regression testing have began looking to performance analysis and machine learning to aid software engineering [1] and in this paper we propose a method that joins performance analysis [2], machine

G. Ruhe and Y. Zhang (Eds.): SSBSE 2013, LNCS 8084, pp. 158–171, 2013.
© Springer-Verlag Berlin Heidelberg 2013

learning [3] and genetic algorithms [4] to predict the outcome of unexecuted regression tests in a large regression test suite. A contribution of our work is the inclusion of a set of unique execution metrics measured from the dynamic execution path of the program to compliment the pass/fail and coverage metrics used in previous work [5]. Since the dynamic execution paths corresponding to different test inputs on the same program, to greater or lesser degrees, overlap, this information is useful for modelling the interrelationships between tests and therefore for predicting test outcomes as we will soon show.

One problem with modelling interactions based on execution paths is that even small programs can have a very high execution path trace length and therefore there can be an extremely large number of dynamic metrics describing even a simple test's execution [6]. We solve this problem by using dynamic analysis tools to compress the program's execution trace information into a set of key metrics that we consider could be important determiners and then we use a genetic algorithm to select the best subset of these metrics for a final predictive model as detailed later in this paper.

Our results show that it is indeed possible to predict, with high accuracy, which future regression tests will fail. Additionally we present results showing which of our measurement metrics has the greatest impact on model prediction accuracy. For software engineers, the results presented in this paper demonstrate that the proposed approach could be useful for either ranking tests (e.g. in order to execute those most likely to fail first) or for skipping tests (e.g. in order to avoid executing both tests in a pair if the test outcomes have high correlation). For dynamic instrumentation tool makers and quality assurance professionals the results indicate the value of key performance analysis metrics and could help focus future research in dynamic measurement tool development.

2 Dynamic Performance Analysis

Before we introduce our algorithm to predict regression test correlations, we first present an overview of the Open Performance Analysis Toolkit (OpenPAT) [2] which provides the dynamic execution path measurements we need. OpenPAT [2] is an open source performance analysis toolkit that analyses program execution paths.

OpenPAT is derived from 3S [7,8] and, like its predecessor, OpenPAT instruments programs by inserting measurement stubs at critical points in a program's assembly code as illustrated in Figure 1(a). At runtime, the stubs back-up the main program's state and measure characteristics such as timing information which they pass on to one or more analysis tools for consolidation and later reporting as illustrated in Figure 1(b).

The approach of static assembly instrumentation and dynamic analysis can be used with any program that compiles to assembly [7,8] and combines the low execution overhead advantages of traditional one time instrumentation toolkits such as SUIF [9] with the dynamic performance measurement accuracy advantages of modern frameworks such as Gilk [10], Valgrind [11] and Pin [12]. OpenPAT

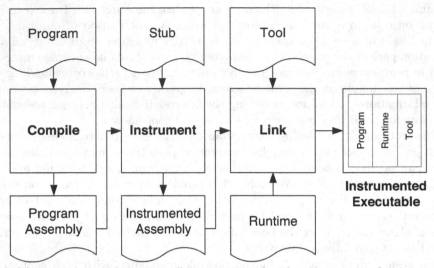

(a) Source assembly is statically instrumented with stubs at critical points.

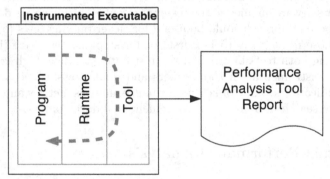

(b) Stubs pass dynamic measurements (dotted line) on to analysis tools at runtime.

Fig. 1. The Open Performance Analysis Toolkit (OpenPAT) approach of combining static instrumentation with dynamic analysis

extends the 3S meaning of a "program that compiles to assembly" to include programs that compile to assembly bytecodes running on a virtual machine [2] such as .NET and Java so that the same tools can be used to analyse programs targeted for native and interpreted environments. In addition to allowing the same tools to gather runtime measurements for a wide range of languages, OpenPAT adds several other features that can be of value for regression testing including test case code coverage metrics, ranged instrumentation and assembly block to source code correspondence information [2].

OpenPAT comes with a number of analysis tools that provide unique dynamic and structural analysis metrics. We will concentrate on the metrics provided by just one of these tools, the OpenPAT version 3.0.0 `hotspot` tool discussed further in Section 3.2, which will be sufficient for demonstrating that we can provide high regression test prediction accuracy with our approach of combining dynamic performance metrics with machine learning and genetic algorithms which we describe next.

3   Approach to Predicting Regression Test Failures

We now describe the framework we have constructed for building predictive models of regression test outcomes based on dynamic execution measurements. We begin with an overview of the framework followed by a subsection describing the role of evolutionary search in our approach.

3.1   Framework Overview

Our framework for predicting test failures and ranking tests is explained with reference to Figure 2. The hypothesis underlying our framework is that dynamic execution metrics measured for a correct execution of a program contain characteristics that describe how the program needs to operate internally in order to produce valid outputs and that machine learning can use this information to better discern the relationships between different tests than simply relying on the test code coverage intersection metrics of previous work [5].

The basic framework process is to run a suite of initial regression tests on a program at a time when the program is known to be correct and to save the correct test results for future comparison as in an unguided traditional testing approach. At the same time, we also record dynamic and structural metrics for the program's execution for every test case using OpenPAT. These additional OpenPAT metrics are referred to as "per test metrics" in Figure 2.

After the program has been modified we re-run the same tests. If the modification has introduced a bug in previous tested features one or more tests will fail. As each test completes, our framework takes the set of tests that have already been executed (where the executed tests are labelled with either "P" or "F" for pass or fail respectively), combines them with the dynamic metrics measured for the correct version of the program, and constructs a table of labelled examples suitable for machine learning.

The table consists of one row for each test that has been executed with columns corresponding to the metrics measured by OpenPAT for the original "correct" version of the program and the known pass/fail results from the "incorrect" version. The table is used to build a dynamically predictive model of test failure as shown in Figure 2. This model in turn is used to label all of the remaining outstanding tests with a failure probability based on the original OpenPAT measurements that can be used to rank tests.

With the test failure rank predictions, a developer is equipped to decide whether to:

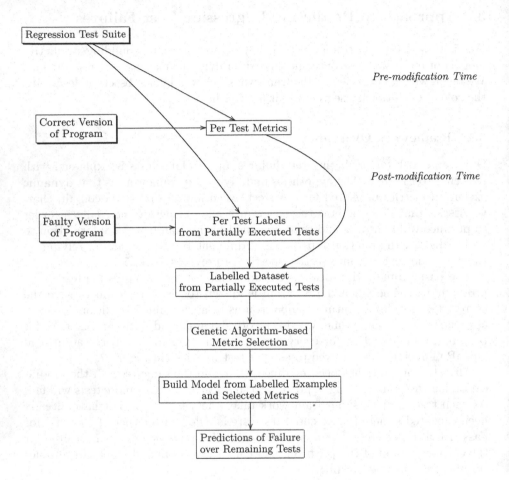

Fig. 2. Flow of information in the test failure prediction system. The inputs are the regression test suite and two versions of the program, one correct and one faulty.

Table 1. Structural and dynamic metrics measured by our version of the OpenPAT `hotspot` tool. We added the `ticks_min` and `ticks_max` timing metrics to the basic `hotspot` tool provided in the OpenPAT version 3.0.0 pre-release 1 distribution our selves by simply inserting min and max counters in the `_OP_MEASUREMENT_T` and per entrance updates in the OpenPAT version 3.0.0 `hotspot` `_OP_TOOL_ANALYSE` function.

Metric	Class	Description
`source_file`	Structural	Source file where a code section is located
`source_line`	Structural	Line in the source file being executed
`instructions`	Structural	Number of assembly instructions in a code section
`order`	Dynamic	Order in which code sections were first executed
`entries`	Dynamic	Number of times a code section was executed
`ticks_min`	Dynamic	Minimum CPU cycles a code section took to execute
`ticks_max`	Dynamic	Maximum CPU cycles a code section took to execute
`ticks_sum`	Dynamic	Total CPU cycles to execute a code section

1. execute the remaining tests that are most likely to fail first in order to provide additional information to support their debug process or
2. execute the remaining tests that are *not* likely to fail first to identify if unrelated features are affected or
3. execute the remaining tests that the learning classifier is not sure about (probability of failure around 50%) in order to strengthen the prediction probabilities for the remaining tests, which requires retraining the model.

The exact decision will be developer, context and business process dependent, but the decision is supported by our algorithm's predictions which we need to be of high quality to be of any practical value.

3.2   Program Test Metrics

The OpenPAT toolkit includes a wide range of metrics available at a fine-grained level for each code section aka "assembly basic block", in the program. Because a typical program can have a large number of code sections [22], we can quickly obtain an extremely high dimensionality (that being code sections times metrics per section) in the dataset. Unfortunately, many machine learning algorithms do not perform well when data dimensionality is high compared to the number of labelled examples used for training [21]. Therefore it is desirable to reduce the data dimensionality somehow and we discuss our use of a genetic algorithm for metric selection later in this work. First however, we describe the specific OpenPAT metrics that we used to measure each program's execution per-test.

The OpenPAT 3.0.0 `hotspot` tool provides a number of useful program analysis metrics that we use for machine learning. These metrics fall broadly into two categories: structural metrics and dynamic metrics. These are described in Table 1.

The `source_file` and `source_line` structural measures of the `hotspot` tool together with the dynamic `entries` measure give, in effect, test coverage information. Specifically, each code section that is executed will have an `entries` figure of at least one and as the static metrics map the number of `entries` back to specific code lines we know that every code section that is executed by a test will have `entries` ≥ 1 and 0 otherwise.

The structural `instructions` metric can be considered a measure of source line complexity. Code that is more complex such as long formulas will, in general, expand to more assembly instructions than simpler code and so the number of assembly instructions associated with a code section can be an important indicator of potential logical issue points.

The dynamic `order` metric is a program execution path indicator. Program code sections that execute earlier in a program's execution path are assigned an earlier execution order by OpenPAT. For example, if a program consists of three code sections A, B and C, and A is executed first, then B executes in a loop 100 times followed finally by C, the OpenPAT execution order for the three blocks would be 1, 2 and 3 respectively (with B having an `entries` figure of 100 because of the loop). While it is true that a program's execution path can be test input data dependent, the internal path of tests is expected to provide information about dependent chains of sub-feature tests through predictable sub-path patterns. Thus (a possibly shifted) `order` metric chain can be useful in identifying test dependencies in addition to the traditional measure of the structural intersection of covered lines which is also identified by the `hotspot` tool as explained above.

The dynamic `ticks_min`, `ticks_max` and `ticks_sum` metrics provide actual CPU execution cycle measurements for the blocks of code executing in a program. The `ticks_min` and `ticks_max` can be used to ascertain information about cache and data access patterns in a program's execution. For example, if code section B executes repeatedly in a loop on a single set of data obtained from main memory, then the second time B executes it could take considerably less time than the first if the data being operated on is still in the CPU's cache. As another example, if the same data is used by A and B and A executes before B then B's `ticks_max` figure could be close to its `ticks_min` figure because the overhead of initial cache loading was suffered by A. The `ticks_sum` metric is the total time a code section takes to execute and can compliment the `instructions` and `entries` figures in providing an execution time dimension to the computational complexity for a line of source code.

While the eight metrics of Table 1 are expected to provide useful information for test case outcome correlation prediction for the reasons outlined above, some can be expected to be of more predictive importance than others. Thus we will evaluate the importance of the different metrics as predictors of regression test set outcomes in Section 4.5 using a genetic search to find the best subset of the metrics to train a machine learning classifier with.

4   Evaluation

In this section we describe the actual implementation of our framework concept and provide comprehensive practical evaluation results.

Table 2. Siemens HR Variant v 2.2 [14, 15] programs and their test suites. The Code Lines column is the source lines excluding comments and blank lines in the program, the Code Sections column refers to OpenPAT version 3.0.0 compiled program basic blocks, #Faulty Versions is the number of faulty versions of the programs supplied, #Tests is the number of feature tests in the benchmark suite and #Failing Tests is the average number of failing feature tests for each of the faulty program versions.

Program Name	Code Lines	Code Sections	#Faulty Versions	#Tests	#Failing Tests
print_tokens	472	315	7	4,072	69
print_tokens2	399	286	10	4,057	224
replace	512	442	31	5,542	107
schedule	292	244	8	2,638	96
schedule2	301	264	9	2,638	33
tcas	141	150	41	1,592	39
tot_info	440	259	23	1,026	84

4.1 Programs and Regression Test Suites

In order to evaluate our method, we need one or more programs, each with a corresponding suite of regression tests. We require correct and faulty versions of the programs so that pass and fail test results can be used to test the predictive power of our approach. To this end, we used the public benchmark of faulty programs originally developed by Siemens and discussed in [14, 15].

Table 2 describes the program suite. There are in total seven different programs, all written in the C programming language, each program accompanied by over a thousand feature tests. Each program also comes with a varying number of faulty, buggy variants.

The figures in Table 2 reflect some minor adjustments we made to the original dataset. In particular, there are three faulty versions that fail no tests. This leaves 129 buggy variants of the seven programs in total. Many of the test suites also have a small number of duplicate tests, and the number of tests in the table reflects the test suite sizes after removal of these duplicates.

4.2 Metric Volume and Balance for the Benchmarks

We took measurements for the correct versions of each program as they executed every test. These measurements were used to compute the metrics for our datasets.

We then compiled each faulty program and re-ran the tests again, this time to determine which tests would pass or fail as a consequence of the bugs injected into the faulty versions. These pass/fail outcomes became the ground truth labels for our datasets. Note that there are 129 datasets in total, one for each faulty program version, with the number of instances in each dataset being equal to the number of (non-duplicate) tests in the corresponding program's test suite.

The dynamic performance execution measurements that we used were acquired using OpenPAT's `hotspot` tool. Specifically, we measured the eight metrics of

Table 1 for each code section in the program as described in Section 3.2. As the number of code sections in the benchmark set ranged from 150 for `tcas` to 442 for `replace`, the total metric measurements for each program test case ranged from 1,262 to 3,653. Such a large number of metrics can cause issues for machine learning algorithms [21] as introduced in Section 3.2 and is the justification for our inclusion of Genetic Algorithms in this work which we discuss further in Section 4.4.

In addition to the large number of metrics caused by the fine measurement granularity available in OpenPAT, there was also quite a large degree of class imbalance in the datasets as the number of failing tests for the faulty benchmarks of Table 2 is only a small proportion of the total number of regression tests for each program. This class imbalance has severe impact on how any predictive modelling scheme can be evaluated as discussed in the next section.

4.3   Prediction Quality Assessment

In order to evaluate the effectiveness of our method, it was necessary to decide on a scheme for measuring and comparing regression test outcome predictions made by different implementations of our basic approach. The simplest measure, prediction accuracy, is not ideal for the Siemens test suite [14, 15] because there are only a small percentage of failing tests for each program as shown in Table 2. In fact the average number of failing tests is only 3% for the programs of Table 2, so even a naïve prediction scheme that simply classified all tests as passing would already achieve an average accuracy of around 97% for the regression test suite.

An alternative, and the prediction quality metric we use in this paper, is to report Area Under the Curve (AUC) [16], a different machine learning performance metric that focusses on the trade-off between true positives and false positives as the classification threshold changes. AUC reports a number between 0.5 (for a random classifier) and 1.0 (for a perfect classifier). The advantage of this metric is that it is not sensitive to class imbalance, and therefore a classifier predicting that all tests pass will achieve the worst possible AUC of 0.5.

4.4   Predictive Algorithm Selection

In total, we evaluated nine different combinations of test class (pass/fail) prediction algorithms on our datasets, as detailed in Table 3. The prediction algorithms consist of three machine learning approaches: Naive Bayes [18], a simple bayesian classifier that assumes conditional independence of metrics; Sequential Minimal Optimization [19], a linear support vector machine classifier; and Random Forests [20], a state-of-the-art method based on an ensemble of trees. We used the implementations of these algorithms from Weka 3.7.7 [3] with all default settings, except for the Random Forests algorithm that had its number of trees set to 100.

To allow us to evaluate the relative importance of different dynamic measurement metrics on regression test prediction quality we used three versions of each

Table 3. The nine algorithmic combinations used to predict regression test outcomes. Each of the machine learning algorithms has three forms: one with all eight Open-PAT dynamic metrics as input, a second with the metrics pre-selected by a Genetic Algorithm and the third with coverage-only metrics.

Class Prediction Algorithm		Metric Selection Algorithm
NB: Naive Bayes		ALL eight hotspot metrics or
SMO: Sequential Minimal Opt.	×	GA: metrics selected by a Genetic Algorithm or
RF: Random Forests		CV: Coverage only metrics

dataset for each of the three machine learning approaches: the first dataset version comprised all of the OpenPAT metric measurement information; the second version comprised a subset of the metric information; and the third supplied only the coverage information from Table 1. To select the metric subset for the second variant of the datasets we used a Simple Genetic Algorithm [4] with a fitness function that rewards correlation of the metrics with the test outcomes (i.e. pass or fail) while explicitly penalising redundancy between metrics as described in Hall [13]. Our genetic algorithm (GA) was again a Weka 3.7.7 implementation and was a simple binary GA with "1" on a chromosome to indicate the presence of a particular OpenPAT metric or coverage feature and a "0" to indicate its absence. The GA was executed for 100 generations with all other default settings, and it was applied only to the training split of the dataset as described below.

We trained and tested each combination of class prediction and metric selection algorithm with randomly selected subsets of the regression tests for each of the faulty versions of the benchmark programs. In all cases, the selected training tests comprised 25% of the total tests (simulating 25% of the regression suite being executed), and the remainder of the tests (i.e. 75%) were used for evaluating the model's predictive power.

We performed ten randomised training and predictive power assessment runs for each of the nine algorithmic combinations of Table 3 and the 129 faulty program versions of our test suite yielding a total of $129 \times 10 \times 9 = 11,610$ individual experimental runs. Prediction quality figures were computed to assess the quality of each experimental run as discussed next.

4.5   Results

The average Area Under the Curve (AUC) performance quality results of our nine experimental runs across the 129 faulty program versions and nine algorithm combinations are presented in Table 4 below. The best performing classifier algorithm for each program has been emphasised in the tables for the reader's convenience.

From the table, three observations can be made. Firstly, the Random Forests algorithm is clearly the best performing classification method. The linear support vector machine classifier Sequential Minimal Optimization frequently comes a close second, but overall it is unable to improve on Random Forests. The Naive

Table 4. Average Area Under the Curve (AUC) prediction quality results by program and algorithmic classifier. Each column provides results for one of the machine learning classifiers used with a subset of OpenPAT metric data from Table 3. For example the first three columns give the results for the Naive Bayes machine learning classifier used with all the OpenPAT metrics, a subset of the metrics selected by a Genetic Algorithm (GA) and just the OpenPAT coverage metrics (CV) respectively as discussed in Section 4.4.

program	Naive Bayes			Seq. Min. Opt.			Random Forests		
	ALL	GA	CV	ALL	GA	CV	ALL	GA	CV
print_tokens	0.614	0.677	0.500	0.793	0.807	0.761	0.866	**0.872**	0.810
print_tokens2	0.820	0.858	0.500	0.934	0.937	0.931	**0.968**	0.967	0.936
replace	0.726	0.812	0.500	0.917	0.914	0.884	0.913	**0.916**	0.877
schedule	0.644	0.718	0.500	0.817	0.823	0.789	0.831	**0.843**	0.791
schedule2	0.613	0.714	0.500	0.856	0.851	0.778	**0.879**	0.872	0.845
tcas	0.820	0.857	0.500	0.868	0.864	0.734	0.860	0.857	**0.883**
tot_info	0.765	0.823	0.500	0.925	0.931	0.879	**0.944**	**0.944**	0.887

Bayes classifier is universally the worst classifier. It is also apparent that the best algorithmic classifier's predictive abilities are always much more accurate than random guessing.

Secondly, the inclusion of the OpenPAT metrics improves performance in most cases compared to using simple code coverage. This is most obvious in the case of Naive Bayes, where code coverage (i.e. CV) features alone are insufficient to train the model at all, as demonstrated by the AUC measures being at 0.5 which indicates no predictive power.

The third observation is that for four of seven benchmarks, the best prediction quality was achieved using a Genetic Algorithm to select a subset of the Open-PAT metrics so as not to "overwhelm" the machine learning algorithm with all the OpenPAT metrics as discussed in Section 4.2. In fact, considering each of the machine learning algorithms in isolation, we see that the GA variant of the classification algorithm gives the best results for:

1. all seven of the benchmarks using the Naive Bayes algorithm
2. four of the seven benchmarks using Sequential Minimal Optimization and
3. four of the seven benchmarks using Random Forests

which indicates the value of the GA metric sub-selector in these tests.

In order to examine the performance of the GA more closely, we looked at the OpenPAT metrics selected by it during all runs for Naive Bayes over all 129 datasets. The results are shown in Table 5, and they give the probability of each metric being selected by the GA, averaged over faulty version and run. The results show that while the different metrics are selected fairly uniformly, there is a slight bias towards ticks_sum, entries and order. It is also valuable to note that while the GA only selects 30% of the available attributes for use with the Naive Bayes algorithm, the predictive quality of the GA variant is better

Table 5. Importance of the OpenPAT `hotspot` tool metrics as indicated by the probability that each metric was selected by the Genetic Algorithm for the Naive Bayes machine learning algorithm

Metric	Class	GA Selection Prob.
source_file	Structural	29%
source_line	Structural	29%
instructions	Structural	29%
order	Dynamic	30%
entries	Dynamic	31%
ticks_min	Dynamic	29%
ticks_max	Dynamic	29%
ticks_sum	Dynamic	31%

than the Naive Bayes approach using all the available metrics as shown by the ALL column of Table 4 for every benchmark considered here.

As previously indicated, the genetic algorithm allows the Naive Bayes classifier to perform better with larger initial metric volumes (number of metrics used times program code sections the metrics are measured for) than would otherwise be possible. While the GA metric subset selection improvement was less pronounced for the other machine learning algorithms for these small benchmarks, the Genetic Algorithm improvements are already valuable for these benchmarks and are expected to become more pronounced for larger commercial and open source programs as the metric volume increases [22].

5   Conclusion

We have presented a framework for using dynamic execution measurements taken during the regression testing of correct versions of a program for predicting future regression test failures using genetic search and machine learning algorithms. Our experiments demonstrate that combining dynamic performance metric information with machine learning and genetic algorithms can provide improved test result accuracy predictions over approaches that use test code coverage metric intersections alone. This increased prediction accuracy could lead to reductions in regression testing time and allow regression testing to be more frequently applied to feature modifications to support on-line software quality assessment.

While we restricted our experiments to the well known Siemens test suite [14, 15] and eight OpenPAT metrics [2] in this paper, the approach as presented is directly applicable to larger software programs and additional dynamic program analysis metrics. Future work may consider incorporating dynamic metric information gathered during testing (not just prior information gathered for the correct program version) into the method, adding new dynamic measurement metrics from OpenPAT including for example detailed internal control flow information, evaluating the accuracy of the approach with different training sets sizes, different prediction quality metrics, and different code section sizes, and evaluating the benefits of the GA metric selection feature with different machine learning algorithms on larger commercial and open-source programs [22].

References

1. Nori, A.V., Rajamani, S.K.: Program analysis and machine learning: A win-win deal. In: Yahav, E. (ed.) Static Analysis. LNCS, vol. 6887, pp. 2–3. Springer, Heidelberg (2011)
2. The OpenPAT Project. The Open Performance Analysis Toolkit, http://www.OpenPAT.org (accessed March 20, 2013)
3. Hall, M., Frank, E., Holmes, G., Pfahringer, B., Reutemann, P., Witten, I.H.: The WEKA data mining software: An update. SIGKDD Explorations 11(1), 10–18 (2009)
4. Goldberg, D.E.: Genetic algorithms in search, optimization and machine learning. Addison-Wesley (1989)
5. Harman, M., McMinn, P., de Souza, J.T., Yoo, S.: Search Based Software Engineering: Techniques, Taxonomy, Tutorial. In: Meyer, B., Nordio, M. (eds.) Empirical Software Engineering and Verification. LNCS, vol. 7007, pp. 1–59. Springer, Heidelberg (2012)
6. Spacey, S., Wiesmann, W., Kuhn, D., Luk, W.: Robust software partitioning with multiple instantiation. INFORMS Journal on Computing 24(3), 500–515 (2012)
7. Spacey, S.: 3S: Program instrumentation and characterisation framework. Technical Paper, Imperial College London (2006)
8. Spacey, S.: 3S Quick Start Guide. Technical Manual, Imperial College London (2009)
9. Aigner, G., Diwan, A., Heine, D., Lam, M., Moore, D., Murphy, B., Sapuntzakis, C.: An overview of the SUIF2 compiler infrastructure. Technical Paper, Stanford University (2000)
10. Pearce, D.J., Kelly, P.H.J., Field, T., Harder, U.: GILK: A dynamic instrumentation tool for the Linux kernel. In: Field, T., Harrison, P.G., Bradley, J., Harder, U. (eds.) TOOLS 2002. LNCS, vol. 2324, pp. 220–226. Springer, Heidelberg (2002)
11. Nethercote, N., Seward, J.: Valgrind: A program supervision framework. Electronic Notes in Theoretical Computer Science 89(2), 44–66 (2003)
12. Luk, C.-K., Cohn, R., Muth, R., Patil, H., Klauser, A., Lowney, G., Wallace, S., Reddi, V.J., Hazelwood, K.: Pin: Building customized program analysis tools with dynamic instrumentation. In: Proc. of the ACM SIGPLAN Conference on Programming Language Design and Implementation, pp. 190–200 (2005)
13. Hall, M.A.: Correlation-based Feature Subset Selection for Machine Learning. Ph.D. Thesis, University of Waikato, Hamilton, New Zealand (1998)
14. Siemens, HR Variants v 2.2. http://pleuma.cc.gatech.edu/aristotle/Tools/subjects/
15. Hutchins, M., Foster, H., Goradia, T., Ostrand, T.: Experiments on the effectiveness of dataflow- and controlflow-based test adequacy criteria. In: Proc. of the 16th International Conference on Software Engineering, pp. 191–200 (1994)
16. Fawcett, T.: An introduction to ROC analysis. Pattern Recognition Letters 27, 861–874 (2006)

17. Yoo, S.: Evolving human competitive spectra-based fault localization techniques. In: Fraser, G., Teixeira de Souza, J. (eds.) SSBSE 2012. LNCS, vol. 7515, pp. 244–258. Springer, Heidelberg (2012)
18. John, G.H., Langley, P.: Estimating Continuous Distributions in Bayesian Classifiers. In: Proceedings of the Eleventh Conference on Uncertainty in Artificial Intelligence, pp. 338–345. Morgan Kaufmann, San Mateo (1995)
19. Platt, J.C.: Fast training of support vector machines using sequential minimal optimization. In: Schölkopf, B., Burges, C., Smola, A. (eds.) Advances in Kernel Methods – Support Vector Learning. MIT Press (1998)
20. Breiman, L.: Random Forests. Machine Learning 45(1), 5–32 (2001)
21. Domingos, P.: A Few Useful Things to Know about Machine Learning. Communications of the ACM 55(10), 78–87 (2012)
22. Spacey, S., Luk, W., Kuhn, D., Kelly, P.H.J.: Parallel Partitioning for Distributed Systems using Sequential Assignment. Journal of Parallel and Distributed Computing 73(2), 207–219 (2013)

A Recoverable Robust Approach
for the Next Release Problem

Matheus Henrique Esteves Paixão and Jerffeson Teixeira de Souza

Optimization in Software Engineering Group, State University of Ceará,
1700 Avenida Paranjana, 60.714-903, Fortaleza, Brazil
{matheus.paixao,jerffeson.souza}@uece.br

Abstract. Selecting a set of requirements to be included in the next
software release, which has become to be known as the Next Release
Problem, is an important issue in the iterative and incremental software
development model. Since software development is performed under a
dynamic environment, some requirements aspects, like importance and
effort cost values, are highly subject to uncertainties, which should be
taken into account when solving this problem through a search technique.
Current robust approaches for dealing with these uncertainties are very
conservative, since they perform the selection of the requirements considering all possible uncertainties realizations. Thereby, this paper presents
an evolution of this robust model, exploiting the recoverable robust optimization framework, which is capable of producing recoverable solutions
for the Next Release Problem. Several experiments were performed over
synthetic and real-world instances, with all results showing that the recovery strategy handles well the conservatism and adds more quality to
the robust solutions.

Keywords: Recoverable robustness, next release problem, search based
software engineering.

1 Introduction

In an iterative and incremental software development model, the selection of a
set of requirements to be added to the next software release is known as the
Next Release Problem (NRP). In such problem, each requirement is represented
by an importance, which refers to the value aggregated to the client when the
requirement is included in the next release, and a cost value, related to the effort
required to implement the requirement. In that context, the next release problem
consists in selecting a subset of requirements in such a way that the sum of their
importance is maximized, with the cost needed to implement those requirements
respecting the release's available budget [1].

Therefore, in order to employ a search technique to solve the NRP, it is necessary to obtain the importance and cost values of each requirement. The importance values could be indicated by the client and the costs determined by the
development team. In both cases, these values are acquired through estimations,

G. Ruhe and Y. Zhang (Eds.): SSBSE 2013, LNCS 8084, pp. 172–187, 2013.
© Springer-Verlag Berlin Heidelberg 2013

which can be hard to make due to the dynamic environment in which software development takes place.

In fact, changes in the requirements characteristics can be fairly dangerous for the whole system development. As can be perceived in the sensitivity analysis by Harman et. al [2], small changes in the requirements features may have a high impact on requirements selection. Thereby, it is paramount to consider the uncertainties related to the requirement's importance and cost when solving the NRP through optimization techniques [3].

The robust optimization is an operational research framework that identifies and quantifies uncertainties in generic optimization problems [4]. It started to gain more visibility after the first works in [5] and [6]. The robust optimization framework consists of two steps. The first step seeks to identify and quantify all uncertainties related to the problem. Using these information about the uncertainties, the second step consists of building a model which seeks robust solutions, that is, solutions which are feasible for every realization of the uncertainties.

The robust optimization framework has been previously applied to the NRP [7]. In that paper, it was considered that the requirements importance could assume different values due to the occurrence of certain events. The requirement's importance was then calculated by taking into account all these possible values and the respective occurrence probabilities. In order to examine the cost uncertainties, it was defined a *robustness control parameter*, which indicated the expected level of failure in the team cost estimations. This parameter actually stipulates how many requirements will have their real cost higher than the original estimate. Since there is no way to know in advance which requirements will have different real cost values, this approach guaranteed that, even if the team missed the cost of the most expensive requirements, the produced solution would still be feasible. Experiments showed that the penalization with regard to solution quality due to robustness is relatively small. This approach, however, can still be considered conservative, because it assumes that, invariably, some requirements are wrongfully estimated, and their real costs will be as high as possible. Since the requirements selection is made considering the worst possible cost uncertainty values, any different requirements' cost realization will cause a waste of resources.

In the work by Liebchen et. al [8], seeking to handle the conservatism of the "classical" robust optimization, named *strict robustness*, it was introduced a new concept of robustness, the *recoverable robustness*. A recoverable robust solution is the one which, for a limited set of uncertainties realizations, can be made feasible or *recovered*, by a limited effort [9]. Accordingly, the recoverable robustness framework can improve the model in [7], producing a more "realist" requirements selection for the next release problem.

In this context, this papers aims at answering the following research questions:

- RQ_1: How to model the Next Release Problem considering the recoverable robustness framework?
- RQ_2: How much is gained in solution quality with the new recoverable robust model when compared with the strict robust model?

Consequently, the original and main contribution of this paper relates to the tackling of the uncertainties in the Next Release Problem using the recoverable robustness framework.

The remaining of this paper is organized as follows: in Section 2 the recoverable robustness framework is explained in more details, while in Section 3, the recoverable robust NRP model is evolved. Section 4 exhibits and examines the experiments designed to evaluate the proposed formulation. Finally, Section 5 concludes the paper and points out some future research directions.

2   The Recoverable Robustness Framework

The recoverable robustness framework is composed of three main steps, as discussed in [9] and presented next:

1. Identify the uncertainties related to the problem (step Ω)
2. Develop a model which produces recoverable solutions (step M)
3. Define a set of possible recovery algorithms (step A)

These three steps are intrinsically connected. The model M is developed by considering the uncertainties identified in Ω. The recovery algorithms A recover solutions generated by M. Therefore, the triple (Ω, M, A) does not only states that recovery is possible, but explicitly demonstrates how this recovery can be performed.

For steps Ω and M, different modeling techniques can be employed from the strict robustness literature, however, step A is a little trickier and can be formalized as follows:

Definition 1. *Let F_ω be the set of feasible solutions under uncertainties realization ω. A recovery algorithm A is the one which for every solution x under realization ω, it generates a feasible solution, i.e., $A(x,\omega) \in F_\omega$*

Therefore, the output of a recoverable robust problem is genuinely a pair (x, A), called *precaution*, which is composed of the solution x and a recovery algorithm A. In the case where some uncertainty realization makes the solution x unfeasible, it can be recovered by applying the algorithm A.

A generic recoverable robust problem can then be stated as follows:

$$\text{optimize: } f(x)$$
$$\text{subject to: } \forall \omega \subseteq \Omega : A(x,\omega) \in F_\omega$$

In a practical context, one way to limit the effort needed to recover a solution is to consider the number of changes to that solution during the recovery process. Employing this bound in the recovery phase, the concept of *k-recoverable robustness* was proposed by Büsing et. al [10][11]. This new approach is an attempt to control the recovery phase. The recovery control parameter k acts as a limit to the recovery algorithm, i.e., $A(x,\omega,k)$ must recover the solution making at most k changes to the original solution. A k-recoverable robust problem can be stated as:

$$\text{optimize: } f(x)$$
$$\text{subject to: } \forall \omega \subseteq \Omega : A(x, \omega, k) \in F_\omega$$

In the next section, this framework will be employed to the Next Release Problem.

3 Evolving a Recoverable Robust Next Release Problem Formulation

Given a set of requirements $R = \{r_1, r_2, \ldots, r_N\}$, the requirement r_i importance and cost values are represented by v_i and c_i, respectively. A classic formulation of the Next Release Problem is presented next:

$$\text{maximize: } \sum_{i=1}^{N} v_i x_i \tag{1}$$

$$\text{subject to: } \sum_{i=1}^{N} c_i x_i \leq b \tag{2}$$

where b is the release budget. The solution X can be represented as a vector $\{x_1, x_2, \ldots, x_N\}$ where $x_i = 1$ indicates that the requirement r_i is included in the next release, $x_i = 0$ otherwise.

As discussed earlier, the occurrence of certain events can change some requirements' characteristics, including the importance value. Thereby, this type of uncertainty seems adequate to be treated in a discrete and probabilistic way, using the concept of scenarios, as in [7].

A scenario can be defined as a set of importance values due to the occurrence of certain event. Thus, it is defined a set of scenarios $S = \{s_1, s_2, \ldots, s_M\}$, where each scenario is represented by $s \subset S | s = \{v_1^s, v_2^s, \ldots, v_N^s\}$, with v_i^s indicating the importance of requirement r_i under scenario s. The range a requirement importance value can vary is discrete and depends on the set of scenarios. In the assignment of these importance values, the probability of each event taking place can be considered. Thus, for each scenario s it is defined an occurrence probability p_s, with $\sum_{s=1}^{M} p_s = 1$. The requirement importance value v_i is then defined as:

$$v_i = \sum_{s=1}^{M} v_i^s p_s \tag{3}$$

The uncertainty related to the requirement's cost is different. Usually, the cost variation is different from one requirement to another and this difference may not be discrete. Thus, it is unlikely that one would be able to raise a set of scenarios based on possible events. Thereby, the requirement's cost uncertainty will be quantified in a continuous and deterministic way. Let c_i be the estimated requirement cost. It is defined a value $\hat{c}_i$, which indicates the maximum expected cost variation. These values are used to generate lower and upper bounds to the real requirement cost $\bar{c}_i$, so that $c_i - \hat{c}_i \leq \bar{c}_i \leq c_i + \hat{c}_i$.

An alternative robust formulation to the release total cost is presented next:

$$\sum_{i=1}^{N} c_i x_i + \sum_{i=1}^{N} \hat{c}_i x_i \tag{4}$$

In the above case, besides the requirements' costs, it is also considered the cost variation of all requirements selected to the next release. This approach guarantees that, even in the worst possible case, i.e., when all requirements will cost their upper bounds $(c_i + \hat{c}_i)$, the budget constraint will be satisfied. Clearly, this model is very conservative since it assumes that the development team will miss all cost estimates by the maximum amount.

In order to minimize this conservatism, the release cost considered in the NRP robust formulation proposed in [7] can be seen below:

$$\sum_{i=1}^{N} c_i x_i + max_{W \subseteq R, |W| \leq \Gamma} \sum_{i \in W} \hat{c}_i x_i \tag{5}$$

In this model, a control parameter Γ is defined, indicating the maximum number of requirements that may have real costs different from the original estimates. For instance, in a situation where the development team estimates are historically 20% incorrect, in a project with 50 requirements, the control parameter would be $\Gamma = 10$. In order to calculate the release total cost, the variation of all requirements will no longer be considered, but only the variation of the Γ requirements in which the cost variation sum is maximum, represented by the subset $W \subseteq R$. This model guarantees that, even if the team misses the costs of the requirements with highest variations, the generated solution would still be feasible.

Both robust approaches assume that some requirements cost estimates are wrong, and the real cost of these requirements will be the highest possible. From these assumptions, these models find solutions to all possible uncertainties realizations, which characterize them as strict robust approaches. As stated earlier, these kind of robust solutions are still conservative and may waste a considerably amount of resources.

This paper evolves the formulation in [7] by proposing a k-recoverable robust model to the NRP. This improved model would be able to find non-conservative solutions when the requirements costs are correctly estimated, i.e, solutions as close as possible to the classic NRP model. At the same time, if some cost uncertainty realization makes the solution unfeasible due to budget constraints, the solution would be recovered by removing at most k requirements. In order to model the release total cost so that the produced solution has the aforementioned characteristics, the following functions are defined:

$$basicCost(X) = \sum_{i=1}^{N} c_i x_i \tag{6}$$

$$uncertaintyLoss(X, \Gamma) = max_{W \subseteq R, |W| \leq \Gamma} \sum_{i \in W} \hat{c}_i x_i \tag{7}$$

$$recoveryGain(X, k) = min_{Y \subseteq R, |Y|=k} \sum_{i \in Y} c_i x_i \tag{8}$$

The function $basicCost()$ returns the classic NRP release total cost, i.e, the cost sum of all requirements selected to the next release. The function $uncertaintyLoss(\Gamma)$ represents the *robustness level* [7] and calculates the sum of the Γ maximum requirements cost variations. Finally, $recoveryGain(k)$ is controlled by the *recovery parameter* k and can be considered as the *recovery level*. It represents the sum of the k minimum requirements cost estimates. For a certain solution, this recovery level indicates the minimum cost that can be removed from the release in case of recovery.

Thus, in the recoverable robust NRP model proposed in this paper, the release total cost is computed as:

$$max(basicCost(X), basicCost(X) + uncertaintyLoss(X, \Gamma) - recoveryGain(X, k)) \tag{9}$$

The robustness parameter Γ indicates how many requirements could have been wrongfully estimated while the recovery parameter k denotes the number of requirements that can be removed during the recovery operation. Depending on the robustness and recovery paramaters configuration, the value of $recoveryGain(k)$ may be bigger than the $uncertaintyLoss(\Gamma)$ value, which would cause a robust release cost smaller than the classic release cost. Such solution would be necessary to recover even if all requirements costs were correctly estimated, which does not make sense in a practical next release planning environment. In order to avoid this situation, the above release cost formulation guarantees that a solution will not have its total cost lower than the classic NRP model.

Interestingly, this recoverable robust formulation for the release cost can be seen as a generalization of the strict robust and classic models. When considering the recovery parameter $k = 0$, meaning that recovery is not allowed, we get the same robust formulation present in [7]. Using $k = 0$ and $\Gamma = N$, there is no recovery and all cost variations will be considered, characterizing the conservative case shown in Equation (4). Finally, considering $k = \Gamma = 0$, the model falls back into the classic NRP model in Equation (2).

Accordingly to the importance and cost uncertainties quantification (step ω) presented above, it is presented next the proposed formal model that seeks k-recoverable solutions to the Next Release Problem (step M), partially answering the research question RQ_1.

The proposed formulation generates a feasible solution to the NRP, guaranteeing that, even if some cost uncertainty realization makes this solution unfeasible due to budget constraints, by removing at most k requirements, the solution will be recovered to be once again feasible. To perform this recovery, the proposed algorithm (Algorithm 1) can recover a solution by losing the minimum importance amount.

$$\text{maximize: } \sum_{i=1}^{N} \sum_{s=1}^{M} v_i^s p_s x_i$$

subject to: $max(basicCost(),$

$$basicCost() + uncertaintyLoss(\Gamma) - recoveryGain(k)) \leq b$$

where, $basicCost() = \sum_{i=1}^{N} c_i x_i$

$$uncertaintyLoss(\Gamma) = max_{W \subseteq R, |W| \leq \Gamma} \sum_{i \in W} \hat{c}_i x_i$$

$$recoveryGain(k) = min_{Y \subseteq R, |Y| = k} \sum_{i \in Y} c_i x_i$$

$x_i \in \{0, 1\}$

R is the set of requirements

N is the number of requirements

M is the number of scenarios

p_s is the scenario s occurrence probability

v_i^s is the value of requirement r_i in scenario s

c_i is the cost of requirement r_i

$\hat{c}_i$ is the cost variation of r_i

Γ is the robustness control parameter

k is the recovery control parameter

b is the release budget

Algorithm 1. Minimum Value Loss Recovery Algorithm

---
while release is unfeasible **do**
   remove the less valuable requirement
   if new release cost $\leq b$ **then**
     return recovered solution
   end if
end while

This recovery algorithm is straightforward and consists in removing less valuable requirements until the solution becomes feasible once again. As the model guarantees that any k requirements can be removed, the model can recover the release by losing the minimum importance value as possible.

This proposed recovery algorithm represents the last step (step A) in the application of the recoverable robustness framework to the NRP, fully answering the research question RQ_1.

4   Experimental Evaluation

In order to ensure robustness to a solution, some loss regarding quality is inevitable. This measure of loss has become to be known in the literature as the "price of robustness" [12]. As mentioned earlier, strict robust models are conservative approaches that usually waste a significant amount of resources. Under specific conditions, these models may present a relatively high "price of robustness". The research question RQ_2 is related to how much is gained in solution quality when we employ the proposed recoverable robustness model instead of the strict model presented in [7].

In order to permit the full replication of all experiments, all synthetic and real-world instances are available at the paper supporting webpage - http:// www.larces.uece.br/ jeff/recoverablenrp -, which also contains all results that have to be omitted from this paper due to space constraints.

4.1   Settings

Experiments were performed over 7 synthetic and 14 real-world instances. In the synthetic instance set, each instance has 3 scenarios in which the requirements importance values v_i^s can assume integer values between 1 and 10. The effort cost also varies from 1 to 10. The instances were generated with different numbers of requirements, from 50 to 200. In this paper, the synthetic instance name is in the format I_S_R, where R is the number of requirements. The instance I_S_120, for example, is a synthetic one and has 120 requirements. The real-world instances were adapted from the work by Xuan et. al [13]. These instances were extracted from bug repositories of two big open source projects, Eclipse (a java integrated development environment) [14] and Mozilla (a set of web applications) [15]. Each bug is considered a requirement. Its importance is calculated by the number of users that commented on that bug report. The bug severity is mapped to the requirement's cost. Both importance and cost values were normalized to the 1 to 10 interval. Seven instances were extracted from each bug repository. The instances are formed by the most important requirements and contain from 50 to 200 requirements. The real-world instance name is in the format I_Re_P_R, where P represents the project (E for Eclipse and M for Mozilla) and R indicates the number of requirements. The instance I_Re_M_200, for example, was extracted from the Mozilla bug repository and has 200 requirements.

For all instances, synthetic and real, the cost variation $\hat{c}_i$ of each requirement was configured as a random number between 0 and 50% of the respective requirement cost c_i. To make the selection problem more complex, we ensure that it is not possible to select all requirements to the next release by setting the release available budget to 70% of the sum of all requirements' costs.

Different configurations of the robustness parameter Γ and the recovery parameter k were evaluated. For each instance, the parameter Γ was set to $\Gamma = \{0, 0.2N, 0.4N, \ldots, N\}$, where N is the number of requirements, while the recovery parameter k was set to $k = \{0, 0.1N, 0.2N, \ldots, N\}$.

In [7], both Genetic Algorithm and Simulated Annealing were employed to solve the NRP strict robust model. Since the Genetic Algorithm [16] achieved better results overall, in this paper we apply only this metaheuristic. In our GA, the population is composed by N (number of requirements) individuals. The initial population is randomly generated. All individuals that have a release cost bigger than the available budget are discarded and new individuals are randomly generated. This process is repeated until the initial population is composed only by feasible individuals. Crossover probability is set to 0.9, using one point crossover. Mutation is performed for each requirement with a $1/(10N)$ probability. It consists of a single requirement inclusion/exclusion. Both crossover and mutation operators might generate invalid individuals. Therefore, a repairing method was designed, randomly removing requirements from the individual until the solution becomes feasible. The implementation employs the elitism strategy, with 20% of the best individuals in the population being automatically included in the next generation. The algorithm returns the best individual after 10000 generations. These parameters were all set based on the results of experiments specifically designed to this purpose.

All results, including fitness value averages and standard deviations, were obtained from 10 executions of the algorithm for each instance.

As mentioned early, ensuring robustness to a solution causes some loss regarding quality. In order to measure this "price of robustness", a 'reduction metric' is introduced, which indicates the percentage of loss in fitness value in a certain configuration of the parameters k and Γ, when compared with the classic NRP model ($k = \Gamma = 0$). Thus, assuming α_j^i as the fitness value average for $k = i.N$ and $\Gamma = j.N$, the 'reduction metric' δ_j^i is calculated as follows:

$$\delta_j^i = 100 \times (1 - \frac{\alpha_j^i}{\alpha_0^0}) \tag{10}$$

4.2   Results and Analysis

Table 1 presents the fitness values computed by the Genetic Algorithm for some of the synthetic instances. The $\Gamma = 0$ rows represent the classic NRP while the $k = 0$ column presents the results for the strict robust model in [7].

Considering the results for the strict robust model in [7], as the robustness parameter Γ increases, there is a loss in solution quality. By allowing recovery, the proposed recoverable model improves the solutions. As the recovery parameter k increases, there is a gain in solution quality when compared with the strict model fitness values. For a recovery level of 20%, for example, the generated solutions are in average 2.9% better in terms of quality. Also, in average, a 10% recovery level represents a 1.5% improvement in fitness value, when comparing the proposed recoverable model with the strict model in [7].

Table 1. Fitness values results for some of the synthetic instances, regarding different values for both robustness and recovery parameters

Instance	Γ	k					
		0	0.2N	0.3N	0.5N	0.7N	N
I_S_50	0	256.83 ± 0.30	256.83 ± 0.30	256.83 ± 0.30	256.83 ± 0.30	256.83 ± 0.30	256.83 ± 0.30
	0.2N	243.69 ± 0.00	251.78 ± 0.43	256.93 ± 0.00	256.81 ± 0.36	256.93 ± 0.00	256.93 ± 0.00
	0.4N	237.31 ± 0.55	246.08 ± 0.00	253.61 ± 0.41	256.83 ± 0.30	256.93 ± 0.00	256.93 ± 0.00
	0.6N	233.93 ± 0.41	242.33 ± 0.49	250.34 ± 0.53	256.69 ± 0.48	256.93 ± 0.00	256.93 ± 0.00
	0.8N	233.03 ± 0.25	241.13 ± 0.30	249.05 ± 0.00	256.93 ± 0.00	256.93 ± 0.00	256.93 ± 0.00
	N	233.08 ± 0.26	241.25 ± 0.07	249.05 ± 0.00	256.93 ± 0.00	256.93 ± 0.00	256.93 ± 0.00
I_S_120	0	581.21 ± 0.38	581.21 ± 0.38	581.21 ± 0.38	581.21 ± 0.38	581.21 ± 0.38	581.21 ± 0.38
	0.2N	544.49 ± 0.70	563.05 ± 0.75	578.32 ± 0.49	581.37 ± 0.31	581.34 ± 0.46	581.53 ± 0.25
	0.4N	531.82 ± 0.62	549.96 ± 0.28	564.25 ± 0.66	581.37 ± 0.34	581.24 ± 0.58	581.45 ± 0.19
	0.6N	526.27 ± 0.70	544.28 ± 0.53	559.02 ± 0.41	581.45 ± 0.44	581.08 ± 0.76	581.51 ± 0.32
	0.8N	525.98 ± 0.49	543.27 ± 0.56	557.17 ± 0.61	581.54 ± 0.29	581.32 ± 0.48	581.15 ± 0.60
	N	525.58 ± 0.58	543.51 ± 0.43	557.70 ± 0.31	581.43 ± 0.53	581.55 ± 0.43	581.46 ± 0.40
I_S_200	0	946.62 ± 1.24	946.62 ± 1.24	946.62 ± 1.24	946.62 ± 1.24	946.62 ± 1.24	946.62 ± 1.24
	0.2N	886.95 ± 0.69	923.70 ± 1.12	947.08 ± 1.05	947.37 ± 0.76	946.96 ± 1.04	947.92 ± 0.58
	0.4N	861.32 ± 1.51	898.55 ± 1.13	928.37 ± 1.15	947.55 ± 1.12	946.56 ± 0.96	946.95 ± 0.80
	0.6N	851.83 ± 0.97	887.56 ± 1.44	917.67 ± 0.68	947.54 ± 0.86	947.36 ± 1.33	947.61 ± 1.05
	0.8N	850.16 ± 1.17	885.93 ± 0.90	915.04 ± 0.93	947.72 ± 1.38	947.08 ± 1.17	947.84 ± 0.77
	N	850.64 ± 1.01	885.93 ± 1.29	914.99 ± 1.70	946.94 ± 0.79	946.99 ± 1.18	946.77 ± 1.27

As the recovery level grows, the fitness values converge to the classic NRP model. The recovery stability point is around 40% for most instances. Thereby, a lower robustness parameter (a small quantity of wrongfully estimated requirements) reaches the classic NRP model with a lower recovery parameter.

It is also noteworthy the considerably low standard deviation presented by the Genetic Algorithm. For most experimental results shown in the table, the standard deviation is less than 1, reaching no more than 1.7.

Figure 1 presents the fitness results for some of the instances that were not shown in Table 1. The solutions clearly converge to the classic NRP as k increases, as stated above. Since $k = 0$ represents the fitness value for the strict model in [7], for all robustness parameters values, every recovery level increase adds quality to the solution.

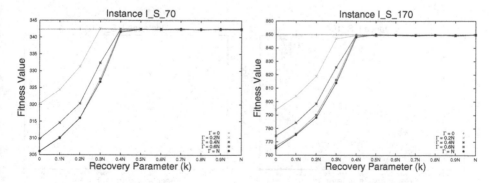

Fig. 1. Fitness value results for synthetic instances I_S_70 and I_S_170

Table 2 presents the reduction factors for some of the synthetic instances. As it has been mentioned, this value indicates the percentage of fitness value loss of some robust solution when compared to the classic NRP ($\Gamma = k = 0$).

Table 2. Reduction factor results for some of the synthetic instances, regarding different values for both robustness and recovery parameters

Instance	Γ	k					
		0	0.2N	0.3N	0.5N	0.7N	N
I_S_50	0.2N	5.12	1.97	0.04	0.01	0.04	0.04
	0.4N	7.60	4.19	1.25	0.00	0.04	0.04
	0.6N	8.92	5.65	2.52	0.06	0.04	0.04
	0.8N	9.26	6.11	3.03	0.04	0.04	0.04
	N	9.25	6.07	3.03	0.04	0.04	0.04
I_S_120	0.2N	6.32	3.12	0.50	0.03	0.02	0.06
	0.4N	8.50	5.38	2.92	0.03	0.01	0.04
	0.6N	9.45	6.35	3.82	0.04	0.02	0.05
	0.8N	9.50	6.53	4.14	0.06	0.02	0.01
	N	9.57	6.49	4.04	0.04	0.06	0.04
I_S_200	0.2N	6.30	2.42	0.05	0.08	0.04	0.14
	0.4N	9.01	5.08	1.93	0.10	0.01	0.03
	0.6N	10.01	6.24	3.06	0.10	0.08	0.10
	0.8N	10.19	6.41	3.34	0.12	0.05	0.13
	N	10.14	6.41	3.34	0.03	0.04	0.02

The conservatism of the strict model in [7] produces a reduction factor higher than 9% for most of the robustness levels. By allowing recovery, the proposed model becomes less conservative and there is an improvement in the reduction factor measure. In average, the reduction factor is 40% lower for each 10% recovery level increase. As the recovery stability point is reached, the reduction factor is almost none, i.e, the solution is virtually equal to the one generated by the classic NRP model. These results are consistent to state the improvement in solution quality for all recovery levels, even the small ones.

Figure 2 presents the reduction factors for some of the synthetic instances. The results are very similar to those presented in Table 2, as the reduction factor has a 40% decrease for each 10% recovery level increase, in average.

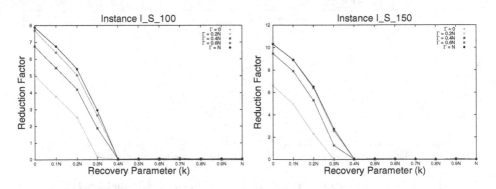

Fig. 2. Reduction factor results for synthetic instances I_S_100 and I_S_150

Table 3 presents the fitness values for some real-world instances. Due to space constraints, only one instance from each bug repository is presented.

Table 3. Fitness values results for real-world instances I_Re_E_100 and I_Re_M_150

Instance	Γ	k					
		0	0.2N	0.3N	0.5N	0.7N	N
I_Re_E_100	0	296.73 ± 0.60	296.73 ± 0.60	296.73 ± 0.60	296.73 ± 0.60	296.73 ± 0.60	296.73 ± 0.60
	0.2N	270.55 ± 1.01	286.64 ± 0.71	297.00 ± 0.42	296.73 ± 0.45	296.82 ± 0.61	296.82 ± 0.45
	0.4N	259.73 ± 1.52	274.45 ± 0.76	294.09 ± 0.61	296.91 ± 0.60	296.36 ± 0.70	296.82 ± 0.73
	0.6N	254.45 ± 1.31	268.82 ± 1.08	288.36 ± 0.36	296.82 ± 0.73	296.82 ± 0.45	296.73 ± 0.83
	0.8N	254.55 ± 1.35	267.00 ± 1.41	286.82 ± 0.45	296.64 ± 0.58	296.82 ± 0.61	296.55 ± 0.89
	N	254.55 ± 1.22	268.36 ± 0.79	286.82 ± 0.45	296.73 ± 0.45	296.45 ± 0.76	296.55 ± 0.68
I_Re_M_150	0	423.64 ± 0.59	423.64 ± 0.59	423.64 ± 0.59	423.64 ± 0.59	423.64 ± 0.59	423.64 ± 0.59
	0.2N	394.93 ± 0.50	419.00 ± 0.97	423.93 ± 0.48	423.93 ± 0.36	423.93 ± 0.58	424.00 ± 0.35
	0.4N	379.64 ± 0.73	402.79 ± 0.87	423.71 ± 0.62	423.93 ± 0.36	423.79 ± 0.56	423.71 ± 0.62
	0.6N	375.57 ± 0.43	397.29 ± 0.70	423.43 ± 0.53	424.07 ± 0.46	423.86 ± 0.35	424.14 ± 0.43
	0.8N	375.43 ± 0.80	396.50 ± 0.59	422.57 ± 0.65	424.00 ± 0.65	423.79 ± 0.33	424.14 ± 0.29
	N	374.93 ± 0.67	396.57 ± 0.83	422.71 ± 0.77	424.00 ± 0.57	424.00 ± 0.65	423.86 ± 0.47

As can be seen, the proposed recoverable model performs nearly the same for both synthetic and real-world instances, which helps to validate the first results. When recovery is not allowed, the fitness value tends to get worse as the robustness level increases. As recovery is enabled, this conservatism is handled and the solutions converge to the classic NRP. Once again, even for small recovery levels, there is already a gain in solution quality when compared with the strict model in [7]. The standard deviation remains considerably small, reaching at most 1.41.

Figure 3 presents fitness value results for some real-world instances, where one instance of each bug repository is presented. The behavior of these real instance results are very similar to the synthetic ones, as could have been seen in Table 3. There is a gain in solution quality for all recovery levels under all robustness parameters values.

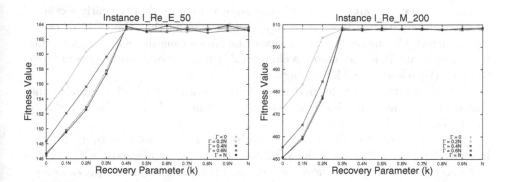

Fig. 3. Fitness value results for real-world instances I_Re_E_50 and I_Re_M_200

Table 4 presents the reduction factor results for some real-world instances. The conservatism of the model in [7], regarding the real instances, produced a reduction factor even higher than the synthetic instances, reaching more than

Table 4. Reduction factor results for real-world instances I_Re_E_100 and I_Re_M_150

Instance	Γ	k					
		0	0.2N	0.3N	0.5N	0.7N	N
I_Re_E_100	0.2N	8.82	3.40	0.09	0.00	0.03	0.03
	0.4N	12.47	7.51	0.89	0.06	0.12	0.03
	0.6N	14.25	9.41	2.82	0.03	0.03	0.00
	0.8N	14.22	10.02	3.34	0.03	0.03	0.06
	N	14.22	9.56	3.34	0.00	0.09	0.06
I_Re_M_150	0.2N	6.78	1.10	0.07	0.07	0.07	0.08
	0.4N	10.39	4.92	0.02	0.07	0.03	0.02
	0.6N	11.35	6.22	0.05	0.10	0.05	0.12
	0.8N	11.38	6.41	0.25	0.08	0.03	0.12
	N	11.50	6.39	0.22	0.08	0.08	0.05

14% in some cases. The proposed recoverable robust model behavior was nearly identical of the synthetic instances, despite the high reduction factor when $k = 0$, a recovery level of 20% decreased the reduction almost to the half.

In conclusion, all results are consistent to show that the proposed recoverable robust model have improved previous robust models to the NRP, in order to handle the conservatism by allowing a release recovery. Results are very similar for both synthetic and real-world instances, pointing out the model's reliability and applicability.

Finally, all presented results have helped in answering the research question RQ_2, stating the improvement in solution quality when using the new recoverable robust model for the Next Release Problem.

4.3   Recovery Analysis

In this section, it will be analysed the fitness value behavior when some requirements are wrongfully estimated and, consequently, recovery becomes necessary to fulfill the budget constraint.

The fitness value *before recovery* is the same as presented in the early sections. The fitness value *after recovery* is computed assuming that the costs of the Γ requirements with highest variations were the ones wrongfully estimated, forcing the recovery algorithm to remove a considerably number of requirements in order to make the release feasible once again.

Since the proposed model performs nearly identical for both synthetic and real-world instances, as shown in previous sections, only a synthetic instance will be considered in the analysis.

Table 5 presents the fitness value results before and after recovery for the instance I_S_120, with the results after recovery being highlighted.

Since the fitness values before recovery are the same as in this previous sections, as the recovery parameter k increases, the fitness values converge to the classic NRP. However, the fitness values after recovery behaves the opposite, since as the recovery levels grow, the solutions lose in quality if the recovery is performed, as can be seen in the table. That behavior highlights an interesting characteristic of the recoverable robust framework, that is, the recovery possibility can be considered a bet, that is, if the requirements' costs are correctly

Table 5. Before and after recovery fitness values comparison for the instance I_S_120

Instance	Γ	k					
		0	0.2N	0.3N	0.5N	0.7N	N
I_S_120	0	581.21 ± 0.38	581.21 ± 0.38	581.21 ± 0.38	581.21 ± 0.38	581.21 ± 0.38	581.21 ± 0.38
		581.21 ± 0.38	581.21 ± 0.38	581.21 ± 0.38	581.21 ± 0.38	581.21 ± 0.38	581.21 ± 0.38
	0.2N	544.49 ± 0.70	563.05 ± 0.75	578.32 ± 0.49	581.37 ± 0.31	581.34 ± 0.46	581.53 ± 0.25
		544.49 ± 0.70	533.24 ± 3.58	521.99 ± 3.95	515.28 ± 7.82	517.84 ± 4.76	510.28 ± 7.45
	0.4N	531.82 ± 0.62	549.96 ± 0.28	564.25 ± 0.66	581.37 ± 0.34	581.24 ± 0.58	581.45 ± 0.19
		531.82 ± 0.62	522.84 ± 2.98	510.81 ± 5.07	486.17 ± 5.10	484.22 ± 6.75	482.69 ± 6.01
	0.6N	526.27 ± 0.70	544.28 ± 0.53	559.02 ± 0.41	581.45 ± 0.44	581.08 ± 0.76	581.51 ± 0.32
		526.27 ± 0.70	518.04 ± 2.67	509.58 ± 4.55	480.49 ± 7.82	478.16 ± 5.39	478.11 ± 6.70
	0.8N	525.98 ± 0.49	543.27 ± 0.56	557.17 ± 0.61	581.54 ± 0.29	581.32 ± 0.48	581.15 ± 0.60
		525.98 ± 0.49	518.07 ± 1.39	509.17 ± 3.28	482.48 ± 7.41	478.70 ± 3.40	485.00 ± 5.51
	N	525.58 ± 0.58	543.51 ± 0.43	557.70 ± 0.31	581.43 ± 0.53	581.55 ± 0.43	581.46 ± 0.40
		525.58 ± 0.58	518.89 ± 2.43	509.38 ± 4.35	478.75 ± 4.28	481.24 ± 5.74	480.83 ± 8.82

estimated, the solutions will behave very similarly to the ones from the classic NRP and significantly better than the results produced by the original robust framework. On the other hand, if the requirements' costs are wrongfully estimated, the solution after recovery will be worse than the conservative robust model. The decision maker must be aware of this trade-off to choose the robustness and recovery parameters which fit better in a particular release planning situation.

It is also worthwhile to highlight the considerable increase in the standard deviation for the fitness values after recovery. While for the before recovery values the highest standard deviation is 0.76, when considering the after recovery values, the highest standard deviation was 8.82.

Due to space constraints, it is not possible to show more after recovery results and analyis in this paper, but all results and instances are available at the paper supporting webpage, as mentioned previously.

5   Conclusion and Future Works

The Next Release Problem is an important activity in the iterative and incremental software development model. Since the requirements' characteristics, such as importance and cost, may change during the release development, robust approaches have been proposed to address this uncertainty in the NRP. However, the current robust methods to the NRP are very conservative because they select a subset of requirements in order to fulfill all possible uncertainties realizations.

This paper proposed an improvement to the state-of-art robust models to the NRP by considering the recoverable robust optimization framework. This modeling technique can handle the conservatism of the classic robust methods by adding a recovery possibility to the solution. If some cost uncertainty realization make the solution unfeasible due to budget constraints, the release can be recovered removing a controlled quantity of requirements.

The improved recoverable robust method was applied to both synthetic and real-world instances, varying the number of requirements in each instance. The real-world instances were extracted from bug repositories of two big open source projects, Eclipse and Mozilla. Experiments were performed in order to measure how much is the gain in solution quality when using the improved recoverable model instead of the conservative robust models.

For all instances and for all robustness level configurations, a small recovery level allows the production of solutions with more quality than the conservative strict robust models. Furthermore, as the recovery possibility increases, there is more gain in solution quality. However, if recovery is necessary, depending on the uncertainty realization, the solution quality after recovery can be worse than the conservative model. Therefore, the recovery possibility is a risky decision to make and it is fundamental to perform a deep analysis in order to choose the best robustness and recovery levels for each situation.

As a future research direction, the recoverable robust optimization framework can be used to tackle other problems that have to cope with uncertainty in the SBSE field. Specifically related to the next release problem, the interdependencies between requirements could be considered. Furthermore, other experiments could be performed, varying the release available budget and using other strategies to cope with the cost uncertainty.

Acknowledgment. This paper is a partial result of the UbiStructure project supported by CNPq (MCT/CNPq 14/2011 - Universal) with number 481417/2011-7.

References

1. Bagnall, A., Rayward-Smith, V., Whittley, I.: The next release problem. Information and Software Technology 43, 883–890 (2001)
2. Harman, M., Krinke, J., Ren, J., Yoo, S.: Search based data sensitivity analysis applied to requirement engineering. In: Proceedings of the 11th Annual Conference on Genetic and Evolutionary Computation, pp. 1681–1688. ACM (2009)
3. Zhang, Y.-Y., Finkelstein, A., Harman, M.: Search based requirements optimisation: Existing work and challenges. In: Rolland, C. (ed.) REFSQ 2008. LNCS, vol. 5025, pp. 88–94. Springer, Heidelberg (2008)
4. Beyer, H., Sendhoff, B.: Robust optimization–a comprehensive survey. Computer Methods in Applied Mechanics and Engineering 196, 3190–3218 (2007)
5. Bai, D., Carpenter, T., Mulvey, J.: Making a case for robust optimization models. Management Science 43, 895–907 (1997)
6. Mulvey, J., Vanderbei, R., Zenios, S.: Robust optimization of large-scale systems. Operations Research 43, 264–281 (1995)
7. Paixao, M., Souza, J.: A scenario-based robust model for the next release problem. In: ACM Genetic and Evolutionary Computation Conference (GECCO 2013) (to appear, 2013)
8. Liebchen, C., Lübbecke, M., Möhring, R.H., Stiller, S.: Recoverable robustness (2007)
9. Liebchen, C., Lübbecke, M., Möhring, R., Stiller, S.: The concept of recoverable robustness, linear programming recovery, and railway applications. In: Ahuja, R.K., Möhring, R.H., Zaroliagis, C.D. (eds.) Robust and Online Large-Scale Optimization. LNCS, vol. 5868, pp. 1–27. Springer, Heidelberg (2009)
10. Büsing, C., Koster, A.M., Kutschka, M.: Recoverable robust knapsacks: the discrete scenario case. Optimization Letters 5, 379–392 (2011)

11. Büsing, C., Koster, A.M.C.A., Kutschka, M.: Recoverable robust knapsacks: γ-scenarios. In: Pahl, J., Reiners, T., Voß, S. (eds.) INOC 2011. LNCS, vol. 6701, pp. 583–588. Springer, Heidelberg (2011)
12. Bertsimas, D., Sim, M.: The price of robustness. Operations Research 52, 35–53 (2004)
13. Xuan, J., Jiang, H., Ren, Z., Luo, Z.: Solving the large scale next release problem with a backbone-based multilevel algorithm. IEEE Transactions on Software Engineering 38, 1195–1212 (2012)
14. Eclipse (January 2013), http://www.eclipse.org/
15. Mozilla (January 2013), http://www.mozilla.org/
16. Holland John, H.: Adaptation in natural and artificial systems: an introductory analysis with applications to biology, control, and artificial intelligence. University of Michigan, USA (1975)

A Systematic Review of Software Requirements Selection and Prioritization Using SBSE Approaches

Antônio Mauricio Pitangueira[1,3], Rita Suzana P. Maciel[1], Márcio de Oliveira Barros[2], and Aline Santos Andrade[1]

[1] Federal University of Bahia
Computer Science Department
{antoniomauricio,aline}@ufba.br, ritasuzana@dcc.ufba.br
[2] Post-graduate Information Systems Program
marcio.barros@uniriotec.br
[3] Federal Institute of Bahia
antoniomauricio@ifba.edu.br

Abstract. Selection and prioritization of software requirements represents an area of interest in Search-Based Software Engineering (SBSE) and its main focus is finding and selecting a set of requirements that may be part of a software release. This paper uses a systematic review to investigate which SBSE approaches have been proposed to address software requirement selection and prioritization problems. The search strategy identified 30 articles in this area and they were analyzed for 18 previously established quality criteria. The results of this systematic review show which aspects of the requirements selection and prioritization problems were addressed by researchers, the methods approaches and search techniques currently adopted to address these problems, and the strengths and weaknesses of each of these techniques. The review provides a map showing the gaps and trends in the field, which can be useful to guide further research.

Keywords: requirements selection, requirement prioritization, systematic review.

1 Introduction

Requirements engineering is the branch of software engineering concerned with the real-world goals for functions and constraints on software systems. It is also concerned with the relationship of these factors to precise specifications of software structure, behavior, and to their evolution over time and across software families (Zave, 1997).

Requirements engineering process goals are to create and maintain system requirement artifacts. In this process multiple activities are performed, such as requirements elicitation, analysis and management of changes throughout the software development life-cycle (Somerville, 2007).

Software engineering practices aim to ensure that a software product meets the needs of its users (Cheng & Atlee, 2007). Software requirements should express the

G. Ruhe and Y. Zhang (Eds.): SSBSE 2013, LNCS 8084, pp. 188–208, 2013.
© Springer-Verlag Berlin Heidelberg 2013

needs and constraints fixed for a software product that contribute to the solution of some real world problem (Kotonya & Sommerville, 1998). Software is becoming complex and the number of requirements that must be met is increasing and consequently software development processes are commonly performed in an incremental way. An increment is composed of a set of requirements that form an operational product a version of software, for the user (Pressman, 2002). Thus, the requirements engineer is faced with a scenario that will have several decisions, constraints (such as, budgetary limitations and technical issues) and specifications regarding the selection of requirements that will be part of the next version of the software.

Consequently, the main objective in selecting software requirements is to identify optimal choices for a set of requirements and to exploit trade-off decision-making to satisfy the demands of stakeholders, while at the same time making sure that there are sufficient resources to undertake the selected task (Zhang ,2010).

In a requirements engineering process a human expert faces a scenario in which there are several decisions and considerations to be taken into account, such as requirement interdependencies, project costs, different kinds of customers, budget constraints, etc. An analysis of software requirements, selection and prioritization of them is important because mistakes and misunderstandings as this early stage in the software development lifecycle can be extremely costly (Zhang, 2010).

Several approaches have been proposed in the literature to support selecting and prioritizing requirements in software development projects (Karlsson et al. 1998), such as Analytical Hierarchy Process(Saaty, 1980), Cost-Value (Karlsson & Ryan, 1997), B-tree(Heger, 2004), and other traditional methods (Aasem et al. 2010; Wiegers, 1999; Fellow & Hooks, 1998; Boehm et al., 2001). Some of these approaches use techniques that can assist in finding a better set of software requirements according to a set of goals and constraints.

Recently, non-exhaustive and automated search methods have emerged as an alternative strategy to solve some problems of software requirements selection to meet the demands of the users of software. A well known strategy to solve this problem is Next Release Problem (NRP). According to Bagnall (Bagnall et al, 2001), the objective of NRP is to select a set of requirements that are deliverable within a company budget and which meet the demands of their customers. According to Zhang (Zhang, 2010) this objective allows stakeholders to receive an increment that is a complete system as soon as possible and ensures that the most important requirements are delivered first. Thus, new software requirements can be released during each increment according to stakeholder' feedback.

NRP is an area within a field named Search-Based Software Engineering (SBSE). Currently, several types of these techniques have been proposed and significant results have been obtained in the selection process of software requirements. It is therefore necessary to understand how applications are being used in this area, what techniques are being used, the type of modeling to use in addressing this selection problem and what the current trends are in this area focusing on requirements selection and prioritization. As there is still no consensus about which techniques to apply, a systematic review was performed in order to obtain a better understanding and comprehension about software requirements selection and prioritization and trends in this area.

In the systematic review presented in this paper we are interested in understanding what has been proposed to solve the problems about the selection and prioritization of requirements using Search-Based Software Engineering. This review followed the guidelines proposed by Kitchenham et al (2004) and (Kitchenham, 2004). The paper is structured as follows. The next section has some background about requirements selection and prioritization with the SBSE approach. Section 3 formally presents the systematic review process. The results obtained and discussions about these are described in Section 4. Finally, in section 5 conclusions are drawn and future work is proposed.

2   Software Requirements Selection and Prioritization

In the context of software development, the systematic review conducted here focuses on the selection of a set of requirements for the release of the next version of software (Harman et al. 2012). More specifically, this approach was launched when Bagnall (Bagnall et al. 2001) formulated the "Next Release Problem" (NRP) as a search problem.

This problem is illustrated in Figure 1, which can be identified by a set $R = \{r1, r2, r3, ... rn\}$ software requirements, which are offered by another set $C = \{c1, c2, c3,..., cn\}$ formed by customers. It is assumed that all requirements are independent, i.e. no requirements depend on requirements.

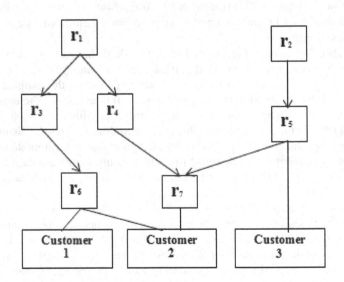

Fig. 1. The structure of the next release problem (Bagnall, 2001)

With these two sets, Bagnall assumed that there is a cost vector for the requirements in R called $cost = [cost1, cost2, cost3,..., costn]$. Each cost c_i is associated to fulfilling the requirement r_i.

As each customer has a degree of importance for the company, there is the existence of a set of relative weights $W = \{w1, w2, w3, ..., wn\}$ associated with each customer in the set C. In various situations, the same requirements are desired by more than one customer, however, its importance may be different for each customer (Del Sagrado et al, 2011). Thus, the importance that a requirement r_i has for customer i is given by *value (ri, ci)* where a value higher than 0 means the customer c_i gets the requirement r_i and 0 otherwise (Harman et al., 2012). Under these assumptions, the overall satisfaction or score is measured as a weighted sum of its importance values for all the customers and this can be formalized as:

$$score = \sum_{i=1}^{n} wi \cdot value\ (ri, ci).$$ (1)

In general, the single-objective NRP can be modeled as follows:

$$Maximize\ \sum_{i=1}^{n} wi \cdot value\ (ri, ci)$$ (2)

subject to

$$\sum_{i=1}^{n} costi \cdot ci \leq B$$ (3)

where B is the budget designated by the company and $c_i = 1$ means if the customer i will have its requirements satisfied and $c_i = 0$ otherwise.

Consequently, NRP consists of selecting a set among all the requirements of a software package such that the cost, in terms of money or resources, of fulfilling these requirements is minimum and the satisfaction of all the users of that system is maximum (Durillo et al,, 2009). Thus, it ensures that the most important requirements are released first so that the maximum attainable benefits of the new system are gained earliest (Zhang et al. 2008).

From this initial comprehension of the problem new studies have emerged in the area with a more specific focus, for example using more than one objective to be optimized (Zhang et al., 2007), requirements interdependencies (Carlshamre et al., 2001), requirement selection and scheduling (Li et al, 2007), requirements interaction (Del Sagrado et al., 2011) and release planning (Van den Akker, 2008; Greer & Ruhe, 2004).

2.1   SBSE Techniques Applied to the Software Requirements Selection and Prioritization

To obtain solutions for software requirements selection and prioritization through SBSE approaches, there is a need for techniques that assist in the process of understanding, analyzing, and interpreting results obtained for inclusion of requirements for the next version of the software. The types of techniques can be differentiated according to the way they approach the problem, e.g. single or multiple objective (Harman et al., 2012). In the simplest cases (single objective), a fair comparison between some algorithms (for example, simulated annealing and Hill Climbing) observing the amount of effort required by each search and elementary statistical analysis can be used to analyze the best solution for a set of requirements (Harman et al., 2012) to here.

However, in practice, a software engineer is more likely to have many conflicting objectives to address when determining the set of requirements to include in the next release of the software. As such, the multiple objective formulation is more likely to be appropriate than the single objective NRP (Zhang et al. 2007). Therefore, when the goal of modeling the problem is the optimization of multiple objectives and multiple constraints, there is a need for more advanced techniques to improve the search for solutions, because, contrary to single objective optimization, the solution of a multi-objective problem is not a single point, but a set of solutions. One technique is the use of Pareto Optimal, in which several optimization objectives are combined, but without needing to decide which takes precedence over the others (Harman et al., 2012, Harman, 2007). Given its efficiency, several studies have emerged using this technique in software requirements (Durillo et al., 2009, Saliu & Ruhe, 2007, Zhang et al.,2007).

Another type of technique that has been widely used by researchers in this area is Genetic Algorithm (GA), a bio-inspired search algorithm based on the evolution of the collection of individuals resulting from natural selection and natural genetics (Goldberg, 1989). According to Talbi (Talbi, 2009), A GA usually applies a crossover operator to two solutions which play a major role, plus a mutation operator that randomly modifies the individual contents to promote diversity.

One of the most commonly used is NSGA-II developed by Deb (Deb et al., 2002), which is often used in complex problems involving the selection and prioritization of requirements (Zhang & Harman, 2010, Finkelstein et al.2008).

Another way of approaching NRP problems is the use of hybridisation. According to Harman (Harman et al., 2012), hybridisation with non-SBSE techniques can also be beneficial, for example, the Greedy algorithm (Talbi, 2009) has been used to inject solution into other evolutionary algorithms in order to accelerate the process of finding solutions.

3   Systematic Review Process

A systematic review (SR) is a technique to identify, evaluate and interpret relevant research in a particular area of interest, a research question or a specific phenomenon of interest (Kitchenham 2004). More specifically, systematic reviews provide a concise summary of evidence available regarding a given area of interest. This approach uses explicit and rigorous methods to identify, critically evaluate and synthesize relevant studies on a particular topic (Dyba et al. 2007). There are several reasons for performing a systematic review (Kitchenham 2004), for example to summarize the available evidence regarding a treatment of a technology; identify gaps in current research in order to suggest areas to promote new research and provide a framework in order to properly position new research activities.

A SR usually comprises the steps of a) planning (identification of the need for a review and development of a review protocol), b) conducting (identification of research, selection of primary studies, study quality assessment, data extraction and data synthesis) and c) report writing.

This systematic review is for a PhD project, showing the strengths and weaknesses of software requirements selection and prioritization using SBSE approaches and identifying possible research trends and fields of interest. The phases of the work are demonstrated and discussed. Two researchers participated in the process: a doctoral student who was responsible for carrying out the three steps outlined above, and a senior researcher who was responsible for validating the review protocol and monitoring all the steps comprising the systematic review.

3.1   Planning the Review – Fundamental Questions

As previously mentioned, a systematic review requires a well specified protocol that describes the dynamics of the process. One of the most important activities at the planning stage is the proper formulation of a research question or specific questions that must be answered by the systematic review. All other phases of the process are dependent on this formulation (Dyba et al. 2007).

The aim of our study was to examine the current state of software requirements selection and prioritization methods, focusing in Search-Based software engineering methods. From this, our research question (RQ) for this systematic review is:

"What is the state of the art for the application of search-based optimization in the process of software requirements selection and prioritization?"

This is a topic of scientific and professional importance because this is becoming increasingly used, given the power to support the attainment of (close to) optimum solutions in a problem as complex as the selection and prioritization of requirements in software projects (Zhang et al. 2008). This question can be split into other questions:

— RQ1: What types of modeling are being used in selection and prioritization of software requirements with a focus on SBSE?
— RQ2: What methods are used for selection and prioritization of software requirements with a focus on SBSE?
— RQ3: What search techniques are used for the process of selecting and prioritizing requirements with a focus on SBSE?

In RQ1 aspects concerning modeling relate to how the problem of software requirements selection and prioritization are covered and how they are addressed to find possible solutions. In other words, how organized the fitness function and the constraints are to form the model representation (Harman & Jones 2001).

Regarding methods (RQ2), these can be understood as a way of obtaining solutions to the problem at hand, in general, such as meta-heuristics or hybridization. In this case, approaches to operations research techniques can be used as a solution to the problem of selecting and prioritizing software requirements (Harman, 2007). Finally, RQ3 addresses search techniques for selecting and prioritizing software requirements. In this case, the term search technique refers to the ways to tackle the problem by observing their proposed goals and objectives, for example, the use of a genetic algorithm or exact algorithm. The question RQ3 is derived from RQ2 showing in details the search techniques that were used in methods of approach.

These questions were essential for determining the structure and content of this review, and also for guiding the process because all other parts of this systematic review are derived from these issues.

3.2   Identification of Research – Search Strategy

In order to perform an exhaustive search for primary studies, our search strategy consisted of a manual search in the major conference and online search in relevant libraries. To ensure the quality of this review, we manually searched in the major conference in this area, the Symposium on Search-Based Software Engineering (SSBSE) (2009-2012). After this, the following electronic databases were searched as we considered these to be most relevant: IEEE Xplore, ACM Digital Library, ISI Web of Science, SpringerLink, and Science Direct.

For the online search in digital libraries, search keywords are very important to obtain good results, so they have to be chosen carefully. Finding an answer to the research question includes selecting appropriate information resources and executing an accurate search strategy. Then, based on our research question, we experimented with different search criteria using different combinations of strings. The following basic search strings were considered the most appropriate for the SR:

1. Software requirements AND selection
2. Software requirements AND prioritization
3. Search Based AND requirements optimization
4. Search Based and requirements selection
5. Search Based AND requirements prioritization

All these search terms were combined by using the Boolean "OR" operator, which implies that an article only had to include any one of the terms to be retrieved. That is, we searched: 1 OR 2 OR 3 OR 4 OR 5. The search terms "software requirements", "selection" and "prioritization" are derived from the terms of the specific area. The inclusion of the term "Search Based" was due to the need to restrict the search to articles that were in the area of software engineering with SBSE approach, to avoid recovering articles that focused on requirements selection and/or prioritization in research fields other than SBSE. We applied the search terms to the titles, abstracts, and keywords of the articles in the identified electronic databases.

Due to the different functions and features of search engines, the search strings for the digital libraries were similar and we had to implement the search strategy individually for each database. This created considerable extra work as we had to perform several trial searches only to find out how each of the databases handled different Boolean expressions. The stages of the study can be seen in Figure 2.

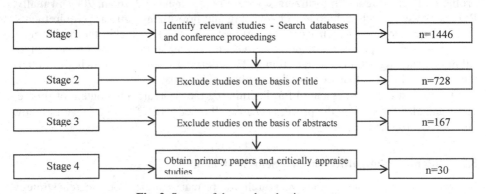

Fig. 2. Stages of the study selection process

3.3   Study Selection Criteria and Procedures

The inclusion and exclusion criteria were defined in the review protocol that we developed for this systematic review. The included primary studies should belong to one of the following categories:

- Category A: Studies which propose a new model or approach using SBSE that can be applied in software requirement selection and/or prioritization; or
- Category B: Studies which apply existing models and techniques to software requirement selection and/or prioritization using SBSE.

The following studies would be excluded during the study selection phase:

- Studies on software requirements selection or prioritization that do not use a Search-Based Software Engineering approach
- Studies on training, editorials, article, summaries, interviews, prefaces, news, reviews, correspondence, tutorials, poster session, workshops and panels.

Thus, studies were eligible for inclusion in our review if they presented all the characteristics from SBSE and passed the minimum quality threshold (Table 1- Section Quality Assessment). The SR included studies published from 2001 to 2012 and only studies written in English were included.

The reason for choosing studies from 2001 was due to usage optimization methods in software engineering as described in (Harman & Jones 2001), when the term SBSE was created and the studies in this area were categorized in the SBSE field.

As can be seen in Figure 2, our study selection started searching for relevant studies based on their titles, abstracts and keywords. Relevant studies are the potential candidates for primary studies and the full papers were fully analyzed. We reviewed each relevant study to determine whether it was a primary study. This was necessary because in the software requirements engineering area, title, abstract and keywords are not usually enough to determine the content of a paper. Therefore, we reviewed the full paper before making a final decision on whether to include or exclude it. More specifically, at stage 1, duplicate citations were identified and removed. In the second stage, we excluded studies that were clearly not about software engineering requirements. Titles that were clearly outside the scope of the systematic review were removed. However, in case of doubt, some articles were considered for the third stage. In this phase, studies were excluded on the basis of abstracts if their focus was not software requirements selection or prioritization using the SBSE approach. However, some abstracts are poor or misleading and several gave little information about what was in the article. Therefore, at this stage we included all the studies that shared some characteristics with our proposed SR. Finally, if the article was not clear from the title, abstract and keywords it was included for a deep quality assessment.

3.4   Quality Assessment

We chose eighteen criteria to obtain and assess each primary study resulting from stage 4. These criteria were based on a study presented in (Barros & Dias-neto, 2011) in which the authors developed a systematic approach to assess experimental studies in the SBSE field.

From this, we developed a checklist in which every question has "yes" or "no" answer. Table 1 presents this study quality assessment checklist. For a better understanding of the evaluation, we decided to divide these criteria into five groups. The first one refers to general aspects and structural information about the article and is to assess whether the selected work is within the context of experiments in the area of software engineering (Jedlitschka & Pfahl, 2005; Kitchenham et al., 2010; Sjoberg, Hannay, Hansen & Kampenes, 2005).

Table 1. Quality Criteria

Quality Criteria
General
1- Is there a proper introduction to the article?
2-Does it have a clear idea of the research objectives?
3- Is there a clear statement of the results?
4- Are there any limitations or restrictions on the results?
5- Does the study make a projection of value for research and practice?
Internal Validity
6- Is the source code used in the study discussed and made available to other researchers?
7- Does the article details the procedure for collecting the data used in the experiment?
8-Does the article present an explicit definition of the target instance (random and real)?
Conclusion Validity
9- Does the experiment consider random variations (different runs) in the algorithms presented?
10- Is the hypothesis of the study formally presented?
11- Are statistical inference tests used?
12- Is there a significant basis for comparison between the techniques used and the best known solutions?
Construction Validity
13- Does the article discuss the model adopted for the optimization process?
14- Does the article discuss the validity of effectiveness measures?
External Validity
15- Does the study clearly show the strategy of selecting instances? (real data or randomly generated)
16- Does the study treat the variation in the complexity of the instances used in the experiment?
17- Does the study use real world instances in the experiment?
18- Does the study present the parameter values used in the experiment?

The other groups are related to threats to the validity of experiments in SBSE. As proposed by Wohlin (Wohlin et al, 2000) threats to validity are risks associated with the design, implementation and analysis of results from experimental studies. The criteria included in the group of internal validity are to evaluate if the relationship is between the observed treatment and the outcome. That is, the experiment must ensure that it is a relationship of cause and not the result of a factor over which the researcher has no control.

The group about conclusion validity contains criteria that relate treatment and outcomes, therefore statistical procedures must be used to evaluate the significance of results (Barros & Dias-neto, 2011).The construction validity group contains criteria concerned with the relationship between theory and observation (Wohlin et al., 2000). Finally, the last set of criteria deals with external validity by focusing on the generalization of the results observed in an experiment for a larger population, beyond the instances that make up the sample used in the study (Barros & Dias-neto, 2011).

In the remainder of this work, each quality criterion is identified with the Q and the number of the criteria, for example, Q1 refers to the first Quality criteria in Table 1.

4   Results and Discussion

We identified 30 studies on software requirements selection and prioritization. Table 2 presents the articles that were selected after applying the inclusion and exclusion criteria depicted in our systematic review protocol. As can be seen in this table, the selected studies are sorted and given an identification number (id), year of publication, and paper title.

First of all, the quantitative data (Figures 3 to 8) relating to the problem of selecting and prioritizing software requirements are presented in the following sequence: (i) problem addressed discussed in the selected studies, (ii) methods/approaches used for solving the problem, (iii) search techniques adopted and, finally, (iv) analysis of articles through quality criteria adopted for assessment of experimental studies in SBSE (Table 1).

After the presentation of these results, the qualitative data extracted was analyzed, showing recent trends and possibilities, strengths and weaknesses in the field. Initially, the results indicated a growing number of publications from 2009 (Table 2). In this case, this is the result of the increase in the total publication number, due to the creation of the International Symposium on Search-Based Software Engineering, where the program adopted multiple areas, and specifically in 2010 when an area was dedicated to requirements selection and prioritization alone.

With regard to problem addressed in software requirements selection, Figure 3 shows quantitative data about selection and prioritization requirements approaches presented in the selected papers. Five kinds of works were identified: NRP (Next Release Problem), MONRP (Multiple Objective Next Release Problem), RP (Release Planning), Prior (Prioritization of requirements), RIM (Requirements Interaction Management). The most frequently addressed problem is the Next Release Problem, however, more recent articles show a growing interest in MONRP.

These data answer the first research question (RQ 1) about what types of modeling are being used in selection and prioritization of software requirements with a focus on SBSE. Observing Table 2 and the data in Figure 3, it can be seen that initially the studies focused on single objective modeling. However, MONRP is a recent trend as in 2007 (Zhang, Harman, & Mansouri, 2007) published their work arguing that the multi-objective formulation is more realistic than the single objective one, because requirements engineering is characterized by the presence of many complex and conflicting demands.

Table 2. Selected Studies

Year	Title	References
2009	Search Based Data Sensitivity Analysis applied to Requirement Engineering	Harman, M., Krinke, J., Ren, J., Yoo, S.
2010	Search Based Optimization of Requirements Interaction Management	Zhang, Y, Harman, M
2007	The Multi-Objective Next Release Problem	Zhang, Y, Harman, M. & Mansouri, S.A
2009	A Study of The Multi-Objective Next Release Problem	Durillo, J.J. et al
2008	Software Product Release Planning Through optimization and what-if Analysis.	Van den Akker, M. et al
2010	Using Interactive GA for Requirements Priorization	Tonella, P., Susi, A. & Palma, F
2001	The Next Release Problem	Bagnall, A., Rayward-Smith, V.;Whittley, I
2004	Software Release Planning: an evolutionary and iterative approach	Greer, D ;Ruhe, G
2011	Software Next Release Planning Approach Through Exact Optimization	Freitas, F., Coutinho, D. & T. Souza, J.,.
2009	A New Approach to The Software Release Planning	Colares, F. et al.
2010	An Integrated Approach for Requirement Selection and Scheduling in Software Release Planning	Li, C. et al
2007	Flexible Release Planning using Integer Linear Programming	Van Den Akker, J.M. et al
2009	A search based approach to fairness analysis in requirement assignments to aid negotiation, mediation and decision making	Finkelstein, A., Harman, M., Mansouri, S. A., Ren, J., Zhang, Y.
2008	A systematic approach for solving the wicked problem of software release planning	Ngo-The, A,Ruhe, Guenther
2011	A Study of The Bi-Objective Next Release Problem	Durillo, J.J. et al.
2010	Comparing The Performance of Metaheuristics for the Analysis of Multi-stakeholder Tradeoffs in Requirements Optimisation	Zhang, Y. et al.
2012	Empirical Evaluation of Search Based Requirements Interaction Management	Zhang, Y., Harman, M., Lim, S.L
2006	Search Based Approaches to Component Selection and Priorization for the Next Release Problem	Baker et al.
2007	Bi-Objective Release Planning for Evolving Software	Saliu, M. Ruhe, G
2010	Ant Colony Optimization for the Next Release Problem	Del Sagrado, J., Del Aguila, I., Orellana, F.
2003	Quantitative Studies in Software Release Planning under Risk and Resource Constraints	Ruhe, Günther, Greer, Des
2005	Supporting Software Release Planning Decision for Evolving Systems	Saliu, O.,Ruhe, G
2010	A Hybrid ACO Algorithm for The Next Release Problem	Jiang, H., Zhang, J., et al..
2012	Software Requirements Selection using Quantum-inspired Elitist Multi-objective Evolutionary Algorithm	Kumari, A.C., Srinivas, K. & Science, C
2005	Determination of the Next Release of a Software product: an Approach using Integer Linear Programming	Van Den Akker,J.M et al.
2012	Interactive Requirements Priorization using a Genetic Algorithm	Tonella, P., Susi, A,Palma, F
2012	Solving the Large Scale Next Release Problem with a Backbone-based Multilevel Algorithm	Xuan, J. et al.
2005	Software Release Planning for Evolving Systems	Saliu, Omolade,Ruhe, Guenther
2010	Approximate Backbone Based Multilevel Algorithm for Next Release Problem	Jiang, H., Xuan, J. , Ren, Z.
2011	An Ant Colony Optimization Approach to the software Release Planning Problem with Dependent Requirements	Souza, J.T. et al

Regarding Research Question 2 (RQ2), about what methods are used for selection and prioritization of software requirements with a focus on SBSE, the results can be seen in Figure 4. They can be divided into four groups: 1) Metaheuristics 2) exact search techniques to obtain optimal solutions 3) hybrid methods containing both the meta-heuristics and exact search techniques; and 4) a new formulation created to tackle the problem. It was observed that meta-heuristics is arguably the most commonly applied method in experiments in search of solutions for requirements selection and prioritization problems. Indeed, given the complex interrelationships between requirements, generally it is quite costly to find an optimal solution. Therefore, the use of meta-heuristics may be more appropriate when there is uncertainty and difficulty in finding a single optimal solution.

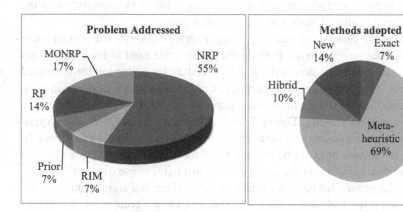

Fig. 3. Problem addressed   Fig. 4. Methods adopted

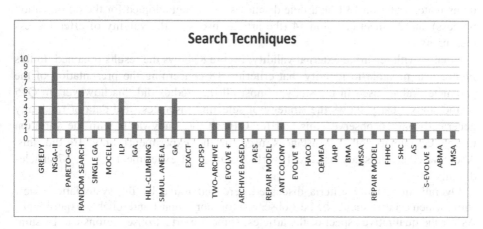

Fig. 5. Search Techniques

With regard to which methods are used for the process of selecting and prioritizing requirements with a focus on SBSE (RQ 3), the results obtained in our systematic review can be seen in Figure 5. Multiple search techniques are used in experiments to obtain good solutions. According to the data obtained, it is evident that the NSGA-II (Non-Sorted Genetic Algorithm II) is the most frequently used algorithm, followed by Genetic Algorithm, Integer Linear Programming, and Greedy.

Random Search is used for comparison of results and is not considered as a method to solve the problem of selecting and prioritizing requirements. Many authors consider NSGA-II to be the fastest and most effective solution for a search in large and complex spaces, therefore the choice of this method is probably the most remembered.

With respect to the constructs of quality criteria (see Table 1), initially, as to the general validity, practically all items showed excellent rates.

Figure 6 shows the results obtained regarding internal validity. These data show that nearly half of the articles do not provide the source code used in the experiments (Q6) and more than 20 articles do not detail the procedure for collecting the data used in the experiment (Q7). Regarding question 8, definition of instance destination (random or real), more than 20 studies meet this criterion.

Regarding conclusion validity, Figure 7 shows the data. About Q9 (if the experiment consider random variations (different runs) in the algorithms presented), only 16 papers did this. In the case of Q10 (the hypothesis of the study formally presented), 19 papers do not do this. Concerning the quality criterion 11 (Q11- use of statistical inference test), only 12 papers did this, and finally, Q12- if there is a significant basis for comparison between the techniques used and the best known solutions), 17 articles fulfill this.

In relation to items that address construct validity, good numbers are obtained, 29 items match criterion 13 (the article discusses the model adopted for the optimization process) and 24 meet criterion 14 (the article discusses the validity of effectiveness measures).

Finally, with regard to external validity, Figure 8 shows the results obtained. In this Figure it is possible to identify that criterion 18 concerning the presentation of the parameter values used in the study, almost all the studies did this however, in Q15 (if the study clearly shows the strategy of selecting instances (real data or randomly generated) only 16 observed this and for Q16 (if the study deals with the variation in the complexity of the instances used in the experiment) only 10 did this. About whether the study used real world instances in experiment (Q17), 17 articles did this.

Overall, the quality criteria discussed here and found by the systematic review show which criteria should be best observed for more robust and reliable experiments. As for the qualitative aspect of the articles, some important observations can be summarized:

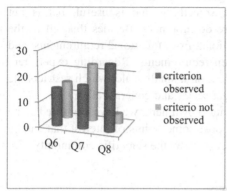

Fig. 6. Internal Validity

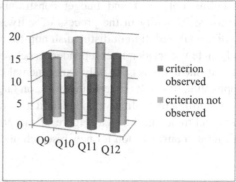

Fig. 7. Conclusion Validity

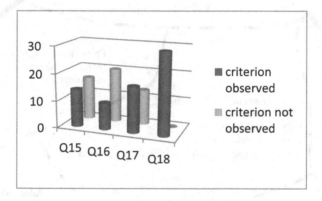

Fig. 8. External Validity

(a) Recent trend to use of multi-objective modeling
(b) Incorporation of new search techniques
(c) Focus on randomly generated data
(d) Little comparison between real and experimental data
(e) Lack of generalization of the models
(f) Experiments with data on a small scale
(g) No categorization of requirements (functional or nonfunctional)
(h) Few studies consider interdependency between software requirements
(i) Modeling consideration only restriction related to budget or costs.

In the studies analyzed in this systematic review it can be seen that there is a recent trend for the use of multi-objective modeling, something to be expected given the power of this type of modeling to solve many conflicting objectives relating to a set of requirements to include in the next release of the software.

Additionally new techniques have been incorporated to help obtain solutions, especially from technical Metaheuristics (see Figure 5). However, many still consider modeling only cost and budget constraints, something that is useful, but is not practiced in reality in the process of software development. Besides this, all of the studies analyzed did not distinguish non-functional from functional requirements, and only a few consider interdependence between requirements. Regarding experiment format, most studies use only experimental data on a small scale, which restricts the application of results in real situations, on larger scales and generalization.

According to qualitative and quantitative data shown here, we have identified some gaps and trends in the area (Figure 9) and propose some points of interest that can be taken into consideration for new research undertaken by the scientific community.

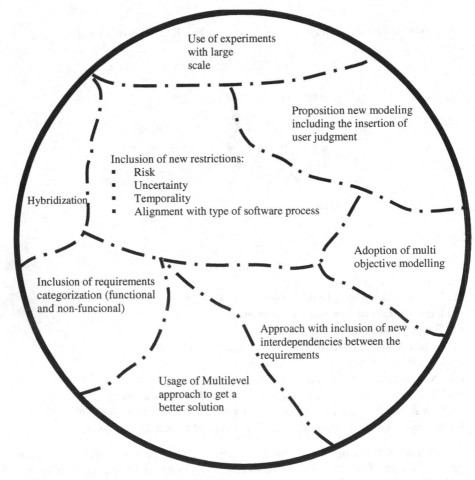

Fig. 9. Gaps and tendencies in SBSE focusing on requirements selection and prioritization

Some items are being researched, such as: (i) the adoption of multi-objective modeling, (ii) usage of hybrid methods to get better solutions, for example, the Hill Climbing Local search in conjunction with Ant Colony Optimization (Jiang, Zhang, et al, 2010), (iii) the interdependencies between requirements, exploring the most common interaction types, such as, precedence, value-related, cost-related, AND operator and exclusive OR, and (iv) usage of experiments on a large scale and multilevel approach, however, there are few studies that use these features. Therefore, there is the possibility of using exact optimization (e.g. mathematical programming and constraint programming) combined with several metaheuristic, such as, evolutionary algorithms, parallel metaheuristics to improve the results obtained in a search.

Recently, a multilevel approach proposes to solve large scales NRP instances exploring iteratively the search spaces by multilevel reductions and refinements (Jiang, Xuan & Ren, 2010). It is a recent trend in SBSE filed and may be further explored in cases of experiments on a large scale experiments.

In terms of innovation for the area three factors may contribute to performing experiments closer to the reality of a software engineer:

(i)   Conduct experiments in SBSE that categorize and differentiate functional and non-functional requirements given that there are differences between them, thus, further experiments can be performed and the results obtained may correspond the reality of the software industry. Currently, there are no studies in NRP that achieves this differentiation and its consequences,

(ii) Add user judgment in modeling the problem of selecting and prioritizing requirements. This may lead to better results and experiments closer to the user requirements,

(iii) The inclusion of new restrictions could make the experiments closer to the reality of the software industry, where uncertainties, risks, factors related to project deadlines and the use of software process have a significant impact on software development.

A promising area that can be observed for software requirements selection is robust optimization, where various aspects of risks and uncertainties are added to optimization models. According to Ben-Tal and Nemirovski (Ben-Tal & Nemirovski, 2001), Robust Optimization is a modeling methodology, combined with computational tools, to process optimization problems in which the data are uncertain and is only known to belong to some uncertainty set. This method can be very effective in the engineering process requirements since human experts faces a scenario with multiple decisions where there are several associated uncertainties and risks.

Figure 9 presents the gaps and tendencies in SBSE focusing on requirements selection and prioritization according to the results obtained in this systematic review. It is important to note that the eight areas present in that figure can be used in conjunction, may enable studies and experiments in the selection and prioritization of software requirements more effective, achieving better results and closer to the reality of the software industry.

5   Conclusions

Requirements engineering is a complex discipline that covers multiple activities in the software development process. Some important tasks such as selecting and prioritization requirements can be an extremely arduous and exhaustive task throughout the process, depending on the size of the software features of the application domain, interdependence between requirements, among others.

In order to support the search for automated and less exhaustive solutions Search-Based Software Engineering has emerged with the characteristic to address the problems of software engineering as a search based optimization problem.

Given the growth of this approach and obtaining meaningful results, the work developed here studied and identified the state of the art applications of optimization in the process of software requirements selection and prioritization using SBSE approach.

It was possible to identify the techniques and approaches which are already established in the area, such as mono-objective modeling and NSGA-II, as well as identify some gaps in conducting experiments and possible future trends in this field.

This systematic review not only identified the techniques and methods most frequently used in the experiments, but also analyzed some quality criteria that must be taken into consideration when approaching the arduous task of selecting and prioritizing requirements. Some key points can be considered for further experiments:

- Insertion of statistical inference tests that can support the results obtained.
- Formal presentation of the hypothesis for a better understanding of what is the desired result
- Adoption of real world instances (for example, data from the software industry) to be closer to software industry reality.

From the qualitative results extracted from the analyzed articles it can be seen that multi-goal modeling is a trend that is growing in the current studies, however, there is much room to create models even closer to the reality of software engineers. Insertion of the user judgment and the inclusion of new restrictions, such risks and uncertainties, constitute an open field for exploration. Consideration of the interdependence between requirements already being used, however, still requires further elaboration.

Future work includes studying the use of robust optimization to include new fitness functions and new restrictions in the modeling process.

References

Aasem, M., Ramzan, M., Jaffar, A., Islamabad, E.S.: Analysis and optimization of software requirements prioritization techniques. In: Information and Emerging Technologies (ICIET) (2010)

Bagnall, A.J., Rayward-Smith, V.J., Whittley, I.M.: The next release problem. Information and Software Technology 43(14), 883–890 (2001)

Baker, et al.: Search Based approaches to Component Selection and prioritization for the Next Release Problem. In: 22nd IEEE International Conference on Software Maintenance (ICSM 2006), pp. 176–185 (2006)

Barros, M.D.O., Dias-neto, A.C.: Developing a Systematic Approach to Evaluation of Experimental Studies on Search-Based Software Engineering. Brazilian Conference on Software: Theory and Practic (2011) (in Port uguese)

Ben-Tal, A., Nemirovski, A.: Robust Optimization – methodology and applications. Mathematical Programming 92(3), 453–480 (2002)

Boehm, B., Grunbacher, P.: Developing Groupware for Requirements Negotiation:Lessons Learned. IEEE Software 18(2) (2001)

Carlshamre, P., Sandahla, K., Lindvallb, M., Regnellc, B., Natt, J.: An Industrial Survey of Requirements Interdependencies in Software Product Release Planning. In: Fifth IEEE International Symposium on Requirements Engineering (RE 2001), pp. 84–92 (2001)

Cheng, B., Atlee, J.: Research Directions in Requirements Engineering. In: Future of Software Engineering Conference (FOSE 2007) (2007)

Colares, F., et al.: A New Approach to the Software Release Planning. In: XXIII Brazilian Symposium on Software Engineering, pp. 207–215 (2009)

Deb, K., Pratap, A., Agarwal, S., Meyarivan, T.: A Fast and Elitist Multiobjective Genetic Algorithm: NSGA-II. IEEE Transactions on Evolutionary Computation 6(2), 182–197 (2002)

Del Sagrado, J., Del Aguila, I.M., Orellana, F.J.: Ant Colony Optimization for the Next Release Problem: A Comparative Study. In: 2nd International Symposium on Search Based Software Engineering, pp. 67–76 (2010)

Del Sagrado, J., Águila, I.M., Orellana, F.J.: Requirements Interaction in the Next Release Problem. In: GECCO 2011, pp. 241–242 (2011)

Durillo, J.J., et al.: A Study of the Bi-objective Next Release Problem. Empirical Software Engineering 16(1), 29–60 (2011)

Durillo, J.J., et al.: A Study of the Multi-objective Next Release Problem. 1st International Symposium on Search Based Software Engineering, 49–58 (2009)

Dyba, T., Dingsoyr, T., Hanssen, G.K.: Applying Systematic Reviews to Diverse Study Types: An Experience Report. In: First International Symposium on Empirical Software Engineering and Measurement (ESEM 2007) (2007)

Felows, L., Hooks, I.: A Case for Priority Classifying Requirements. In: 8th Annual International Symposium on Systems Engineering, Seattle, Washington (1998)

Finkelstein, A., Harman, M., Mansouri, S.A., Ren, J., Zhang, Y.: A search based approach to fairness analysis in requirement assignments to aid negotiation, mediation and decision making. Requirements Engineering 14(4), 231–245 (2009)

Finkelstein, A., Harman, M., Mansouri, S., Ren, J., Zhang, Y.: Fairness Analysis in Requirements Assignments. In: Proceedings of the 16th IEEE International Requirements Engineering Conference (RE 2008), September 8-12, pp. 115–124. IEEE Computer Society, Barcelona (2008)

Freitas, F., Coutinho, D.P., Souza, J.T.: Software Next Release Planning Approach through Exact Optimization. International Journal of Computer Applications 22(8), 1–8 (2011)

Goldberg, D.E.: Genetic Algorithms in Search, Optimizatiom, and Machine Learning. Adisson-Wesley, EUA (1989)

Greer, D., Ruhe, G.: Software release planning: an evolutionary and iterative approach. Information and Software Technology 46(4), 243–253 (2004)

Harman, M.: The Current State and Future of Search Based Software Engineering The Current State and Future of Search Based Software Engineering. Techniques (2007)

Harman, M., Jones, B.F.: Search-based software engineering. Information and Software Technology 43(14), 833–839 (2001)

Harman, M., Krinke, J., Ren, J., Yoo, S.: Search Based Data Sensitivity Analysis Applied to Requirement Engineering. Analysis, 1681–1688 (2009)

Harman, M., McMinn, P., de Souza, J.T., Yoo, S.: Search Based Software Engineering: Techniques, Taxonomy, Tutorial. In: Meyer, B., Nordio, M. (eds.) LASER Summer School 2008-2010. LNCS, vol. 7007, pp. 1–59. Springer, Heidelberg (2012)

Heger, D.A.: A Disquisition on The Performance Behavior of Binary Search Tree Data Structures. European Journal for the Informatics Professional (2004)

Jedlitschka, A., Pfahl, D.: Reporting Guidelines for Controlled Experiments in Software Engineering Dietmar Pfahl. In: ISESE, pp. 95–104 (2005)

Jiang, H., Zhang, J., et al.: A Hybrid ACO Algorithm for the Next Release Problem. In: Proceedings of 2nd International Conference on Software Engineering and Data Mining (SEDM 2010), pp. 166–171 (2010)

Jiang, H., Xuan, J., Ren, Z.: Approximate backbone based multilevel algorithm for next release problem. In: Proceedings of the 12th Annual Conference on Genetic and Evolutionary Computation (GECCO 2010), p. 1333 (2010)

Karlsson, J., Wohlin, C., Regnell, B.: An evaluation of methods for prioritizing software requirements. Information and Software Technology 39(14-15), 939–947 (1998)

Karlsson, J., Ryan, K.: A Cost-Value Approach for Prioritizing Requirements. IEEE Software 14(5), 67–74 (1997)

Kitchenham, B.: Procedures for Performing Systematic Reviews (p. 28). Keele UniversityTecnical Report TR/SE-0401 ISSN:1353-776, Australia (2004)

Kitchenham, B.A., Dybå, T., Jorgensen, M.: Evidence-based Software Engineering. In: Proceedings of 26th International Conference on Software Engineering. IEEE Computer Society (2004)

Kitchenham, B., Sjøberg, D.I.K., Brereton, O.P., Budgen, D., Dybå, T., Höst, M., Pfahl, D., et al.: Can we evaluate the quality of software engineering experiments? In: Proceedings of the ACM-IEEE International Symposium on Empirical Software Engineering and Measurement (ESEM 2010) (2010)

Kotonya, G., Sommerville, I.: Requirements Engineering: Processes and Techniques. Wiley (1998)

Kumari, A.C., Srinivas, K., Science, C.: Software Requirements Selection using Quantum inspired Elitist Multi-objective Evolutionary Algorithm. In: IEEE ICAESM (2012)

Li, C., van den Akker, J.M., Brinkkemper, S., Diepen, G.: Integrated Requirement Selection and Scheduling for the Release Planning of a Software Product. In: Sawyer, P., Heymans, P. (eds.) REFSQ 2007. LNCS, vol. 4542, pp. 93–108. Springer, Heidelberg (2007)

Li, C., et al.: An integrated approach for requirement selection and scheduling in software release planning. Requirements Engineering 15(4), 375–396 (2010)

Ngo-The, A., Ruhe, G.: A systematic approach for solving the wicked problem of software release planning. Soft Computing 12(1), 95–108 (2007)

Pressman, R.: Software Engineering, 5th edn. McGraw-Hill (2002)

Ruhe, G., Greer, D.: Quantitative Studies in Software Release Planning under Risk and Resource Constraints University of Calgary. Empirical Software Engineering, 1–10 (2003)

Saaty, T.L.: The Analytic Hierarchy Process, McGraw-Hill, Inc. (1980)

Saliu, M., Ruhe, G.: Bi-Objective Release Planning for Evolving Software Systems. In: Proceedings of the 6th Joint Meeting of the European Software Engineering Conference and the ACM SIGSOFT International Symposium on Foundations of Software Engineering (ESEC/FSE), pp. 105–114 (2007)

Saliu, O., Ruhe, G.: Supporting Software Release Planning Decisions for Evolving Systems. In: 29th Annual IEEE/NASA Software Engineering Workshop, pp. 14–26 (2005)

Saliu, O., Ruhe, G.: Software release planning for evolving systems. Innovations in Systems and Software Engineering 1(2), 189–204 (2005)

Sjøberg, D.I.K., Hannay, J.E., Hansen, O., Kampenes, V.B.: A Survey of Controlled Experiments in Software Engineering. ISESE 31, 733–753 (2005)

Sommerville, I.: Software Engineering, 8th edn. Pearson-Addison Wesley (2007)

De Souza, J.T., et al.: An Ant Colony Optimization Approach to the Software Release Planning with Dependent Requirements. In: Proceedings of the Third International Conference on Search Based

Talbi, E.-G.: Metaheuristics: from design to implementation. John Wiley & Sons (2009)

Tonella, P., Susi, A., Palma, F.: Interactive Requirements Prioritization using a Genetic Algorithm. Information and Software Technology, 1–15 (2012)

Tonella, P., Susi, A., Palma, F.: Using Interactive GA for Requirements Prioritization. In: 2nd International Symposium on Search Based Software Engineering (Section II), pp. 57–66 (2010)

Van Den Akker, J.M., et al.: Determination of the Next Release of a Software Product: an Approach using Integer Linear. In: Proceedings of CAISE 2005, vol. 03018, pp. 119–124 (2005)

Van Den Akker, J.M., et al.: Flexible Release Planning using Integer Linear Programming. In: Proceedings of the 11th International Workshop on Requirements Engineering for Software Quality (RefsQ 2005) (2005)

Van den Akker, M., et al.: Software product release planning through optimization and what-if analysis. Information and Software Technology 50(1-2), 101–111 (2008)

Wiegers, K.: First Thing First: Prioritizing Requirements. Software Developmnet (September 1999)

Wohlin, C., Runeson, P., Host, M., Ohlsson, M., Regnell, B., Wesslen, A.: Experimentation in Software Engineering; An Introduction. Kluwer Academic Publishers (2000)

Xuan, J., et al.: Solving the Large Scale Next Release Problem with a Backbone-Based Multilevel Algorithm 38(10), 1–18 (2012)

Zave, P.: Classification of Research Efforts in Requirements Engineering. ACM Computing Studis 29(4), 315–321 (1997)

Zhang, Y., et al.: Comparing the performance of metaheuristics for the analysis of multi-stakeholder tradeoffs in requirements optimisation. Information and Software Technology 53(7), 761–773 (2011)

Zhang, Y., Harman, M.: Search Based Optimization of Requirements Interaction Management. In: 2nd International Symposium on Search Based Software Engineering, pp. 47–56 (2010)

Zhang, Y.: Multi-Objective Search-based Requirements Selection and Optimisation. King's College London, UK (2010)

Zhang, Y., Harman, M., Lim, S.L.: Empirical evaluation of search based requirements interaction management. Information and Software Technology (2012)

Zhang, Y., Harman, M., Mansouri, S.A.: The multi-objective next release problem. In: Proceedings of the 9th Annual Conference on Genetic and Evolutionary Computation (GECCO 2007), p. 1129 (2007)

Zhang, Y.-Y., Finkelstein, A., Harman, M.: Search Based Requirements Optimisation: Existing Work and Challenges. In: Rolland, C. (ed.) REFSQ 2008. LNCS, vol. 5025, pp. 88–94. Springer, Heidelberg (2008)

Regression Testing for Model Transformations: A Multi-objective Approach

Jeffery Shelburg, Marouane Kessentini, and Daniel R. Tauritz

Department of Computer Science
Missouri University of Science and Technology, Rolla, MO, USA
{jssdn2,marouanek}@mst.edu, dtauritz@acm.org

Abstract. In current model-driven engineering practices, metamodels are modified followed by an update of transformation rules. Next, the updated transformation mechanism should be validated to ensure quality and robustness. Model transformation testing is a recently proposed effective technique used to validate transformation mechanisms. In this paper, a more efficient approach to model transformation testing is proposed by refactoring the existing test case models, employed to test previous metamodel and transformation mechanism versions, to cover new changes. To this end, a multi-objective optimization algorithm is employed to generate test case models that maximizes the coverage of the new metamodel while minimizing the number of test case model refactorings as well as test case model elements that have become invalid due to the new changes. Validation results on a widely used transformation mechanism confirm the effectiveness of our approach.

Keywords: search-based software engineering, testing, model transformation, multi-objective optimization.

1 Introduction

Model-Driven Engineering (MDE) considers models as first-class artifacts during the software lifecycle. The number of available tools, techniques, and approaches for MDE are growing that support a wide variety of activities such as model creation, model transformation, and code generation. The use of different domain-specific modeling languages and diverse versions of the same language increases the need for interoperability between languages and their accompanying tools [1]. Therefore, metamodels are regularly updated along with their respective transformation mechanism.

Afterwards, the updated transformation mechanism should be validated to assure quality and robustness. One efficient validation method proposed recently is model transformation testing [1,2] which consists of generating source models as test cases, applying the transformation mechanism to them, and verifying the result using an oracle function such as a comparison with an expected result. Two challenges are: (1) the efficient generation of test cases, and (2) the definition of the oracle function. This paper focuses on the efficient generation of test cases in the form of source models.

G. Ruhe and Y. Zhang (Eds.): SSBSE 2013, LNCS 8084, pp. 209–223, 2013.
© Springer-Verlag Berlin Heidelberg 2013

The generation of test case models for model transformation mechanisms is challenging because many issues need to be addressed. As explained in [3], testing model transformation is distinct from testing traditional implementations; the input data are models that are complex when compared to simple data types which complicates the generation and evaluation of test case models [4]. The basis of the work presented in this paper starts from the observation that most existing approaches in testing evolved transformation mechanisms regenerate all test cases from scratch. However, this can be a very fastidious task since the expected output for all test cases needs to be completely redefined by hand. Furthermore, when the number of changes made between metamodel versions is relatively small in comparison to metamodel sizes, redefining all test case output is inefficient. A better strategy is to revise existing test cases to cover new changes in metamodels to reduce the effort required to manually redefine expected test case output.

In this paper, a multi-objective search-based approach is used to generate test case models that maximizes the coverage of a newly updated metamodel while minimizing the number of refactorings applied to existing test case models in addition to minimizing the number of test case model elements that have become invalid due to the new changes. The proposed algorithm is an adaptation of multi-objective simulated annealing (MOSA) [5] and aims to find a Pareto optimal solution consisting of test case model refactorings that will yield the new test case models when applied to existing test case models of the previous version metamodel that best satisfy the three criteria previously mentioned. This approach is implemented and evaluated on a known case of transforming UML 1.4 class diagrams to UML 2.0 class diagrams [6]. Results detailing the effectiveness of the proposed approach are compared to results of a traditional simulated annealing (SA) approach (whose single objective is to maximize metamodel coverage) to create UML 2.0 test case models in two scenarios: (1) updating test case models for UML 1.4 and (2) creating new test case models from scratch. Results indicate that the proposed approach holds great promise as using MOSA from previous test case models attains slightly less metamodel coverage than using SA with, however, significantly less refactorings and invalid model elements while always outperforming both methods starting from scratch.

The primary contributions of this paper are summarized as follows: (1) A novel formulation of the model transformation testing problem is introduced using a novel multi-objective optimization technique, and (2) results of an empirical study comparing the proposed MOSA approach to a traditional SA approach in scenarios starting from previous test case models and from scratch are reported. The obtained results provide evidence supporting the claim that the proposed MOSA approach requires less manual effort to update expected output than SA and starting from existing test case models is more effective than regenerating all test case models from scratch.

2 Methodology

In this section, the three main components of any search-based approach are defined: the solution representation, change operators, and objective function.

2.1 Solution Representation

Since the proposed approach needs to modify test case models in response to changes at the metamodel level, the solution produced should yield a modified version of the original test case models that best conforms to the updated metamodel. This can be done primarily in one of two different ways: the solution could either consist of the actual updated test case model itself, or represent a structure that, when applied to the original test case models, produces the updated test case models. The latter was chosen for this problem in the form of lists of model refactorings, because it allows a sequence of refactorings to be modified at any point in the sequence.

For example, if a search-based method was employed to generate the new test case models and a suboptimal refactoring was included in the best found test case model solution at some point in the search process, it would be difficult to reverse the application of the suboptimal refactoring to the best found test case model solution if the test case model was modified directly. This is because it would need to search and find the refactoring in the space of all possible refactorings to apply to the test case model to reverse or change the suboptimal refactoring. By modifying a list of model refactorings, it is easier for the search process to remove or modify the suboptimal refactoring because it has direct access to the model refactorings included in the best found solution. Furthermore, maintaining a list of the best sequence of refactorings found during the search process gives direct information about what exactly was changed from the previous version test case models that makes updating the expected output a simpler task.

Each element in the lists of refactorings solution representation is a list of model refactorings that corresponds to a test case model. Each list of model refactorings is comprised of model refactorings that are applied to the corresponding test case model in the order in which they appear in the list. Applying these refactorings transforms the existing test case models into the updated test case models for the updated metamodel. An example of model refactorings that can be applied to UML class diagrams are shown in Table 1. Figure 1 shows an example of a possible list of UML refactorings for a test case model that moves method *getAge* from class *Employee* to class *Person*, adds a *Salary* field to the *Employee* class, and then removes the *Job* class, in that order.

| MoveMethod(getAge, Employee, Person) | AddField(Salary, Employee) | RemoveClass(Job) |

Fig. 1. Example list of UML class diagram model refactorings

Table 1. UML class diagram model refactorings

Add Field	Add Association	Move Field	Push Down Field
Add Method	Add Generalization	Move Method	Push Down Method
Add Class	Remove Method	Extract Class	Pull Up Field
Remove Field	Remove Association	Extract Subclass	Pull Up Method
Remove Class	Remove Generalization	Extract Superclass	Collapse Hierarchy
Change Bi- to Uni-Directional Association		Change Uni- to Bi-Directional Association	

2.2 Change Operators

The only change operator employed in MOSA is mutation. When mutating a given test case model's list of refactorings, the type of mutation to perform is first determined from a user-defined probability distribution that chooses between inserting a refactoring into the list, removing a refactoring from the list, or modifying a refactoring in the list. When inserting a refactoring into a list of refactorings, an insertion point between refactorings is first chosen, including either ends of the list. The refactorings that appear in the list before the insertion point are first applied to the test case model in the order in which they appear in the list. A refactoring is then randomly generated for the refactored test case model as it exists at the selection point, applied to the model, and inserted into the list at the insertion point. The refactorings that appear after the insertion point in the list are then validated in the order in which they appear by first checking their validity and subsequently applying them to the test case model if they are valid. If a refactoring is found to be invalid due to a conflict caused by the insertion of the new refactoring into the list, the refactoring is removed from the list. An invalid refactoring could occur, for example, if a new refactoring is inserted into the front of a list that removes a specific class attribute that is referenced in an existing refactoring later in the list. If such an occurrence happened, the existing refactoring that references the now-removed class attribute will be removed from the list. When performing a mutation that removes a refactoring from a list of refactorings, a refactoring is selected at random and removed from the list. Validation is performed in the same manner as when inserting a refactoring for those refactorings that appear after the removed refactoring in the list of refactorings.

When mutating a refactoring in the list of refactorings, a refactoring is first randomly selected. Then, one of three types of mutations is selected for application to the selected refactoring using a user-defined probability distribution: (1) replace the selected refactoring with a new randomly-generated refactoring, (2) replace the selected refactoring with a new randomly-generated refactoring of the same refactoring type (e.g., replace a *MoveField* refactoring with a new randomly generated *MoveField* refactoring), or (3) mutate a parameter of the selected refactoring. An example of a refactoring parameter mutation is changing the target class of a *MoveMethod* refactoring to another randomly chosen class in the model. Validation for all three types of refactoring mutations are performed in the same manner as described previously.

2.3 Objective Functions

Objective functions are a very important component of any search-based algorithm, because they define the metrics upon which solutions are compared that ultimately guides the search process. In the context of determining the quality of lists of refactorings to be applied to test case models in response to metamodel changes, three objective functions that define characteristics of a good solution are: (1) maximize updated metamodel coverage, (2) minimize model elements that do not conform to the updated metamodel, and (3) minimize the number of refactorings used to refactor the existing test case models.

Maximizing the coverage of the updated metamodel is imperative because the sole purpose of test case models is to ensure that the model transformation mechanisms are robust. Minimizing the number of invalid test case model elements due to metamodel changes ensures that the test case models themselves are free of defects in order to properly assess the quality of the model transformation mechanism being tested. Finally, minimizing the number of refactorings used to refactor the test case models reduces the amount of effort required to update the expected output for the test case model transformations.

Metamodel Coverage. Since UML metamodels are utilized in the experimentation described in this paper, UML metamodel coverage is described here; however, note that different methods of calculating metamodel coverage may exist for different metamodel types. The method used to derive UML metamodel coverage was first introduced in [4]. This method begins by a priori performing partition analysis in which the types of coverage criteria taken into consideration for a given problem are chosen. For metamodel coverage, an adaptation of the same three coverage criteria from [4] are used. These criteria are association-end multiplicities (AEM), class attributes (CA), and generalizations (GN). AEM refers to the types of multiplicities used in associations included in a metamodel such as *0..1, 1..1,* or *1..N*. CA refers to the types of class attributes included in a metamodel such as *integer, string,* or *boolean*. Since the metamodels used in the empirical tests in this paper support class operations in addition to attributes, class method return types are included in CA. GN refers to the coverage of classes that belong to each of the following categories: *superclass, subclass, both superclass and subclass,* and *neither superclass nor subclass*.

Each coverage criterion must be partitioned into logical partitions that, when unioned together, represent all the value types each criterion could take on. These partitions are then assigned representative values to represent each coverage criterion partition. For example, if a metamodel allows for classes to have an *integer* attribute, then the *integer* class attribute element is included in the CA coverage criterion. The values an *integer* class attribute can take on can be split into partitions whose representative values are *<-1, -1, 0, 1,* and *>1*, for example. An example of partition analysis and a subset of the coverage items generated from its representative values are shown in Table 2 and Table 3, respectively.

After representative values are defined, a set of coverage items for the updated metamodel is created. In our adaptation of the coverage item set creation method

Table 2. Partition analysis example showing associated representative values for given coverage criteria

Coverage Criteria	Representative Values
CA: *boolean*	*true, false*
CA: *integer*	*<-1, -1, 0, 1, >1*
CA: *float*	*<-1.0, -1.0, 0.0, 1.0, >1.0*
CA: *string*	*Null, '', 'something'*
AEM: *1..1*	*1*
AEM: *1..N*	*1, N*
GN	*sub, super, both, neither*

Table 3. Subset of coverage items created from representative values found in Table 2

Coverage Items	
CA: *-1*	AEM: *N*
CA: *'something'*	GN: *super*
AEM: *1*	AEM: *N*
AEM: *1*	GN: *neither*
CA: *false*	CA: *>1.0*
CA: *Null*	AEM: *1*

introduced in [4], this is done by calculating all possible 2-tuple combinations of representative values from all partitions of all coverage criteria types that are included in the updated metamodel. The only exception to this are coverage items containing two different GN representative values, because they would be impossible to satisfy. This is done to ensure the robustness of the model transformation mechanism for all possible valid combinations of representative values. The metamodel coverage objective value for given test case models and updated metamodel is determined by calculating the percentage of metamodel coverage items the test case models satisfy. For example, if a given updated metamodel included associations with end multiplicities of *1..1* → *1..N*, then the derived coverage items would include associations with end-multiplicities of *1* → *1* and *1* → *N*. Additionally, if a given updated metamodel also included *boolean* class attributes, then the additional coverage items would include classes with a *boolean* attribute and association end multiplicity of *true* and *1*, *false* and *1*, *true* and *N*, and *false* and *N*, respectively. For a more in-depth example of a model and the coverage items it would satisfy, refer to Figure 2 and Table 4, respectively.

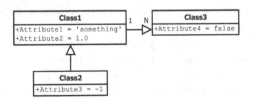

Fig. 2. Example test case model

Table 4. Coverage items satisfied by the example shown in Figure 2

Coverage Items	
CA: *'something'*	CA: *1.0*
CA: *'something'*	AEM: *1*
CA: *1.0*	AEM: *1*
CA: *'something'*	GN: *super*
CA: *1.0*	GN: *super*
AEM: *1*	GN: *super*
CA: *-1*	GN: *sub*
CA: *false*	AEM: *N*
AEM: *1*	AEM: *N*
AEM: *N*	GN: *neither*
CA: *false*	GN: *neither*

Metamodel Conformity. Unlike the bacteriological approach used to automatically generate test case models from scratch in [4], the proposed approach is initialized with test case models that were created to conform to a metamodel that may contain metamodel elements that are not compatible with the updated metamodel. Because of this, there may exist test case model elements that do not conform to the updated metamodel, and if so, should be removed or modified to improve the validity of the test case models by reducing the number of invalid model elements. Calculating the metamodel conformity objective value of given test case models and updated metamodel is done by summing up the number of test case model elements from all test case models that do not conform to the updated metamodel. For example, say Metamodel v1.0 includes *integer* class attributes while Metamodel v2.0 does not. All *integer* model elements from the test case models for Metamodel v1.0 are invalid in Metamodel v2.0, so they need to be removed or modified to a valid class attribute type to improve the validity of the test case models themselves.

Number of Refactorings. While automatically generating test case models in an attempt to maximize metamodel coverage has been previously explored and improving metamodel conformity of test case models by itself can be accomplished trivially by removing or modifying nonconforming test case model elements, performing these tasks by finding a minimal number of refactorings to apply to existing test case models has not yet been explored to our knowledge. By minimizing the number of refactorings required to update existing test case models for an updated metamodel, the task of updating expected test case model transformation output is simplified. The challenge of finding a minimal set of refactorings to apply to test case models to maximize metamodel coverage and minimize the number of nonconforming test case model elements stems from the fact that there are a multitude of different refactoring sequences that can be applied to achieve the same resulting test case models. Calculating the number of refactorings is done by summing up the number of refactorings in the lists of refactorings.

2.4 Search-Based Approach

Simulated Annealing (SA). SA is a local search heuristic inspired by the concept of annealing in metallurgy where metal is heated, raising its energy and relieving it of defects due to its ability to move around more easily. As its temperature drops, the metal's energy drops and eventually it settles in a more stable state and becomes rigid. This technique is replicated in SA by initializing a temperature variable with a "high temperature" value and slowly decreasing the temperature for a set number of iterations by multiplying it by a value α every iteration, where $0 < \alpha < 1$. During each iteration, a mutation operator is applied to a copy of the resulting solution from the previous iteration. If the mutated solution has the same or better fitness than the previous one, it is kept and used for the next iteration. If the mutated solution has a worse fitness, a probability of keeping the mutated solution and using it in the next iteration is calculated using an acceptance probability function. The acceptance probability function takes as input the difference in fitness of the two solutions as well as the current temperature value and outputs the acceptance probability such that smaller differences in solution fitness and higher temperature values will yield higher acceptance probabilities. In effect, this means that for each passing iteration, the probability of keeping a mutated solution with worse fitness decreases, resulting in a search policy that, in general, transitions from an explorative policy to an exploitative policy. The initial lenience towards accepting solutions with worse fitness values is what allows simulated annealing to escape local minima/maxima.

Multi-Objective Simulated Annealing (MOSA). Traditional SA is not suitable for the automatic test case model generation as described previously because a solution's fitness consists of three separate objective functions and SA cannot directly compare solutions based on multiple criteria. Furthermore, even if SA had the ability to determine relative solution fitness, there would still be the problem of quantifying the fitness disparity between solutions as a scalar value for use in the acceptance probability function. MOSA overcomes these problems. When comparing the relative fitness of solutions, MOSA utilizes the idea of Pareto optimality using dominance as a basis for comparison. Solution A is said to dominate solution B if: (1) every objective value for solution A is the same or better than the corresponding objective value for solution B, and (2) solution A has at least one objective value that is strictly better than the corresponding objective value of solution B. If solution A does not dominate solution B and solution B does not dominate solution A, then these solutions are said to belong to the same non-dominating front. In MOSA, the mutated solution will be kept and used for the next iteration if it dominates or is in the same non-dominating front as the solution from the previous iteration. To determine the probability that the mutated solution dominated by the solution from the previous iteration will be kept and used for the next iteration of MOSA, there are a number of possible acceptance probability functions that can be utilized. Since previous work has noted that the average cost criteria yields good performance [5], we have utilized it. The average cost criteria simply takes the average of the differences of each objective value between two solutions, i and j, over all objectives D, as shown in Equation 1. The final acceptance probability function used in MOSA is shown in Equation 2.

$$c(i,j) = \frac{\sum_{k=1}^{|D|}(c_k(j) - c_k(i))}{|D|} \quad (1) \qquad AcceptProb(i,j,temp) = e^{\frac{-abs(c(i,j))}{temp}} \quad (2)$$

MOSA Adaptation for Generating Test Case Models. When using the number of refactorings fitness criterion along with mutations that add, modify, or remove refactorings in MOSA, a slight modification of the definition of dominance is required in order to obtain quality results. The problem with using the traditional definition of dominance in this case is that "remove refactoring" mutations will always generate a solution that is at least in the same non-dominated front as the non-mutated solution because it utilizes less refactorings, thus making it strictly better in at least one objective. In MOSA, this means that the non-mutated solution will always be discarded in favor of the mutated solution that it will use in the following iteration. The problem with this is that the probability of an add refactoring or modify refactoring mutation yielding a mutated solution that is in the same non-dominated front or better is much less than that of a mutation removing a refactoring (100%). This is because the only way an add or modify refactoring mutation could at least be in the same non-dominated front is if it satisfied a previously unsatisfied metamodel coverage item, removed an invalid model element, or modified an invalid model element to make it valid. As a result, solutions tend to gravitate towards solutions with less refactorings that eventually results in solutions with the least possible number of refactorings, one refactoring per each test case model. This was found to be the case in experiments executed with the traditional dominance implementation. The problem is alleviated by modifying how dominance is determined in MOSA such that a mutated solution with less refactorings and less metamodel coverage or more invalid model elements than the non-mutated solution is considered to be dominated by the non-mutated solution. In other words, MOSA will only transition from the non-mutated solution from the previous iteration to the new mutated solution (using the "remove refactoring" mutation) with 100% probability if the mutated solution dominates the non-mutated solution. If the mutated solution has less refactorings but also less metamodel coverage or more invalid model elements, then it will only be accepted and used for the next iteration given the probability calculated by the acceptance probability function.

The second problem to overcome is how to use the metamodel coverage, number of invalid model elements, and number of refactoring values in the acceptance probability function in a meaningful way. As they are, these three values take on values in different scales: metamodel coverage takes on values between 0% and 100% (0.0 and 1.0), number of invalid model elements takes on values between 0 and the initial number of invalid model elements before MOSA begins, and the number of refactorings takes on the value of any nonnegative integer. In order to make the average of differences between fitness criteria values meaningful, normalization is performed. Metamodel coverage does not require any normalization as its values already lie between 0.0 and 1.0 and thus all differences between metamodel coverage values will as well. The only operation necessary is to take the absolute value of the difference to ensure it is positive as shown in Equation 3. To normalize the difference between numbers of invalid model elements, simply take the absolute value of the difference between the number of invalid model elements values and divide by the number of invalid model elements from the initial test case models as shown in Equation 4.

$$CovDiff = abs(Cov(i) - Cov(j)) \quad (3) \quad InvDiff = \frac{abs(Inv(i) - Inv(j))}{Inv_0} \quad (4)$$

To normalize the difference in number of refactorings, the maximum number of refactorings should be used as a divisor. Since there is theoretically no upper bound to the possible number of refactorings that the lists of refactorings could have, a reasonable estimate is required. For this estimate, the sum of the initial number of unsatisfied coverage items and the number of invalid model elements of the starting test case models is used because it assumes that each coverage item and invalid model element will take one refactoring to satisfy and remove, respectively. As shown in Equation 5, the normalization of the difference in number of refactorings is calculated by taking the absolute value of the difference in number of refactorings divided by the sum of the initial number of unsatisfied coverage items and the number of invalid model elements of the starting test case models.

$$NumRefDiff = \frac{abs(NumRef(i) - NumRef(j))}{UnsatCovItems_0 + Inv_0} \tag{5}$$

2.5 Implementation

Before using MOSA to generate the lists of refactorings, a maximum model size must be declared to ensure a balance between the size of the test cases and the number of test cases is maintained. As explained in [4], smaller test cases allow for easier understanding and diagnosis when an error arises while the number of test cases should be reasonable in order to maintain an acceptable execution time and amount of effort for defining an oracle function.

After the maximum model size is declared, the automatic test case model generation begins. The algorithm iterates through all test case models once. For each test case model, its corresponding list of refactorings is initialized with one randomly-generated refactoring before the adapted MOSA algorithm is executed. After the algorithm has iterated over every test case model, the final lists of refactorings for each test case model are output along with the resulting test case models yielded from the application of the refactorings. The pseudocode for this algorithm is shown in Algorithm 1. It is important to note that although search is done for refactorings at the test case model level, the objective functions are executed on the overall running solution of the entire set of updated test case models at any given iteration. This means that, for example, if the space of refactoring lists for a particular test case model is being searched and a mutation is performed that covers a new coverage item for that test case model, but a list of refactorings for another test case model from a previous iteration already covered that particular coverage item, then there is no increase in the metamodel coverage objective function. The value yielded from the metamodel coverage objective function will only increase if a coverage item is covered that has not already been covered by any other test case model with their refactorings in the overall solution.

Algorithm 1. Pseudocode for adapted MOSA for generating test case models

---

function MOSA(testCaseModels, maxModelSize, initialTemperature, α)
    ListOfRefactorings.setMaxModelSize(maxModelSize)
    solution ← list()
    for testCaseModel in testCaseModels **do**
        refactorings ← ListOfRefactorings(testCaseModel)
        temp ← initialTemperature
        for iteration = 1 → maxIterations **do**
            newRefactorings ← copy(refactorings)
            newRefactorings.mutate()
            if newRefactorings.dominates(refactorings) **then**
                refactorings ← newRefactorings
            else if $u[0.0,1.0]$ < AcceptProb(refactorings,newRefactorings,temp) **then**
                refactorings ← newRefactorings
            temp ← temp × α
        solution.push(refactorings)
    return listsOfRefactorings

---

3 Experimentation

3.1 Experimental Setting

To test the effectiveness of the proposed approach, experiments were carried out to evolve test case models for the UML 2.0 metamodel. In the implementation used, the UML 2.0 metamodel generated 857 coverage items that needed to be satisfied in order to obtain 100% metamodel coverage. To discover if initializing the test case models with those of a previous metamodel version was beneficial, experiments were done starting from a set of test case models that conform to UML 1.4 as well as a set of new test case models. Each test case model in the set of UML 1.4 test case models consists of between 17 and 23 model elements that collectively satisfy 46.58% of the UML 2.0 metamodel coverage items and have 60 model elements that are invalid with respect to the UML 2.0 metamodel, while each test case model in the set of new test case models consists of only five class model elements, collectively satisfy 0% of the UML 2.0 metamodel coverage items, and have no invalid model elements. Both sets are comprised of 20 test case models each.

To justify the multi-objective approach proposed in this paper, the same experiments were carried out using an SA approach utilizing only metamodel coverage like in previous works [4]. All experiments were run 30 times in order to establish statistical significance. For each of the 20 test case models, 10,000 iterations of SA were performed with a starting temperature of 0.0003 and an alpha value of 0.99965. The starting temperature and alpha values were chosen because they yielded the best results in empirical preliminary tests for both SA and MOSA. All probability distributions used by the search process (e.g., to determine the type of mutation to execute or refactoring to generate) were such that each discrete possibility had equal chance of being selected.

3.2   Results

The complete results from all four experiment configurations can be found in Table 5. The SA approaches outperformed the corresponding MOSA approaches in the metamodel coverage objective as shown in Figure 3 while, however, using a far greater number of refactorings as shown in Figure 5. Figure 4 shows that the MOSA experiment that started with the UML 1.4 test case models removed all 60 test case model elements every run while the corresponding SA experiment removed less than half of the invalid test case model elements on average. All differences in results were determined to be statistically significant employing a two-tailed t-test with $\alpha = 0.05$.

Table 5. Empirical results with standard deviations in parentheses

	From Scratch		From Existing Models	
	SA	**MOSA**	**SA**	**MOSA**
Coverage	83.82% (0.05%)	63.36% (0.04%)	96.20% (<0.01%)	91.70% (0.01%)
Invalid	-	-	35.47 (4.03)	0.00 (0.00)
Num. Ref.	1185.87 (176.69)	315.17 (18.08)	726.87 (34.15)	348.90 (13.60)

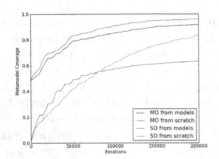

Fig. 3. Metamodel coverage versus iterations

Fig. 4. Invalid model elements versus iterations

3.3   Discussion

With respect to the metamodel coverage objective, it is intuitive that the SA approaches would outperform the MOSA approaches, albeit by a relatively small margin when starting from existing test case models, because the MOSA approaches must balance conflicting objectives while the SA approaches do not. As a result, the lists of refactorings yielded from the MOSA approaches are more effective in terms of metamodel coverage per refactoring than the ones yielded from SA. Combined with the fact that the total number of refactorings yielded by the MOSA approaches are drastically less than those yielded by the SA approaches, this means that the effort required to implement the changes

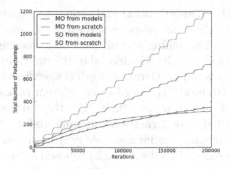

Fig. 5. Refactorings versus iterations

to expected output is less and overall more effective using the MOSA approach under the assumption that an increase in refactorings made to test case models increases the amount of effort required to update the test case expected output.

Furthermore, the results show that the approaches that start with existing test case models of a previous metamodel version outperform the same approaches that generate completely new models. This also helps reduce the effort required to update the expected test case output because portions of the expected output for the existing test cases will not need to be modified. Furthermore, if a user is already familiar with the previous test case models that were initially used as a basis for the new test case models, that knowledge can be leveraged to further decrease the amount of effort required to update expected output.

4   Related Work

Fleurey et al. [4,7] and Steel et al. [8] discuss the reasons why testing model transformations is distinct from testing traditional implementations: the input data are models that are complex in comparison to simple data types. Both papers describe how to generate test data in MDE by adapting existing techniques, including functional criteria [2] and bacteriologic approaches [3]. Lin et al. [9] propose a testing framework for model transformation built on their modeling tools and transformation engine that offers a support tool for test case construction, test execution, and test comparison; however, the test case models are manually developed in this work.

Some other approaches are specific to test case generation for graph transformation mechanisms. Küster [10] addresses the problem of model transformation validation in a way that is very specific to graph transformation by focusing on the verification of transformation rules with respect to termination and confluence. This work is concerned with the verification of transformation properties rather than the validation (testing) of their correctness. Darabos et al. [11] investigate the testing of graph transformations by considering graph transformation rules as the transformation specification and propose to generate test data from this specification. Darabos et al. propose several faulty models that can occur when performing pattern matching as well as a test case generation technique that targets those particular faults. Compared to the multiobjective search-based approach proposed in this paper, Darabos' work is specific to graph-based transformation testing. Mottu et al. [1] describe six different oracle functions to evaluate the correctness of an output model. In [12], the authors suggest manually determining the expected transformation outcome and comparing it with the actual transformation outcome using a simple graph-comparison algorithm.

The multi-objective search-based approach proposed in this paper is inspired by contributions in the domain of Search-Based Software Engineering (SBSE) [13]. SBSE uses search-based approaches to solve optimization problems in software engineering, and once a software engineering task is framed as a search problem, many search algorithms can be applied to solve that problem. These search-based approaches are also used to solve problems in software testing [14,15,12]. The general idea behind the proposed approach is that possible test case model refactorings define a search space and multiple conflicting test case model criteria are integrated into multiple objective functions. These components guide the search approach in an attempt to find an optimal set of test case model refactorings that yields a set of adequate updated test case models.

Although the problem of generating test cases at the code level is well-studied, there are few works that generate test cases at the model level to test transformation mechanisms. To our knowledge, there is currently no other work that utilizes existing test case models of a previous metamodel to generate test case models for an updated metamodel. Furthermore, this is the first adaptation of heuristic search algorithms to take into consideration multiple objectives when generating source models (test cases) similar to the data that will be transformed.

5   Conclusion and Future Work

Empirical results show that MOSA can automatically generate quality test case models from existing test case models in response to metamodel changes. The new test case models are generated with minimal refactorings so the effort required to update expected test case model transformation output is reduced. While SA is able to achieve slightly better overall metamodel coverage, the number of refactorings, and thus required effort, is substantially greater. Furthermore, the MOSA approach is able to reliably remove test case model elements that become invalid due to metamodel changes.

To generalize our proposed approach and ensure its robustness, we plan to extend our validation to other metamodels such as Petri nets and relational schema. Furthermore, comparative studies will be performed between different multiobjective metaheuristic algorithms as well as between processing all test case models at once to yield an overall single list of refactorings and the proposed method of processing each test case model one at a time.

References

1. Mottu, J., Baudry, B., Le Traon, Y.: Model Transformation Testing: Oracle Issue. In: IEEE International Conference on Software Testing Verification and Validation Workshop, ICSTW 2008, pp. 105–112 (2008)
2. Brottier, E., Fleurey, F., Steel, J., Baudry, B., le Traon, Y.: Metamodel-based Test Generation for Model Transformations: An Algorithm and a Tool. In: 17th International Symposium on Software Reliability Engineering, ISSRE 2006, pp. 85–94 (2006)
3. Baudry, B., Fleurey, F., Jezequel, J.M., Traon, Y.L.: Automatic Test Cases Optimization Using a Bacteriological Adaptation Model: Application to.NET Components. In: Proceedings of ASE 2002 (Automated Software Engineering), Edinburgh (2002)
4. Fleurey, F., Steel, J., Baudry, B.: Validation in Model-Driven Engineering: Testing Model Transformations. In: Proceedings of First International Workshop on Model, Design and Validation, pp. 29–40 (2004)
5. Nam, D., Park, C.H.: Multiobjective Simulated Annealing: A Comparative Study to Evolutionary Algorithms. International Journal of Fuzzy Systems 2(2), 87–97 (2000)
6. Brosch, P., Egly, U., Gabmeyer, S., Kappel, G., Seidl, M., Tompits, H., Widl, M., Wimmer, M.: Towards Scenario-Based Testing of UML Diagrams. In: Brucker, A.D., Julliand, J. (eds.) TAP 2012. LNCS, vol. 7305, pp. 149–155. Springer, Heidelberg (2012)
7. Fleurey, F., Baudry, B., Muller, P.A., Traon, Y.: Qualifying Input Test Data for Model Transformations. Software & Systems Modeling 8(2), 185–203 (2009)
8. Steel, J., Lawley, M.: Model-based Test Driven Development of the Tefkat Model-Transformation Engine. In: 15th International Symposium on Software Reliability Engineering, ISSRE 2004, pp. 151–160 (2004)
9. Lin, Y., Zhang, J., Gray, J.: A Testing Framework for Model Transformations. In: Research and Practice in Software Engineering - Model-Driven Software Development, pp. 219–236. Springer (2005)
10. Küster, J.M., Abd-El-Razik, M.: Validation of Model Transformations – First Experiences using a White Box Approach. In: Kühne, T. (ed.) MoDELS 2006. LNCS, vol. 4364, pp. 193–204. Springer, Heidelberg (2007)
11. Darabos, A., Pataricza, A., Varr, D.: Towards Testing the Implementation of Graph Transformations. In: Proceedings of the 5th International Workshop on Graph Transformations and Visual Modeling Techniques, pp. 69–80. Elsevier (2006)
12. McMinn, P.: Search-based Software Test Data Generation: A Survey: Research Articles. Softw. Test. Verif. Reliab. 14(2), 105–156 (2004)
13. Harman, M., Mansouri, S.A., Zhang, Y.: Search-based Software Engineering: Trends, techniques and applications. ACM Comput. Surv. 45(1), 11:1–11:61 (2012)
14. Baresel, A., Binkley, D., Harman, M., Korel, B.: Evolutionary Testing in the Presence of Loop-Assigned Flags: A Testability Transformation Approach. In: Proceedings of the 2004 ACM SIGSOFT International Symposium on Software Testing and Analysis, ISSTA 2004, pp. 108–118. ACM, New York (2004)
15. Baresel, A., Sthamer, H., Schmidt, M.: Fitness Function Design To Improve Evolutionary Structural Testing. In: Proceedings of the Genetic and Evolutionary Computation Conference, GECCO 2002, pp. 1329–1336. Morgan Kaufmann Publishers Inc., San Francisco (2002)

Provably Optimal and Human-Competitive Results in SBSE for Spectrum Based Fault Localisation

Xiaoyuan Xie[1], Fei-Ching Kuo[1], Tsong Yueh Chen[1], Shin Yoo[2],
and Mark Harman[2]

[1] Swinburn University, John St, Hawthorn VIC3122, Australia
{xxie,dkuo,tychen}@swin.edu.au
[2] University College London, Gower Street, London WC1E 6BT, UK
{shin.yoo,mark.harman}@ucl.ac.uk

Abstract. Fault localisation uses so-called risk evaluation formulæ to guide the localisation process. For more than a decade, the design and improvement of these formulæ has been conducted entirely manually through iterative publication in the fault localisation literature. However, recently we demonstrated that SBSE could be used to automatically design such formulæ by recasting this as a problem for Genetic Programming(GP). In this paper we prove that our GP has produced four previously unknown globally optimal formulæ. Though other human competitive results have previously been reported in the SBSE literature, this is the first SBSE result, in any application domain, for which human competitiveness has been formally proved. We also show that some of these formulæ exhibit counter-intuitive characteristics, making them less likely to have been found solely by further human effort.

1 Introduction

Early work demonstrated the wide applicability of SBSE to many different software engineering domains, perhaps surprising some software engineers, who had previously thought computational search inadmissible in their areas of activity. However, now that SBSE is a mature [7] and well-established 'standard' approach to software engineering [9,11], the SBSE research agenda should become more ambitious in order to continue to stimulate further development.

One area in which more work is needed lies in the development of techniques that are human competitive, a long-sought goal of all optimisation approaches. Such results are inherently compelling demonstrations of the value of SBSE for which the scientific evidence should be sufficient to convince even the most skeptical software engineer.

Recent work has produced specific claims for human competitive results in SBSE [19], while much other SBSE work is already implicitly partly human competitive, since it automates aspects of software engineering for which human effort is simply too expensive [11, 15, 17]. In this paper we seek to go a step further. We seek not only to demonstrate that our SBSE results are human

G. Ruhe and Y. Zhang (Eds.): SSBSE 2013, LNCS 8084, pp. 224–238, 2013.
© Springer-Verlag Berlin Heidelberg 2013

competitive, but also that we have provably optimal results in an area for which many years of human effort have been expended by very capable scientists to construct just such optimal results.

The area for which we are able to demonstrate provably optimal and human competitive results is fault localisation. We focus on Spectrum-Based Fault Localisation (SBFL), a well-known and widely-studied fault localisation approach. SBFL ranks statements according to a risk evaluation formula. The faulty statement should ideally be ranked at the top. Designing an effective risk evaluation formula has been one of the most widely studied aspects of SBFL: known formulæ include Tarantula [14], Ochiai [1], Wong [20] and many others.

There has been more than a decade of risk evaluation formulæ development, all of which has remained entirely manual. This development has called upon the considerable ingenuity of many different groups of researchers, all of which have peer-reviewed expertise and results on the introduction of each of their proposed formulæ. Therefore, any approach which could automatically find an equivalent or better performing formula would clearly be human competitive, and at the highest level of intellectual challenge too.

Recently, Genetic Programming (GP) has been successfully applied to automatic design of risk evaluation formulæ [23]. Empirical results showed that, among the 30 GP-evolved formulæ, six are very effective and can outperform some human-designed formulæ. However, this analysis was entirely empirical; we cannot be *sure* that the evaluation formulæ found by our GP approach are always superior.

Fortunately, Xie et al. developed a framework to support the theoretical analysis of risk evaluation formulæ performance [21,22]. Xie et al. analysed 30 manually designed risk evaluation formulæ, identifying a fault localisation effectiveness hierarchy between formulæ. The results of the theoretical analysis showed that there exist two maximal groups of human defined formulæ, namely ER1 and ER5, for programs with single fault.

In this paper, we apply the same theoretical framework to the 30 GP-evolved formulæ discovered by GP and reported by Yoo at SSBSE 2012 [23]. The results show that, among these 30 GP-evolved formulæ, four formulæ, namely GP02, GP03, GP13, and GP19 are optimal: GP13 is proved to be equivalent to the human-discovered optima ER1, while the remaining three formulæ form three distinct and entirely new groups of optima.

Interestingly, some of the optimal GP-evolved formulæ display characteristics that are best described as 'unintuitive'. This is a common observation for computational search; it finds niche results that are not always obvious and sometimes highly counter-intuitive; SBSE is no exception [11]. Since our results are both optimal, yet counter-intuitive, they are not only human competitive with respect to the past decade of human effort, but also unlikely to have been discovered by further decade of human effort.

The contributions of this paper are as follows:

- We prove that one of the risk-evaluation formulæ from the previous work [23] belongs to the same equivalence group as two known maximal formulæ, extending the maximal group ER1 [21] to ER1'. This shows provable human competitiveness for the first time in SBSE.

- We also prove that three other formulæ from the previous work [23] form their own maximal groups.
- Our analysis of the evolved formulæ shows the flexibility of GP in designing risk evaluation formulæ. For some formulæ, GP follows the same design intuition as humans; for others, GP does not conform to the human intuition but still produces maximal formulæ.

The rest of the paper is organised as follows. Section 2 describes the foundations of Spectrum-Based Fault Localisation (SBFL) and the theoretical framework that uses set-membership to provably compare risk evaluation formulæ. Section 3 contains proofs of maximality for GP02, GP03, GP13, and GP19. Section 4 discusses the insights gained from an in-depth analysis of GP-evolved formulæ. Section 5 presents related work and Section 6 concludes.

2   Background

2.1   Spectrum-Based Fault Localisation (SBFL)

SBFL uses testing results and program spectrum to do fault localisation. The testing result is whether a test case is *failed* or *passed*. While the program spectrum records the run-time profiles about various program entities for a specific test suite. The program entities could be statements, branches, paths, etc.; and the run-time information could be the binary coverage status, the execution frequency, etc. The most widely used program spectrum involves statement and its binary coverage status in a test execution [2,14].

$$
\begin{array}{cc}
 & \text{TS:} \quad \begin{pmatrix} t_1 \ t_2 \ \ldots \ t_m \end{pmatrix} \\[4pt]
\text{PG:} \begin{pmatrix} s_1 \\ s_2 \\ \cdot \\ \cdot \\ \cdot \\ s_n \end{pmatrix} & \text{MS:} \begin{pmatrix} 1/0 \ 1/0 \ \ldots \ 1/0 \\ 1/0 \ 1/0 \ \ldots \ 1/0 \\ \cdots \\ \cdots \\ \cdots \\ 1/0 \ 1/0 \ \ldots \ 1/0 \end{pmatrix} \\[4pt]
 & \text{RE:} \quad \begin{pmatrix} p/f \ p/f \ \ldots \ p/f \end{pmatrix}
\end{array}
$$

Fig. 1. Information for conventional SBFL

Consider a program $PG=<s_1, s_2, ..., s_n>$ with n statements and a test suite of m test cases $TS=\{t_1, t_2, ..., t_m\}$. Figure 1 shows the information required by SBFL. RE records all the testing results, in which p and f indicate *passed* and *failed*, respectively. Matrix MS represents the program spectrum, where the (i^{th}, j^{th}) element represents the coverage information of statement s_i, by test case t_j, with 1 indicating s_i is executed, and 0 otherwise. In fact, the jth column represents the *execution slice* of t_j.

For each statement s_i, its relevant testing result can be represented as a tuple $i=(e_f^i, e_p^i, n_f^i, n_p^i)$, where e_f^i and e_p^i represent the number of test cases in TS that execute it and return the testing result of *failure* or *pass*, respectively; n_f^i and n_p^i denote the number of test cases that do not execute it, and return the testing result of *failure* or *pass*, respectively. A risk evaluation formula R is then applied to the tuple corresponding to each statement s_i to calculate the *suspiciousness* score that indicates its risk of being faulty. Ideally, the faulty statement should be at or near the top of the ranking, so that the developer can save time if the program statements are examined following the ranking order.

The most commonly adopted intuition in designing risk evaluation formulæ is that statements associated with more *failed* or less *passed* testing results should not have lower risks. Formulæ that comply with this intuition include Tarantula [12], Jaccard [4], Ochiai [1], Naish1 and Naish2 [16], among others.

2.2   Theoretical Framework

With the development of more and more risk evaluation formulæ, people began to investigate their performance. Xie et al. [21] have recently developed a theoretical framework to analysis the performance between different formulæ. Since we will apply this theoretical framework in this paper, thus we briefly describe it before presenting the analysis on GP-evolved formulæ.

Definition 1. *Given a program with n statements $PG=<s_1, s_2, ..., s_n>$, a test suite of m test cases $TS=\{t_1, t_2, ..., t_m\}$, and a risk evaluation formula R, which assigns a risk value to each program statement. For each statement s_i, a vector $i=<e_f^i, e_p^i, n_f^i, n_p^i>$ can be constructed from TS, and $R(s_i)$ is a function of i. For any faulty statement s_f, following three subsets are defined.*

$$S_B^R = \{s_i \in S | R(s_i) > R(s_f), 1 \leq i \leq n\}$$
$$S_F^R = \{s_i \in S | R(s_i) = R(s_f), 1 \leq i \leq n\}$$
$$S_A^R = \{s_i \in S | R(s_i) < R(s_f), 1 \leq i \leq n\}$$

That is, S_B^R, S_F^R and S_A^R consist of statements of which the risk values are higher than, equal to and lower than the risk value of s_f, respectively.

In practice, a tie-breaking scheme may be required to determine the order of the statements with same risk values. The theoretical analysis only investigates consistent tie-breaking schemes, which are defined as follows.

Definition 2. *Given any two sets of statements S_1 and S_2, which contain elements having the same risk values. A tie-breaking scheme returns the ordered statement lists O_1 and O_2 for S_1 and S_2, respectively. The tie-breaking scheme is said to be consistent, if all elements common to S_1 and S_2 have the same relative order in O_1 and O_2.*

The effectiveness measurement is referred to as Expense metric, which is the percentage of code that needs to be examined before the faulty statement is identified [23]. A lower Expense of formula R indicates a better performance.

Let E_1 and E_2 denote the Expenses with respect to the same faulty statement for risk evaluation formulæ R_1 and R_2, respectively. We define two types of relations between R_1 and R_2 as follows.

Definition 3 (Better). R_1 *is said to be* better *than R_2 (denoted as $R_1 \rightarrow R_2$) if for any program, faulty statement s_f, test suite and consistent tie-breaking scheme, we have $E_1 \leq E_2$.*

Definition 4 (Equivalent). R_1 *and R_2 are said to be* equivalent *(denoted as $R_1 \leftrightarrow R_2$), if for any program, faulty statement s_f, test suite and consistent tie-breaking scheme, we have $E_1 = E_2$.*

It is obvious from the definition that $R_1 \rightarrow R_2$ means R_1 is equal to or more effective than R_2. As a reminder, if $R_1 \rightarrow R_2$ holds but $R_2 \rightarrow R_1$ does not hold, $R_1 \rightarrow R_2$ is said to be a strictly *"better"* relation. In the theoretical framework, there are several assumptions, which are listed as follows.

1. A testing oracle exists, that is, for any test case, the testing result of either *fail* or *pass* can be decided.
2. We have the assumption of perfect bug detection that the fault can always be identified once the faulty statement is examined.
3. We exclude omission faults, because SBFL is designed to assign risk values to the existent statements.
4. We assume that the test suite contains at least one passing test case and one failing test case.

As a reminder, our analysis only focuses on statements that are covered by the given test suite (that is, any statement s_i such that $e_p^i + e_f^i > 0$). This is because a statement that is never covered by any test case in the given test suite cannot be the faulty statement that triggers the observed failure and hence should be ignored (or effectively deemed to have the lowest risk values). For readers who are interested in all the detailed justifications, validity and impacts of the above assumptions, please refer to [21].

Given a test suite TS, let T denote its size, F denote the number of *failed* test cases and P denote the number of *passed* test cases. Immediately after the definitions and the above assumptions, we have $1 \leq F < T$, $1 \leq P < T$, and $P + F = T$, as well as the following lemmas.

Lemma 1. *For any $i = <e_f^i, e_p^i, n_f^i, n_p^i>$, we have $e_f^i + e_p^i > 0$, $e_f^i + n_f^i = F$, $e_p^i + n_p^i = P$, $e_f^i \leq F$ and $e_p^i \leq P$.*

Lemma 2. *For any faulty statement s_f with $f = <e_f^f, e_p^f, n_f^f, n_p^f>$, if s_f is the only faulty statement in the program, we have $e_f^f = F$ and $n_f^f = 0$.*

A sufficient condition for the equivalence between two risk evaluation formulae is as follows.

Theorem 1. *Let R_1 and R_2 be two risk evaluation formulæ. If we have $S_B^{R_1} = S_B^{R_2}$, $S_F^{R_1} = S_F^{R_2}$ and $S_A^{R_1} = S_A^{R_2}$ for any program, faulty statement s_f and test suite, then $R_1 \leftrightarrow R_2$.*

Xie et al. [21] have applied the above theoretical framework on 30 manually designed formulæ, identifying two groups of most effective formulæ for programs with single fault, namely the maximal groups of formulæ. The definition of *maximal formula* is as follows.

Definition 5. *A risk evaluation formula R_1 is said to be a maximal formula of a set of formulæ, if for any element R_2 of this set of formulæ, $R_2 \rightarrow R_1$ implies $R_2 \leftrightarrow R_1$.*

3   Theoretical Analysis of GP-Evolved Risk Evaluation Formulæ

3.1   Risk Evaluation Formulæ Generated by GP

Yoo [23] has generated 30 GP-evolved formulæ. There are 10 out of the 30 formulæ which need unreasonable additional assumptions, and, hence, are excluded in this study[1]. Therefore, our investigation will focus on the remaining 20 formulæ (namely, GP01, GP02, GP03, GP06, GP08, GP11, GP12, GP13, GP14, GP15, GP16, GP18, GP19, GP20, GP21, GP22, GP24, GP26, GP28 and GP30). As a reminder, the following analysis is for programs with single fault.

The above mentioned theoretical framework has proved the equivalence of the formulae within ER1 (consists of Naish1 and Naish2) and ER5 (consists of Wong1, Russel & Rao, and Binary), as well as their maximality, for programs with single fault [22]. By using the theoretical framework above, we are able to prove that among the 20 GP-evolved formulæ, GP02, GP03, GP13 and GP19 are maximal formulæ for programs with single fault. More specifically, GP02, GP03 and GP19 are distinct maximal formulæ to ER1 and ER5; while GP13 is equivalent to ER1. In the following discussion, the group which consists of Naish1, Naish2 and GP13 will be referred to as ER1'. We have also proved that ER1' is strictly better than all the other remaining 16 GP-evolved formulæ under investigation. However, since the focus of this paper is to identify the maximal (that is, maximally effective) GP-evolved formulæ, we will only provide the detailed proofs for the maximality of GP02, GP03, GP13 and GP19. Definitions of the involved formulæ are listed in Table 1.

3.2   Maximal GP-Evolved Risk Evaluation Formulæ

Before presenting our proof, we need the following lemmas for ER1 (consists of Naish1 and Naish2) and GP13.

---

[1] The reason for exclusion is primarily to avoid division by zero. For example, GP04 [23] contains $\frac{1}{e_p - n_p}$, i.e., it assumes $e_p \neq n_p$. We consider assumptions of this kind unrealistic.

Table 1. Investigated formulæ

	Name	Formula expression
ER1'	Naish1	$\begin{cases} -1 & \text{if } e_f < F \\ P - e_p & \text{if } e_f = F \end{cases}$
	Naish2	$e_f - \frac{e_p}{e_p + n_p + 1}$
	GP13	$e_f(1 + \frac{1}{2e_p + e_f})$
ER5	Wong1	e_f
	Russel & Rao	$\frac{e_f}{e_f + n_f + e_p + n_p}$
	Binary	$\begin{cases} 0 & \text{if } e_f < F \\ 1 & \text{if } e_f = F \end{cases}$
GP02		$2(e_f + \sqrt{n_p}) + \sqrt{e_p}$
GP03		$\sqrt{|e_f^2 - \sqrt{e_p}|}$
GP19		$e_f\sqrt{|e_p - e_f + n_f - n_p|}$

Lemma 3. *For Naish1 and Naish2, which are shown to be equivalent to each other in the previous work [22], we have $S_B^{N1} = S_B^{N2} = X^{Op}$, $S_F^{N1} = S_F^{N2} = Y^{Op}$ and $S_A^{N1} = S_A^{N2} = Z^{Op}$, where*

$$X^{Op} = \{s_i | e_f^i = F \text{ and } e_p^f > e_p^i, 1 \leq i \leq n\} \tag{1}$$

$$Y^{Op} = \{s_i | e_f^i = F \text{ and } e_p^f = e_p^i, 1 \leq i \leq n\} \tag{2}$$

$$Z^{Op} = S \backslash X^{Op} \backslash Y^{Op} \tag{3}$$

Lemma 4. *For GP13, we have $S_B^{GP13} = X^{Op}$, $S_F^{GP13} = Y^{Op}$ and $S_A^{GP13} = Z^{Op}$, respectively.*

Proof. Since $e_f^f = F$, it follows immediately from the definition of GP13 that

$$S_B^{GP13} = \{s_i | e_f^i(1 + \frac{1}{2e_p^i + e_f^i}) > F(1 + \frac{1}{2e_p^f + F}), 1 \leq i \leq n\} \tag{4}$$

$$S_F^{GP13} = \{s_i | e_f^i(1 + \frac{1}{2e_p^i + e_f^i}) = F(1 + \frac{1}{2e_p^f + F}), 1 \leq i \leq n\} \tag{5}$$

1. To prove that $S_B^{GP13} = X^{Op}$.
   (a) To prove $X^{Op} \subseteq S_B^{GP13}$.
   For any $s_i \in X^{Op}$, we have $F(1 + \frac{1}{2e_p^i + F}) > F(1 + \frac{1}{2e_p^f + F})$ because $e_p^f > e_p^i$ and $F > 0$. Since $e_f^i = F$, we have $e_f^i(1 + \frac{1}{2e_p^i + e_f^i}) > F(1 + \frac{1}{2e_p^f + F})$, which implies $s_i \in S_B^{GP13}$. Thus, we have proved $X^{Op} \subseteq S_B^{GP13}$.
   (b) To prove $S_B^{GP13} \subseteq X^{Op}$.
   For any $s_i \in S_B^{GP13}$, we have $e_f^i(1 + \frac{1}{2e_p^i + e_f^i}) > F(1 + \frac{1}{2e_p^f + F})$. Let us consider the following two exhaustive cases.

- Case (i) $e_f^i < F$. First, consider the sub-case that $e_f^i = 0$. Then we have $e_f^i(1 + \frac{1}{2e_p^i + e_f^i}) = 0$. It follows from the definition of S_B^{GP13} that $0 > F(1 + \frac{1}{2e_p^f + F})$, which is however contradictory to $F > 0$ and $e_p^f \geq 0$. Thus, it is impossible to have $e_f^i = 0$. Now, consider the sub-case that $0 < e_f^i < F$. After re-arranging the terms, the expression $e_f^i(1 + \frac{1}{2e_p^i + e_f^i}) - F(1 + \frac{1}{2e_p^f + F})$ becomes $(\frac{e_f^i}{2e_p^i + e_f^i} - \frac{F}{2e_p^f + F}) - (F - e_f^i)$. Since $0 < e_f^i < F$, this expression can be further re-written as $(\frac{1}{1 + 2\frac{e_p^i}{e_f^i}}$

  $- \frac{1}{1 + 2\frac{e_p^f}{F}}) - (F - e_f^i)$. Since $\frac{e_p^i}{e_f^i} \geq 0$ and $\frac{e_p^f}{F} \geq 0$, we have $0 < \frac{1}{1 + 2\frac{e_p^i}{e_f^i}} \leq 1$ and $0 < \frac{1}{1 + 2\frac{e_p^f}{F}} \leq 1$. As a consequence, we have $(\frac{1}{1 + 2\frac{e_p^i}{e_f^i}} - \frac{1}{1 + 2\frac{e_p^f}{F}}) < 1$. Since both F and e_f^i are positive and non-negative integers, respectively, $e_f^i < F$ implies $(F - e_f^i) \geq 1$. Thus, we have $(\frac{1}{1 + 2\frac{e_p^i}{e_f^i}} - \frac{1}{1 + 2\frac{e_p^f}{F}}) - (F - e_f^i)$

  < 0, which however is contradictory to $e_f^i(1 + \frac{1}{2e_p^i + e_f^i}) > F(1 + \frac{1}{2e_p^f + F})$. Therefore, it is impossible to have $0 < e_f^i < F$. Therefore, we have proved that if $s_i \in S_B^{GP13}$, we cannot have $e_f^i < F$.

- Case (ii) $e_f^i = F$. Assume further $e_p^i \geq e_p^f$. Obviously, we have $F(1 + \frac{1}{2e_p^i + F}) \leq F(1 + \frac{1}{2e_p^f + F})$, which can be re-written as $e_f^i(1 + \frac{1}{2e_p^i + e_f^i}) \leq F(1 + \frac{1}{2e_p^f + F})$. However, this is contradictory to $F(1 + \frac{1}{2e_p^i + F}) > F(1 + \frac{1}{2e_p^f + F})$. Thus, the only possible case is $e_p^f > e_p^i$.

Therefore, we have proved that if $s_i \in S_B^{GP13}$, then $e_f^i = F$ and $e_p^f > e_p^i$, which imply $s_i \in X^{Op}$. Therefore, $S_B^{GP13} \subseteq X^{Op}$.

In conclusion, we have proved $X^{Op} \subseteq S_B^{GP13}$ and $S_B^{GP13} \subseteq X^{Op}$. Therefore, $S_B^{GP13} = X^{Op}$.

2. To prove that $S_F^{GP13} = Y^{Op}$.

(a) To prove $Y^{Op} \subseteq S_F^{GP13}$.

For any $s_i \in Y^{Op}$, we have $e_f^i(1 + \frac{1}{2e_p^i + e_f^i}) = F(1 + \frac{1}{2e_p^f + F})$ because $e_f^i = F$ and $e_p^f = e_p^i$. After the definition of S_F^{GP13}, $s_i \in S_F^{GP13}$. Thus, we have proved $Y^{Op} \subseteq S_F^{GP13}$.

(b) To prove $S_F^{GP13} \subseteq Y^{Op}$.

For any $s_i \in S_F^{GP13}$, we have $e_f^i(1 + \frac{1}{2e_p^i + e_f^i}) = F(1 + \frac{1}{2e_p^f + F})$. Let us consider the following two exhaustive cases.

- Case (i) $e_f^i < F$. First, consider the sub-case that $e_f^i = 0$. Then we have $e_f^i(1 + \frac{1}{2e_p^i + e_f^i}) = 0$. It follows from the definition of S_F^{GP13} that $0 = F(1 + \frac{1}{2e_p^f + F})$, which is however contradictory to $F > 0$ and $e_p^f \geq 0$. Thus, it is impossible to have $e_f^i = 0$. Now, consider the sub-case that $0 < e_f^i < F$. Similar to the above proof of $S_B^{GP13} \subseteq X^{Op}$, we can prove that $(\frac{1}{1+2\frac{e_p^i}{e_f^i}}-\frac{1}{1+2\frac{e_p^f}{F}})<(F-e_f^i)$, which is however contradictory to $e_f^i(1+\frac{1}{2e_p^i+e_f^i})=F(1+\frac{1}{2e_p^f+F})$. Therefore, it is impossible to have $0<e_f^i<F$. Therefore, we have proved that if $s_i{\in}S_F^{GP13}$, then we cannot have $e_f^i<F$.

- Case (ii) $e_f^i=F$. Assume further $e_p^i{\neq}e_p^f$. Obviously, we have $F(1+\frac{1}{2e_p^i+F}){\neq}F(1+\frac{1}{2e_p^f+F})$, which can be re-written as $e_f^i(1+\frac{1}{2e_p^i+e_f^i}){\neq}F(1+\frac{1}{2e_p^f+F})$. However, this is contradictory to $e_f^i(1+\frac{1}{2e_p^i+e_f^i})=F(1+\frac{1}{2e_p^f+F})$. Thus, the only possible case is $e_p^f=e_p^i$.

We have proved that if $s_i{\in}S_F^{GP13}$, then $e_f^i=F$ and $e_p^f=e_p^i$, which imply $s_i{\in}Y^{Op}$. Therefore, $S_F^{GP13}{\subseteq}Y^{Op}$.

In conclusion, we have proved $Y^{Op}{\subseteq}S_F^{GP13}$ and $S_F^{GP13}{\subseteq}Y^{Op}$. Therefore, we have $S_F^{GP13}=Y^{Op}$.

3. To prove that $S_A^{GP13}=Z^{Op}$.

After Definition 1, we have $S_A^{GP13}=S{\setminus}S_B^{GP13}{\setminus}S_F^{GP13}$ and $Z^{Op}=S{\setminus}X^{Op}{\setminus}Y^{Op}$, where S denotes the set of all investigated statements. Since we have proved $S_B^{GP13}=X^{Op}$ and $S_F^{GP13}=Y^{Op}$, it is obvious that $S_A^{GP13}=Z^{Op}$.

Now, we are ready to prove that GP13, Naish1 and Naish2 belong to the same group of equivalent formulæ (referred to as ER1').

Proposition 1. *GP13 $\leftrightarrow$ Naish1 and GP13 $\leftrightarrow$ Naish2.*

Proof. Refer to Lemma 3 and Lemma 4, we have $S_B^{N1}=S_B^{N2}=S_B^{GP13}$, $S_F^{N1}=S_F^{N2}=S_F^{GP13}$ and $S_A^{N1}=S_A^{N2}=S_A^{GP13}$, respectively. After Theorem 1, GP13 $\leftrightarrow$ Naish1 and GP13 $\leftrightarrow$ Naish2.

Apart from GP13, we have three new maximal GP-evolved formulæ for programs with single fault, namely, GP02, GP03 and GP19. Unlike GP13, these three formulæ do not belong to ER1' or ER5.

Proposition 2. *GP02, GP03, GP19, ER1' and ER5 are distinct maximal formulæ (or groups of equivalent formulæ).*

Proof. To prove this, we will demonstrate that neither $R_1 \rightarrow R_2$ nor $R_2 \rightarrow R_1$ is held, where R_1 and R_2 are any two of these five formulæ (or groups of equivalent formulæ). Consider the following two program PG_1 and PG_2 as shown in Figure 2 and Figure 3, respectively. Suppose two test suites $TS1_1$ and $TS1_2$ are applied on PG_1 and two test suites $TS2_1$ and $TS2_2$ are applied on PG_2. Vector i with respect to these test suites and programs are listed in Table 2.

Table 3 lists the statement divisions for these five formulæ with respect to $TS1_1$ and $TS1_2$ applied on PG_1, while Table 4 lists the statement divisions for these five formulæ with respect to $TS2_1$ and $TS2_2$ applied on PG_2.

Suppose we adopt the "ORIGINAL ORDER" as the tie-breaking scheme. Then the corresponding rankings of the faulty statement for these five formulæ are as Table 5. From this table, we have demonstrated that

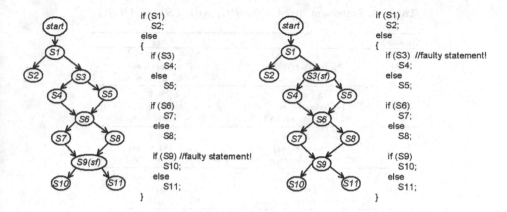

Fig. 2. Program PG_1 **Fig. 3.** Program PG_2

Table 2. i for PG_1 and PG_2 with different test suites

Statement	$i=<e_f^i, e_p^i, n_f^i, n_p^i>$			
	$TS1_1$	$TS1_2$	$TS2_1$	$TS2_2$
s_1	$<1,6,0,0>$	$<1,8,0,0>$	$<2,15,0,0>$	$<10,15,0,0>$
s_2	$<0,1,1,5>$	$<0,6,1,2>$	$<0,1,2,14>$	$<0,1,10,14>$
s_3	$<1,5,0,1>$	$<1,2,0,6>$	$<2,14,0,1>$	$<10,14,0,1>$
s_4	$<1,4,0,2>$	$<1,1,0,7>$	$<1,7,1,8>$	$<9,0,1,15>$
s_5	$<0,1,1,5>$	$<0,1,1,7>$	$<1,7,1,8>$	$<1,14,9,1>$
s_6	$<1,5,0,1>$	$<1,2,0,6>$	$<2,14,0,1>$	$<10,14,0,1>$
s_7	$<1,4,0,2>$	$<1,1,0,7>$	$<1,8,1,7>$	$<5,6,5,9>$
s_8	$<0,1,1,5>$	$<0,1,1,7>$	$<1,6,1,9>$	$<5,8,5,7>$
s_9	$<1,5,0,1>$	$<1,2,0,6>$	$<2,14,0,1>$	$<10,14,0,1>$
s_{10}	$<1,4,0,2>$	$<1,1,0,7>$	$<1,9,1,6>$	$<1,12,9,3>$
s_{11}	$<0,1,1,5>$	$<0,1,1,7>$	$<1,5,1,10>$	$<9,2,1,13>$

- With $TS1_2$ ER1' $\rightarrow$ GP02 does not hold; with $TS2_1$ GP02 $\nrightarrow$ ER1' does not hold.
- With $TS1_2$ ER5 $\rightarrow$ GP02 does not hold; with $TS2_1$ GP02 $\nrightarrow$ ER5 does not hold
- With $TS1_1$ ER1' $\rightarrow$ GP03 does not hold; with $TS1_2$ GP03 $\nrightarrow$ ER1' does not hold.
- With $TS1_1$ ER5 $\rightarrow$ GP03 does not hold; with $TS1_2$ GP03 $\nrightarrow$ ER5 does not hold.
- With $TS1_1$ ER1' $\rightarrow$ GP19 does not hold; with $TS1_2$ GP19 $\nrightarrow$ ER1' does not hold.
- With $TS1_1$ ER5 $\rightarrow$ GP19 does not hold; with $TS1_2$ GP19 $\nrightarrow$ ER5 does not hold.

Table 3. Statement division for PG_1 with $TS1_1$ and $TS1_2$

Statement	$TS1_1$	$TS1_2$
ER1'	$S_B^R = \{s_4, s_7, s_{10}\}$ $S_F^R = \{s_3, s_6, s_9\}$ $S_A^R = \{s_1, s_2, s_5, s_8, s_{11}\}$	$S_B^R = \{s_4, s_7, s_{10}\}$ $S_F^R = \{s_3, s_6, s_9\}$ $S_A^R = \{s_1, s_2, s_5, s_8, s_{11}\}$
ER5	$S_B^R = \emptyset$ $S_F^R = \{s_1, s_3, s_4, s_6, s_7, s_9, s_{10}\}$ $S_A^R = \{s_2, s_5, s_8, s_{11}\}$	$S_B^R = \emptyset$ $S_F^R = \{s_1, s_3, s_4, s_6, s_7, s_9, s_{10}\}$ $S_A^R = \{s_2, s_5, s_8, s_{11}\}$
GP02	$S_B^R = \{s_4, s_7, s_{10}\}$ $S_F^R = \{s_3, s_6, s_9\}$ $S_A^R = \{s_1, s_2, s_5, s_8, s_{11}\}$	$S_B^R = \emptyset$ $S_F^R = \{s_3, s_6, s_9\}$ $S_A^R = \{s_1, s_2, s_4, s_5, s_7, s_8, s_{10}, s_{11}\}$
GP03	$S_B^R = \{s_1\}$ $S_F^R = \{s_3, s_6, s_9\}$ $S_A^R = \{s_2, s_4, s_5, s_7, s_8, s_{10}, s_{11}\}$	$S_B^R = \{s_1, s_2, s_5, s_8, s_{11}\}$ $S_F^R = \{s_3, s_6, s_9\}$ $S_A^R = \{s_4, s_7, s_{10}\}$
GP19	$S_B^R = \{s_1\}$ $S_F^R = \{s_3, s_6, s_9\}$ $S_A^R = \{s_2, s_4, s_5, s_7, s_8, s_{10}, s_{11}\}$	$S_B^R = \{s_1, s_4, s_7, s_{10}\}$ $S_F^R = \{s_3, s_6, s_9\}$ $S_A^R = \{s_2, s_5, s_8, s_{11}\}$

- With $TS1_1$ GP02 $\to$ GP03 does not hold; with $TS1_2$ GP03 $\to$ GP02 does not hold.
- With $TS1_1$ GP02 $\to$ GP19 does not hold; with $TS1_2$ GP19 $\to$ GP02 does not hold.
- With $TS2_1$ GP03 $\to$ GP19 does not hold; with $TS2_2$ GP19 $\to$ GP03 does not hold.

In summary, we have proved that for any two of these five formulæ (or groups of equivalent formulæ) R_1 and R_2, neither $R_1 \to R_2$ nor $R_2 \to R_1$ is held. Therefore, GP02, GP03, GP19, ER1' and ER5 are five distinct maximal formulæ (or groups of equivalent formulæ).

4   Discussion

Yoo [23] used a small number of programs and faults to evolve new risk evaluation formulæ: more precisely, four subject programs and 20 mutants for evolution. To quote Yoo, "the results should be treated with caution" since "there is no guarantee that the studied programs and faults are representative of all possible programs and faults".

In this paper, we use the theoretical framework recently proposed by Xie et al. [21] to analyse Yoo's GP-evolved risk evaluation formulæ for programs with single fault. Among Yoo's formulæ, four have been proved to be maximal, namely, GP02, GP03, GP13 and GP19, where GP13 forms a new maximal group of equivalent formulæ with Naish1 and Naish2. This new maximal group is referred to as ER1'); while GP02, GP03 and GP19 are distinct to ER1' and ER5. Moreover, ER1' is strictly better than the remaining 16 GP-evolved formulæ under investigation.

Results in this paper are exempt from the inherent disadvantages of experimental studies, and hence are definite conclusions for any program and fault

Table 4. Statement division for PG_2 with $TS2_1$ and $TS2_2$

Statement	$TS2_1$	$TS2_2$
ER1'	$S_B^R = \emptyset$ $S_F^R = \{s_3, s_6, s_9\}$ $S_A^R = \{s_1, s_2, s_4, s_5, s_7, s_8, s_{10}, s_{11}\}$	$S_B^R = \emptyset$ $S_F^R = \{s_3, s_6, s_9\}$ $S_A^R = \{s_1, s_2, s_4, s_5, s_7, s_8, s_{10}, s_{11}\}$
ER5	$S_B^R = \emptyset$ $S_F^R = \{s_1, s_3, s_6, s_9\}$ $S_A^R = \{s_2, s_4, s_5, s_7, s_8, s_{10}, s_{11}\}$	$S_B^R = \emptyset$ $S_F^R = \{s_1, s_3, s_6, s_9\}$ $S_A^R = \{s_2, s_4, s_5, s_7, s_8, s_{10}, s_{11}\}$
GP02	$S_B^R = \{s_4, s_5, s_7, s_8, s_{10}, s_{11}\}$ $S_F^R = \{s_3, s_6, s_9\}$ $S_A^R = \{s_1, s_2\}$	$S_B^R = \{s_4, s_{11}\}$ $S_F^R = \{s_3, s_6, s_9\}$ $S_A^R = \{s_1, s_2, s_5, s_7, s_8, s_{10}\}$
GP03	$S_B^R = \{s_2, s_4, s_5, s_7, s_8, s_{10}, s_{11}\}$ $S_F^R = \{s_3, s_6, s_9\}$ $S_A^R = \{s_1\}$	$S_B^R = \emptyset$ $S_F^R = \{s_3, s_6, s_9\}$ $S_A^R = \{s_1, s_2, s_4, s_5, s_7, s_8, s_{10}, s_{11}\}$
GP19	$S_B^R = \{s_1\}$ $S_F^R = \{s_3, s_6, s_9\}$ $S_A^R = \{s_2, s_4, s_5, s_7, s_8, s_{10}, s_{11}\}$	$S_B^R = \{s_1, s_4, s_{11}\}$ $S_F^R = \{s_3, s_6, s_9\}$ $S_A^R = \{s_2, s_5, s_7, s_8, s_{10}\}$

Table 5. Rankings of faulty statement for five formulæ

Statement	PG_1 ($s_f{=}s_9$)		PG_2 ($s_f{=}s_3$)	
	$TS1_1$	$TS1_2$	$TS2_1$	$TS2_2$
ER1'	6	6	1	1
ER5	6	6	2	2
GP02	6	3	7	3
GP03	4	8	8	1
GP19	4	7	2	4

under the assumptions that are commonly adopted by the SBFL community. It is a surprise that without exhausting all possible programs and faults, GP can still deliver maximal formulæ. Moreover, the process of evolving a risk evaluation formula is totally automatic and does not need any human intelligence. Thus, the cost of designing risk evaluation formulæ can be significantly reduced.

From analysing formulæ in ER1', we note some common features. First, they all involve two independent parameters[2] e_f and e_p. Secondly, all these three formulæ comply with the commonly adopted intuition that statements associated with more *failed* or less *passed* testing results should never have lower risks. Finally, in all these three formulæ, any statement s_i with $e_f^i{<}F$ always has lower risk value than statement s_j with $e_f^j{=}F$. With respect to ER1', the evolved formula follows the known intuition. However, interestingly enough, the other maximal formulæ, GP02, GP03, and GP19, do not conform to the same intuition. Let us elaborate. Given two statements, s_1 and s_2:

---

[2] By definition, $n_p = P-e_p$ and $n_f = F-e_f$.

- **GP02**: If $e_p{}^1=e_p{}^2$, then $e_f{}^1>e_f{}^2$ implies GP02(s_1)>GP02(s_2), which is consistent with the commonly adopted intuition. However, if $e_f{}^1=e_f{}^2$, then $e_p{}^1<e_p{}^2$ does not necessarily imply GP02(s_1)≥GP02(s_2). For example, $e_f{}^1 = e_f{}^2 = 1$, $P=8$, $e_p{}^1=1$ and $e_p{}^2=2$, then we have GP02(s_1)=2·(1+$\sqrt{8-1}$)+1, which is less than GP02(s_2)=2 · (1 + $\sqrt{8-2}$) + $\sqrt{2}$. This does not comply with the commonly adopted intuition.
- **GP03**: If $e_p{}^1 = e_p{}^2$, then $e_f{}^1 > e_f{}^2$ does not necessarily imply GP03(s_1) ≥ GP03(s_2). For example, $e_p{}^1=e_p{}^2=25$, $e_f{}^1=2$ and $e_f{}^2=1$, then we have GP03(s_1)=1, which is less than GP03(s_2)=2. This does not comply with the commonly adopted intuition. Moreover, if $e_f{}^1=e_f{}^2$, then $e_p{}^1<e_p{}^2$ does not necessarily imply GP03(s_1)≥GP03(s_2). For example, $e_f{}^1=e_f{}^2=1$, $e_p{}^1=16$ and $e_p{}^2=25$, then we have GP03(s_1)=$\sqrt{3}$, which is less than GP03(s_2)=2. As a consequence, the commonly adopted intuition is not complied.
- **GP19**: If $e_p{}^1=e_p{}^2$, then $e_f{}^1>e_f{}^2$ does not necessarily imply GP19(s_1) ≥ GP19(s_2). For example, $P=20$, $e_p{}^1=e_p{}^2=10$; $F=4$, $e_f{}^1=2$ and $e_f{}^2=1$, then we have GP19(s_1)=0, which is less than GP19(s_2)=$\sqrt{2}$. This example demonstrates that the commonly adopted intuition is not complied. Moreover, if $e_f{}^1=e_f{}^2$, then $e_p{}^1<e_p{}^2$ does not necessarily imply GP19(s_1)≥GP19(s_2). For example, $F=2$, $e_f{}^1=e_f{}^2=1$; $P=10$, $e_p{}^1=8$ and $e_p{}^2=9$, then we have GP19(s_1)=$\sqrt{6}$, which is less than GP19(s_2)=$\sqrt{8}$. This does not comply with the commonly adopted intuition.

Formulæ defined by human beings are more likely to be confined to the perceived intuition and background of the designer. Thus, it is possible that some maximal formulæ may be overlooked by humans. However, GP does not suffer from this problem and has the advantage of being unbiased. As explained in the above examples for GP02, GP03 and GP19, GP is able to define maximal formulæ based on intuitions that humans would rarely consider.

5   Related Work

Spectrum-Based Fault Localisation (SBFL) is also referred to as statistical fault localisation: it aims to identify statements that are suspected to contain the root cause for software failure by examining a large number of passing and failing test executions. Tarantula [14] was the first SBFL risk evaluation formula that originally started its life as a visualisation tool. Many other formulaæ followed, applying different statistical analysis to compute the ranking of suspiciousness statements [2, 3, 5, 18, 20], all of which have been designed manually: Yoo [23] is the first to use Genetic Programming to automatically evolve an SBFL formula.

The predominant method for evaluating SBFL risk evaluation formulæ in the literature has been empirical studies [6, 13, 24]. However, recent advances in theoretical analysis of SBFL have provided optimality proof for specific program structures [16], as well as proofs of equivalence/dominance relations for arbitrary combinations of faulty source code and test suites [21].

6   Conclusion

Search-based techniques have been widely used in software engineering, such as testing, maintenance, etc [8,10]. Recently, Yoo [23] has successfully utilized a search-based technique, namely, Genetic Programming, to generate effective risk evaluation formulæ for SBFL. In this paper, by using the recently developed theoretical framework by Xie et al. [21] on Yoo's GP-evolved formulæ, we have demonstrated that four formulæ are maximal for programs with single fault, namely, GP02, GP03, GP13 and GP19. The results provide a strong support that Genetic Programming can be an ideal tool for designing risk evaluation formulæ. GP not only can deliver maximal formulæ having the same features as some maximal formulæ designed by humans, but also can help to provide novel insights and intuitions about effective formulæ that humans may overlook.

Acknowledgement. This work was partly funded by the Engineering and Physical Sciences Research Council [grant no. EP/J017515/1] and the Australian Research Council [grant no. DP 120104773].

References

1. Abreu, R., Zoeteweij, P., van Gemund, A.J.C.: An evaluation of similarity co-efficients for software fault localization. In: Proceedings of the 12th Pacific Rim International Symposium on Dependable Computing, pp. 39–46. Riverside, USA (2006)
2. Abreu, R., Zoeteweij, P., van Gemund, A.J.C.: An observation-based model for fault localization. In: Proceedings of the 2008 International Workshop on Dynamic Analysis: Held in Conjunction with the ACM SIGSOFT International Symposium on Software Testing and Analysis (ISSTA 2008), WODA 2008, pp. 64–70. ACM, New York (2008)
3. Artzi, S., Dolby, J., Tip, F., Pistoia, M.: Directed test generation for effective fault localization. In: Proceedings of the 19th International Symposium on Software Testing and Analysis, ISSTA 2010, pp. 49–60. ACM, New York (2010)
4. Chen, M., Kiciman, E., Fratkin, E., Fox, A., Brewer, E.: Pinpoint: problem determi-nation in large, dynamic internet services. In: Proceedings of the 32th IEEE/IFIP International Conference on Dependable Systems and Networks, Washington DC, USA, pp. 595–604 (2002)
5. Dallmeier, V., Lindig, C., Zeller, A.: Lightweight bug localization with ample. In: Proceedings of the Sixth International Symposium on Automated Analysis-driven Debugging, AADEBUG 2005, pp. 99–104. ACM, New York (2005)
6. DiGiuseppe, N., Jones, J.A.: On the influence of multiple faults on coverage-based fault localization. In: Proceedings of the 2011 International Symposium on Software Testing and Analysis, ISSTA 2011, pp. 210–220. ACM, New York (2011)
7. de Freitas, F.G., de Souza, J.T.: Ten years of search based software engineering: A bibliometric analysis. In: Cohen, M.B., Ó Cinnéide, M. (eds.) SSBSE 2011. LNCS, vol. 6956, pp. 18–32. Springer, Heidelberg (2011)
8. Harman, M., Jones, B.: Search based software engineering. Information and Soft-ware Technology 43(14), 833–839 (2001)

9. Harman, M.: The current state and future of search based software engineering. In: FOSE 2007: 2007 Future of Software Engineering, pp. 342–357. IEEE Computer Society, Washington, DC (2007)

10. Harman, M.: The relationship between search based software engineering and predictive modeling. In: Proceedings of the 6th International Conference on Predictive Models in Software Engineering, Timişoara, Romania, pp. 1:1–1:13 (2010)

11. Harman, M., Mansouri, S.A., Zhang, Y.: Search-based software engineering: Trends, techniques and applications. ACM Computing Surveys 45(1), 11:1–11:61 (2012)

12. Jones, J.A., Harrold, M.J., Stasko, J.: Visualization of test information to assist fault localization. In: Proceedings of the 24th International Conference on Software Engineering, Florida, USA, pp. 467–477 (2002)

13. Jones, J.A., Harrold, M.J.: Empirical evaluation of the tarantula automatic fault-localization technique. In: Proceedings of the 20th International Conference on Automated Software Engineering (ASE 2005), pp. 273–282. ACM Press (2005)

14. Jones, J.A., Harrold, M.J., Stasko, J.T.: Visualization for fault localization. In: Proceedings of ICSE Workshop on Software Visualization, pp. 71–75 (2001)

15. McMinn, P.: Search-based software test data generation: A survey. Software Testing, Verification and Reliability 14(2), 105–156 (2004)

16. Naish, L., Lee, H.J., Ramamohanarao, K.: A model for spectra-based software diagnosis. ACM Transactions on Software Engineering Methodology 20(3), 11:1–11:32 (2011)

17. Räihä, O.: A survey on search-based software design. Computer Science Review 4(4), 203–249 (2010)

18. Renieres, M., Reiss, S.: Fault localization with nearest neighbor queries. In: Proceedings of the 18th International Conference on Automated Software Engineering, pp. 30–39 (October 2003)

19. de Souza, J.T., Maia, C.L., de Freitas, F.G., Coutinho, D.P.: The human competitiveness of search based software engineering. In: Proceedings of 2nd International Symposium on Search based Software Engineering (SSBSE 2010), pp. 143–152. IEEE Computer Society Press, Benevento (2010)

20. Wong, W.E., Qi, Y., Zhao, L., Cai, K.Y.: Effective fault localization using code coverage. In: Proceedings of the 31st Annual International Computer Software and Applications Conference, COMPSAC 2007, vol. 1, pp. 449–456. IEEE Computer Society, Washington, DC (2007)

21. Xie, X.Y., Chen, T.Y., Kuo, F.C., Xu, B.W.: A Theoretical Analysis of the Risk Evaluation Formulas for Spectrum-Based Fault Localization. Accepted by the ACM Transactions on Software Engineering and Methodology (2012)

22. Xie, X.: On the analysis of spectrum-based fault localization. Ph.D. thesis, Swinburne University of Technology (May 2012)

23. Yoo, S.: Evolving human competitive spectra-based fault localisation techniques. In: Fraser, G., Teixeira de Souza, J. (eds.) SSBSE 2012. LNCS, vol. 7515, pp. 244–258. Springer, Heidelberg (2012)

24. Yu, Y., Jones, J.A., Harrold, M.J.: An empirical study of the effects of test-suite reduction on fault localization. In: Proceedings of the International Conference on Software Engineering (ICSE 2008), pp. 201–210. ACM Press (May 2008)

On the Synergy between Search-Based and Search-Driven Software Engineering

Colin Atkinson, Marcus Kessel, and Marcus Schumacher

University of Mannheim, Software Engineering Group,
68131 Mannheim, Germany
{atkinson,kessel,schumacher}@informatik.uni-mannheim.de
http://swt.informatik.uni-mannheim.de/

Abstract. Two notions of "search" can be used to enhance the software engineering process — the notion of searching for optimal architectures/designs using AI-motivated optimization algorithms, and the notion of searching for reusable components using query-driven search engines. To date these possibilities have largely been explored separately within different communities. In this paper we suggest there is a synergy between the two approaches, and that a hybrid approach which integrates their strengths could be more useful and powerful than either approach individually. After first characterizing the two approaches we discuss some of the opportunities and challenges involved in their synergetic integration.

Keywords: Search-Based Software Engineering, Search-Driven Software Engineering, Software Metric, Software Measurement, Test-Driven Search.

1 Introduction

The concept of "search-based" software engineering (SBSE) [1] has gained a great deal of traction over the last few years as a paradigm for software development driven by the use of sophisticated optimization algorithms to find the "best" realization of a software system according to some quantified measure of quality or goodness [2]. There is a well-established research community pursuing this vision with a successful workshop (now symposium[1]) series bearing this name. However, this is not the only meaningful and useful interpretation of "search" in connection with software engineering. Another interpretation of the term, which has its roots in the software reuse community, is software engineering driven by engines and tools that "search" for components, tests and other useful software artefacts within the vast amounts of software available in public and private repositories. In this second interpretation, "search" is meant in the sense of google-like search engines rather than "search" algorithms from the realm of artificial intelligence. This second interpretation, which we will refer to

---

[1] e.g. SSBSE, http://ssbse.org/

G. Ruhe and Y. Zhang (Eds.): SSBSE 2013, LNCS 8084, pp. 239–244, 2013.
© Springer-Verlag Berlin Heidelberg 2013

in the remainder of the paper as "search-driven" software engineering (SDSE), also has an active research community, with associated workshops[2], although the term has not become the label for that community. At first glance SBSE and SDSE might appear to be unrelated, and perhaps even incompatible. It is certainly true that they have different foci and use different concepts, tools and techniques to fulfil their goals. However, we believe that far from being unrelated and incompatible, the two interpretations are in fact highly synergistic and reinforce each other's strengths whilst compensating for each other's weaknesses.

The main weakness of SBSE approaches is *scalability*. Optimizing fitness measures over all possible realizations of a software system, right down to the smallest grained components, is not a practical proposition for all but the smallest systems because of the sheer number of possible realizations to consider. This is why research based on the use of optimization algorithms in software engineering has tended to focus on high-level architectural choices rather than on detailed component implementations. The latest generation of software-search engines, in contrast, can support rapid searches over vast indexes of software components, often with very high precision. For example, merobase[3] currently has an index of around nine million components and has the ability, in certain circumstances, to return results with 100% precision [3].

The main weakness of SDSE is *lack of goal orientation*. More specifically, the current generation of search engines and code recommendation tools based on them provide little help to developers to select the "best" component from the many candidates in the result set. Although they do employ ranking algorithms (e.g. [4][5]) to try to prioritize components according to "how well" they match the search query, the ranking algorithms are application independent and developers usually have to browse through the returned candidates manually and make ad hoc judgements about their "fitness" to their application. This, however, is precisely the strength of artificial intelligence (AI) based optimization algorithms [6] — finding the best solution for the problem in hand in a goal driven way.

Combining the goal orientation of SBSE approaches with the efficiency of SDSE approaches therefore has the potential to yield more scalable approaches that are able to more effectively find optimum solutions to software engineering problems using reusable components. The key to achieving this synergy is to find the optimal interface between SBSE (AI-based) search algorithms and SDSE (query-driven) search engines based on the right kinds of metrics [7]. The key is to find the most effective criteria and level of granularity to decide when to call upon a query-driven search engine from within a goal-driven, optimization algorithm, and to align the metrics that they use to rank components or solutions.

In the remainder of this paper we present a vision for how such a hybrid approach might be realized and how it might be used. For want of a better term we refer to it as "search-enhanced software engineering" (SESE).

---

[2] e.g. SUITE, http://resuite.org/
[3] http://merobase.com/

2   Realizing Search-Enhanced Software Engineering

Figure 1 provides a schematic picture of how SESE might work. The top left of the picture shows two alternative ways of architecting a system, S, from components. The top architecture of S has three types of components, A, B, and C, while the bottom architecture has two types of components X and Y. The top center of the picture schematically represents functionality matching reusable components that have been discovered by a code search engine. Thus, for example, A1, A2 and A3 are different realizations of A with different implementations and non-functional properties. An example of such a non-functional property might be energy efficiency. Ideally the search engine ranks the components according to their energy efficiency. The top right of the figure shows different energy efficiency curves for different possible ways of building S from alternative combinations of the reusable candidates. The figure shows that the configuration with the highest global maximum is composed of X1 and Y2, even though Y2 is not the most energy efficient variant of Y.

A code search engine (i.e. SDSE) by itself could not arrive at such a conclusion because it is not able to optimize the selection of components based on the global, emergent properties of the different architecture. An AI search algorithm (i.e. SBSE) could in principle arrive at such a conclusion but only if it walked over all components in the index of the search engine, which is usually in the millions. In practice this is not possible within a reasonable time frame. The only effective way of finding the best architecture and component configuration is therefore to combine SDSE and SBSE, as indicated in the bottom part of the figure. This shows the general situation in which the lower level components in the eventual architecture have been "discovered" by a search engine while the best higher level composition of the candidate components has been "discovered" by the AI search algorithm. While this hybrid approach may theoretically miss a possible optimum, in practice it facilitates the consideration of a significantly larger number of possible configurations. The key challenge, therefore is to find the optimal level of granularity at which to integrate SDSE into SBSE. If the level is too high, too many possible global optimal solutions could be missed, but if the level is too low, the time taken to reach a conclusion could be too long.

To realize such a vision of SESE, the code search engines that support the SDSE ingredient must have two important properties which currently lie outside the capabilities of most search engines at the current time — the ability to return search results with very high precision (i.e. that match the requirements) and the ability to rank components according to some purpose-relevant criteria.

High-Precision Search Results. Most of the code search engines available today still use relatively simple text-based queries (similar to those of general purpose search engines like google) which have very low precision. The latest generation of code search engines support more sophisticated interface and signature based queries which offer much better results [8], but these are still too imprecise to drive the SESE scenario described above because the likelihood of any individual in the result set being fit for purpose is too low. What is required,

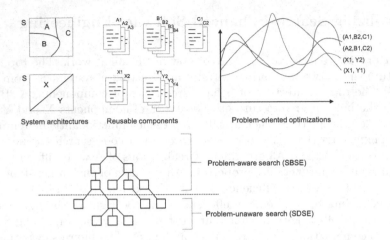

Fig. 1. Schematic illustration of envisioned hybrid SESE approach

ideally, is a search engine that is able to deliver results that are 100% certain to be "fit-for-purpose" from a functional perspective. At the present time the only practical, working example of a search mechanism able to return results with this level of precision is test-driven search (TDS) [3]. As its name implies, a test-driven search takes a test definition, similar to those used in test-driven development approaches [9], and applies it to each of the candidates returned in a standard search to filter out those components that do not pass. The resulting filtered result set therefore contains only those components that are fit-for-purpose according to the tests [10]. Merobase is the only code search engine which currently offers such a TDS capability online.

Purpose-Relevant Ranking. TDS addresses the problem of returning components that are 100% fit-for-purpose according to the tests defined for them. However, it does not address the problem that the returned components are not ranked according to criteria that match the overall optimization goals of the project. The aim of the ranking algorithms used in the current generation of code search engines is to order components according to how likely they are to match the functionality that the searcher is looking for [4]. In other words they rank the components according to functional rather than non-functional criteria. For example, Hummel [5] ranks the set of candidates according to the "closeness" of their syntactic matches, leading to the presentation of candidates with high syntactic matches first. When TDS is used as the basis for establishing the result set, however, such a ranking approach is superfluous because the components are guaranteed to be functionally fit-for-purpose. It is therefore possible to rank the components according to non-functional criteria such as metrics used in the SBSE optimization algorithms (i.e. "Metrics as Fitness Functions" [7], [11]).

While it is relatively easy to determine so called "internal", structural metrics on components (e.g. lines of code, cyclomatic complexity etc.) it is much more difficult to determine "external", user-relevant metrics that could serve as the basis for a fitness function. The only class of metrics for which this is possible are dynamic metrics that can be measured by observing running software (e.g. execution time, energy usage). By definition, therefore, TDS provides a perfect foundation for calculating such metrics because it involves the execution of each component in the initial result set returned by a basic search. Nevertheless, instrumenting software execution platforms to measure useful properties is a non-trivial task. One of our current research goals at the University of Mannheim is to obtain energy-usage metrics for components during the TDS processes by using specially instrumented hardware.

3   Bottom-Up, Optimized Development

The SBSE approach described in the previous section essentially assumes a top-down process of software development in which the candidate architectures are first designed independently, without any knowledge of the available components, and then code search engines are used to explore the component repository to see if any suitable components are available. This is acceptable if the architecture is just represented by a component diagram, but when a lot of effort has to be put into defining the architecture and desired components (e.g. test cases) this approach becomes itself suboptimal. It would be much better if the architecture candidates could be designed with some knowledge of the available components — in other words, if the process could proceed in a more bottom-up way. This, however, creates the new challenge of defining metrics that make it possible to compare the non-functional properties of components with different functionality — so called "Functionality-independent Metrics" (FIMs).

Coming up with end-user relevent FIMs is a major challenge because some technique is needed to judge the "work done" [12] by components in order to indicate whether one operates in a "better" way than another even it does something different. For example, to compare the effective power of two types of car it is much better to use the power-to-weight ratio than the raw power metric. To support such FIMs for software components some abstract way of comparing functionality such as "feature points" is needed. This is another one of the challenges we are working on at the University of Mannheim. By observing software components during TDSs and applying various static analysis techniques, we are in the processes of creating a database of profiles and metrics for the merobase component repository. This provides the basis for calculating FIMs to support the efficient, bottom-up development of optimized software architectures.

Optimization algorithms in SBSE are chosen depending on the individual optimization problem under investigation [6]. To use FIM-based fitness functions in SBSE approaches, it is therefore necessary to select an appropriate optimization algorithm. This, in general means that single- as well as multi-objective optimization problems need to be accommodated. Single optimization problems exist in cases where only one FIM is applied. Experiments are required to determine a well-suited optimization algorithm based on FIM-based fitness functions. Multi-objective optimization problems exist, for instance, if several FIM dimensions need to be optimized. Pareto optimality [6] may be a candidate for such a case, for example, as it supports the optimization of multiple, possibly conflicting dimensions.

4 Conclusion

In this paper we have explained why we believe that a hybrid mix of SBSE and SDSE technologies offer the most effective way of creating optimized software systems based on the available reusable components. However, to support such a hybrid approach, which we refer to as SESE, enhanced code search engines providing high precision results, ranked according to user-relevant, non-functional metrics are needed. Ideally, they should also support the use of functionality-independent metrics. When such search engines become available the challenge will be to integrate them effectively into SBSE optimization algorithms. At the University of Mannheim we are focussing on the SDSE aspect of this challenge by developing suitable metrics and ranking approaches.

References

1. Harman, M., Jones, B.F.: Search-based software engineering. Information and Software Technology 43(14), 833–839 (2001)
2. Harman, M., Mansouri, S.A., Zhang, Y.: Search based software engineering: A comprehensive analysis and review of trends techniques and applications. Department of Computer Science, Kings College London, Tech. Rep. TR-09-03 (2009)
3. Hummel, O., Janjic, W., Atkinson, C.: Code conjurer: Pulling reusable software out of thin air. IEEE Software 25(5), 45–52 (2008)
4. Inoue, K., Yokomori, R., Yamamoto, T., Matsushita, M., Kusumoto, S.: Ranking significance of software components based on use relations. IEEE Transactions on Software Engineering 31(3), 213–225 (2005)
5. Hummel, O.: Semantic component retrieval in software engineering, vol. 151 (2008)
6. Harman, M., McMinn, P., de Souza, J.T., Yoo, S.: Search based software engineering: Techniques, taxonomy, tutorial. In: Meyer, B., Nordio, M. (eds.) LASER Summer School 2008-2010. LNCS, vol. 7007, pp. 1–59. Springer, Heidelberg (2012)
7. Harman, M., Clark, J.: Metrics are fitness functions too. In: Proceedings of the 10th International Symposium on Software Metrics, 2004, pp. 58–69. IEEE (2004)
8. Hummel, O., Janjic, W., Atkinson, C.: Evaluating the efficiency of retrieval methods for component repositories. In: SEKE, pp. 404–409 (2007)
9. Beck, K.: Test driven development: By example. Addison-Wesley Professional (2003)
10. Hummel, O., Atkinson, C.: Extreme harvesting: Test driven discovery and reuse of software components. In: Proceedings of the 2004 IEEE International Conference on Information Reuse and Integration, IRI 2004, pp. 66–72. IEEE (2004)
11. Ó Cinnéide, M., Tratt, L., Harman, M., Counsell, S., Hemati Moghadam, I.: Experimental assessment of software metrics using automated refactoring. In: Proceedings of the ACM-IEEE International Symposium on Empirical Software Engineering and Measurement, pp. 49–58. ACM (2012)
12. Johann, T., Dick, M., Naumann, S., Kern, E.: How to measure energy-efficiency of software: Metrics and measurement results. In: 2012 First International Workshop on Green and Sustainable Software (GREENS), pp. 51–54 (2012)

Preference-Based Many-Objective Evolutionary Testing Generates Harder Test Cases for Autonomous Agents

Sabrine Kalboussi[1], Slim Bechikh[1], Marouane Kessentini[2], and Lamjed Ben Said[1]

[1] SOIE Lab, ISG-Tunis, University of Tunis, Tunisia
{sabrine.kalboussi,slim.bechikh}@gmail.com,
lamjed.bensaid@isg.rnu.tn
[2] CS, Missouri University of Science and Technology, Missouri, USA
marouanek@mst.edu

Abstract. Despite the high number of existing works in software testing within the SBSE community, there are very few ones that address the problematic of agent testing. The most prominent work in this direction is by Nguyen et al. [13], which formulates this problem as a bi-objective optimization problem to search for hard test cases from a robustness viewpoint. In this paper, we extend this work by: (1) proposing a new seven-objective formulation of this problem and (2) solving it by means of a preference-based many-objective evolutionary method. The obtained results show that our approach generates harder test cases than Nguyen et al. method ones. Moreover, Nguyen et al. method becomes a special case of our method since the user can incorporate his/her preferences within the search process by emphasizing some testing aspects over others.

Keywords: Agent testing, many-objective optimization, user's preferences.

1 Introduction

Software testing is a software development phase that aims to evaluate the product quality and enhance it by detecting errors and problems [11]. Despite the big efforts performed in the software testing research field, such activity remains complex and so expensive from the effort viewpoint and also the cost one. For this reason, researchers have proposed a new testing approach called *Search-Based Software Testing* (*SBST*) [7]. The latter consists in modeling the software testing problem as an optimization problem and then solving it by using a particular search method (usually metaheuristic) such as Evolutionary Algorithms (EAs), tabu search, etc. The SBST approach is a sub area of Search Based Software Engineering (SBSE) [7] and it is applied to several testing types [9], [10]. It has shown a great effectiveness and efficiency in achieving the testing goals.

There is little work in testing autonomous agents in regard what has already achieved in software testing [4], [14]. The pro-activity characteristic of software agent makes its test a hard task since it may react in different manners for the same input over time. Recently, Nguyen et al. [13] have proposed a search-based method to test autonomous agents. In fact, Nguyen et al. identified two soft goals that are *robustness*

G. Ruhe and Y. Zhang (Eds.): SSBSE 2013, LNCS 8084, pp. 245–250, 2013.
© Springer-Verlag Berlin Heidelberg 2013

and *efficiency* to test an autonomous Cleaner agent that has to keep clean a square area of an airport. However, they detailed/used only the robustness soft goal by proposing only two objective functions that drive the used multi-objective EA (i.e., NSGA-II [5]). The proposed Evolutionary Testing (ET) method has demonstrated its effectiveness in finding test cases that reply to the two considered objective functions belonging to the robustness soft goal.

In this paper, we propose a Preference-based Many-Objective Evolutionary Testing (P-MOET) method which corresponds to an extension of Nguyen et al.'s work [13]. The main idea is to propose additional objective functions corresponding to different soft goals with the aim to generate *harder* test cases (a hard test case is a test case that urges the agent to not achieve the soft goals) than Nguyen et al.'s method ones, and then solving the new obtained problem by considering all objective functions *simultaneously*. The main contributions of this work are as follows: (1) proposing five additional objective functions corresponding to different soft goals, (2) solving the obtained problem in a many-objective fashion [8], (3) Offering the user the ability to incorporate his/her preferences by emphasizing some objectives (testing aspects) over others by means of the use of the reference point concept [3], [2] and (4) outperforming in average an existing approach [13] when generating test cases on the same experimental environment.

2   Proposed Approach

2.1   New Many-Objective Formulation for Autonomous Agent Testing Problem

We propose a new many-objective formulation for the ET problem that considers simultaneously *seven* objectives. This formulation is stated as follows:

$$Min f(u) = [f_1(u), f_2(u), ..., f_7(u)]^T \qquad (1)$$

where the test case u is encoded as follows $u = (x_1, y_1, x_2, y_2, ..., x_n, y_n)$ such that x_i and y_i are respectively the abscissa and the ordinate of the object i in the area to clean. Table 1 summarized the seven used objective functions (the two first ones are defined in [13] and the five new ones are proposed by us). The latter are classified into four families based on the ensured soft goal where $TPC(u)$ is the Total Power Consumption, $NEO(u)$ is the Number of Encountered Obstacles, $ACW(u)$ is the Amount of Collected Waste during a specified amount of time that we fixed to 10 seconds in this work, $NDNW(u)$ is the Number of times that the agent Drops to collect the Nearest Waste, $NDND(u)$ is the Number of times that the agent Drops to put the waste in the Nearest Dustbin, $NDNC(u)$ is the Number of times that the agent Drops to go to the Nearest Charging station when its battery is low, and $NRSD(u)$ is the Number of times that the agent does not Respect the Safety Distance. All these quantities are computed when executing the Cleaner agent on the test case u. The expected outcomes are hard test cases that obstruct the agents under test from reaching the soft-goals under consideration. When multiple soft-goals are considered at once, we expect to obtain test cases that satisfy multiple *hard-to-find conditions* simultaneously.

Table 1. Classification of used objectives with their objective functions

Soft goal family	Objective	Objective function
Robustness	Maintain battery	$f_1(u) = 1/TPC(u)$
	Avoid obstacle	$f_2(u) = 1/NEO(u)$
Efficiency	Clean up waste	$f_3(u) = ACW(u)$
Stability	Collect the nearest waste	$f_4(u) = 1/NDNW(u)$
	Put the waste into the nearest dustbin	$f_5(u) = 1/NDND(u)$
	Go to the nearest charging station	$f_6(u) = 1/NDNC(u)$
Safety	Maintain a separation distance from obstacle	$f_7(u) = 1/NRSD(u)$

2.2   P-MOET: Preference-Based Many-Objective Evolutionary Testing Method

To solve our many-objective ET problem, we use a proposed preference-based MOEA, called *r-NSGA-II* (reference solution-based NSGA-II) [3]. Fig. 1 describes the adaptation of r-NSGA-II algorithm to our many-objective autonomous agent testing problem. The algorithm basic iteration begins by generating the parent population P_t of size N. After that, each test case from P_t is executed on the Cleaner agent module. Once all P_t test cases are evaluated, we apply binary tournament selection and genetic operators (crossover and mutation) to generate the offspring population Q_t of

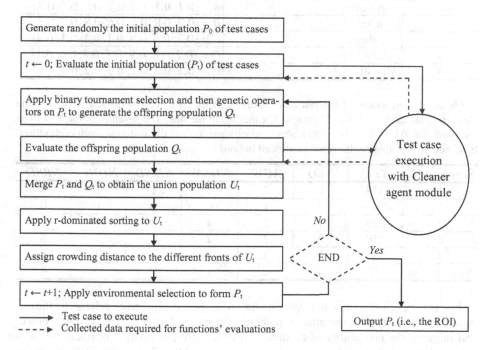

Fig. 1. Adaptation schema of r-NSGA-II to the many-objective agent testing problem

size N. We form U_t by merging P_t and Q_t (the size of U_t is then $2N$). We apply non-r-dominated sorting based on the r-dominance relation to sort U_t into several non-r-dominated fronts. After that, P_{t+1} is filled with individuals of the best non-r-dominated fronts, one at a time. Since overall population size is $2N$, not all fronts may be accommodated in N slots available in the new population P_{t+1}. When the last allowed front is being considered, it may contain more solutions than the remaining available slots in P_{t+1}. Hence, only least crowded solutions of the last considered front are saved and the others are rejected. Concerning the Cleaner agent module, we have downloaded it from its authors' Web site via the URL [12], and then we have *adjusted* it to our work. We note that the overall adaptation of r-NSGA-II to the many-objective autonomous agent testing problem is named *P-MOET*.

3   Experimental Study

When generating test cases for agents based on the considered soft goals or goals (objectives), the user may prefer: (1) emphasizing some soft goals/goals over others or (2) emphasizing all soft goals/goals simultaneously. For this reason, different scenarios are used and summarized in table 2.

Table 2. Used scenarios with their reference points

Scenario N°	Preferred soft goal(s)	Used reference point
1	Robustness	$A = (\mathbf{0.1}, \mathbf{0.1}, 0.9, 0.7, 0.8, 0.7, 0.8)$
2	Efficiency	$B = (0.7, 0.8, \mathbf{0.1}, 0.6, 0.8, 0.7, 0.8)$
3	Stability	$C = (0.7, 0.8, 0.9, \mathbf{0.1}, \mathbf{0.1}, \mathbf{0.1}, 0.8)$
4	Safety	$D = (0.7, 0.8, 0.9, 0.7, 0.8, 0.6, \mathbf{0.1})$
5	All soft goals	$E = (\mathbf{0.1}, \mathbf{0.2}, \mathbf{0.1}, \mathbf{0.2}, \mathbf{0.2}, \mathbf{0.1}, \mathbf{0.1})$

Table 3. Median values of the test case hardness metrics for the 5 P-MOET scenarios and Nguyen et al. work [13] over 51 runs on Cleaner agent module. The *p-values* of the Wilcoxon test, with $\alpha = 0.05$, have shown that all the results are statistically different from each others. Best values regarding hardness are mentioned in bold.

Scenario N°	TPC	NEO	ACW	NDNW	NDND	NDNC	NRSD
1	**335**	**4**	2	1	1	1	4
2	300	2	**1**	0	0	1	0
3	295	1	2	**4**	**3**	**3**	2
4	250	3	2	2	1	1	**8**
5	330	3	2	3	2	2	6
Nguyen et al.	**335**	**4**	2	1	0	0	4

For instance, for *scenario 1*, we emphasize only the objectives related to the *robustness* soft goal with the aim to generate test cases that consume so much power and increase the probability of crashing with the different existing obstacles. This is achieved by using the reference point $A= (\mathbf{0.1}, \mathbf{0.1}, 0.9, 0.7, 0.8, 0.7, 0.8)$ where we emphasize just the *two first* objectives (mentioned with bold numbers) by fixing them

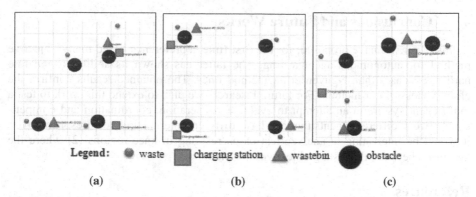

Legend: ● waste   ■ charging station   ▲ wastebin   ● obstacle

(a)   (b)   (c)

Fig. 2. Representative test cases for: (a) scenario 3, (a) scenario 5 and (b) Nguyen et al. work

to a low value (< 0.4) and the other aspiration (i.e., desired) values are set to high values (> 0.6). We restricted each objective value to the normalized interval [0,1] in order to ease the expression of user's preferences. For each scenario, we run the P-MOET method with a population of 50 individuals for 100 generations. Then we select *randomly* a representative test case from the obtained ROI [1]. The difficulties related to the obtained test cases are assessed based on the following metrics: (1) *TPC*, (2) *NEO*, (3) *ACW*, (4) *NDNW*, (5) *NDND*, (6) *NDNC* and (7) *NRSD*. In fact, each scenario test case is executed 51 times on the Cleaner agent module and the different metrics' values are recorded. After that, we record the median values in table 3. Due to the stochastic aspects of the results, we use the Wilcoxon rank sum hypothesis test in a pairwise comparison fashion, with a 95% confidence level ($\alpha = 0.05$), in order to detect whether the results are significant or not. According to table 3, we observe that the P-MOET method has demonstrated its ability and flexibility in replying to the requirements of each scenario. For example, scenario 3 has the maximal values regarding the stability metrics (*NDNW*, *NDND* and *NDNC*). This observation shows the effectiveness of our method in solving the 7-objective agent testing problem while respecting user's preferences. Similar observations are obtained for the scenarios 1, 2 and 4. Although scenario 5 does not present any best value regarding the test case hardness metrics, it seems to be the scenario that provides the hardest test case set. In fact, this scenario emphasizes all the soft goals simultaneously, which is demanding. Consequently, it makes a compromise between: (1) robustness, (2) efficiency, (3) stability and (4) safety. For this reason, it furnishes the hardest test cases. This result is emphasized by fig. 2(a-b) which illustrates two test cases for the third scenario and the fifth one.

Next, we compare the P-MOET scenario 5 against Nguyen et al.'s work. From table 3, we remark that Nguyen et al. method's representative test case has the maximal values for the *TPC* and *NEO* metrics. The same observation is obtained for scenario 1. We can say that the P-MOET can reproduce the Nguyen et al. method test cases by running scenario 1. Fig. 2(c) illustrates the test case of Nguyen et al. method. When comparing the latter with the test case of P-MOET scenario 5, we remark that although the fifth scenario test case does not present any best value in terms of the considered hardness metrics in table 3, we observe from fig. 2(b-c) that the scenario 5 test case is harder than Nguyen et al. method one. This is illustrated by the locations of the different objects in the environment for each test case in regard to the semantic meaning of objects' locations.

4   Conclusions and Future Works

In this paper, we have proposed, for the first time, a preference-based many-objective method for autonomous agent testing. The latter has shown its ability to generate harder test cases than Nguyen et al. method ones. The obtained results confirm the effectiveness of our method. For future research, we plan to extend this work to test a multi-agent system in an attempt to evaluate cooperation, coordination and competition between different agents that can have different internal architectures. Moreover, it would be interesting to analyze test cases residing in knee regions [2] where the trade-offs between the testing objectives are maximal.

References

1. Adra, S.F., Griffin, I., Fleming, P.J.: A Comparative Study of Progressive Preference Articulation Techniques for Multiobjective Optimisation. In: Obayashi, S., Deb, K., Poloni, C., Hiroyasu, T., Murata, T. (eds.) EMO 2007. LNCS, vol. 4403, pp. 908–921. Springer, Heidelberg (2007)
2. Bechikh, S., Ben Said, L., Ghédira, K.: Searching for Knee Regions of the Pareto Front using Mobile Reference Points. Soft Computing 15(9), 1807–1823 (2011)
3. Ben Said, L., Bechikh, S., Ghédira, K.: The r-Dominance: A New Dominance Relation for Interactive Evolutionary Multicriteria Decision Making. IEEE Trans. on Evolutionary Computation 14(5), 801–818 (2010)
4. Coelho, R., Kulesza, U., Staa, A., Lucena, C.: Unit Testing in Multi-agent Systems using Mock Agents and Aspects. In: International Workshop on Software Engineering for Large-Scale Multi-agent Systems, pp. 83–90 (2006)
5. Deb, K., Pratap, A., Agarwal, S., Meyarivan, T.: A Fast and Elitist Multiobjective Genetic Algorithm: NSGA-II. IEEE Trans. on Evolutionary Computation 6(2), 182–197 (2002)
6. Harman, M., Ph, U., Jones, B.F.: Search-Based Software Engineering. Information and Software Technology 43, 833–839 (2001)
7. Harman, M., Mansouri, S.A., Zhang, Y.: Search-Based Software Engineering: Trends, Techniques and Applications. ACM Computing Surveys 45(1), 11 (2012)
8. Hughes, E.J.: Evolutionary Many-objective Optimization: Many Once or One Many? In: IEEE Congress on Evolutionary Computation, pp. 222–227 (2005)
9. McMinn, P.: Search-Based Software Testing: Past, Present and Future. In: 4th International Workshop on Search-Based Software Testing, pp. 153–163 (2011)
10. McMinn, P.: Search-based software test data generation: A survey. Software Testing, Verification and Reliability 14(2), 105–156 (2004)
11. McMinn, P., Harman, M., Lakhotia, K., Hassoun, Y., Wegener, J.: Input Domain Reduction through Irrelevant Variable Removal and Its Effect on Local, Global, and Hybrid Search-Based Structural Test Data Generation. IEEE Trans. on Software Engineering 38(2), 453–477 (2012)
12. Nguyen, C.D.: Web page, tools, http://selab.fbk.eu/dnguyen/public/cleaner-agent.tgz
13. Nguyen, C.D., Miles, S., Perini, A., Tonella, P., Harman, M., Luck, M.: Evolutionary Testing of Autonomous Software Agents. Autonomous Agents and Multi-Agent Systems 25(2), 260–283 (2012)
14. Nunez, M., Rodriguez, I., Rubio, F.: Specification and Testing of Autonomous Agents in E-Commerce Systems. Software Testing, Verification and Reliability 15(4), 211–233 (2005)

Efficient Subdomains for Random Testing

Matthew Patrick[1], Rob Alexander[1], Manuel Oriol[1,2], and John A. Clark[1]

[1] Department of Computer Science, University of York, UK
{mtp,rda,manuel,jac}@cs.york.ac.uk
[2] ABB Corporate Research, Baden-Dättwil, Switzerland
manuel.oriol@ch.abb.com

Abstract. Opinion is divided over the effectiveness of random testing. It produces test cases cheaply, but struggles with boundary conditions and is labour intensive without an automated oracle. We have created a search-based testing technique that evolves multiple sets of efficient subdomains, from which small but effective test suites can be randomly sampled. The new technique handles boundary conditions by targeting different mutants with each set of subdomains. It achieves an average 230% improvement in mutation score over conventional random testing.

1 Introduction

Random testing is a straightforward and inexpensive software testing technique [1]. It generates a large number of test cases, then verifies the results using an automated oracle. Although formal analysis has shown random testing can be efficient [2], experienced practitioners still see it as ineffective [3]. This paper uses meta-heuristic search to identify sets of input subdomains whose sampling increases fault finding capability and efficiency. The evolved subdomains can be used for program analysis and regression testing. In common with much testing research, we adopt mutation score as the measure of fault finding effectiveness; for details of mutation testing the reader is referred to Jia and Harman [4].

A subdomain is a specific range within the program input domain. Generating tests from the entire domain can require an infeasible number of test cases, so subdomains are used to make random testing more efficient. It can be difficult to determine a priori which subdomains to use in random testing. The well known Triangle program, commonly used in testing research, has three integer inputs (a, b and c) and its branches contain conditions such as $a=b=c$. Michael et al. [5] selected over 8000 test cases from the entire input domain, but exercised less than half of the branches. Duran [1] selected 25 test cases from the subdomains ((1..5), (1..5), (1..5)) and exercised all the branches. We address the following problems of conventional random testing by evolving efficient subdomains:

1. **It is inefficient for faults that require specific boundary conditions**
   – We evolve multiple sets of subdomains to target boundary conditions more efficiently than sampling over a single large subdomain.
2. **Without an automated oracle, random testing is labour intensive**
   – Our technique requires fewer test cases than is typical for random testing, thus reducing the human effort required to create test oracles.

G. Ruhe and Y. Zhang (Eds.): SSBSE 2013, LNCS 8084, pp. 251–256, 2013.
© Springer-Verlag Berlin Heidelberg 2013

2   Background

2.1   Evolution Strategies

Evolution strategies are optimisation algorithms inspired by the process of adaptation in nature [6]. In contrast to some genetic algorithms, they optimise numerical values rather than bit strings and emphasise mutation over recombination [6]. New candidate solutions are produced by applying a (typically Gaussian) update function (F) to existing sets of values, $x'_1 \ldots x'_n = F(x_1 \ldots x_n)$. Evolution strategies are suited to fine tuning numerical properties, as disruption from crossover is largely avoided. Amongst many other applications, they have been used to optimise image compression [7], network design [8] and web crawling [9].

2.2   CMA-ES

Covariance Matrix Adaptation Evolution Strategies (CMA-ES) represent the search neighbourhood with a multivariate normal distribution [10]. They use a mean vector for the currently favoured solution, a scaling factor for the step size and a covariance matrix for the shape. Adaptation is performed to achieve fast, but not premature convergence, taking into account pairwise dependencies in the covariance matrix and fitness in both time and space [10].

CMA-ES are popular because they can solve difficult optimisation problems without the need for manual parameter tuning. CMA-ES have been shown to be particularly effective at non-linear optimisation. In a recent black-box comparison study with 25 benchmark functions, CMA-ES outperformed eleven other algorithms in terms of the number of function evaluations before the global optimum value is reached [11].

3   Subdomain Optimisation

In previous work [12] we evolved a single subdomain for each input parameter. This increased the mutation score of eight benchmark programs. Yet, one of the programs (Tcas) required manual scaling of its constants and another program (Replace) still had less than 50% mutation score. In the new approach, multiple sets of subdomains are evolved for each program. Each set targets a different group of mutants. This enables us to kill more mutants with fewer test cases.

A candidate solution consists of subdomains in the following three forms:

Numerical subdomains
    are represented with a lower and upper value. Test input values are selected only between these two values (inclusive).
Boolean probability values
    are described with an integer value between 0 and 100. This value represents the percentage probability that a generated parameter value is 'true'.
Character array distributions
    are fixed in length (by default to five characters). Each special character (wildcard, closure etc.) is given its own probability of inclusion.

Algorithm 1. Optimisation for subdomains $[a_l..a_u]$, $[b_l..b_u]$, .. $[N_l..N_u]$

1: Select initial random values for a_l, a_u, b_l, b_u, .. N_l and N_u.
2: **repeat**
3:    **for** $s = 1 \to 100$ **do**
4:       Generate 5 test cases from $[a_l..a_u]$, $[b_l..b_u]$, .. $[N_l..N_u]$.
5:       Count and record the number of times each mutant is killed by the test cases.
6:    **end for**
7:    Calculate subdomain fitness (see Equation 1).
8:    Sample new values from multivariate normal distribution centred around current best candidate: $(a_l, a_u, b_l, b_u, ..N_l, N_u, \sigma^2) \to (a'_l, a'_u, b'_l, b'_u, ..N'_l, N'_u, \sigma^2)$.
9: **until** $\exists m \in M, TimesKilled(m) \geq 95$

Algorithm 1 outlines the main process used in searching for subdomains. Due to limitations in space, only numerical subdomains are described, but a similar process occurs with Boolean probabilities and character array distributions. Subdomains are preferred that consistently kill the same group of mutants. This is achieved by maximising variance in the number of times each mutant is killed and minimising variance in the number of times the same mutant is killed (see Equation 1). A mutant is considered to be covered if it is killed at least 95 times out of 100 by 5 test cases sampled from the subdomains. Once subdomains are found to cover a group of mutants, the search continues with the remaining mutants. If no new mutants have been covered after 50 generations, the program is stretched to make one of the mutants easier to kill. We terminate the search if, after the stretching process is completed, no new mutants have been covered.

$$\sum_{s \in S} \sum_{m \in M} \frac{(K_{s,m} - \bar{K}_m)^2}{(\bar{K}_m - \bar{K})^2} \tag{1}$$

(S is the set of test suites, M is the set of mutants, K is the number of kill events)

4   Program Stretching

Stretching a program [13] involves transformation of its code and a new fitness function. Instead of targeting a group of mutants, we maximise the number of times a particular single mutant is killed, targeting mutants that have been killed the most number of times first. By gradually restoring the program back to the original mutant, we drag the subdomain values along with it.

The following three 'stretch' modes are used in this research:

Path stretching
   forces branch conditions leading up to a mutant to be true or false, depending on whether the branch was taken the last time the mutant was killed.

Mutation stretching
   alters the mutation by an offset of 100, for example $x >= y \to x > y$ becomes $x > y + 100$ with the aim of increasing its impact on the program.

Branch condition stretching
   adds an offset of 100 to a difficult branch condition in order to make it easier to meet, for example $x == y$ becomes $(x <= y + 100)\&\&(y <= x + 100)$.

Path stretching is applied first to ensure the mutation is reached. If the mutant still cannot be killed a sufficient number of times, the mutation is stretched. Once the stretched mutant has been covered, it is gradually unstretched by decrementing the mutation offset and removing restrictions on the branch conditions. If restoring a branch condition prevents the mutant from being covered, the difficult branch condition is also stretched then gradually restored. The aim in program stretching is to dynamically alter the fitness landscape so as to make the necessary subdomain values more readily available to the search process. Once stretching is completed, the main fitness function is reapplied to take advantage of the stretching process on other mutants that are killed by similar input values.

5   Experiments

We applied the new technique to four programs (see Table 1). Tcas has 10 numerical and 2 Boolean input parameters. Its subdomains can be represented with 10 lower and upper values, along with 2 percentage probabilities. Replace requires a search pattern, a replacement string and a source file. We limit the search and replacement strings to 5 characters and the source file to 10 characters (or copies of the search string). SingularValueDecomposition and SchurTransformation take matrices. We generate diagonals of a four-by-four matrix for SingularValueDecomposition and values of a three-by-three matrix for SchurTransformation.

Table 1. Test programs used in the experiments)

Program	Mutants	LOC	Function
Tcas	267	120	Air traffic control
Replace	1632	500	Substring replacement
SingularValueDecomposition	2769	298	Matrix decomposition
SchurTransformation	2125	497	Matrix transformation

6   Results

We compared our approach for evolving multiple sets of subdomains with our previous approach [12] (which evolves a single set without program stretching) and random testing in the interval [0..100]. The results are presented graphically in Figure 1 and numerically in Table 2. To allow a fair comparison, we used the same number of test cases in each approach. The number of test cases is determined by sampling 5 test cases from each subdomain in the new approach.

Multiple sets of subdomains achieved 33% higher mutation score on average than single sets and 230% higher than random testing. The new technique is particularly effective at meeting difficult branch conditions. To achieve the results shown in Figure 1, single sets required manual parameter scaling [12]. Multiple sets did not need this. Unlike the single set approach, multiple sets achieved a higher mutation score for Tcas and Replace than previous experiments with dynamic symbolic execution [12]. Random testing outperformed multiple sets on SchurTransformation, but each approach scored close to 100% on this program.

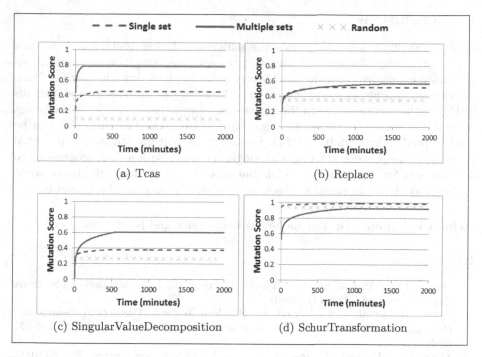

Fig. 1. Percentage of mutants covered by evolved subdomains (averaged over 100 trials)

On average, the time required to evolve multiple sets of subdomains is 11.6% greater than single sets. Yet, on a case by case basis there are more significant differences. It took over seven times longer to evolve single sets of subdomains for Tcas than multiple sets, but almost twice as long to evolve multiple sets for Replace than single sets. Depending on the program under test, there are cogent advantages to using multiple sets for mutation score and computational expense.

Similar mutation scores were previously achieved for random testing and the single set approach using fewer test cases [12]. It seems sensible to consider whether the number of subdomains in the multiple sets approach can be reduced. We can use k-means clustering to select a diverse subset of subdomains. Selecting 10 sets of subdomains (50 test cases) for Replace gave a mutation score of 0.549, higher than that of the single set approach, but lower than that for the complete set of subdomains. This compares with a mutation score of 0.514 when selecting 10 subdomains at random.

Table 2. Summary of results (averaged over 100 trials)

Program	Mutation Score		Time (mins)		Test Cases
	Single	Multiple	Single	Multiple	
Tcas	0.457	0.780	364	50.6	205
Replace	0.520	0.566	746	1410	455
SingularValueDecomposition	0.397	0.632	524	546	125
SchurTransformation	0.986	0.920	958	885	45

7   Conclusions

Evolving multiple sets of subdomains achieved a higher mutation score than single sets, except for one trivially easy to test program. It was computationally more expensive to evolve multiple sets for Replace, but cheaper for Tcas. Subdomain optimisation is expensive to perform but cheap to re-use and it significantly reduces human cost in the absence of an automated oracle. It is efficient at meeting boundary conditions (e.g. those in the Tcas program) and can be used to predict fault-finding ability. Further work will investigate the potential for a two-stage process, starting with single set optimisation then progressing to multiple sets for more difficult to kill mutants. Research effort will also be spent finding ways to select smaller subsets of subdomains to minimise labour cost.

Acknowledgment. Dr Yue Jia for his suggestions and helpful discussion.

References

1. Duran, J.W.: An Evaluation of Random Testing. IEEE Transactions on Software Engineering 10(4), 438–444 (1984)
2. Arcuri, A., Iqbal, M.Z., Briand, L.: Random Testing: Theoretical Results and Practical Implications. IEEE Transactions on Software Engineering 38(2), 258–277 (2012)
3. Myers, G.J., Badgett, T., Sandler, C.: The Art of Software Testing. Wiley (2011)
4. Jia, Y., Harman, H.: An Analysis and Survey of the Development of Mutation Testing. IEEE Transactions on Software Engineering 37(5), 649–678 (2011)
5. Michael, C.C., McGraw, G., Schatz, M.A.: Generating Software Test Data by Evolution. IEEE Transactions on Software Engineering 27(12), 1085–1110 (2001)
6. Bäck, T.: Evolutionary Algorithms in Theory and Practice, pp. 66–90. Oxford (1996)
7. Babb, B., Moore, F., Aldridge, S., Peterson, M.R.: State-of-the-Art Lossy Compression of Martian Images via the CMA-ES Evolution Strategy. In: International Society for Optics and Photonics, vol. 8305, pp. 22–26. SPIE (2012)
8. Nissen, V., Gold, S.: Survivable Network Design with an Evolution Strategy. In: Jung, J., Shan, Y., Bui, L.T. (eds.) Success in Evolutionary Computation. SCI, pp. 263–283. Springer, Heidelberg (2008)
9. Jung, J.: Using Evolution Strategy for Cooperative Focused Crawling on Semantic Web. J. Neural Comput. Appl. 18(3), 213–221 (2009)
10. Hansen, N.: The CMA Evolution Strategy: A Comparing Review. In: Lozano, J.A., Larrañaga, P., Inza, I., Bengoetxea, E. (eds.) Towards a New Evolutionary Computation. StudFuzz, vol. 192, pp. 75–102. Springer, Heidelberg (2006)
11. Hansen, N., Auger, A., Ros, R., Finck, S., Posik, P.: Comparing Results of 31 Algorithms from BBOB-2009. In: 12th Genetic and Evolutionary Computation Conference, pp. 1689–1696. ACM (2010)
12. Patrick, M., Alexander, R., Oriol, M., Clark, J.A.: Using Mutation Analysis to Evolve Subdomains for Random Testing. In: 8th International Workshop on Mutation Analysis. IEEE (2013)
13. Ghani, K., Clark, J.: Widening the Goal Posts: Program Stretching to Aid Search Based Software Testing. In: 1st International Symposium on Search Based Software Engineering, SSBSE (2009)

Applying Genetic Improvement to MiniSAT

Justyna Petke, William B. Langdon, and Mark Harman

CREST Centre, University College London,
Gower Street, London,
WC1E 6BT,
United Kingdom

Abstract. Genetic Programming (GP) has long been applied to several SBSE problems. Recently there has been much interest in using GP and its variants to solve demanding problems in which the code evolved by GP is intended for deployment. This paper investigates the application of genetic improvement to a challenging problem of improving a well-studied system: a Boolean satisfiability (SAT) solver called MiniSAT. Many programmers have tried to make this very popular solver even faster and a separate SAT competition track has been created to facilitate this goal. Thus genetically improving MiniSAT poses a great challenge. Moreover, due to a wide range of applications of SAT solving technologies any improvement could have a great impact. Our initial results show that there is some room for improvement. However, a significantly more efficient version of MiniSAT is yet to be discovered.

Keywords: Genetic Improvement, GISMOE, SAT.

1 Introduction

Genetic improvement [2,8,9,12,15] seeks to use SBSE to automatically improve programs according to one or more fitness function. Typically, an evolutionary algorithm has been used based on genetic programming [2,12,15] or a hybrid of genetic programming and other techniques [8,9].

This paper investigates the application of genetic improvement to a challenging problem of improving the MiniSAT [5] system. This is a significant challenge, because MiniSAT has been iteratively improved over many years by expert human programmers, to address the demand for more efficient SAT solvers and also in response to repeated calls for competition entries in the MiniSat hack track of SAT competitions [1].

We therefore chose MiniSAT because it represents one of the most stringent challenges available for automated genetic improvement using SBSE. Our goal is to investigate the degree to which genetic improvement can automatically improve a system that has been very widely and well studied and for objectives that have been repeatedly attacked by expert humans.

We report initial results of experiments aimed at the genetic improvement of MiniSAT using the GISMOE approach to genetic improvement [8]. Our primary findings are that one can achieve a more efficient version of MiniSAT by simply getting rid off assertions and statements related to statistical data. Moreover, deleting certain optimisations leads to faster runs on some SAT instances. However, a significantly more efficient version of the system is yet to be discovered.

G. Ruhe and Y. Zhang (Eds.): SSBSE 2013, LNCS 8084, pp. 257–262, 2013.
© Springer-Verlag Berlin Heidelberg 2013

2   MiniSAT

MiniSAT is a well-known open-source C++ solver for Boolean satisfiability problems (SAT). It implements the core technologies of modern SAT solving, including: unit propagation, conflict-driven clause learning and watched literals [13], to name a few. The solver has been widely adopted due to its efficiency, small size and availability of ample documentation. It is used as a backend solver in several other tools, including Satisfiability Modulo Theories (SMT) solvers, constraint solvers and solvers for deciding Quantified Boolean Formulae (QBF) . MiniSAT has also served as a reference solver in SAT competitions.

In the last few years progress in SAT solving technologies involved only minor changes to the solvers' code. Thus in 2009 a new track has been introduced into the SAT competition, called MiniSAT hack track. In order to enter this track one needs to modify the code of MiniSAT. This solver has been improved by many expert human programmers over the years, thus we wanted to see how well an automated approach scales. We used genetic improvement in order to find a more efficient version of the solver. In our experiments we used the latest version of the solver - MiniSAT-2.2.0[1].

3   Our Approach to the Genetic Improvement of MiniSAT

Our objective is to find a version of MiniSAT that is correct, i.e answers whether an instance is satisfiable or not, and that is faster than the unmodified solver. We used test cases from SAT competitions[2]. The training test suite was divided into five groups: satisfiable/unsatisfiable instances on which MiniSAT runs for less than 1 second, satisfiable/unsatisfiable instances on which MiniSAT runs for between 1 and 10 seconds and a mixture of satisfiable and unsatisfiable SAT instances on which MiniSAT runs for between 10 and 20 seconds.

We modified the SAT solver at the level of source code. We used a specialised BNF grammar to make sure that the evolved code is syntactically correct. Thus individuals produced have a good chance of compiling and thus high chances of running. We used time-outs to force termination of individuals which run significantly longer than the unmodified solver. We changed the code by using three operations:

- *copy* : copies a line of code in another place,
- *replace* : replaces a line of code with another line of code,
- *delete* : deletes a line of code.

There were a few special cases involving loops and `if` conditions, namely the same three operations (*copy*, *replace* and *delete*) were applied to conditions in `if` statements, `while` and `for` loops[3].

---

[1] Solver available at: `http://minisat.se/MiniSat.html`.

[2] Instances available at: `http://www.satcompetition.org/`.

[3] Note here, however, that a part of a `for` loop, for instance, could have only been replaced with the same part of another `for` loop. For instance, '$i + +$' could have been replaced with '$j + +$', but not '$j = 0$'.

We modified two C++ files: Solver.cc, containing the core solving algorithm (321 out of 582 lines of code), and SimpSolver.cc, which simplifies the input instance (327 out of 480 lines of code).

Furthermore, we were evolving a list of changes, that is, a list of *copy*, *replace* and *delete* instructions. We only kept such lists in memory, instead of multiple copies of an evolved source code.

For each generation the top half of the population was selected. These were either mutated, by adding some of the three operations mentioned above, or crossover was applied, which simply merged two lists of changes together. Mutation and crossover took place with 50% probability each. New individuals were created by selecting one of the three mutation operations.

For each generation five problems were randomly chosen from the five groups of test cases. Fitness was evaluated as follows: if correct answer was returned by an individual, 2 points were added; if, additionally, the modified program was faster, 1 more point was added. Only individuals with 10 or more points were considered for selection. In order to avoid environmental factors, we counted the number of lines used to establish whether a mutated program was more efficient than the original one. The whole process is presented in Figure 1.

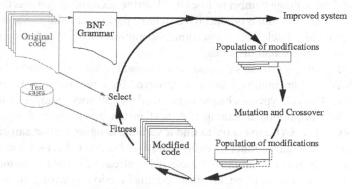

Fig. 1. GP improvement of MiniSAT

4   Initial Results

A summary of our results is shown in Table 1. We refer to versions of MiniSAT that run faster than the unmodified solver on the maximum set of instances as 'best individuals'.

We ran our experiments on a test suite with 71 test cases taken from the 2011 SAT competition. Each generation contained 20 individuals. Time limit was set to 25 seconds and it took 14 hours to produce 100 generations. We only modified the Solver.cc file, containing the core solving algorithm. Of all programs generated 73% of them compiled. The best one was more efficient than the unmodified solver on 70 SAT instances, in terms of lines of code used. However, the modified versions mostly just removed assertions as well as some statistical data. Some optimisations have also been deleted, but these in turn led to longer runtimes on certain instances.

Next, we selected the test cases from only the application tracks of SAT competitions. MiniSAT was able to find an answer for 107 problems out of 500 instances tested within

Table 1. Results of genetically improving MiniSAT. The 'Improved' column shows the number of test cases on which the best generated version of the solver was more efficient. The 'Best improvement' column shows the highest decrease in lines used for some test case, not necessarily achieved by the best individual.

Test cases	Type	Population size	Generations	Compiles	Improved	Best improvement
71	various	20	100	73%	70	0.937%
107	application	20	100	73%	107	0.859%
107	application	100	20	66%	106	0.858%

the time limit, which was set to 25 seconds for each instance. Therefore, the 107 SAT problems were used for GP. Again we set population size to 20 and the number of generations to 100 and around 73% of individuals compiled. In 34 generations there was an individual that was more efficient than the unmodified solver on all five randomly selected test cases. The best one was more efficient on all 107 instances. However, it only removed assertions and operations on variables used for statistical purposes. We also ran the experiments with population size 100 for 20 generations and achieved similar results (with the exception that 66% of modified programs compiled). In all cases the number of lines used by a 'better' version of MiniSAT generated was less by at most 1% and the average number of lines used during each solver run was in the order of 10^{10}. None of the individuals produced led to large performance improvements. Most of the changes involved deletion of assertions, operations used for gathering statistical data or deletion of minor optimisations.

To sum up, in our experiments genetic improvement has mostly found ways to pare down MiniSAT implementation. This was achieved by removing non-essential code like assertions. Another type of change performed by GP was removal of minor optimisations. We will provide an example: A SAT instance is composed of constraints called *clauses*, hence SAT solvers try to find a variable assignment that satisfies all the clauses. MiniSAT contains a function called `satisfied` that checks the satisfiability of a clause and removes it from the database if it's already satisfied by some variable assignment that cannot be changed. GP disabled this function by setting the second part of the main `for` loop to zero. Thus, during a run of such a modified solver at each variable assignment all clauses were checked for satisfiability, even though some of them could have already been satisfied. On the other hand, the main body of the `satisfied` function was not executed.

5   Related Work

Genetic Programming (GP) has long been applied to several SBSE problems including project management and testing.

More recently, there has been much interest in using GP and variants and hybrids of GP to solve demanding problems in which the code evolved by GP is intended for deployment, rather than merely as a source of decision support (but not ultimate deployment as a working software system). Much of the recent upsurge in interest in GP can be traced back to the seminal work of Arcuri and Yao on bug fixing using GP [3] and the development of this agenda into practical, scalable systems for automated program repair [11,14]. Recent results indicate that these automated repairs may prove to be as maintainable as human generated patches [6] and that the patches can be computed cheaply using cloud computing [7].

While previous work on bug fixing has already scaled to large real world systems, work on whole system genetic improvement has not previously scaled as well. However, recently Langdon and Harman [10] demonstrated scalability of whole program genetic improvement for a system of 50,000 Lines of Code on a real-world bioinformatics system. They were able to use a GP hybrid to find new evolved versions of the DNA sequence analysis system Bowtie2 that are, on average, 70 times faster than the original (and semantically slightly improved) when applied to DNA sequences from the 1,000 genome dataset.

A general framework of genetic improvement in set out on the ASE 2012 keynote paper by Harman et al. [8]. In the work reported here we adapt the approach developed by Langdon and Harman [10] applied to the Bowtie2 system to seek to optimise the MiniSAT system. Any improvements for implementations of SAT solving that we are able to achieve may have benefits for the wide and diverse applications of SAT solving. Even if we can only optimise a SAT solver for a subdomain of application (such as all constraints of a particular type), then this may allow us to use genetic improvement to achieve a kind of partial evaluation [4]. Such partial evaluation of SAT solving by genetic improvement may be useful in specific applications for which a known subset of formulae of the desired type are prevalent.

6 Conclusions and Future Work

Genetic improvement has successfully been applied to systems such as Bowtie2, leading to significant speed-ups. Therefore, we wanted to investigate if this could be achieved on a well-known software system that is easy to analyse and has been engineered by many expert human programmers. Hence we chose MiniSAT, a very popular Boolean satisfiability (SAT) solver that has been thoroughly studied. MiniSAT hack track of SAT competitions was specifically designed to encourage people to make minor changes to MiniSAT code that could lead to significant runtime improvements, and hence some new insights into SAT solving technology. We wanted to check how an automated approach scales.

If Genetic Programming (GP) is allowed to only apply mutations and crossover at the level of lines of source code, it turns out that little can be done to improve the current version of MiniSAT. Most changes simply pare down MiniSAT implementation. These involve deletion of assertions as well as operations used for producing statistical data. Some minor optimisations have also been removed by GP. A version of the solver that is significantly more efficient than the unmodified MiniSAT solver is yet to be discovered. We intend to conduct further experiments. We plan to remove assertions from the GP process and also conduct mutations on smaller constructs than a line of code. One possibility is to mutate mathematical expressions. Further experiments with varying population and generation size are also desirable. Furthermore, using a certain type of test cases, exhibiting, for instance, similar structure, could help find improvements specific for such classes of problems. We have already started experiments in this direction by considering test cases from the application tracks of SAT competitions. However, other classes of problems are yet to be investigated.

References

1. MiniSAT hack competition. In 2013 this is part of the 16th International Conference on Theory and Applications of Satisfiability Testing (2013)
2. Arcuri, A., White, D.R., Clark, J., Yao, X.: Multi-objective Improvement of Software Using Co-evolution and Smart Seeding. In: Li, X., et al. (eds.) SEAL 2008. LNCS, vol. 5361, pp. 61–70. Springer, Heidelberg (2008)
3. Arcuri, A., Yao, X.: A novel co-evolutionary approach to automatic software bug fixing. In: Wang, J. (ed.) 2008 IEEE World Congress on Computational Intelligence, Hong Kong, June 1-6. IEEE Computational Intelligence Society, IEEE Press (2008)
4. Bjørner, D., Ershov, A.P., Jones, N.D.: Partial evaluation and mixed computation. North–Holland (1987)
5. Eén, N., Sörensson, N.: An extensible SAT-solver. In: Giunchiglia, E., Tacchella, A. (eds.) SAT 2003. LNCS, vol. 2919, pp. 502–518. Springer, Heidelberg (2004)
6. Fry, Z.P., Landau, B., Weimer, W.: A human study of patch maintainability. In: International Symposium on Software Testing and Analysis (ISSTA 2012), Minneapolis, Minnesota, USA (July 2012) (to appear)
7. Goues, C.L., Dewey-Vogt, M., Forrest, S., Weimer, W.: A systematic study of automated program repair: Fixing 55 out of 105 bugs for $8 each. In: International Conference on Software Engineering (ICSE 2012), Zurich, Switzerland (2012)
8. Harman, M., Langdon, W.B., Jia, Y., White, D.R., Arcuri, A., Clark, J.A.: The GISMOE challenge: Constructing the pareto program surface using genetic programming to find better programs (keynote paper). In: 27th IEEE/ACM International Conference on Automated Software Engineering (ASE 2012), Essen, Germany (September 2012)
9. Langdon, W.B., Harman, M.: Evolving a CUDA kernel from an nVidia template. In: Sobrevilla, P. (ed.) 2010 IEEE World Congress on Computational Intelligence, Barcelona, July 18-23, pp. 2376–2383. IEEE (2010)
10. Langdon, W.B., Harman, M.: Genetically improving 50000 lines of C++. Research Note RN/12/09, Department of Computer Science, University College London, Gower Street, London WC1E 6BT, UK (September 19, 2012)
11. Le Goues, C., Nguyen, T., Forrest, S., Weimer, W.: GenProg: A generic method for automatic software repair. IEEE Transactions on Software Engineering 38(1), 54–72 (2012)
12. Orlov, M., Sipper, M.: Flight of the FINCH through the Java wilderness. IEEE Transactions on Evolutionary Computation 15(2), 166–182 (2011)
13. Silva, J.P.M., Lynce, I., Malik, S.: Conflict-driven clause learning SAT solvers. In: Biere, A., Heule, M., van Maaren, H., Walsh, T. (eds.) Handbook of Satisfiability. Frontiers in Artificial Intelligence and Applications, vol. 185, pp. 131–153. IOS Press (2009)
14. Weimer, W., Nguyen, T.V., Goues, C.L., Forrest, S.: Automatically finding patches using genetic programming. In: International Conference on Software Engineering (ICSE 2009), Vancouver, Canada, pp. 364–374 (2009)
15. White, D.R., Arcuri, A., Clark, J.A.: Evolutionary improvement of programs. IEEE Transactions on Evolutionary Computation 15(4), 515–538 (2011)

Using Contracts to Guide the Search-Based Verification of Concurrent Programs

Christopher M. Poskitt[1] and Simon Poulding[2]

[1] ETH Zürich, Switzerland
chris.poskitt@inf.ethz.ch
[2] University of York, UK
simon.poulding@york.ac.uk

Abstract. Search-based techniques can be used to identify whether a concurrent program exhibits faults such as race conditions, deadlocks, and starvation: a fitness function is used to guide the search to a region of the program's state space in which these concurrency faults are more likely occur. In this short paper, we propose that contracts specified by the developer as part of the program's implementation could be used to provide additional guidance to the search. We sketch an example of how contracts might be used in this way, and outline our plans for investigating this verification approach.

1 Introduction

Concurrency is often necessary if programs are to make the most efficient use of modern computing architectures. In particular, multiprocessor manufacturers have shifted focus from increasing CPU clock speeds to producing processors with multiple cores in the pursuit of better performance. For a program to realise this potential performance improvement it must be able to use more than one of the cores at the same time.

However, multi-threaded programs may exhibit concurrency-specific faults which are both difficult to avoid during development and to identify during testing. *Race conditions* can occur when more than one thread manipulates a shared data structure simultaneously, potentially resulting in the corruption of the data structure and consequential functional faults in the program. Race conditions may be avoided by an arbitration mechanism, such as locking, that controls access to shared resources. However, such mechanisms may give rise to non-functional faults such as *deadlocks* when a cycle of threads are each waiting to acquire a lock held by the next thread in the cycle and so none of them are able to proceed; and *starvation* when one thread is continually denied access to a shared resource as a result of the method of arbitration.

Verification of concurrent programs is thus complicated by the need to consider not only input data, but also the relative times at which key events occur, such as lock acquisitions and accesses to shared resources, across all of the program's threads. The temporal order of such events is referred to as an *interleaving* of the threads. The timings of such key events are not typically constrained and

G. Ruhe and Y. Zhang (Eds.): SSBSE 2013, LNCS 8084, pp. 263–268, 2013.
© Springer-Verlag Berlin Heidelberg 2013

so each invocation of the program can have a different interleaving as a result of non-determinism in the hardware and software platform on which the program runs. Therefore verification techniques—both dynamic testing as well as more formal static approaches—must consider many possible interleavings in order to assess the likelihood of a concurrency fault.

A number of effective search-based techniques have been demonstrated for this purpose, each using a fitness function to guide the search algorithm to interleavings that could cause concurrency faults.

In this short paper, we propose that contracts provided by the developer could provide additional information with which to guide the search, and therefore improve the practicality of verifying concurrent programs using search-based techniques.

2   Background and Related Work

One approach to detecting concurrency faults is *model checking*, a static technique that builds an abstract model of the concurrent program from its design or implementation. The model is used to determine all possible states of the program and the valid transitions between these states. By exhaustively analysing all reachable model states for the existence of concurrency faults, all thread interleavings—not just those that occurred in a single invocation of the program—may be verified. However, since the set of model states is formed by a product of the states of each thread in the program, the number of states to be checked grows very quickly with the size of the program and the number of threads.

Alternatively, the set of possible interleavings can be explored during *dynamic testing* of the program itself by exerting control over the relative timings of key events in each thread. This can be achieved by inserting instructions that introduce delays around critical operations such as the acquisition of locks. However, as for the model checking, the number of potential interleavings that must be explored grows very quickly with the program size.

Search-based techniques can be used to locate counterexamples—specific thread interleavings (or equivalently, model states) in which concurrent faults arise—rather than an exhaustive exploration of the entire space. Such an approach does not guarantee the *absence* of such faults, but can demonstrate the *presence* of faults. If the metaheuristic algorithm can efficiently locate regions of the search space (i.e. the set of possible thread interleavings or model states) that potentially give rise to concurrency faults, this is a practical alternative to exhaustive exploration of all possible interleavings/model states.

An important factor that determines the efficiency of a search is the fitness function which guides the metaheuristic algorithm. For many types of concurrency faults, the fault either exists or it does not: for example, a deadlock cannot be 'partial'. Thus a fitness function based only on the existence of the fault itself would provide no guidance to the metaheuristic algorithm, and the function must instead utilise other information to identify interleavings/model states that are 'closer' to one that exhibits the concurrency fault.

For example, Godefroid and Khurshid [4], Alba et al. [1], and Shousha et al. [7], each describe the use of a genetic algorithm to locate deadlocks in models of concurrent programs; Staunton and Clark [8] describe an estimation of distribution algorithm using N-grams with the same objective. The fitness function used by Godefroid and Khurshid utilises the total number of transitions out of model states visited on the path to the current state. The rationale is that minimising this sum will guide the search to states with no outgoing transitions: such a state represents a deadlock. The fitness functions used by the other three algorithms all utilise the number of blocked threads (those waiting to acquire locks) in the current state as one of the metrics to guide the search. The rationale in this case is that the more threads that are waiting to acquire locks, the more likely a deadlock state is to occur.

Bhattacharya et al. [2] use hill climbing and simulated annealing to identify potential race conditions through dynamic testing. A simulator is used to execute the program as this allows control of the thread interleaving by injecting timing delays while removing other sources of non-determinism. The fitness function is based on the timing between write accesses to the same memory location by different threads. The rationale is that by reducing the gap between write accesses, a race condition is more likely to arise.

3 Using Contracts to Guide Search

3.1 Our Proposed Use of Contracts

The search-based techniques discussed in the previous section used a fitness function to efficiently guide the search to regions of the space of thread interleavings/model states in which concurrency faults are most likely to occur. Nevertheless, some of the fitness functions return values from only a small range of discrete values. For example, the metric of the number of blocked threads— used in the functions that guide the search to deadlock states during model checking—takes only integer values between 0 and the total number of threads in the program. Thus many states may have the same fitness, and the search is provided with no guidance as to how to choose between them in order to reach a state that has, in this example, more blocked threads.

We propose that there is opportunity to provide additional guidance to the search by utilising developer-specified contracts. The objective would be to improve the efficiency of the search algorithm by incorporating additional information into the fitness function.

We do not envisage contracts taking the form of exhaustive specifications. Instead we propose the use of formal contracts of the type used in the *Design by Contract* approach to software development. Examples of this type of contract are the preconditions, invariants and postconditions specified in the Eiffel programming language using the **require, invariant,** and **ensure** constructs respectively [5]; and equivalent constructs in the Java Modeling Language (JML) [3]. Such contracts do not necessarily change the semantics of a program unless the developer chooses to enable runtime checking for contract violations (for example, in order to localise bugs in development builds), and there is no requirement on them to be exhaustive. However they do document the behaviour of the program intended and assumed by the developer in a form that might not otherwise be easily inferable from the program code itself. It is this information that we believe could be used to guide the search.

For example, a contract could document the assumption that the developer has made as to how other threads will access the shared resources used by a particular section of code. The search could then attempt to locate thread interleavings that break this assumption using a fitness function derived automatically from the contract. The rationale would be that if the assumption made by the developer can be invalidated, it is likely that such interleavings could give rise to concurrency faults.

Alternatively, a contract could be used to guide the search to particular *data* states that increase the likelihood of concurrency faults. This possibility is motivated by the observation that most of the existing fitness functions consider only metrics related to interleavings—such as the number of blocked threads or time between access to a shared memory location—but not the data that, for example, satisfies guards on code that performs operations likely to cause concurrency faults. This additional information in the fitness function could be used to guide the selection of input data as well as thread interleavings.

Our proposal to use developer-specified assumptions in search-based algorithms contrasts with their use in more analytical approaches. For example, the approach of [10] uses an SMT solver to construct sequences of interfering instructions that drive a program under test to break the assumptions.

3.2 An Example

As a motivating example, we consider a program written in concurrent Eiffel with SCOOP (for Simple Concurrent Object-Oriented Programming). SCOOP [5,6] is an experimental object-oriented concurrency model which has contracts as a central concept, making it an interesting starting point for our work.

An object in the model can be declared with a special type using the keyword **separate**, meaning that applications of routines to it may occur on a different *processor* (an abstraction of threads, physical cores, etc.), and that calls to commands (i.e. routines that do not return results) are executed asynchronously. Every object belongs to exactly one processor; no other processor can access its state. Calls to **separate** objects are only allowed if the current processor *controls* the processors owning those objects; this is guaranteed if they are passed as arguments, in which case they are automatically and exclusively locked for the duration of the routine's execution.

SCOOP supports pre- and postconditions for routines (preceded by **require** and **ensure** respectively). In a sequential setting, preconditions are (optionally) checked before executing the routine. In a concurrent setting, preconditions are interpreted as *wait conditions*. That is, the execution of the routine is delayed until simultaneously the precondition is satisfied and the processors handling the **separate** objects controlled.

Suppose we have a simple program that has a bounded buffer, on which we can store integers and from which we can consume them—provided that respectively, the buffer is not full or empty. We give possible implementations of a `store` routine below, using both the Eiffel SCOOP model (left) and Java (right). Both implementations involve waiting if the buffer is full. In the SCOOP version, an (asynchronous) execution would first wait for the separate `a_buffer` object to become available and for the precondition to hold; then, the buffer is locked, a new element is pushed, and the lock released. The Java version is intended to do the same, but when waiting for buffer space to become available (with the call to `buffer.wait()`), relies on an (unspecified) consumer object notifying this `store` thread that it has consumed an element from the buffer.

```
store (a_buffer: separate                public void store(BBuffer<Integer>
   BOUNDED_BUFFER [INTEGER];                buffer, int element) {
   an_element: INTEGER)                  synchronized(buffer) {
require                                     while (!(buffer.size() <
   a_buffer.count < a_buffer.size                  buffer.maxSize()))) {
do                                          try {
   a_buffer.put (an_element)                  buffer.wait();
ensure                                      } catch
   not a_buffer.is_empty                    (InterruptedException e) {}
   a_buffer.count = old a_buffer.          }
      count + 1                           buffer.push(element);
end                                      } }
```

We have only given fragments of the whole programs, but already, with the precondition in the SCOOP version, we can infer a "region of interest" in the state space, i.e. a region where concurrency bugs may be more likely to reveal themselves. In our example, this region involves states in which the buffer is approaching its bound. A poor design of the SCOOP program might, for example, lead to a call of `store` waiting for an unacceptably long time, e.g. if consumers are starved of access to a full buffer. In the Java version, threads that are blocked because of a full buffer may never be awoken, for example, if the implementation of consumers fails to notify threads when the buffer is no longer full. These bugs would not be observed outside of that region of interest, and with a sufficiently large bound on the buffer, naive testing strategies might not encounter them. The information provided by the precondition should be incorporated into the fitness function to guide the search towards this region of interest, perhaps by converting the contract's Boolean condition to a metric similar in nature to the branch distance [9] used in other forms of search-based testing. Note that the precondition is essentially exposing information that is present in the Java program, but would be more difficult for search to extract in that form.

This is a simple motivating example, and though illustrated with SCOOP, we hope that the approach will generalise to other concurrent object-oriented languages by allowing routines to be annotated with some notion of contract. Furthermore, the example we considered used a *functional* precondition. We are also interested in how search might be guided by a contract language offering *non-functional* preconditions, such as expressions about patterns of access or deadlock-free resource usage.

4　Conclusions and Next Steps

In this short paper, we have proposed the use of contracts in concurrent programs for guiding search-based techniques towards regions of the state space where concurrency faults may be more likely. We placed our proposal within the context of the state-of-the-art, and sketched an example in a concurrent object-oriented programming model to discuss how contracts might be exploited.

Our next step is to empirically evaluate our proposal on realistic software with preconditions expressed in JML, the wait conditions of SCOOP, or another suitable language. We also plan to investigate whether and how search-based techniques can benefit from simple non-functional contracts in the code.

Acknowledgements. This work is funded in part by ERC grant agreement no. 29138, CME: Concurrency Made Easy, and by EPSRC grant EP/J017515/1, DAASE: Dynamic Adaptive Automated Software Engineering.

References

1. Alba, E., Chicano, F., Ferreira, M., Gomez-Pulido, J.: Finding deadlocks in large concurrent Java programs using genetic algorithms. In: Proc. 10th Annual Conference on Genetic and Evolutionary Computation, pp. 1735–1742 (2008)
2. Bhattacharya, N., El-Mahi, O., Duclos, E., Beltrame, G., Antoniol, G., Le Digabel, S., Guéhéneuc, Y.-G.: Optimizing threads schedule alignments to expose the interference bug pattern. In: Fraser, G., Teixeira de Souza, J. (eds.) SSBSE 2012. LNCS, vol. 7515, pp. 90–104. Springer, Heidelberg (2012)
3. Chalin, P., Kiniry, J.R., Leavens, G.T., Poll, E.: Beyond assertions: Advanced specification and verification with JML and ESC/Java2. In: de Boer, F.S., Bonsangue, M.M., Graf, S., de Roever, W.-P. (eds.) FMCO 2005. LNCS, vol. 4111, pp. 342–363. Springer, Heidelberg (2006)
4. Godefroid, P., Khurshid, S.: Exploring very large state spaces using genetic algorithms. In: Tools and Algorithms for the Construction and Analysis of Systems, pp. 266–280. Springer (2002)
5. Meyer, B.: Object-Oriented Software Construction, 2nd edn. Prentice Hall (1997)
6. Nienaltowski, P.: Practical framework for contract-based concurrent object-oriented programming. Ph.D. thesis, ETH Zürich (2007)
7. Shousha, M., Briand, L.C., Labiche, Y.: A UML/MARTE model analysis method for uncovering scenarios leading to starvation and deadlocks in concurrent systems. IEEE Transactions on Software Engineering 38(2), 354–374 (2012)
8. Staunton, J., Clark, J.A.: Searching for safety violations using estimation of distribution algorithms. In: Proc. 3rd International Workshop on Search-Based Software Testing, pp. 212–221 (2010)
9. Tracey, N.J.: A Search-Based Automated Test-Data Generation Framework for Safety-Critical Software. Ph.D. thesis, The University of York (2000)
10. West, S., Nanz, S., Meyer, B.: Demonic testing of concurrent programs. In: Aoki, T., Taguchi, K. (eds.) ICFEM 2012. LNCS, vol. 7635, pp. 478–493. Springer, Heidelberg (2012)

Planning Global Software Development Projects Using Genetic Algorithms

Sriharsha Vathsavayi, Outi Sievi-Korte, Kai Koskimies, and Kari Systä

Department of Pervasive Computing, Tampere University of Technology,
Tampere, Finland
`firstname.lastname@tut.fi`

Abstract. Planning a Global Software Development project is a challenging task, as it involves balancing both technical and business related issues. On the other hand, the selected software architecture also influences the distributed development, making the separate development of components either easier or more difficult. This kind of planning problem with multiple variables is difficult to solve using deterministic methods. In this work, we propose an approach based on genetic algorithms for planning global software projects.

Keywords: global software development, work assignment, work scheduling, project planning, software architecture, genetic algorithms.

1   Introduction

Global Software Development (GSD) is a major trend in software engineering. GSD is usually characterized by engagements with different national and organizational cultures in different geographic locations and time zones, using various traditional and IT-enabled means to collaborate [1]. Project planning activities such as work assignment and work scheduling need to be performed carefully in GSD, because performing them improperly may increase the cost and duration of the project. Planning of GSD is challenging, because it involves multiple choices related not only to assigning and scheduling the work in a heterogeneous environment but also to the ways software architecture supports the work division. While planning a GSD project, the communication problems caused by geographical, time-zone, and socio-cultural distances between the teams [1] should be considered. Moreover, the software architecture decisions that support the work assignment should also be taken into account.

Software architecture may ease or hamper distributed development [2]. In order to assign the work, first the target system needs to be divided into a set of components, which can be developed as independently as possible. Since the architecture dictates the decomposition of the system and dependencies between the components, it determines the potential work units, too. In particular, the solutions that influence coupling between components are important for the work allocation: the more loosely coupled two components are, the easier it is to develop them separately [3]. Here we call such decisions *decoupling solutions*.

G. Ruhe and Y. Zhang (Eds.): SSBSE 2013, LNCS 8084, pp. 269–274, 2013.
© Springer-Verlag Berlin Heidelberg 2013

Given the large variety of different, partly conflicting factors that have to be taken into account in finding an optimal GSD work plan and the huge search space, using a deterministic search method is difficult. For example, the problem of assigning 10 tasks to 10 available teams has a search space of 10 billion (10^{10}). In this paper we propose a genetic algorithm (GA) based approach as a novel method to solve the GSD work plan optimization problem. The approach takes information about the target system and the organization as input and finds a near-optimal work assignment plan and work schedule, together with supporting decoupling solutions.

Several studies, such as [4] and [5], have applied genetic algorithms in the area of project management. However, we have not found any studies that applied genetic algorithms to project management problems in GSD. Moreover, our study differs from those concerning project management by taking into account architectural solutions and considering the team distribution effect on cost and duration of the project.

The paper is structured as follows. In the following section we formulate the problem to be solved by the proposed approach. In Section 3 we present our GA-based approach for solving the GSD optimization problem. The results from early experiments are discussed in Section 4. Finally, we conclude with some remarks on future work in Section 5. We assume that the reader is familiar with the basics of GAs, as given, e.g., by Michalewicz [6].

2   GSD Optimization Problem and Work Plan

2.1   GSD Optimization Problem

The GSD optimization problem can be formally expressed as a tuple (C, T), where C is a component graph and T is the team graph. The component graph C is a labeled graph representing two relationships between the components (nodes): dependency and precedence (edges). Dependency relationships are determined based on the functional decomposition of system, which is assumed to be decided by the architect. If component c_1 needs the services of component c_2, then c_1 depends on c_2. This implies that when developing component c_1, some information is needed of component c_2 (e.g. service interfaces, service protocols, and the meaning of services), implying need for communication between the teams developing the components. On the other hand, precedence is a relationship expressing the preferred development order of the components: if component c_1 precedes component c_2, then c_1 should be developed before c_2. The precedence relationships are assumed to be determined by the architect based on various facts known about the components. For example, a situation where component c_1 produces large data entities used by component c_2, implies that component c_1 precedes component c_2. Using this relationship, the architect or project manager can express various types of additional information concerning the development order, which cannot be deduced by any automatic means.

The team graph T is a labeled graph, where the teams are nodes connected by edges representing the communication between the teams. Each edge is labeled by the communication distance [7] of the two teams. The communication distance is assumed to take into account factors like geographical, time-zone, language, cultural and social differences. The communication distance is assumed to be estimated by the project manager using appropriate coarse scale (e.g. short, medium, long).

Each component c_i in the component graph is characterized by several attributes. These attributes include the estimated effort and skills required for developing the component. We assume that the effort can be estimated using any known software cost estimation method, such as COCOMO II [8]. Similarly, each team has several characteristics. These include the capacity of the team in person hours per day, the set of skills possessed by the team, average cost of the team per day and maximum number of hours the team can spend on the project.

2.2 Work Plan

The solution produced by the genetic algorithm is expressed in the form of a *work plan*. A work plan provides the decoupling solutions introduced between the components, allocation of components to suitable teams and a schedule specifying the order in which teams should develop the components. Moreover, a work plan should satisfy the following constraints: every component should be assigned to a team that has necessary skills to develop it and no team should be assigned more work than the maximum number of hours they can spend on the project. The work plan can be formally expressed as a tuple (C', wf), where C' is a component graph extended with decoupling solutions and wf is the work allocation function: wf(c) = (i, k) indicates that component c will be developed by team i as its k:th work item. In the component graph C', some of the dependency relationships of C have been refined into specific decoupling solution relationships, indicating that the components are interacting through a particular decoupling solution.

2.3 Decoupling Solutions

Above we have assumed that decoupling solutions can be applied between components to reduce the need for communication between the teams. There are different decoupling solutions, such as various message-based communication techniques [9] (like JMS [10] or IBM WebSphere MQ [11]), REST interfaces [12], broker-based service infrastructures like CORBA [13] or Web services [14], Publisher-Subscriber solutions [3], or just well-defined, documented and properly maintained interfaces. Messaging is typically used in system integration as a powerful decoupling pattern [3], reducing the mutual dependencies of subsystems. The application of REST interfaces also reduces the coupling between components, as components interact through uniform interfaces rather than using specific methods. Similarly, brokers detach the client and server components from each other. The application of each decoupling solution influences the amount of coupling between the components, and therefore the amount of communication needed to develop the components. For example, if two components are communicating using messages, they rely only on the messaging infrastructure and can be developed to large extent independently. In this work, we use two decoupling solutions, taken from the opposite ends of the spectrum: messaging (representing strong decoupling) and well-defined interfaces (representing weak decoupling).

3   A GA Based Approach to Solve GSD Optimization Problem

The overall setup is presented in Fig. 1. The *initial work plan* is given as input to the approach. The initial work plan consists of a component graph (without decoupling solutions) and a random assignment of components to teams and a random development order for the teams. The initial work plan is encoded into a *chromosome* form by specifying the information about each available component. The chromosome is then used to generate an initial population of chromosomes (i.e., work plans).

During the evolution, the work plans are subjected to mutations and crossover. The *mutations* include introducing or removing a decoupling solution between the components, changing the assignment of a component from one team to another team, and changing the schedule, i.e., changing the position of the component in the team's development order. The mutation that changes the team assignment is applied only if the application does not violate the constraints to be satisfied by a work plan. The *crossover* operation is implemented as a traditional one-point crossover. Each mutation is selected with a *roulette wheel* selection [6]. Null mutation and crossover are also included in the wheel. The size of each slice of the wheel is in proportion to the given probability of the respective mutation.

In each generation, the *fitness function* is used to evaluate the goodness of the work plan in terms of cost and duration. In calculating the duration, the basic effort of the component, the effort required by the component for communicating with components in other teams, the effort required by the component for using the introduced decoupling solution, and the time spent by the team waiting before developing the preceded component are taken into account. The communication distance between the teams and coupling resulted due to the applied decoupling solution are considered in calculating the communication effort required by a component. In calculating the effort required for using a decoupled solution, the complexity of the applied decoupling solution is considered. The team's development order is used in calculating the waiting time spent by the team. The cost is calculated by summing the money paid to the teams for the time they spent on the project. For each generation, the *Selection* of the individuals for each generation is made with the same kind of roulette wheel method as was used for choosing the mutations.

As the result, the genetic algorithm produces a work plan proposal, which contains work assignment plan and schedule plan along with the applied decoupling solutions. Moreover, it also estimates the duration and cost required to realize the work plan.

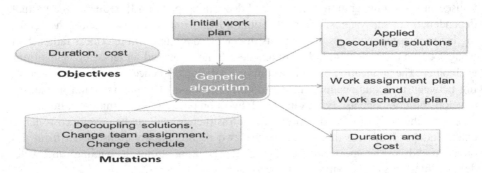

Fig. 1. GA based approach to solve GSD optimization problem

4   Preliminary Experiments

To experiment with our approach, we use an example project in which a sketched home control system is planned to be developed with four teams, which are T_1, T_2, T_3 and T_4. The communication distance is short between teams T_1-T_3, medium between teams T_2-T_4, and long between teams T_1-T_2, T_1-T_4, T_3-T_2, T_3-T_4. The average cost per day is high for teams T_1 and T_3, medium for team T_2, low for team T_4. As discussed earlier, each team is also given additional characteristics such as skills possessed by the team, maximum time the team can spend on the project, etc. The component graph of home control system contains 12 components, 15 dependency relationships and 8 precedence relationships. Moreover, each component is given an estimated effort and skill required to develop the component. The initial work plan for home control system is obtained by randomly assigning each component to a team and giving it a random position in the team's development order.

In the experiments, our main interest was to study whether GA produces work plans that are in line with common sense reasoning when either cost or duration is emphasized over the other. To study this phenomenon, we performed two different tests using the initial work plan of home control system. Each test was run for 10 times and for both the tests GA was executed with a population of 100 individuals for 250 generations.

In the first test, we emphasized duration over cost. In this test, the GA favored solutions that have few inter-team dependencies between distant teams (T_1-T_4, T_3-T_4), and moved majority of work to closer teams (T_1, T_3). The decrease in the inter-team dependencies decreases the need for communication effort, which decreases the duration of the planned software. However, the cost of the planned software increased as the majority of work was moved to expensive teams (T_1, T_3). The cost was emphasized over duration in the second test. In this test, the GA favored solutions in which majority of work was moved to low cost team (T_4). This decreased the cost of the planned software, but increased the duration, as the number of inter-team dependencies between distant teams (T_1-T_2, T_1-T_4, T_3-T_2, T_3-T_4) were increased. The generated work plans showed that GA was behaving in a sensible way demonstrating the conflicting nature of cost and duration, i.e., duration required to realize the work plan can be decreased at the expense of cost and vice-versa.

5   Conclusions

We have proposed a GA based approach to plan GSD projects. Planning a GSD project is challenging as it involves organization, personnel, business and architecture. For this kind of problem, the project manager does not necessarily want to just see an optimal solution produced by a tool, but rather she needs guidance on how prioritizing or constraining different factors will influence the result. A major advantage of the proposed approach is that it can be used to develop a guidance tool for choosing the right balance of the different factors. Developing this kind of tool support is our main research objective in the future. Furthermore, our future work involves applying the approach on industrial data, and evaluating the results together with practitioners.

References

1. Hossain, E., Bannerman, P.L., Jeffery, D.R.: Scrum practices in global software development: a research framework. In: Proceedings of the 12th International Conference on Product-Focused Software Process Improvement, Berlin, Heidelberg, pp. 88–102 (2011)
2. Clerc, V., Lago, P., van Vliet, H.: Global Software Development: Are architectural Rules the Answer? In: Proc. of ICGSE 2007, pp. 225–234. IEEE CS Press (2007)
3. Hohpe, G., Woolf, B.: Enterprise Integration Patterns. Addison-Wesley (2004)
4. Di Penta, M., Harman, M., Antoniol, G.: The use of search-based optimization techniques to schedule and staff software projects: an approach and an empirical study. Software: Practice and Experience, 495–519 (2011)
5. Alba, E., Chicano, F.: Software Project Management with Gas. Information Sciences 177, 2380–2401 (2007)
6. Michalewicz, Z.: Genetic Algorithms + Data Structures = Evolutionary Programs. Springer (1992)
7. Herbsleb, J.D., Grinter, R.E.: Architectures, coordination, and distance: Conway's law and beyond. IEEE Software, 63–70 (1999)
8. Boehm, B., Abts, C., Brown, A., Chulani, S., Clark, B., Horowitz, E., Madachy, R., Reifer, D., Steece, B.: Software Cost Estimation with COCOMO II. Prentice Hall (2000)
9. Shaw, M., Garlan, D.: Software Architecture - Perspectives on an Emerging Discipline. Prentice Hall (1996)
10. Java Messaging service, http://www.oracle.com/technetwork/java/jms/index.html
11. IBM WebSphere MQ, http://www.ibm.com/software/integration/wmq/
12. Architectural Styles and the Design of Network-based Software Architectures, http://www.ics.uci.edu/~fielding/pubs/dissertation/top.htm
13. Object Management Group, The Common Object Request Broker: Architecture and Specification, Revision 3.3 (November 2012)
14. Web service architecture, http://www.w3.org/TR/ws-arch/

What Can a Big Program Teach Us about Optimization?

Márcio de Oliveira Barros[1] and Fábio de Almeida Farzat[2]

[1] Post-graduate Information Systems Program – PPGI/UNIRIO
Av. Pasteur 458, Urca – Rio de Janeiro, RJ – Brazil
[2] Computers and System Engineering Program – COPPE/UFRJ
Cx Postal 68501, Cidade Universitária – Rio de Janeiro, RJ – Brazil
marcio.barros@uniriotec.br, ffarzat@cos.ufrj.br

Abstract. In this paper we report on the evolution of Apache Ant, a build automation tool developed in Java. We observed a typical case of architectural mismatch in this system: its original simple design was lost due to maintenance and addition of new features. We have applied SBSE techniques to determine whether the search would be able to recover at least parts of the original design, in a metrics-based optimization. We observed that current SBSE techniques produce complex designs, but they also allow us to study the limitations of present design metrics. In the end, we propose a new research perspective joining software clustering and refactoring selection to improve software evolution.

Keywords: Apache Ant, Hill Climbing search, software module clustering.

1 Assessing the Evolution of Apache Ant's Architecture

Apache Ant (or simply Ant) is a build automation tool frequently used to support continuous integration (CI). CI is a software development practice in which members of a team integrate their work frequently, usually once per day and person [1]. Integration involves executing a set of tasks, which build and verify the software. Some of these tasks are mechanical and repetitive, and a build automation tool (such as Ant) automates their execution. Ant uses XML files to describe what tasks must be executed (and in which order) during integration. These tasks typically involve downloading code from a version control system, copying files, compiling code, executing unit tests, building deployment descriptors, and so on. They must be properly sequenced and specific persons must be notified if errors are found during their execution.

Twenty-four versions of Ant were released since its inception in 2003, including 9 major and 15 minor versions. All versions were implemented in Java. The first version (v1.1.0) had 102 classes distributed into 4 packages. The software grew over the last years, as a large number of task definitions were added. The current version (v1.9.0, released in March, 2013) surpasses 1,100 classes organized in 60 packages.

Figure 1 presents Ant's conceptual architecture, with its major packages and dependencies among them. The architecture has 3 major components: a utility library (*util*), an automation and notification framework (*ant*), and a set of task definitions (*taskdefs*). Task definitions may use the utility library and the framework to perform their tasks, while the framework may use the libraries to provide its services.

G. Ruhe and Y. Zhang (Eds.): SSBSE 2013, LNCS 8084, pp. 275–281, 2013.
© Springer-Verlag Berlin Heidelberg 2013

Figure 2 shows package dependency charts for 6 versions of Ant: points represent packages and lines represent dependencies between two packages. A package A depends on a package B if at least one class from A depends on at least one class from B to implement its features. Due to space limitation, only versions introducing major architectural changes are presented, and dependency direction and package names are suppressed.

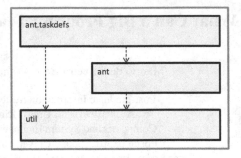

Fig. 1. – Reference architecture for Ant

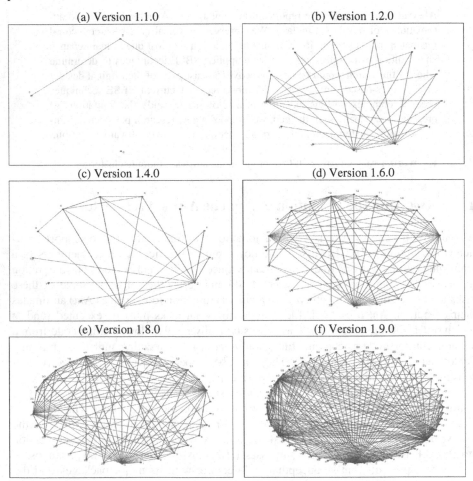

(a) Version 1.1.0   (b) Version 1.2.0

(c) Version 1.4.0   (d) Version 1.6.0

(e) Version 1.8.0   (f) Version 1.9.0

Fig. 2. – Architecture overview for six major versions of Apache Ant

Instead of presenting a detailed description for the project's architecture evolution, the charts in Figure 2 intend to show how complexity is incorporated to originally simple software as it evolves. Many package dependencies were created and the components of the original architecture cannot be easily found in charts for recent versions. This reduces reusability, understandability, and testability. In a typical case of *architectural mismatch* [9], small changes made by developers on a daily basis over the course of the software life-cycle, have increased the distance between the current implementation and the original design. It's a creeping fact of software development: useful software is required to change; changed software (frequently) slowly decays.

2 But, Can SBSE Help Rescuing the Architecture?

Software module clustering addresses the problem of finding a proper distribution for the modules representing domain concepts and computational constructs comprising a program into larger, container-like structures. In this sense, software clustering is strongly associated to the definition of components and their connections in software architectures. Due to the huge number of alternative module distributions for non-trivial programs, this problem has been addressed with SBSE approaches.

The most commonly used mono-objective models for the software clustering problem rely on graphs describing dependencies among classes and optimize (maximize) one of two alternative fitness functions: MQ and EVM. Using different formulations, these fitness functions aim for a balance between coupling (related to the number of dependencies between packages, to be minimized) and cohesion (related to the number of dependencies within packages, to be maximized). For more information on the problem, its models, and fitness functions, the interested reader may refer to [2, 3, 4].

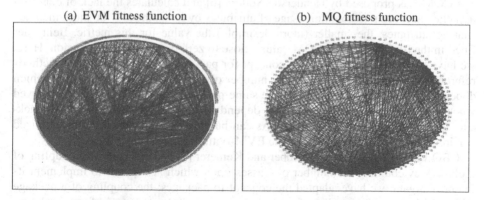

    (a) EVM fitness function   (b) MQ fitness function

Fig. 3. – Optimized architecture for Apache Ant version 1.8.2

We have optimized Ant's version 1.8.2 according both to EVM and MQ in order to improve its module dependency structure and observe whether the search process might reverse the architectural mismatch. Figure 3 presents the solutions found after executing the search based on EVM (Figure 3.a) and MQ (Figure 3.b). We have used a Hill Climbing search with random restarts, consuming a fitness function evaluation budget of 1,000 N^2, where N is the number of classes in the program (1,090 classes for Ant version 1.8.2). This was a large-scale optimization process, considering that published papers addressing the software clustering problem usually report on instances up to 300 modules. Each optimization process (one for EVM, one for MQ) took about 4 days in a dedicated 2.6 GHz Core i7 computer with 4 Gb RAM.

But how can we evaluate whether the optimized versions have improved the design presented of Ant version 1.8.2? One possible way is to consider metrics. Table 1 presents 6 structural metrics for version 1.8.2 and the two module distributions resulting from optimization based on distinct fitness functions. Table columns represent, from left to right, the number of packages on each version, EVM value, MQ value, average class elegance (NAC), and average values for variations of LCOM [6] and CBO [7].

Table 1. – Metrics for the original and optimized versions of Apache Ant

Version	Packages	EVM	MQ	NAC	LCOM	CBO
Original v1.8.2	59	-51,615	21.37	39.2	0.79	55.6
EVM-optimized	363	-8,170	51.71	7.2	0.46	10.6
MQ-optimized	103	-12,336	43.09	14.2	0.71	32.1

Class elegance (NAC) was proposed by Simons and Parmee [5] as a way to evaluate the concentration of classes in a few packages in a software design. It is calculated as the standard deviation of the number of classes on each package and is expected to be a small number, denoting that all packages have roughly the same number of classes. Both optimized versions improve class elegance, which is quite high in the original version. Special attention must be given to the EVM-optimized version, which presents an expressive reduction for this measurement.

LCOM was proposed by Henderson-Sellers [6] and calculates the lack of cohesion in a class according to common usage of attributes by its methods – the more methods sharing attributes, the smaller (more desirable) the value for this metric. Being defined in the [0, 1] interval, LCOM values close to zero denote greater cohesion. Here, we have borrowed and adapted the concept for package cohesion: instead of methods referencing attributes, we consider the number of classes from a given package which depend on other classes residing on the same package. Lack of cohesion is observed when most classes in a package do not depend on other classes from the same package, leading to a large LCOM value. As can be observed in Table 1, both optimized versions improve LCOM, specially the EVM-optimized version.

CBO was introduced by Chidamber and Kemerer [7] and calculates the coupling of a class A by counting the number of classes upon which A depends to implement its features. Again, we have adapted the concept to packages: the coupling of a package A is calculated as the number of packages on which it depends to perform its duties, that is, the number of packages conveying classes upon which classes residing on package A depend to implement their features. Again, both optimized versions improve this measure when compared to the original version. And again, the EVM-optimized version outperforms the MQ-optimized one in improving this metric.

Finally, both optimized versions improve their related fitness functions. The EVM-optimized version even provides a module distribution with better MQ than the

MQ-optimized version. They also improve cohesion (both decrease the original LCOM) and coupling (both decrease the original CBO). Finally, they also increase class elegance when compared to the original version. Thus, from a metrics perspective, both optimized versions seem superior to the original version. But why is their design so complex? Do they really take the software to a state in which maintenance, reusability, and testability are easier than in version 1.8.2? The visual impression given by the meshes of dependencies in Figure 3 do not contribute much to such a perception.

One major problem with the optimized versions is that they excessively increase the number of packages in the design. As a result of this increase, the average package has fewer classes – those few classes which are strongly interrelated (decreasing average LCOM). The increased number of packages also decreases average CBO – there are so many packages and so few classes on each package that the average number of dependencies between packages is relatively small. Finally, the reduced number of classes on each package also contributes to reducing the standard deviation used to calculate NAC, thus yielding a sense of better elegance.

Overall, the optimized versions seem to be "cheating" the software engineer: they are "improving the design" from a metrics point-of-view by spreading the classes along a large number of packages, which might not be a real improvement in the eyes of the development team. To serve as a reference, Lanza and Marinescu [8] suggest that the average number of classes per package in Java programs is 17 (with 6 considered as a lower-bound and 26 as an upper-bound).

3   Then, Can We Conclude that SBSE Is Not Helpful?

That can hardly be true! First and foremost, without performing the optimization we would never be able to observe the behavior of even simple metrics in a large system, such as Apache Ant. Even using simple techniques, it took four days to optimize the program. Finding (close to) optimal solutions would probably be an unfeasible task in any other way except using algorithmic optimization.

Moreover, we have to acknowledge that optimization worked as commanded, though not as expected. EVM and MQ values increased significantly, but as one might pick the shortest path to a given destination, the optimization process opted to increase the number of packages in order to improve metrics. Although a large number of packages with few classes might not be considered a good design [8], the search leveraged on an aspect which was not covered by the selected metrics.

Thus, in the least SBSE helps determining to which extent metrics might be useful in searching for solutions for a given problem. As seen in the former section, it seems that using the simple metrics we teach our students to pursue while designing software may not help in the large. We may need more complex metrics. We may need more than metrics. In this sense, SBSE-style optimization helps to improve our body of knowledge on software architecture and software design.

4   So, Given These Perceptions, What Can We Do?

We have not further investigated the field (though we intend to), but since current metrics seem unable to produce credible optimization results starting from scratch, one possible alternative is to leverage knowledge possessed by developers [12]. Maybe the package organization conceived for the reference architecture of a given program or its present architecture can be used as starting point for module distribution.

One direction we intend to investigate is using Dependency Structure Matrices (DSM), as proposed by Sangal and Waldman [10]. The authors, who have also analyzed Apache Ant, suggest that dependencies between packages might be depicted in the lower triangular part of a square dependency lattice and that dependencies appearing out of this region might be signaled to and corrected (refactored) by developers.

A problem arising from this suggestion is determining which refactoring transformations should be applied to get rid of these undesired dependencies and in which order might they be employed. Considering that we might be able to handle large programs with severely mismatched architectures, the number of possible transformations (along with their permutations) may be huge. Supported by a history of successful attempts to use SBSE approaches to select refactoring strategies [11], search-based techniques may be useful to produce permutations of refactoring transformations sought to recover a project towards its reference architecture.

Acknowledgements. The authors would like to express their gratitude to CNPq, the research agency that financially supported this project. We also acknowledge and are grateful for the discussions held with Prof. Guilherme Travassos regarding the topic addressed in this paper.

References

1. Fowler, M.: Continuous Integration, http://www.martinfowler.com/articles/continuousIntegration.html (last accessed on March 26, 2013)
2. Mitchell, B., Mancoridis, S.: On the automatic modularization of software systems using the bunch tool. IEEE Transactions on Software Engineering 32(3), 193–208 (2006)
3. Harman, M., Swift, S., Mahdavi, K.: An Empirical Study of the Robustness of two Module Clustering Fitness Functions. In: Proceedings of GECCO 2005, Washington, USA (2005)
4. Barros, M.: An Analysis of the Effects of Composite Objectives in Multiobjective Software Module Clustering. In: Proceedings of the Genetic and Evolutionary Computation Conference (GECCO 2012), Philadelphia, USA (2012)
5. Simons, C.L., Parmee, I.C.: Elegant Object-Oriented Software Design via Interactive, Evolutionary Computation. IEEE Transactions on Systems, Man, and Cybernetics, Part C (Applications and Reviews) 42(6), 1797–1805 (2012), doi:10.1109/TSMCC.2012.2225103
6. Henderson-Sellers, B.: Software Metrics. Prentice Hall, Hemel Hempstead (1996)
7. Chidamber, S., Kemerer, C.: A Metrics Suite for Object Oriented Design. IEEE Transactions on Software Engineering 20(6), 476–493 (1994)
8. Lanza, M., Marinescu, R.: Object-oriented Metrics in Practice: using Software Metrics to Characterize, Evaluate, and Improve the Design of Object-Oriented Systems. Springer, Heidelberg (2006)
9. Garlan, D., Allen, R., Ockerbloom, J.: Architectural Mismatch or, Why it's hard to build systems out of existing parts. IEEE Software 12(6), 17–26 (1995)

10. Sangal, N., Waldman, F.: Dependency Models to Manage Software Architecture. CROSSTALK: The Journal of Defense Software Engineering, 8–12 (November 2005)
11. Cinnéide, M.Ó., Tratt, L., Harman, M., Counsell, S., Moghadam, I.H.: Experimental Assessment of Software Metrics Using Automated Refactoring. In: Proc. of the 6th Int. Symposium on Empirical Software Engineering and Measurement, Sweden, pp. 49–58 (2012)
12. Hall, M., Walkinshaw, N., McMinn, P.: Supervised Software Modularisation. In: Proc. of the International Conference on Software Maintenance, Riva del Garda, pp. 472–481 (2012)

eCrash: An Empirical Study
on the Apache Ant Project

Ana Filipa Nogueira[1], José Carlos Bregieiro Ribeiro[2],
Francisco Fernández de Vega[3], and Mário Alberto Zenha-Rela[1]

[1] University of Coimbra,
CISUC, DEI, 3030-290, Coimbra, Portugal
{afnog,mzrela}@dei.uc.pt
[2] Polytechnic Institute of Leiria,
Morro do Lena, Alto do Vieiro, Leiria, Portugal
jose.ribeiro@ipleiria.pt
[3] University of Extremadura,
C/ Sta Teresa de Jornet, 38, Mérida, Spain
fcofdez@unex.es

Abstract. The eCrash tool employs Strongly-Typed Genetic Programming to automate the generation of test data for the structural unit testing of Object-Oriented Java programs. This paper depicts the results attained by utilising eCrash to generate test data for the classes of the Apache Ant project.

Keywords: Evolutionary Testing, Search-Based Test Data Generation, Structural Coverage.

1   Introduction

The application of Evolutionary Algorithms (EAs) to test data generation is often referred to as Evolutionary Testing [8] or Search-Based Test Data Generation [4]. Significant success has been achieved by applying EAs and other metaheuristics to automate the generation of test data for Object-Oriented (OO) software testing. eCrash is a Java-based test data generation tool for OO software, which was developed in order to support the research steps which led to the presentation of Ribeiro's PhD thesis [7]; it embodied the Evolutionary Testing approach proposed and allowed experimenting with novel techniques.

The empirical studies which supported previous research were conducted utilising container classes as Test Objects; these were considered suitable subjects for experimentation in the absence of a set of adequate benchmark programs. This paper depicts the results attained by applying the eCrash tool to generate test data for the (much more complex) Apache Ant[1] project. These results were analysed and compared to those yielded by the Randoop [6] and EvoSuite [1] test data generation tools.

---

[1] https://ant.apache.org/

G. Ruhe and Y. Zhang (Eds.): SSBSE 2013, LNCS 8084, pp. 282–287, 2013.
© Springer-Verlag Berlin Heidelberg 2013

2   The eCrash Tool

The eCrash tool employs EAs to automate the generation of test data for the structural unit testing of OO Java programs. For evolving test data, the Strongly-Typed Genetic Programming (STGP) paradigm [5] is utilized. STGP is especially suited for this purpose: it allows the definition of constraints that eliminate invalid combinations of operations, thus restraining the search space to the set of compilable Test Programs; and has already been extended to support more complex type systems, including generics, inheritance, and polymorphism. The Test Data evaluation process involves instrumenting the Test Object, and executing it using the generated Test Programs as inputs; the trace information collected during execution allows deriving coverage metrics. The aim is that of efficiently guiding the search process towards achieving full structural coverage of the Test Object.

Test Object analysis is performed offline, before Test Data generation takes place. The main tasks involved in this process are those of: defining the Test Cluster, i.e. the transitive set of classes which are relevant for testing the class under test; building the Control Flow Graphs required for assessing the structural coverage attained and the quality of the generated Test Programs; generating the Function Set defining the STGP constraints (automatically and solely with basis on Test Cluster information); and parametrizing the Test Program generation process, namely the ECJ framework [3] which is utilized for evolving individuals.

Test Data generation involves the iterative evolution of potential solutions to the problem with basis on the STGP technique. Test Programs are synthesised with basis on the generated STGP individuals, and then executed and evaluated dynamically. Those Test Programs that exercise previously untraversed structures of the Test Object (i.e., the method under test) are selected for inclusion on the Test Set, which may then be provided to an external unit testing framework (e.g., JUnit). Additional outputs include statistics about the Test Data generation process, such as the level of coverage attained, the number of Test Programs generated, and the time spent performing these tasks.

3   Experimental Study

The experiments detailed in this Section involved the generation of structural test data for the public members of the Apache Ant project, Release 1.8.4 for posterior execution and analysis. The results obtained by eCrash were measured up against those obtained by applying Randoop, a widely-used random testing framework, and EvoSuite, a state of the art search-based test data generation tool, to the same Test Object and in similar conditions. Cobertura[2] was utilised for gathering structural coverage (line and branch) information; even though eCrash and Evosuite provide this data, the usage of Cobertura ensured that the results yielded by the different test data generation tools were analysed in the same manner.

---

[2] http://cobertura.sourceforge.org

3.1   Setup

The Apache Ant project encompasses a total of 1188 classes. However, given that at its current stage of development the eCrash tool is limited (as is Randoop) to generation of test data for the public members (i.e., methods and constructors) of public, concrete and outer classes, the set of classes under test was restricted to the subset of 684 classes which fit these restrictions. The 684 classes tested encompassed a total of 5342 public methods and 861 public constructors. Three runs were executed for each tool, in which each class was tested individually using the set of configurations described in the remaining of this Section.

The stopping criteria considered were: eCrash – achieving full structural coverage of the method under test, or a maximum of 50 generations (each with a population of 30 individuals/test programs); Evosuite – achieving full structural coverage of the class under test (non-public members included), or a maximum of 13605 test programs; and Randoop – reaching a maximum of 13605 test programs per class. The reason for defining an upper limit to the number of test programs per class for the EvoSuite and Randoop tools has to do with the fact that their generation approach is class-oriented, whereas eCrash's is method-oriented; given that the classes under test include an average of 9.07 public members, and that eCrash generated a maximum of 1500 test programs per method, EvoSuite and Randoop where allowed a maximum of 13605 (9.07 * 1500) test programs per class. The other parameters for eCrash remained with their default values, including the probabilities for the GP operators (mutation=0.34, crossover=0.33, reproduction=0.33) and the size for the GP trees (min-size=4, max-size=18).

3.2   Results

This Section summarizes and discusses the results attained in this experimental study. The full data set is available online at:

– `http://eden.dei.uc.pt/~afnog/ssbsechallenge2013.html`

Table 1 presents an overview of the results obtained for each tool. The coverage values achieved by the test set provided in the Apache Ant's distribution are also presented for comparison purposes. In this test set, 261 files contain valid JUnit tests: 218 files correspond to a specific class under test; 41 files seem to test simultaneously features from several classes; and a total of 1828 test cases (methods starting with "test") were identified. The number of members to be tested is difficult to infer due to the structural characteristics of the test code.

The analysis of this data allows concluding that Evosuite's runs achieved the best values for coverage (51% LC and 41% BC by Evosuite, 44% LC and 28% BC by eCrash, and 34% LC and 22% BC), which is, in a way, consistent with our expectations, mostly due to the fact that: (i) Randoop is not oriented towards achieving coverage; and (2) eCrash is still in a prototype stage of development, while Evosuite has evolved greatly in recent years. Even though we may consider it natural for Evosuite to have achieved better results, we must highlight that the results achieved by eCrash are quite remarkable if we take into account its

Table 1. Number of classes and members successfully tested; global percentage of line and branch coverage attained by each tool

Property	Crash	Evosuite	Randoop	Manual
Number of tested classes	652	646	614	>= 218
Number of tested members	5868	7830	3735	N/A
Percentage of global Line Coverage	44%	51%	34%	45%
Percentage of global Branch Coverage	28%	41%	22%	40%

current approach – testing only public members – and some of the eCrash's identified limitations. It is also interesting to note that the test set included in the Apache Ant release achieved a total of 45% BC and 40% LC. No details were provided about the methodology utilised to generate these tests or their purpose, which makes it difficult to make comparisons and draw conclusions; nevertheless, the test set appears to have been defined manually by a software tester, which may explain the higher percentage of BC achieved.

It should be pointed out that all tools faced issues that impeded some classes and members from being tested. eCrash was unable to generate tests for some instance methods which blocked the process (either by stopping it, which was the case with the class Launcher, or by entering an infinite loop), and some static methods in situations in which there were no public constructors providing instances of necessary data types. The former issue is due to a problem with the Test Object, whereas the latter is related with a limitation of the eCrash tool which should be addressed in future releases; nevertheless, they prevented a total of 32 classes from being tested. Likewise, Randoop failed to generate tests for a total of 70 classes for reasons unknown to the authors. Evosuite managed to generate test suites for 646 classes; 24 were qualified as classes with untestable methods; and for 24 classes, the test data generation failed due to classpath related issues which we were unable to solve in a timely manner. In summary, eCrash generated tests for 95.32% of the classes and 94.60% of their public members; Randoop generated tests for 89.77% of the classes and 60.21% of their public members; and Evosuite created test suites for 94.44% of the classes, and tested 88.45% of the methods identified as testable (8852 methods in 646 classes).

Figures 1a and 1b report the box-plots of the coverage values achieved by each tool (eC - eCrash, R - Randoop and Ev - Evosuite) for the set of classes analysed. It is possible to observe that the worst results were obtained by Randoop, and that Evosuite attained the best values. In turn, eCrash has encouraging values: almost 75% of the classes with LC over 40 %; and 50 % of the classes with BC over 40 %. Also, there are no substantial differences in the amount of collateral coverage generated by the tests in the project. Collateral coverage is the coverage obtained for class A during the process of testing class B.

By analysing the classes in which eCrash was unable to achieve BC it is possible to pinpoint some problematic methods, which: use reflection and try to access a particular method or class that is not specified (e.g., TaskAdapter); try to access/load a set of jars or classes (e.g., Launcher, SplitClassLoader); perform logging tasks (e.g., ProfileLogger); deal with input requests and generate tasks and threads (e.g., DemuxInputStream); wait for valid inputs (e.g.,

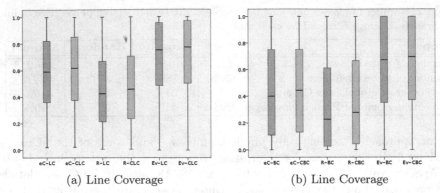

(a) Line Coverage   (b) Line Coverage

Fig. 1. Coverage values for eCrash, Randoop and Evosuite; blue boxes: coverage without collateral coverage; green boxes: coverage values with collateral coverage

DefaultInputHandler); manage files/folders that do not exist, send e-mails or download files (e.g., MimeMailer); implement compilers (e.g., JavacExternal) or extensions for compilers (e.g., ForkingSunRmic); perform operations on compressed files (e.g., Untar); manage, import or execute a set of sequential Apache Ant's tasks (e.g., Sequential); encapsulate Unix commands (e.g., Chown); and deal with audio and image (e.g., Draw). Some of these issues were pointed out in [2] as problems that should be addressed by testing tools.

Randoop and Evosuite also encountered problems to successfully address the hindrances posed by those methods. Randoop was only able to achieve some level of BC in 1/79 classes in which eCrash failed to do so (TaskAdapter: 25%), whereas Evosuite had a higher success rate achieving values for BC in 26/79 classes, e.g.: TaskAdapter (62.50%), Untar (40%) and Sequential (100%).

4   Conclusions

This paper presents an experimental study in which the eCrash Evolutionary Testing tool was utilised to generate structural Test Data for the Apache Ant project. Positive results were achieved, providing strong indicators of the effectiveness and efficiency of the approach, the quality and robustness of the tool, and its applicability to large and complex software products. The results were measured up against those obtained by applying Randoop and EvoSuite. eCrash yielded better coverage results than Randoop; the fact that eCrash utilizes a search-based technique to actively seek the goal of attaining structural coverage makes it more adequate to automate the generation of Test Data that is able to exercise a higher percentage of the Test Object's instructions. When compared to the results yielded by EvoSuite, however, eCrash's performance fell short; it was, nevertheless, promising, and the discussion of the results obtained leads to the conclusion that there is clear potential for improvement.

This was, in fact, the first time that eCrash was applied to a Test Object of this complexity. In future releases, we expect to be able to address several problems, most notably that of including private members and inner classes as search goals. Additional tasks include defining strategies for refining the Test Cluster so as to sample the search space as adequately as possible, e.g. by performing a preliminary static analysis of the Test Object; improving the techniques for dealing with static methods and inner classes; and supporting the testing of classes that handle files and folders, class loaders, and threads. In the past, we have also proposed several techniques for enhancing the automated test data generation process which we did not utilise in this study (e.g., input domain reduction, adaptive constraint selection, object reuse [7]) and that may have a significant impact on the eCrash's performance in future studies.

Future work also includes utilising eCrash in a different scope, namely that of generating Test Data with the intention of gathering information about software properties which are only observable during runtime, for the purpose of obtaining insight about certain software properties (e.g., maintainability).

Acknowledgements. The research reported in this paper has been supported by the Portuguese Foundation for Science and Technology under contract CMU-PT/ELE/0035/2009, Project Affidavit- Automating the Proof of Quality Attributes for Large Scale Software Architectures.

References

1. Fraser, G., Arcuri, A.: Evosuite: automatic test suite generation for object-oriented software. In: Proceedings of the 19th ACM SIGSOFT Symposium and the 13th European Conference on Foundations of Software Engineering, ESEC/FSE 2011, pp. 416–419. ACM, New York (2011)
2. Fraser, G., Arcuri, A.: Sound empirical evidence in software testing. In: 34th International Conference on Software Engineering, ICSE 2012, Zurich, Switzerland, June 2-9, pp. 178–188. IEEE (2012)
3. Luke, S.: ECJ 20: A Java evolutionary computation library (2013), http://cs.gmu.edu/~eclab/projects/ecj/
4. McMinn, P.: Search-based software test data generation: A survey. Software Testing, Verification and Reliability 14(2), 105–156 (2004)
5. Montana, D.J.: Strongly typed genetic programming. Evolutionary Computation 3(2), 199–230 (1995)
6. Pacheco, C., Ernst, M.D.: Randoop: feedback-directed random testing for Java. In: OOPSLA 2007 Companion, Montreal, Canada. ACM (October 2007)
7. Ribeiro, J.C.B.: Contributions for Improving Genetic Programming-Based Approaches to the Evolutionary Testing of Object-Oriented Software. PhD thesis, Universidad de Extremadura, España (November 2010)
8. Tonella, P.: Evolutionary testing of classes. In: ISSTA 2004: Proceedings of the 2004 ACM SIGSOFT International Symposium on Software Testing and Analysis, pp. 119–128. ACM Press, New York (2004)

A Multi-objective Genetic Algorithm for Generating Test Suites from Extended Finite State Machines

Nesa Asoudeh and Yvan Labiche

Department of Systems and Computer Engineering, Carleton University, Ottawa, Canada
{nasoudeh,labiche}@sce.carleton.ca

Abstract. We propose a test suite generation technique from extended finite state machines based on a genetic algorithm that fulfills multiple (conflicting) objectives. We aim at maximizing coverage and feasibility of a set of test cases while minimizing similarity between these cases and minimizing overall cost.

1 Introduction

Extended Finite State Machines (EFSMs) are widely used in system modeling and a great volume of research exists in the area of state-based testing. Due to the presence of guard conditions and action in the EFSM, not all the paths in an EFSM are feasible [1]. Another challenge is decreasing cost and increasing effectiveness of generated test suites to make them scalable to large industrial applications. This can be achieved for instance through increasing test case diversity [2].

Search-Based Software Engineering (SBSE) has emerged in the field of software engineering since the nature of software engineering problems makes them perfect for the application of meta-heuristic search techniques. Search-based methods can be very helpful in solving problems in which there are tradeoffs between different constraints. They can provide solutions when optima are either theoretically impossible or practically infeasible [3]. SBSE has proved to be very successful and there has been a significant increase in the interest and research contributions in this field in the past five years [5]. One of the first applications of SSBSE has been in software testing and dates back to 1976 [6]. In search-based software testing (SBST) a meta-heuristic search method is used to automate or partially automate a testing task [4].

In this paper, we propose an SBST technique for test suite generation from EFSMs. We use a multi-objective genetic algorithm to search for an adequate test suite that is most likely feasible, has minimum cost, and has low similarity between its test paths.

2 Related Work

Others before us have investigated the application of SBST to state-based testing. Hemmati et al. proposed a similarity based test case selection technique that uses search based techniques to maximize test case diversity [2]. In a series of case studies they used different similarity measures as fitness function and considered different

G. Ruhe and Y. Zhang (Eds.): SSBSE 2013, LNCS 8084, pp. 288–293, 2013.
© Springer-Verlag Berlin Heidelberg 2013

search based algorithms: greedy, clustering-based, hill climbing and GA. Kalaji et al. [8] use a GA to generate (likely) feasible test paths from EFSMs and then generate input sequences that trigger those test paths. The GA is used to find a (likely) feasible (their fitness function) test path that executes each transition.

Fraser and Arcuri [12] proposed to generate a complete test suite at once (instead of one test case at a time) from Java program code. To the best of our knowledge, generating a complete test suite from software development artifacts other than code, as we do, has not been addressed before.

Our approach differs from previous contributions in the following aspects. (1) We create an adequate test suite at once rather than one test case at a time. We believe the latter is a sub-optimal strategy/optimization, and that our solution is a more global optimization. This is one among other benefits of generating a complete test suite [12]. (2) We use a multi-objective GA to simultaneously account for test case diversity within the test suite, feasibility of individual test cases, cost and coverage. We note that addressing multiple test objectives is one of the open problems in SBT [4].

3   Proposed Approach

This section presents our solution to the problem of generating a test suite for an EFSM using a multi-objective GA. We first describe what a chromosome and its genes represent (section 3.1) and then discuss the other components of the GA: mutation and crossover operators (sections 3.2 and 3.3), fitness functions (section 3.4). We finish this section by discussing some GA parameters (section 3.5).

3.1   Chromosomes and Genes

A chromosome is a solution to the optimization problem, that is, in our context an entire test suite. The genes are the elements that compose a chromosome (test suite). A gene is therefore a test case, that is, a sequence of transitions of the state model (a.k.a. test path). One of the objectives of test suite construction is to achieve a certain level of coverage according to a selection criterion. Since different adequate (i.e., satisfying a criterion) test suites usually exist and have varying number of test cases, our GA has chromosomes of variable length (i.e., variable number of test cases). The test paths (genes) have variable length too. We generate the initial population randomly. To make every randomly generated traversal of the graph representing an EFSM valid, we use an encoding similar to the one in [8].

3.2   Mutation Operator

Since a chromosome contains many different pieces of information, a chromosome can be mutated in many different ways. We have defined seven different mutation operators. During each mutation one of the following operators is selected randomly with equal probability: (1) Adding a gene to a chromosome, i.e., a randomly generated gene (i.e., test path) is added to the chromosome (test suite); (2) Removing a gene from a chromosome, i.e., a randomly selected gene is removed from the chromosome; (3) Replacing a gene, i.e., a randomly selected gene is replaced by a new randomly generated gene; (4) Removing a transition from a test path (gene), i.e., a randomly selected gene (i.e., test path) is mutated by removing a randomly selected transition from the path; (5) Adding a transition to a test path (gene), i.e., a randomly selected gene is mutated by randomly adding a transition to it; (6) Changing a transition of a test path (gene), i.e., a randomly selected gene is mutated by randomly replacing one of its transitions with a new one; (7) Exchanging randomly selected transitions between randomly selected test paths (genes) of the same test suite (chromosome), a mechanism we borrow from [8]. Each time a test path is modified, we ensure, similarly to the random generation of a entire path, that the resulting path is a valid traversal of the graph representing the EFSM.

3.3   Crossover Operator

Crossover creates two new chromosomes from two existing (parent) chromosomes by exchanging some genetic information, i.e., genes, from/between those parents. Once again, we shall ask ourselves what information can be exchanged between two (parent) chromosomes. Similarly to traditionally defined crossover operators, we can exchange two genes (test paths) between two parent chromosomes (test suites). We can also exchange genetic information at the transition level between test paths. We can select two parent chromosomes, select one gene (test path) in each of those parents, and exchange transition sequence information between those two genes.

3.4   Fitness Functions

As previously mentioned, we are considering four fitness functions: Feasibility, which needs to be maximized, Similarity, which needs to be minimized, coverage, which needs to be maximized and cost, which needs to be minimized.

To determine the **feasibility** of a test path, we reuse previous work that relies on an analysis of data flow dependencies between the transitions of a test path [8]. Different types of data flow dependencies that might exist between two transitions of a test path are assigned penalty values based on their possible effect on feasibility. If a variable is defined in one transition of a path and it is used in a guard condition of one of the subsequent transitions in this path the path can become unfeasible and should be assigned a penalty. This information is used to obtain a feasibility measure for each gene (test path) in a chromosome (test suite) and then to obtain a feasibility measure for the chromosome as the sum of the feasibility values of its genes. This feasibility of a chromosome c_i, made of n genes is then: $feasibility(c_i) = \sum_{j=1}^{n} feasibility(g_j)$ where feasibility(g_j) is computed as explained by Kalaji and colleagues [8].

Our intuition, as well as others' [2], is that test paths should be as dissimilar as possible to increase fault detection. We are therefore interested in computing the **similarities** between pairs of test paths (genes) to obtain a similarity value for a test suite (chromosome). Different similarity measures can be used as fitness function. One of the measures [2], which is not limited to identical length sequences (we have variable length chromosomes), is the Levenshtein distance [9]. To change the distance measure into a similarity measure we reward each match between two sequences by one point and penalize mismatches and gaps by simply ignoring them (i.e., assigning no point). More sophisticated measures (e.g. Needleman-Wunsch) which penalize mismatches and gaps can be used as well. The similarity measure for a test suite (chromosome) is the sum of the similarity measures computed for each pair of test paths (genes) in that chromosome. The objective function needs to be minimized, and is defined as follows: $similarity(c_i) = \sum_{for\ all\ pairs\ of\ genes\ (g_j, g_k)} similarity(g_j, g_k)$.

Different **coverage** criteria can be used as objective function. One possible coverage criterion to compute based on the current encoding is transition coverage. This will be the number of distinct transitions covered by each test suite (chromosome). The fitness function is to minimize the number of uncovered transitions.

The last objective is reducing the **cost** of a test suite as much as possible. We define cost of test path as its length (i.e., number of transitions it exercises). The cost of test suite is the sum of its test paths' cost. This fitness functions is to be minimized.

3.5   Genetic Algorithm Parameters

There are a number of factors that highly affect success of a GA. We selected a population size of 200, which conforms to what has been suggested in the literature [7]: i.e., a value in range [30, 80] (we selected 50) multiplied by the number of objective functions. Based on results from previous studies [11] we selected a crossover rate of 0.7 and a mutation rate of 0.01. The Pareto Fraction parameter controls elitism in a multi-objective GA since it limits the number of individuals on the Pareto set (elite members). Based on a previous study [7], which suggests to set the maximum size of the Pareto set such that the ratio of the Pareto set over the entire population is between ¼ and 4, we set the maximum size of the Pareto set to 0.35.

4   Initial Results

We performed a case study to have an initial evaluation of our proposed approach. We selected a Cruise Control system as a first case study because, although it does not have guards or actions (Fig. 1) and therefore all test paths are feasible (as a consequence we have really three fitness functions), it allowed us to check the correctness of our approach and focus on the three other fitness functions. To run our GA we customized the MATLAB Global Optimization Toolbox [10] multi-objective GA.

Fig. 2 shows a sample Pareto front after running our multi-objective GA for this case study. It plots coverage level versus similarity measure in each test suite belonging to the Pareto front. Numerical values above each point represent the cost of the corresponding test suite (the third fitness function). The point marked with an arrow corresponds to a test suite which consists of the following three test paths:

- Test path 1: < T_1, T_6, T_4, T_5, T_{13}, T_{12}, T_8, T_6, T_7, T_4, T_1, T_2, T_4, T_2, T_5, T_8, T_6, T_2, T_2, T_3, T_5, T_9, T_{14}, T_{16}, T_{18}, T_{21}, T_{24}, T_{28}, T_{17}, T_{20} >
- Test path 2: < $\underline{T_5}$, T_{14}, T_{16}, T_{15}, T_3 >
- Test path 3: < $\underline{T_5}$, T_9, T_{11}, T_{10}, T_{14}, T_{16}, T_{19}, T_{23}, T_{25}, T_{26}, T_{23}, T_{22}, T_6 >

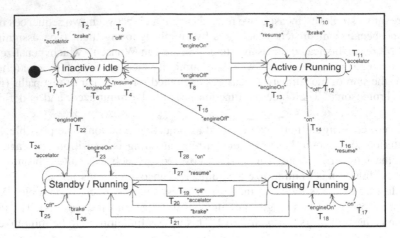

Fig. 1. Cruise Control State Machine

The total number of transitions (cost) in this test suite is 48. Both test paths 2 and 3 start with T5, so similarity measure is one and because T_{27} is not covered coverage penalty is one as well.

5   Plan and Future Work

As previously mentioned, although we have implemented all four fitness functions, we only used three of them in the case study. We are currently working on another case study where paths are not necessarily feasible, thus requiring all four fitness functions. Also we aim at investigating different ways of improving the GA itself (e.g., using test paths that improve one or more fitness measure, instead of randomly generated ones, in the mutation operator, using different mutation operators with different probabilities and observing the effects). We also plan to study other possible

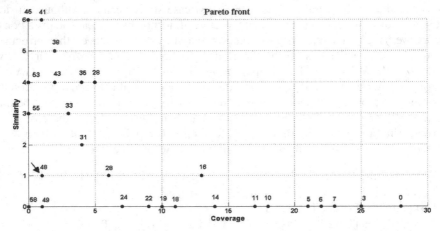

Fig. 2. Pareto front corresponding to cruise control case study

measures to compute coverage (e.g., transition pairs) and similarity (see [2]) of a test suite. Another interesting variation of our GA is one in which fitness functions have different weights. Also we plan to examine different strategies for creating the initial population. Last, we plan on studying the effectiveness at finding faults of the different test suites we generate and compare our test suites with others (e.g., [8]).

Acknowledgment. This work was performed under the umbrella of a NSERC-CRD grant. The authors would like to thank NSERC, CRIAQ, CAE, CMC Electronics, and Mannarino Systems & Software for their financial support.

References

1. Dual, A.Y., Uyar, M.U.: A method enabling feasible conformance test sequence generation for EFSM models. IEEE Transactions on Computers 53(5), 614–627 (2004)
2. Hemmati, H., Arcuri, A., Briand, L.: Achieving scalable model-based testing through test case diversity. ACM Transactions on Software Engineering and Methodology (TOSEM) 22(1) (2013)
3. Harman, M., Jones, B.F.: Search-based software engineering. Information and Software Engineering, 833–839 (2001)
4. MacMinn, P.: Search-based software testing: Past, Present and Future. In: Fourth International Conference on Software Testing, Verification and Validation Workshops, Berlin, Germany (2011)
5. Harman, M., McMinn, P., de Souza, J.T., Yoo, S.: Search based software engineering: Techniques, taxonomy, tutorial. In: Meyer, B., Nordio, M. (eds.) LASER Summer School 2008-2010. LNCS, vol. 7007, pp. 1–59. Springer, Heidelberg (2012)
6. Miller, W., Spooner, D.: Automatic generation of floating point test data. IEEE Transactions on Software Engineering 2(3), 223–226 (1976)
7. Laumanns, M., Zitzler, E., Thiele, L.: On The Effects of Archiving, Elitism, an Density Based Selection in Evolutionary Multi-objective Optimization. In: Zitzler, E., Deb, K., Thiele, L., Coello Coello, C.A., Corne, D.W. (eds.) EMO 2001. LNCS, vol. 1993, pp. 181–196. Springer, Heidelberg (2001)
8. Kalaji, A.S., Hierons, R.M., Swift, S.: An integrated search-based approach for automatic testing from extended finite state machine (EFSM) models. Information and Software Technology 53(12), 1297–1318 (2011)
9. Gusfield, D.: Algorithms on Strings, Trees and Sequences: Computer Sience and Computational Biology. Cambridge University Press, Cambirdge (1997)
10. Global Optimization Toolbox, Mathworks,
    http://www.mathworks.com/products/global-optimization/
    (accessed April 25, 2013)
11. Haupt, R.L., Haupt, S.E.: Practical Genetic Algorithms. Wiley, New york (1998)
12. Fraser, G., Arcuri, A.: Whole test suite generation. IEEE Transactions on Software Engineering 39(2), 276–291 (2013)

An Approach to Test Set Generation for Pair-Wise Testing Using Genetic Algorithms

Priti Bansal, Sangeeta Sabharwal, Shreya Malik, Vikhyat Arora, and Vineet Kumar

Netaji Subhas Institute of Technology, New Delhi, India
bansalpriti@rediffmail.com, ssab23@yahoo.com,
{malik.shreya12,arora.vikhyat}@gmail.com,
vineetmehra_2aug@yahoo.co.in

Abstract. Instead of performing exhaustive testing that tests all possible combinations of input parameter values of a system, it is better to switch to a more efficient and effective testing technique i.e., pair wise testing. In pair wise testing, test cases are designed to cover all possible combinations of each pair of input parameter values. It has been shown that the problem of finding the minimum set of test cases for pair-wise testing is an NP complete problem. In this paper we apply genetic algorithm, a meta heuristic search algorithm, to find an optimal solution to the pair-wise test set generation problem. We present a method to generate initial population using hamming distance and an algorithm to find crossover points for combining individuals selected for reproduction. We describe the implementation of the proposed approach by extending an open source tool PWiseGen and evaluate the effectiveness of the proposed approach. Empirical results indicate that our approach can generate test sets with higher fitness level by covering more pairs of input parameter values.

Keywords: pair-wise testing, genetic algorithms, hamming distance, crossover points.

1   Introduction

For exhaustive testing of a system having n input parameters where, each parameter can take $k_1, k_2,...k_n$ discrete values respectively, a total of $k_1 * k_2 *...k_n$ number of test cases will be required to test all possible combinations of input parameter values. Exhaustive testing is either not feasible or very expensive and time consuming. Instead of performing exhaustive testing, it is better to switch to a more efficient and effective testing technique i.e., combinatorial testing. Combinatorial testing is a technique that is based on the principle that most of the faults in a system are triggered due to the interaction of two or more parameters. Extensive research has been done in the area of applying combinatorial testing techniques for testing traditional applications [1-4] as well as GUI [5] and web applications [6-7]. In combinatorial testing, test sets are generated to cover all possible t-way (2-way, 3-way etc.) combination of input parameters. However, empirical studies show that test set covering all possible 2-way combination of input parameter values is effective for many software systems

G. Ruhe and Y. Zhang (Eds.): SSBSE 2013, LNCS 8084, pp. 294–299, 2013.
© Springer-Verlag Berlin Heidelberg 2013

[1-3]. Pair-wise testing is a combinatorial testing technique that can reduce cost and increase effectiveness of testing by generating test sets to cover every possible pair of input parameter values for a system, without losing much of the fault detection capability [4]. However, the problem of finding minimum number of test cases for pair-wise testing is an NP-complete problem [4]. In this paper, we explore how genetic algorithms (GAs) can be effectively applied to find a solution to pair-wise test set generation problem.

The remainder of this paper is organized as follows. Section 2 briefly presents the related work. Section 3 describes the proposed approach. Section 4 reports some experimental results. Section 5 concludes the paper and future plans are discussed.

2   Related Work

Existing methods to generate optimal test set for pair-wise testing are broadly classified into algebraic methods [8], recursive methods [9], greedy methods [1-4] and meta heuristic methods [10-17]. Since finding an optimal test set is an NP complete problem, hence most of the existing solutions are approximate in a sense that although a solution has been found in reasonable time but it is not necessarily an optimal solution. Algebraic methods mostly used by mathematicians, use an orthogonal array approach to construct covering arrays. In recursive methods, large covering arrays are constructed from smaller ones. Greedy methods generate a test set by creating one test at a time until all the combinations are covered. Meta heuristic methods use stochastic algorithms like simulated annealing [10], tabu search [11], ant colony optimization [12], swarm optimization [13] and GAs [14-17]. Ghazi and Ahmed [14] applied GA to find pair-wise test set. They presented the results of experimental studies; however their input set was small and the generated test set was not optimal. McCraffey [15] proposed a technique, Genetic Algorithm for Pairwise Test Sets (GAPTS) to generate an optimal pair-wise test set. Empirical studies performed by the author in [16] showed that the size of test sets generated by GAPTS were comparable to or better than other algorithms proposed in past. Flores and Cheon [17] applied GA to find an optimal solution to pair-wise test set generation problem. They proposed many variants of crossover and mutation to prevent stagnation and to generate good solution. They developed an open source tool PWiseGen to implement their approach.

3   Pair-Wise Test Set Generation

This paper aims at developing a powerful GA for finding an optimal pair-wise test set to achieve 100% pair-wise combination of input parameter values. As compared to existing GA based approaches, our approach enhances the performance by a) using maximum hamming distance to create an initial population and b) proposing an algorithm to determine crossover points during reproduction. Below we explain these features in detail.

3.1   Initial Population

In GAs, an initial population is created randomly that represents possible solutions to the given problem. In our case, an individual (chromosome) represents a test set, which is a set of test cases wherein the size of a test case is equal to the number of input parameters. A test case contains one value corresponding to each input parameter and we use integer encoding to encode test cases, as suggested in [15]. This paper presents a hamming distance based approach to create an initial population of test sets. Hamming distance between two test cases in a test set is the number of elements in which they differ. Let M be the population size and N be the test set (TS) size. For each test set in M, 50% (first N/2) of the test cases in TS are created randomly. Let tc_1, tc_2 ... tc_i represents the test cases in TS generated till now. To create the next test case tc_j where $j=i+1$, a candidate test case c_j is generated randomly and the hamming distance of c_j from tc_i, for all i: $1 \leq i \leq j-1$, denoted by distance (c_j), is calculated as:

$$distance(c_j) = \sum_{i=1}^{i=j-1} HD(tc_i, c_j) \tag{1}$$

Where, HD (tc_i, c_j) is the hamming distance between tc_i and c_j. An average distance denoted by avg_distance (c_j) is calculated as follows.

$$avg\_distance(c_j) = distance(c_j)/(j-1) \tag{2}$$

Candidate test case c_j is included in the test set TS only if

$$avg\_distance(c_j) \geq \alpha \times N_{IP} \tag{3}$$

Where, α is a diversity factor whose value ranges from 0.3 to 0.4 and N_{IP} is the number of input parameters. Equation 3 implies that a candidate test case c_j is included only if it covers at least 30%-40% distinct input parameter values as compared to those covered by (j-1) test cases. We performed extensive study with varying diversity factor and reached to a conclusion that a value lower than 0.3 will allow almost identical test cases in the test set which may lead to premature convergence to a non optimal solution while a value higher than 0.4 increases the population diversity which leads to slow convergence. The process is repeated until remaining N/2 test cases are generated for the test set TS. Each test set in the population is associated with a fitness value. The fitness function is defined as the number of distinct pairs of input parameter values covered by the test set. The use of hamming distance to create N/2 test cases in each test set enhances the quality of initial population. Although this approach slightly increases the time to generate initial population, but it results in the generation of better quality test set in less number of iterations as compared to random technique used to generate initial population. Hence, there is a trade-off between fitness and time.

3.2   Single or Multipoint Crossover

During crossover, individuals are selected from the population with the intention of producing better individuals by combining features of selected parents. Crossover can be performed either at a single point or at multiple points. A number of variants of single crossover point and multiple crossover points are presented in [17], where the crossover points are either fixed or are determined randomly. An algorithm to determine crossover points is presented in Figure 1. The algorithm takes as input a test set TS and the desired number of crossover points, k. It returns crossover points by selecting test cases in the test set TS that covers least number of distinct pairs. If there is more than one test case that covers least number of distinct pairs, each test case will have equal probability of getting selected for crossover. Application of this algorithm to determine crossover points, either single or multiple, produces offspring with higher fitness values as compared to those produced when random crossover points are used.

begin
    count the number of times each pair is covered by the test set TS
    for each test case $tc_i \in$ TS
        Count the number of unique pairs covered by tc_i and store it in list L
    endfor
    initialize counter i=0
    while (i < k)
        find the test case tc_j that covers least number of unique pairs
        set boundaries of tc_j as crossover point
        mark entry corresponding to tc_j in L as integer.max
    endwhile
end

Fig. 1. Algorithm to find crossover points

4   Experimental Setup and Empirical Evaluation

The key features discussed in previous section are implemented using an open source tool: PWiseGen available at [18]. PWiseGen is an extensible, reusable and configurable tool written in java to generate pair-wise test set using GAs [17]. We extended PWiseGen by adding to it the capability to generate initial population using hamming distance. We created a concrete class *HammingPopulationInitializer ()* which implements the interface *PopulationInitializer()* to create initial population using hamming distance. Next we created a concrete class *crossoverpoint ()* that extends the abstract class *CrossoverStrategy()*, to find crossover points using the algorithm shown in Figure 1. These two features are incorporated in PWiseGen by adding information about the new components in the XML based configuration file.

We studied empirically the effectiveness of the proposed approach by conducting a series of experiments. The experiments were conducted on the existing tool: PWiseGen and its three variants namely a) PWiseGen-I - uses hamming distance to create initial population and crossover points are generated randomly b) PWiseGen-II - initial population is generated randomly and uses algorithm in Figure 1 to find crossover points and c) PWiseGen-III - uses hamming distance to create initial population and algorithm in Figure 1 to find crossover points. The efficiency of proposed approach was evaluated using six benchmark problems of different sizes: 3^4, 3^{13}, $4^{15}3^{17}2^{29}$, $4^13^{39}2^{35}$, 2^{100} and 10^{20} where x^y means a problem with y input parameters, each with x distinct values. These six benchmark input sets were supplied to PWiseGen and its three variants. Single point crossover is used during experimentation. The effectiveness of the proposed approach was evaluated in terms of the fitness level of the generated test set for all the six benchmark problems. The fitness level for each problem is calculated after multiple runs of GA. In all the three variants of PWiseGen, values of other GA parameters (mutation rate, population size etc.) are kept same as in PWiseGen. The results of conducted experiments are shown in Figure 2. As can be seen from Figure 2, PWiseGen-III yields superior or equal results as compared to other variants except in the last case. PWiseGen-I and PWiseGen-II also generates higher fitness test set as compared to PWiseGen.

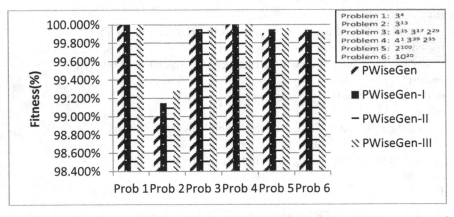

Fig. 2. Comparison of fitness level of test set generated by PWiseGen and its three variants for the six benchmark problems

5   Conclusion and Future Work

In this paper, we have presented an approach to generate test set for pair-wise testing. Our approach has two salient features. First, an approach to generate initial population using hamming distance is employed. Second, an algorithm to determine crossover points is proposed. Empirical results show that the proposed approach generates test set with higher fitness level in less number of iterations as compared to the test set generated when random techniques are used for population initialization and determination of crossover points. In future, we plan to conduct experiments on more input sets to thoroughly check the effectiveness of our approach and explore the trade-off between fitness and time.

References

1. Cohen, D.M., Dalal, S.R., Kajla, A., Patton, G.C.: The automatic efficient test generator. In: Proceedings of the IEEE International Symposium on Software Reliability Engineering, pp. 303–309 (1994)

2. Cohen, D.M., Dalal, S.R., Fredman, M.L., Patton, G.C.: The combinatorial design approach to automatic test generation. IEEE Software, 83–87 (1996)
3. Cohen, D.M., Dalal, S.R., Fredman, M.L., Patton, G.C.: The AETG system: An approach to testing based on combinatorial design. IEEE Transactions on Software Engineering 23(7), 437–443 (1997)
4. Lei, Y., Tai, K.C.: In-parameter-order: A test generation strategy for pairwise testing. In: The 3rd IEEE International Symposium on High-Assurance Systems Engineering, HASE 1998, Washington, DC, pp. 254–261 (1998)
5. Yuan, X., Cohen, M.B., Memon, A.: Covering Array Sampling of Input Event Sequences for Automated GUI Testing. In: Proceedings of the 22nd International Conference on Automated Software Engineering, pp. 405–408 (2007)
6. Wang, W., Sampath, S., Lei, Y., Kacker, R.: An interaction – based test sequence generation approach for testing web applications. In: Proceedings of 11th Int'l IEEE HASE Symposium, pp. 209–218 (2008)
7. Nguyen, C.D., Marchetto, A., Tonella, P.: Combining model-based and combinatorial testing for effective test case generation. In: Proceedings of International Symposium on Software Testing and Analysis, ISSTA, pp. 100–110 (2012)
8. Mandl, R.: Orthogonal Latin Squares: An Application of Experiment Design to Compiler Testing. Communications of the ACM 28(10), 1054–1058 (1985)
9. Hartman, A.: Software and Hardware Testing Using Combinatorial Covering Suites. In: Graph Theory, Combinatorics and Algorithms. Operations Research/Computer Science Interfaces Series, vol. 34, pp. 237–266. Springer, US (2005)
10. Avila-George, H., Torres-Jimenez, J., Hernández, V., Gonzalez-Hernandez, L.: Simulated annealing for constructing mixed covering arrays. In: Omatu, S., Paz Santana, J.F., González, S.R., Molina, J.M., Bernardos, A.M., Rodríguez, J.M.C. (eds.) Distributed Computing and Artificial Intelligence. AISC, vol. 151, pp. 657–664. Springer, Heidelberg (2012)
11. Gonzalez-Hernandez, L., Rangel-Valdez, N., Torres-Jimenez, J.: Construction of Mixed Covering Arrays of Variable Strength Using a Tabu Search Approach. In: Wu, W., Daescu, O. (eds.) COCOA 2010, Part I. LNCS, vol. 6508, pp. 51–64. Springer, Heidelberg (2010)
12. Shiba, T., Tsuchiya, T., Kikuno, T.: Using artificial life techniques to generate test cases for combinatorial testing. In: Proceedings of the 28th Annual International Computer Software and Applications Conference, pp. 72–77. IEEE Computer Society (2004)
13. Jia-Ze, S., Shu-Yan, W.: Generation of Pairwise Test Sets using Novel DPSO algorithm. In: Yang, Y., Ma, M. (eds.) Green Communications and Networks. LNEE, vol. 113, pp. 479–487. Springer, Heidelberg (2012)
14. Ghazi, S.A., Ahmed, M.A.: Pair-wise test coverage using genetic algorithms. In: The 2003 Congress on Evolutionary Computation, vol. 2, pp. 1420–1423. IEEE Computer Society, Australia (2003)
15. McCaffrey, J.D.: Generation of pairwise test sets using a genetic algorithm. In: Proceedings of 33rd Annual IEEE International Computer Software and Applications Conference, pp. 626–631. IEEE Press, Los Alamitos (2009)
16. McCaffrey, J.D.: An empirical study of pairwise test set generation using a genetic algorithm. In: ITNG 2010: 6th International Conference on Information Technology: New Generations, pp. 992–997. IEEE Computer Society, Las Vegas (2010)
17. Flores, P., Cheon, Y.: Pwisegen: Generating test cases for pairwise testing using genetic algorithms. In: IEEE International Conference on Computer Science and Automation Engineering (CSAE), vol. 2, pp. 747–752 (2011)
18. http://code.google.com/p/pwisegen/

Generation of Tests
for Programming Challenge Tasks
Using Helper-Objectives

Arina Buzdalova, Maxim Buzdalov, and Vladimir Parfenov

St. Petersburg National Research University
of Information Technologies, Mechanics and Optics,
49 Kronverkskiy prosp., Saint-Petersburg, Russia, 197101
{abuzdalova,mbuzdalov}@gmail.com,
parfenov@mail.ifmo.ru

Abstract. Generation of performance tests for programming challenge tasks is considered. A number of evolutionary approaches are compared on two different solutions of an example problem. It is shown that using helper-objectives enhances evolutionary algorithms in the considered case. The general approach involves automated selection of such objectives.

Keywords: test generation, programming challenges, multi-objective evolutionary algorithms, multi-objectivization, helper-objectives.

1 Introduction

Programming challenge tasks are given at programming contests [1, 2]. Generally, a task consists of a problem formulation, input data format and output data format. Solutions are checked using pre-written tests. A test represents input data. In order to pass the test, a solution should provide correct output data within certain time and memory limits.

The goal of our research is to automatically generate performance tests. To clarify what exactly a performance test in this paper is, we say that the aim of performance test generation is to create such a test that running time of the tested solution on this tests exceeds the time limit. In order to generate tests, evolutionary algorithms [3] are used, as proposed in our previous work [4].

Although the running time is the objective to optimize, using it as a fitness function is not efficient. We propose using some helper-objectives [5] instead of or along with the running time objective. Such approach is inspired by multi-objectivization and helper-objective optimization techniques [5–7].

The exclusive part of this paper is consideration of helper-objectives for two different solutions and comparative analysis of 10 algorithms which were used to generate tests against these solutions.

G. Ruhe and Y. Zhang (Eds.): SSBSE 2013, LNCS 8084, pp. 300–305, 2013.
© Springer-Verlag Berlin Heidelberg 2013

2   Research Goal

The goal of the research is to explore different evolutionary approaches for performance test generation. The approaches to be explored are listed in Section 3. We generate performance tests against two different solutions of an example programming challenge task. The task, its solutions and corresponding helper-objectives are described below.

2.1   Programming Challenge Task

As in [4], we consider a programming challenge task "Ships. Version 2". This task is located at the Timus Online Judge [2] under the number 1394.

The task formulation is as follows. There are N ships, each of length s_i, and M havens, each of length h_j. It is needed to allocate ships to the havens, such that the total length of all ships assigned to the j-th haven does not exceed h_j. It is guaranteed that the correct assignment always exists. The constraints are $N \leq 99$, $2 \leq M \leq 9$, $1 \leq s_i \leq 100$, $\sum s_i = \sum h_j$. The time limit is one second, and the memory limit is 64 megabytes.

Due to the fact that this problem is NP-hard [8] and the high limits on the input data, it is very unlikely that every possible problem instance can be solved under the specified time and memory limits. However, for the most sophisticated solutions it is very difficult to construct a test which makes them exceed the time limit.

2.2   Helper-Objectives

The target objective to be maximized is running time of a programming challenge task solution. However, it is inefficient to use running time as a fitness function, since it is platform-dependent, quantified and noisy [4]. In order to solve this issue, we suggest including counters in the solution code. The counters can be used as helper-objectives [5]. The pseudocodes of the *Solution-1* and *Solution-2* with the included helper-objectives are shown below.

Solution-1 with included helper-objectives: I, P, R

```
Read the input data
I := 0, P := 0, R := 0
while(solution not found)
    Randomly shuffle ships
    Call the recursive dynamic programming based ship arranging procedure
        For each call to this procedure, R := R + 1
        In each innermost loop, P := P + 1
    if (solution is found)
        Write the answer
    else
        I := I + 1
    end if
end while
```

Solution-2 with included helper-objectives: I, L, Q

```
Read the input data
I := 0, L := 0, last := 0
while (solution not found) do
    Randomly shuffle ships and havens
last := 0
    Call the recursive ship arranging procedure
        For each call to this procedure, last := last + 1
    if (solution is found) then
        Write the answer
    else
        I := I + 1
        L := L + last
        last := 0
    end if
end while
Q := 1000000000 * I + last
```

The main difference between the solutions is the implementation of the ship arranging procedure. Unfortunately, we are not able to put more detailed code in this article, because of the programming challenge rules that prevent publication of solutions. However, it will be obvious from the experiment results that the solutions have different performance.

3   Approach

In this section different evolutionary approaches of test generation are described. Evolutionary algorithms can be used to optimize either a single objective or several ones. The objective can stay the same during the evolutionary algorithm run (a *fixed objective*), or we can select the objective to be optimized at each stage of the optimization process (a *dynamic objective*). The evolutionary algorithms, as well as helper-objective selection strategies are described below.

3.1   Evolutionary Algorithms

Single-Objective Genetic Algorithm (GA). The single-objective evolutionary algorithm is a genetic algorithm (GA) with the population size of 200. To create a new population a tournament selection with tournament size of 2 and the probability of selecting a better individual of 0.9 is used. After that, the crossover and mutation operators similar to [4] are applied with the probability of 1.0. To form a new population, the elitist strategy is used with the elite size of five individuals. If for 1000 generations the best fitness value does not change, then the current population is cleared and initialized with newly created individuals.

Multi-Objective Evolutionary Algorithm (NSGA-II). For optimization of more than one objective, a fast variant of the NSGA-II algorithm [9] proposed in [10] is used. Except for the version of tournament selection and nondominated sorting based selection strategy, which is traditionally used in NGSA-II algorithms, the evolutionary operation pipeline is the same as in the single-objective case.

3.2 Helper-Objective Selection

Selection by M. T. Jensen. We consider two selection methods. The first one was proposed by M. T. Jensen [5]. According to this method, a helper-objective is chosen randomly from the set of helper-objectives and is being optimized for a fixed number of populations. Then the next helper-objective is chosen, and so on. This method implies using two-objective evolutionary algorithm, where the first objective is the running time and the second one is a helper-objective.

Reinforcement Learning Selection (RL). The other selection method is EA + RL method [7]. The fitness function is chosen with reinforcement learning from a set that includes the target objective and the helper ones. The choice is influenced by a reward that depends on the target objective (running time) growth. So the target objective is already taken into account and a single-objective evolutionary algorithm can be used.

In this work, delayed Q-learning algorithm [11] is used. It is restarted every 50 generations, which aims at preventing stagnation. The update period is $m = 5$, the bonus reward is $\varepsilon = 0.001$ and discount factor is $\gamma = 0.1$. The discount parameter used to calculate the reward is set to $k = 0.5$. All the parameter values are set on the basis of preliminary experiment results.

4 Experiment

Tests for each considered solution were generated using all the considered algorithms with each compatible objective. Each algorithm was run for 100 times, then the results were averaged. The termination condition was either evolving of a test that made the solution to exceed the time limit (a *successful run*), or reaching the population number limit, which was 10000 populations.

The results for the Solution-1 are shown in the Table 1. T denotes the running time of the solution, σ is the diversity of the population number in a run. *Populations* refer to the mean number of populations needed to exceed the time limit, the smaller it is the more efficient the corresponding algorithm is. Note that using running time as a fitness function is inefficient, as was expected.

In the fixed objective case, multi-objective optimization significantly outperforms single-objective one, no matter what helper-objective is used. In the dynamic objective case, multi-objective optimization is also good enough. Although in this example NSGA-II with a fixed objective outperforms all the other approaches, using dynamic objective can be more preferable in general, as shown below.

Table 1. Results of test generation for the Solution-1

Algorithm	Fitness functions	Successful runs, %	Populations	
			Mean	σ
Fixed objective				
GA	I	99	2999	1986
GA	R	93	3153	3742
GA	P	54	12621	12770
GA	T	0	–	–
NSGA-II	T, I	100	203	119
NSGA-II	T, R	100	440	381
NSGA-II	T, P	100	448	360
Dynamic objective				
GA + RL	all	65	9636	9538
NSGA-II + RL	all	99	895	1215
NSGA-II + Jensen	all	100	882	786

The results for the Solution-2 are shown in the Table 2. In the fixed objective case, only the objective Q is efficient. Although this objective provides the best performance, we usually do not know this in advance and should perform runs with each helper-objective.

At the same time, all the dynamic objective methods are efficient. In dynamic objective approach one run is enough, the most efficient objective is chosen automatically. So the dynamic helper objective approach is both general and efficient one.

Table 2. Results of test generation for the Solution-2

Algorithm	Fitness functions	Successful runs, %	Generations	
			Mean	σ
Fixed objective				
GA	Q	95	3815	3466
GA	I	54	12669	12873
GA	L	51	13755	14082
GA	T	0	–	–
NSGA-II	T, Q	95	2217	3136
NSGA-II	T, I	45	15861	16723
NSGA-II	T, L	20	41330	44768
Dynamic objective				
GA + RL	all	80	5817	6160
NSGA-II + RL	all	72	6679	7764
NSGA-II+Jensen	all	75	6103	7076

5 Conclusion

A number of approaches for generation of performance tests against programming challenge solutions were compared. It was shown that using helper-objectives significantly improves the optimization process. We suggest using multi-objective evolutionary algorithms with dynamic helper-objectives, which is a general and efficient method. Further work involves formalization of a class of problems that can be efficiently solved using the proposed approach. Another future goal is implementation of automated insertion of helper-objectives in the solution code, since currently such insertion is made manually.

References

1. ACM International Collegiate Programming Contest,
   http://cm.baylor.edu/welcome.icpc
2. Timus Online Judge. The Problem Archive with Online Judge System,
   http://acm.timus.ru
3. Eiben, A.E., Smith, J.E.: Introduction to Evolutionary Computing. Springer (2003)
4. Buzdalov, M.: Generation of Tests for Programming Challenge Tasks Using Evolution Algorithms. In: GECCO Conference Companion on Genetic and Evolutionary Computation, pp. 763–766. ACM, New York (2011)
5. Jensen, M.T.: Helper-Objectives: Using Multi-Objective Evolutionary Algorithms for Single-Objective Optimisation. Journal of Mathematical Modelling and Algorithms 3(4), 323–347 (2004)
6. Knowles, J.D., Watson, R.A., Corne, D.W.: Reducing Local Optima in Single-Objective Problems by Multi-objectivization. In: Zitzler, E., Deb, K., Thiele, L., Coello Coello, C.A., Corne, D.W. (eds.) EMO 2001. LNCS, vol. 1993, pp. 269–283. Springer, Heidelberg (2001)
7. Buzdalova, A., Buzdalov, M.: Increasing Efficiency of Evolutionary Algorithms by Choosing between Auxiliary Fitness Functions with Reinforcement Learning. In: 11th International Conference on Machine Learning and Applications, pp. 150–155. IEEE (2012)
8. Pisinger, D.: Algorithms for Knapsack Problems. PhD Thesis, University of Copenhagen (1995)
9. Deb, K., Pratap, A., Agarwal, S., Meyarivan, T.: A Fast and Elitist Multiobjective Genetic Algorithm: NSGA-II. Transactions on Evolutionary Computation 6(2), 182–197 (2002)
10. D'Souza, Rio G. L., Chandra Sekaran, K., Kandasamy, A.: Improved NSGA-II Based on a Novel Ranking Scheme. Computing Research Repository. ID: abs/1002.4005 (2010)
11. Strehl, A.L., Li, L., Wiewora, E., Langford, J., Littman, M.L.: PAC model-free reinforcement learning. In: 23rd International Conference on Machine Learning, pp. 881–888 (2006)

The Emergence of Useful Bias in Self-focusing Genetic Programming for Software Optimisation

Brendan Cody-Kenny and Stephen Barrett

Distributed Systems Group,
School of Computer Science and Statistics, Trinity College Dublin
{codykenb,stephen.barrett}@scss.tcd.ie

Abstract. The use of Genetic Programming (GP) to optimise increasingly large software code has been enabled through biasing the application of GP operators to code areas relevant to the optimisation of interest. As previous approaches have used various forms of static bias applied before the application of GP, we show the emergence of bias learned within the GP process itself which improves solution finding probability in a similar way. As this variant technique is sensitive to the evolutionary lineage, we argue that it may more accurately provide bias in programs which have undergone heavier modification and thus find solutions addressing more complex issues.

1 Introduction

By posing software modification as a search problem [8], Genetic Programming [16] can be used to modify software for various purposes [17,18,23,21]. A general issue with the use of GP is that when larger programs are considered, the increased number of possible sub-tree and location combinations reduces the chance of finding a solution [6,4]. This poses a problem for the application of GP to source code modification as many programs contain complex interdependencies.

Previous approaches have used node selection bias to shape and scale software to within the practical ability of GP algorithms [21,13]. While bias has been applied statically in these approaches, we inspect how bias can emerge as an integral part of the GP algorithm. In previous work, bias was allocated to nodes involved in offspring generation through observing parent-offspring functionality differences [5] with the effect of dis-improving GP.

In this paper we present a bias allocation rule dependent on the primary software trait of interest, the objective of our optimisation being improvement of performance or reduction in cost of executing the program. The magnitude of bias is calculated from the difference between parent and offspring performance measures as opposed to being fixed [5] or random [2]. Our results show this rule can improve GPs ability to find a better solution and demonstrate the emergence of appropriate bias.

G. Ruhe and Y. Zhang (Eds.): SSBSE 2013, LNCS 8084, pp. 306–311, 2013.
© Springer-Verlag Berlin Heidelberg 2013

2 Related Work

GPs utility for various software modification tasks, including software optimisation, has been demonstrated at different levels of abstraction such as design pattern [19,14], line of code [21], statement [13], Java source code [3,23,5] and bytecode [15]. These works raise the question of there being a tension between the granularity of change and the optimisations that GP can practically find. It would appear that as the granularity of change becomes finer, the search space increases, and GP is less able to adequately search the solution space. If a more coarse granularity is used, GP can make larger jumps across the search space but risks entirely excluding a range of potentially important solutions.

As real-world software may have multiple requirements, and only a single one is required to change as in the case of bug fixing, the portion of the code which needs to be modified can be expected to be small [21,13]. Portions of code which are likely to be relevant can be highlighted through runtime analysis of the code using various test cases for bug fixing [21] or by observing how execution frequency of statements increases with input size for optimisation [13]. The result of analysis provides probabilities for each modification point in the code and determines how likely GP will make a change at each point when applied. The probabilities are specific to the initial version of the software and not to any versions which emerge under evolution. What is distinct about these works is that a software patch is evolved as opposed to the entire program representation.

Finding good locations for modification (good nodes to apply operators to) within programs can be done "online" as part of the GP algorithm and can be achieved in a number of ways. The best offspring program can be found by repeatedly pruning sub-trees [9]. This approach is computationally intensive due to the large number of re-evaluations performed. The usefulness of each sub-tree in a program can be stored in a central location and updated as it occurs in new individuals [12]. This is a sub-tree centric approach mainly concerned with exploration of the search space by avoiding trees which appear correct or have not been executed. By assigning fitness to subtrees, evolutionary search can be focused on subtrees which have a low fitness measure [10].

Measuring the frequency of terminals in successful programs can be used to bias the distribution of these terminals in future programs [7]. This approach is concerned with removing terminals superfluous to the problem at hand. It is unclear how this would help in scenarios where the initial population is seeded with programs which presumably contain mostly relevant terminals. Bias can be introduced at the grammar level to influence how new code segments are generated [22].

Attaching parameters to every node in a program yields bias which can be unique to each program [2]. Updating bias is achieved by the addition of random noise to the parameters at each node and a useful bias is allowed to emerge through standard evolutionary pressure. While Angeline's approach is beneficial, we speculate that a promising individual could be changed in a less-than-optimal location in a non-optimal direction due to arbitrary allocation of noise within the parameter tree.

3   Experimental Setup

Our GP setup involves per-individual node bias [2] applied to a Java implementation of naive bubble-sort [23], using Eclipse's Java Development Tools (JDT)
[20] to modify an Abstract Syntax Tree representation (AST) of the sort and
enforce typing. Primitives for our GP system are gathered from the seed program with the manual addition of the equal to operator ("==") and postfix
decrement operator ("- -"). A population size of 250 is used for 100 generations
created with a crossover rate of 0.8 and a mutation rate of 0.2. The max program
length is set to 20 lines and the max number of operator applications is 100.

The initial GP population is created by repeatedly mutating the seed program
shown in Listing 1.1. Mutation operates by selecting a node from the AST and
then deciding whether to mutate or delete that node. When applying crossover,
a clone is made of the first chosen parent. Our crossover operator selects a node
in the parent clone, and then selects a node of matching type from the second
parent.

The fitness function we use is a value calculated using normalised performance
and functionality measures as shown in Figure 1. We measure performance as
the number of instructions executed by the JVM when the program is passed
a series of test arrays using a bytecode counter [11]. Arrays of size 10, 100 and
1000 are randomly populated with values that are almost sorted, reverse sorted
and completely random in location.

$$F = \frac{C_{\text{individual}}}{C_{\text{seed}}} + 100 \cdot \frac{S_{\text{max}} - S_{\text{individual}}}{S_{\text{max}}} \tag{1}$$

Fig. 1. Fitness is the weighted sum of normalised performance (individual instruction
count over seed instruction count) and functionality score (test case error over max
test case score)

Random node selection is used as the control benchmark against which our
version of node bias and selection is compared. We introduce node selection
bias through the use of a parameter tree [2]. When deciding where to apply
our crossover or mutation operator, we perform tournament selection based on
values in the parameter tree. Parameter tree values are initially set to 1 for every
node in the program. Where mutation is performed on a node, the nodes existing
value is inherited and updated. Where crossover is performed, all values from
the cloned parent are inherited. Values for nodes in the selected subtree from the
second parent are kept as the subtree replaces a subtree in the cloned parent.

We extend previous work [5] with a bias update rule which depends on whether
functionality has been entirely lost after offspring creation. Bias is decreased if all
functionality has been lost by a magnitude of how much functionality has been
lost as per the normalised functionality score. If some functionality is maintained,
bias is increased by the parent fitness over offspring fitness. Bias is updated in
both the parent and offspring.

Listing 1.1 shows a naive version of bubble sort which presents a problem that requires at minimum 2 changes to find the optimisation [23], replacing "i++" with "length- -". While this is a simple problem, it presents an example of imperative code with which we can observe the probability of various GP techniques in finding this optimisation.

Listing 1.1. Inefficient bubble sort

```
public static void sort( Integer[] a, Integer length){
  for (int i=0; i < length; i++) {
    for (int j=0; j < length - 1; j++) {
      if (a[j] > a[j + 1]) {
        int k=a[j];
        a[j]=a[j + 1];
        a[j + 1]=k;
      }
    }
  }
}
```

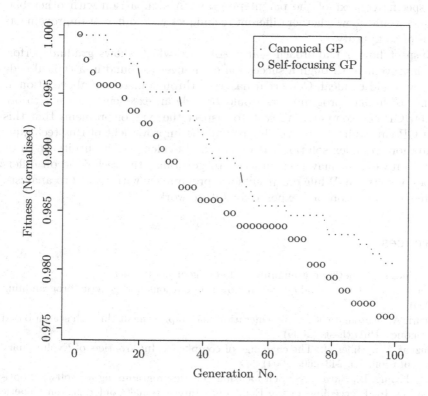

Fig. 2. Comparison of average best fitness for canonical GP against self-focusing GP

Our results as graphed in Figure 2 show the averages of the best fitness-es found in each generation for standard GP and GP with our node bias mechanism. The bias introduced by the rule set outperforms unbiased node selection, and on average has a higher probability of finding the optimisation yielding a lower average fitness.

A post-analysis of bias in programs shows high bias among leaf nodes. Ideally our approach should not just culminate in a bias which only distinguishes between leaf and internal nodes, but should also highlight locations for change throughout all program nodes.

4   Conclusion

As our work and that of Angeline [2] show improvement in GP, we seek to more rigorously inspect how this behaviour emerges. Initially our research will expand our experimentation by tuning the rules we use for allocating bias.

We believe that updating bias as part of the GP algorithm, as opposed to before the application of GP, should allow the algorithm to find improvements in more complex code given that bias can emerge and evolve as the individuals evolve. Bias may remain more predictive for producing offspring if it is updated in the specific context of the parent program. A comparison with other bias techniques would show whether different techniques yield different improvements in terms of complexity.

To inspect how our approach scales, software which shows gradual performance improvement through a succession of changes as found in a typical code repository would be ideal. Code that has gone through incremental evolution at the hands of human programmers would provide an excellent test case to observe how GP can compare. We seek to inspect the type of problems that this form of GP can address with the hope that the improvement of this technique can find more complex solutions. If we can find evidence of its utility on more complex software, we may then proceed to generalise the technique on different types of software. While our results are preliminary with regard to analysis, many research questions are exposed for future work.

References

1. Angeline, P.: Genetic programming and emergent intelligence
2. Angeline, P.: Two self-adaptive crossover operations for genetic programming (1995)
3. Arcuri, A.: Automatic software generation and improvement through search based techniques. PhD thesis (2009)
4. Banzhaf, W., Miller, J.: The challenge of complexity. In: Frontiers of Evolutionary Computation, pp. 243–260 (2004)
5. Cody-Kenny, B., Barrett, S.: Self-focusing genetic programming for software optimisation. In: Proceedings of the Eighteenth International Conference on Genetic and Evolutionary Computation Conference Companion. ACM (2013)

6. de Jong, E., Watson, R., Thierens, D.: On the complexity of hierarchical problem solving. In: Proceedings of the 2005 Conference on Genetic and Evolutionary Computation, pp. 1201–1208. ACM (2005)
7. Friedlander, A., Neshatian, K., Zhang, M.: Meta-learning and feature ranking using genetic programming for classification: Variable terminal weighting. In: 2011 IEEE Congress on Evolutionary Computation (CEC), pp. 941–948. IEEE (2011)
8. Harman, M., Mansouri, S., Zhang, Y.: Search based software engineering: A comprehensive analysis and review of trends techniques and applications. Department of Computer Science, Kings College London, Tech. Rep. TR-09-03 (2009)
9. Hengpraprohm, S., Chongstitvatana, P.: Selective crossover in genetic programming. Population 400, 500 (2001)
10. Jackson, D.: Self-adaptive focusing of evolutionary effort in hierarchical genetic programming. In: IEEE Congress on Evolutionary Computation, CEC 2009, pp. 1821–1828. IEEE (2009)
11. Kuperberg, M., Krogmann, M., Reussner, R.: ByCounter: Portable Runtime Counting of Bytecode Instructions and Method Invocations. In: Proceedings of the 3rd International Workshop on Bytecode Semantics, Verification, Analysis and Transformation, ETAPS 2008, 11th European Joint Conferences on Theory and Practice of Software, Budapest, Hungary, April 5 (2008)
12. Langdon, W., et al.: Directed crossover within genetic programming. Advances in Genetic Programming 2 (1996)
13. Langdon, W.B., Harman, M.: Genetically improving 50000 lines of C++. Research Note RN/12/09, Department of Computer Science, University College London, Gower Street, London WC1E 6BT, UK (September 19, 2012)
14. O'Keeffe, M., Cinnéide, M.: Search-based refactoring: an empirical study. Journal of Software Maintenance and Evolution: Research and Practice 20(5), 345–364 (2008)
15. Orlov, M., Sipper, M.: Flight of the finch through the java wilderness. IEEE Transactions on Evolutionary Computation 15(2), 166–182 (2011)
16. Poli, R., Langdon, W., McPhee, N.: A field guide to genetic programming. Lulu Enterprises UK Ltd. (2008)
17. Räihä, O.: A survey on search-based software design. Computer Science Review 4(4), 203–249 (2010)
18. Ryan, C.: Automatic re-engineering of software using genetic programming, vol. 2. Springer, Netherlands (2000)
19. Simons, C.: Interactive evolutionary computing in early lifecycle software engineering design (2011)
20. The Eclipse Foundation. Java development tools (November 2012), http://www.eclipse.org/jdt/
21. Weimer, W., Forrest, S., Le Goues, C., Nguyen, T.: Automatic program repair with evolutionary computation. Communications of the ACM 53(5), 109–116 (2010)
22. Whigham, P.: Inductive bias and genetic programming (1995)
23. White, D., Arcuri, A., Clark, J.: Evolutionary improvement of programs. IEEE Transactions on Evolutionary Computation (99), 1–24 (2011)

Exploring Optimal Service Compositions in Highly Heterogeneous and Dynamic Service-Based Systems*

Dionysios Efstathiou[1], Peter McBurney[1],
Steffen Zschaler[1], and Johann Bourcier[2]

[1] Department of Informatics, King's College London
{dionysios.efstathiou,peter.mcburney}@kcl.ac.uk, szschaler@acm.org
[2] IRISA, University of Rennes 1
johann.bourcier@irisa.fr

Abstract. Dynamic and heterogeneous service-oriented systems present challenges when developing composite applications that exhibit specified quality properties. Resource heterogeneity, mobility, and a large number of spatially distributed service providers complicate the process of composing complex applications with specified QoS requirements. This PhD project aims at enabling the efficient run-time generation of service compositions that share functionality, but differ in their trade-offs between multiple competing and conflicting quality objectives such as application response time, availability and consumption of resources. In this paper we present a research roadmap towards an approach for flexible service composition in dynamic and heterogeneous environments.

1 Introduction

Pervasive and mobile computation is about systems consisting of a large number of computational nodes with heterogeneous capabilities communicating over highly dynamic networks. *Service composition* [1] is an appropriate paradigm for creating complex applications in such environments where nodes' resources, such as data, network and hardware components, are offered as software services.

Mobile computing and pervasive applications present unique challenges when trying to compose applications with specified QoS due to the resource heterogeneity and high dynamism of both nodes and underlying networks caused by their inherent mobility. When composing services in such systems, continuous adaptation and optimisation must maintain the required functional and QoS levels of the application as the system evolves. The motivating scenario of our research is a fire-fighter decision support system [2]. The goal of the system is to combine services provided by heterogeneous devices such as sensors and tablets, to compose complex applications for assisting fire-fighters to make well-informed decisions within a crisis. For example, during a forest fire, a commanding officer may combine information (e.g. fire position, weather conditions) and prediction

---

* This work has been supported by the European FP7 Marie Curie Initial Training Network "RELATE" (Grant Agreement No. 264840).

G. Ruhe and Y. Zhang (Eds.): SSBSE 2013, LNCS 8084, pp. 312–317, 2013.
© Springer-Verlag Berlin Heidelberg 2013

services for estimating the evolution of the fire. The composed application must exhibit minimum response time to respect the above time-critical scenario.

Traditional approaches try to optimise the QoS of a composite application by considering only the selection of which concrete services to be coordinated by a central orchestrator [3,4]. However, they neglect to consider how the coordination of a composite application may affect its quality. To address this issue, we propose a flexible service composition model which considers the following three *degrees of freedom* (DoFs) for modifying the quality of a composition: (a) service selection, (b) orchestration partitioning, and (c) orchestrator node selection. These DoFs formulate the space of candidate configurations all of which realise the functionality of the targeted composite application, but each of which exhibits different QoS properties. The highly dynamic nature of the studied systems require timely exploration of configurations which best satisfy user's goals. This PhD aims to provide a run-time optimisation-based approach for automatic exploration of trade-off composite applications that share functionality, but where each of them differs in their quality trade-offs.

The paper is organised as follows. Section 2 presents the background to our research followed by Section 3 which states our research problem and roadmap. Section 4 describes the proposed approach. Section 5 discusses related work, before Section 6 summarises the expected contributions of this PhD.

2 Background

Service composition creates complex applications by aggregating services to provide composite functionality that none of the services could provide by itself. We use the concepts of *Concrete Service* (CS) which refers to an invocable service, and *Abstract Service* (AS) which abstractly defines the functionality of a service. Let a composite application be represented as a directed graph, as shown in Fig. 1, consisting of a node set $AS = \langle AS_1, AS_1, \cdots, AS_n \rangle$ of abstract services and an edge set $DF = \langle (AS_i, AS_j) : i \neq j, 1 \leq i \leq n, 1 \leq j \leq n \rangle$ of data flow between abstract services, where AS_i is the source and AS_j the data destination.

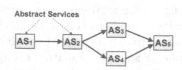

Fig. 1. An example abstract workflow plan

Currently, service composition is identified with *Orchestration* where a central entity coordinates the control and data flow between participating services. *Choreography* defines the interaction protocol between services from a global perspective with an emphasis on P2P collaboration. *Decentralised Orchestration* [5] lies between these two extremes where the coordination of the application is distributed to many nodes. Each orchestrating node integrates a local workflow engine and has only a partial view of the overall composition. The orchestrators cooperate with one another towards realising the complete application.

3   Problem Statement and Our Research Roadmap

In systems consisting of a large number of highly dynamic and heterogeneous nodes, the approaches of centralised orchestration and fully decentralised choreography result in suboptimal configurations [6] as they do not exploit the dynamic resource heterogeneity of both the nodes and the underlying networks.

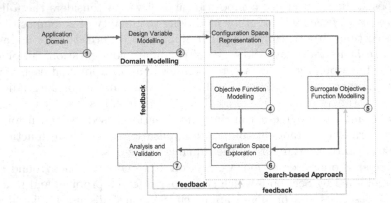

Fig. 2. The research roadmap of this PhD

To fill this gap, we propose the research plan depicted in Fig. 2 where darker colours indicate higher progress achieved so far. The first goal of this PhD project is to select an appropriate application scenario. The chosen scenario is a firefighter decision support system where heterogeneous nodes are deployed in an area of interest and form an ad-hoc network [2]. Then, we focus on providing a service composition model by enabling flexible coordination of composite applications. In step 3, based on the chosen model, we choose an appropriate representation of the space of possible composition configurations. Step 4 concerns the identification of the metrics of interest which will be used as the optimisation objectives towards exploring trade-off configurations. To estimate the real objective function of a configuration we use a resource-consuming simulation. As search algorithms require a large number of objective function evaluations to converge to a set of optimal solutions, we propose the replacement of the expensive simulation by surrogate models for approximating the quality values of a composition configuration (step 5). After choosing the problem representation and an appropriate (surrogate) objective function for guiding the search process, the next step is to define a suitable search algorithm for exploring trade-off, where we will particularly investigate the applicability of stochastic metaheuristics. Finally, we plan to validate the applicability of the overall approach and use the finding to refine the chosen representation, simulation, and optimisation.

4   The Proposed Approach

We now present our approach to enable automated exploration of optimal composite applications in dynamic and heterogeneous service-based environments.

4.1   Modelling Flexible Service Composition

Firstly, we propose a formulation for flexible composition of applications in dynamic and heterogeneous systems. We call the *Degree of Freedom* (DoF) a parameter of a configuration which is free to be varied to affect application's QoS while leaving its functionality unaffected. We propose the consideration of the following three DoFs for modifying a composition configuration: (a) selection of particular concrete services to implement the abstract services of the composition plan; (b) distribution of the control of the overall application into sub-orchestrations; and (c) selection of the nodes to host the various sub-orchestrations. The set of choices for realising a composition is called *service composition configuration*, while the set of all possible configurations is called *design space*.

Current composition approaches try to optimise the quality of a composite application by considering only the selection of particular services to participate in a centralised orchestration. However, in the context of highly mobile resource-constrained systems which are characterised by intermittent connectivity, it is hard to assume that a resource-rich orchestrator has a reliable access to all services in a composition or that such an entity even exists. The proposed approach chooses flexibly the appropriate level of decentralisation for a composite application based on the resource availability of the participating nodes.

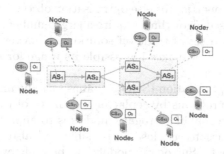

Fig. 3. An example concrete service composition configuration

In Fig. 3, 8 nodes share their services for composing the application in Fig. 1. To define a composition configuration, we have to make decisions for each of the three mentioned DoFs. Firstly, we have to select which concrete services to implement the abstract services of the application (1st DoF). In our example, CS_{12} is chosen for realising AS_1 out of two possible choices (CS_{11} and CS_{12}). Then, the initial composite application is decomposed into two sub-orchestrations (2nd DoF). Finally, $Node_2$ is responsible for coordinating the first sub-orchestration and $Node_4$ for the second one (3rd DoF).

4.2   Formulating Our Optimisation Problem

When considering multiple criteria, such as response time and battery consumption, there is no single optimal solution. Instead, there exist a set of Pareto-optimal solutions. Without having further information about user's goals, none of these trade-off solutions can be said to be better than another. To enable the exploration of trade-off configurations, we define the following:

Definition 1. Distributed Service Orchestration Problem

Given: A set of m abstract services that compose the service composition plan P, a set of n nodes where each node provides a single concrete service and can coordinate a single orchestration, a mapping between concrete service implementations and abstract services, and a set of q quality objectives $Q = \{Q_1, \cdots, Q_q\}$.

Problem: Find a representative set of composition configurations, all of which implement the functionality described by P, but differ in their quality trade-offs according to Q, by using different design options for the mentioned DoFs.

To solve an optimisation problem we have to define two key ingredients [7]: (i) a problem representation, and (ii) an objective function. The last step is to employ an optimisation algorithm for exploring the solution space.

Representation. We have designed a metamodel for specifying the space of possible composition configurations that realise a composite application, which is omitted due to lack of space. Based on this metamodel, we are able to produce model instances like the one described in Fig. 3.

Objective Function. To simulate the studied scenario, we plan to use the NS-3[1] to measure the QoS properties (or else optimisation objectives) of candidate configurations. Search-based algorithms require a large number of objective function evaluations to explore a set of trade-off solutions. However, the high computational cost of the simulator makes impossible its usage for runtime exploration of trade-off configurations.

Surrogate-Based Optimisation (SBO) [8] aims at reducing the computational time of optimisation problems by replacing expensive objective functions with surrogate models. The goal of surrogate models is to approximate the values of the real objective functions as close as possible and also be orders of magnitude cheaper to compute. Surrogate models can be built by using data samples produced by simulation runs for predicting quality properties of composition configurations, such as response time and battery consumption.

4.3   Validation Strategy

The goal is to understand the ability of our approach to explore promising composition configurations by various simulation-based empirical studies. The use of simulation avoids the costly and impractical physical testing of such systems and gives us statistical power by allowing repeated experiments. Firstly, we aim to study the suitability of the proposed formulation for composing applications in highly dynamic and heterogeneous environments. Then, we will investigate the ability of the developed surrogate models to guide the search towards promising areas of the search space. Finally, we plan to study the ability of the developed SBO technique to provide configurations of high-quality during runtime by measuring the execution time for exploring solutions of acceptable quality.

---

[1] http://www.nsnam.org/

5   Related Work

QoS-aware service composition approaches can be grouped into centralised and decentralised. In the first category, the goal is to find the set of concrete services to participate in a centralised orchestration that offer the required functionality, respect user's preferences and constraints, and optimise composition's QoS [3,4]. However, these approaches focus on networks with abundant bandwidth and stationary nodes and neglect to study the problems of centralised orchestration.

On the other hand, Schuhmann et al. [6] proposed a hybrid configuration of distributed applications in the context of pervasive environments by adjusting the level of decentralisation based on the number of available resource-rich nodes. Fdhila et al. [9] proposed a decentralised approach for composing applications by decentralising a composition into partitions of services that communicate frequently, towards optimising the overall QoS of the composition. However, existing approaches do not adapt automatically to changing conditions such as resource availability and network connectivity.

6   Contributions

The expected contributions of this PhD can be summarised as: (i) a design space formulation for flexible composition of applications in highly dynamic and heterogeneous service-based environments; (ii) a search-based approach for efficiently exploring trade-off compositions ; and (iii) a surrogate-assisted approach for accelerating the search process of optimal configurations.

References

1. Papazoglou, M., Georgakopoulos, D.: Introduction: Service-Oriented Computing. Comm. of ACM 46, 24–28 (2003)
2. Efstathiou, D., McBurney, P., Plouzeau, N., Zschaler, S.: Improving the Quality of Distributed Composite Service Applications. In: ICCSW (2012)
3. Canfora, G., Di Penta, M., Esposito, R., Villani, M.L.: An Approach for QoS-Aware Service Composition Based on Genetic Algorithms. In: GECCO (2005)
4. Cardellini, V., Casalicchio, E., Grassi, V., Iannucci, S., Presti, F.L., Mirandola, R.: MOSES: A Framework for QoS Driven Runtime Adaptation of Service-Oriented Systems. TSE 99 (2011)
5. Sheng, Q.Z., Benatallah, B., Dumas, M., Yan Mak, E.O.: SELF-SERV: A Platform for Rapid Composition of Web Services in a Peer-to-Peer Environment (2002)
6. Schuhmann, S., Herrmann, K., Rothermel, K.: Efficient Resource-Aware Hybrid Configuration of Distributed Pervasive Applications. In: The 8th PerCom (2010)
7. Harman, M., McMinn, P., de Souza, J.T., Yoo, S.: Search Based Software Engineering: Techniques, Taxonomy, Tutorial. In: Meyer, B., Nordio, M. (eds.) LASER Summer School 2008-2010. LNCS, vol. 7007, pp. 1–59. Springer, Heidelberg (2012)
8. Jin, Y.: Surrogate-assisted evolutionary computation: Recent advances and future challenges. Swarm and Evolutionary Computation 1(2), 61–70 (2011)
9. Fdhila, W., Dumas, M., Godart, C., García-Bañuelos, L.: Heuristics for Composite Web Service Decentralization. In: SoSyM, pp. 1–21 (2012)

Applying Search in an Automatic Contract-Based Testing Tool

Alexey Kolesnichenko, Christopher M. Poskitt, and Bertrand Meyer

ETH Zürich, Switzerland

Abstract. Automated random testing has been shown to be effective at finding faults in a variety of contexts and is deployed in several testing frameworks. AutoTest is one such framework, targeting programs written in Eiffel, an object-oriented language natively supporting executable pre- and postconditions; these respectively serving as test filters and test oracles. In this paper, we propose the integration of search-based techniques—along the lines of Tracey—to try and guide the tool towards input data that leads to violations of the postconditions present in the code; input data that random testing alone might miss, or take longer to find. Furthermore, we propose to minimise the performance impact of this extension by applying GPU programming to amenable parts of the computation.

1 Introduction

Automated random testing has become widely used, in part because it is inexpensive to run, relatively simple to implement, and most importantly has been demonstrated to be effective at finding bugs in programs; the technique having been implemented in several testing frameworks including AutoTest [7], Korat [1], and Randoop [8]. Using random testing comes with the cost of only using straightforward strategies, and in particular, not leveraging information from previous executions or specifications that—if provided—might otherwise help guide towards test data revealing undiscovered bugs.

The AutoTest framework targets programs written in the object-oriented language Eiffel, which natively supports *contracts* [6], i.e. executable pre- and postconditions for routines (although the framework could be adapted to other contract-equipped languages such as Java with JML). Contracts go hand-in-hand with random testing, with preconditions serving as *filters* for test data, and postconditions serving as *test oracles*. Furthermore, there are techniques to guide the selection of inputs towards ones that satisfy preconditions, e.g. the precondition-satisfaction strategy of AutoTest [12]. We claim in this short paper however that there is still more to be gained from contracts in automated testing. In particular, we propose that contracts are ideal for integration with search-based techniques for test data generation [5]; passing tests could be "measured" against how close they are to violating the postconditions, with *fitness functions* then favouring input data that optimises this measure. This strategy

G. Ruhe and Y. Zhang (Eds.): SSBSE 2013, LNCS 8084, pp. 318–323, 2013.
© Springer-Verlag Berlin Heidelberg 2013

exploits ready-to-use contracts to focus the generation of test data towards objects that get closer to violating postconditions, hence possibly revealing bugs that random testing alone might miss, or take longer to find.

Applying search to test data generation is of course a computationally more expensive task—whilst the envisaged techniques might reveal individual bugs that random testing might miss, the approach quickly loses appeal if the ratio of bugs encountered over time suffers. Hence, we propose to investigate how to implement the computationally expensive parts on modern GPU devices, following on from previous work in the search community (e.g. [13]).

The rest of the paper is structured as follows: Section 2 provides an overview of AutoTest and how search-based techniques might be applied; Section 3 speculates on measuring how "close" input data is to deriving outputs that violate postconditions; Section 4 discusses the application of GPU computation to search; and Section 5 outlines our plans and concludes.

2   Extending the AutoTest Workflow

Having introduced the idea of AutoTest in the previous section, we illustrate its workflow via a simple example. Consider the square root routine in Listing 1; implementation details are not given, but we provide its contract. The precondition, given after **require**, expresses that the input is non-negative; the postcondition, given after **ensure**, expresses the same. Recall that in AutoTest, preconditions are filters and postconditions are oracles. Hence in this example, sqrt is only tested on non-negative inputs, and any negative output indicates that its implementation does not meet its specification.

```
sqrt (a : DOUBLE) : DOUBLE
require
   a >= 0
ensure
   Result >= 0
end
```

Listing 1. Square root contracts

The current workflow of AutoTest is roughly as follows: firstly, random inputs satisfying the routine's precondition are generated. Secondly, the routine is executed on the generated data. If there is a postcondition violation, then the test fails and is recorded. Otherwise, the test passes. The overall picture is shown in Figure 1.

This workflow however does not take into account information from *successful* test cases. Currently, we can say that they satisfied the test oracle; but more interestingly, can we measure how "close" they came to failing it, and use this information in search to derive input data that gets even closer? A high-level picture of the proposed extension to AutoTest is shown in Figure 2. We discuss the issues of search and measuring "closeness" in the following section.

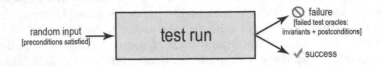

Fig. 1. High-level overview of the AutoTest workflow

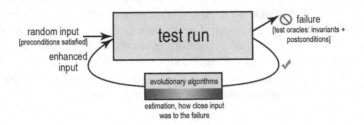

Fig. 2. High-level overview of the proposed extension to the AutoTest workflow

We remark that search was applied to AutoTest previously in [10]; however, their approach differs in that they use genetic algorithms to generate an efficient testing strategy by evolving random ones. Other authors [3] have suggested that condition coverage on postconditions—in a testing tool for Java programs equipped with contracts—seems promising in generating test data, but as far as we know, did not publish implementations or evaluations of such algorithms.

3   Optimising Postcondition Violations

A key part of our proposal involves evaluating how "close" input data is to deriving a postcondition violation. We propose to follow Tracey [11], who defined *objective functions* for logical connectives and relations over data of primitive types. The concepts can be applied to similarly simple contracts, so we illustrate with an example (based on the counter algorithm presented in [11,5]). A *faulty* wrapping counter is shown in Listing 2. It is supposed to take an integer between 0 and 10 (see the precondition), returning that integer incremented by 1 if it was less than 10, and 0 otherwise (see the postcondition).

We can negate the postcondition, and add it in conjunction to the precondition to form a constraint only satisfiable by input data that derives a fault; for example:

$$(n \geq 0 \vee n \leq 10) \wedge \neg((n = 10 \rightarrow Result = 0) \wedge (n \neq 10 \rightarrow Result = n + 1)).$$

We can apply Tracey's objective functions to the relations and connectives of the constraint, yielding a value indicating the "closeness" to satisfying it (smaller values indicating that we are closer). For example, for relations $a = b$, we can define $\mathrm{obj}(a = b)$ to return the absolute difference between the values of a and

```
cyclic_increment (n : INTEGER) : INTEGER
require
  n >= 0 and n <= 10
do
  if (n > 10) then
    Result := 0
  else
    Result := n + 1
  end
ensure
  (n = 10 implies Result = 0) and (n /= 10 implies Result = n + 1)
end
```

Listing 2. Faulty wrapping counter

b. Other relational predicates can be measured in a similar fashion. Objective functions are defined inductively for logical connectives. For example, consider the formula $a \vee b$. A suitable definition of $\mathrm{obj}(a \vee b)$ would be $\min(\mathrm{obj}(a), \mathrm{obj}(b))$, i.e. the minimum value of the two parameters. With a fitness function including such a measure, we hope to apply metaheuristic search techniques [4], optimising the search towards input data that gets closer to violating postconditions (i.e. revealing bugs).

In our wrapping counter example, the smallest output of the objective function should be yielded for $n = 10$, since the implementation incorrectly increments the counter for this value.

For real object-oriented programs, we encounter the challenge of hidden states: objects tend to conceal their implementation details. For example, a routine of a bounded buffer might assert in its postcondition that the buffer is not full. Expressed as buffer.count < buffer.size, we can apply objective functions as we have described. However, the postcondition might instead be expressed as not buffer.is_full, i.e. a Boolean query. Boolean queries are not informative for metaheuristic search because of their "all or nothing" nature. In this example, we cannot distinguish between a buffer that is completely empty and another that is close to being full. Postconditions containing Boolean queries should be transformed into equivalent postconditions that are more amenable for testing. A solution proposed by [2] is to "expand" Boolean queries using their specifications; an approach compatible with our contract-based one. For example, the postcondition of is_full might express that the result is true if and only if count >= size; this being an assertion to which objective functions can be applied more successfully.

4   Performance Considerations

The ideas described in the previous sections do not come for free. Additional computation increases the running time of the tool, and may adversely affect the ratio of bugs found over time. In order to keep the performance as reasonable as possible, we propose to apply GPU computing to speed-up the computationally intensive aspects of the search. Consider for example the family of genetic algorithms (GAs). The population can be encoded as a numerical vector, and the fitness function as a vector function $f \colon \mathbb{R}^n \to \mathbb{R}$.

Essentially, the GA input can be represented as a matrix $m \times n$, where m is the population size, and n is the size of the chromosome vector. Thus, to evaluate a fitness function, one just needs to apply some vector function to each matrix row. A mutation operation (changing chromosomes of some species subset) can also be performed row-wise. Crossover operation is also essentially row-based.

GPUs are very different to conventional CPUs. Whereas CPUs are designed as general-purpose computing devices, with lots of optimisations like branch prediction, multi-level caches, etc., the processing units of GPUs are much simpler. A GPU's processing unit cannot handle the processing of arbitrary data as efficiently as CPUs can; they do not possess sophisticated hardware optimisations. However, there are many more processing cores on a GPU device, compared to the CPU. GPUs are tuned for data parallelism, implementing the SIMD (Single Instruction - Multiple Data) processing model, allowing the execution of thousands of threads in parallel. GPUs have proven to be extremely efficient with matrix-style computations [9], providing a convincing speed-up of 2-3 orders of magnitude.

GPU acceleration was used for the problem of minimising test suite size in [13], and demonstrated that speed-ups of over 25x are possible using GPU computing.

5   Research Plans and Conclusion

The proposed ideas—namely implementing search-based techniques to improve the fault discovery rate of a contract-based random testing tool, and using GPU acceleration to limit the performance hit—need to be carefully evaluated. While we believe that search will enhance the quality of inputs in AutoTest, there are several risks and challenges to be dealt with along the way to confirming or disproving this hypothesis.

A first challenge is the previously mentioned implementation hiding in object-oriented languges, that makes guided search ineffective without first transforming Boolean queries into postconditions that are better suited for objective functions. A second challenge: one should never forget that the goal of testing tools is to reveal as many faults as possible. That is why the enhanced tool needs to be tested against previously successful strategies, e.g. the precondition-satisfaction strategy [12] of AutoTest.

Thirdly, some thought needs to be given as to the particular type of search algorithm to apply (e.g. a genetic algorithm), and how to best encode the objects and data on which these algorithms operate. The final choice will be determined by the quality of inferred data and amenability to GPU-style computations. Finally, one needs to take into account, that GPU acceleration may be overwhelmed by the additional overhead of copying data from main memory to the GPU, and vice versa. Thus, GPU computing should only be applied to computationally intensive parts of the proposed AutoTest workflow.

Acknowledgments. The research leading to these results has received funding from the European Research Council under the European Union's Seventh Framework Programme (FP7/2007-2013) / ERC Grant agreement no. 291389, the Hasler Foundation, and ETH (ETHIIRA). The authors would like to thank Simon Poulding for helpful discussions.

References

1. Boyapati, C., Khurshid, S., Marinov, D.: Korat: automated testing based on Java predicates. In: Proc. International Symposium on Software Testing and Analysis (ISSTA 2002), pp. 123–133. ACM (2002)
2. Cheon, Y., Kim, M.: A specification-based fitness function for evolutionary testing of object-oriented programs. In: Proc. Genetic and Evolutionary Computation Conference (GECCO 2006), pp. 1953–1954. ACM (2006)
3. Cheon, Y., Kim, M., Perumandla, A.: A complete automation of unit testing for Java programs. In: Proc. International Conference on Software Engineering Research and Practice (SERP 2005), pp. 290–295. CSREA Press (2005)
4. Harman, M.: The current state and future of search based software engineering. In: Proc. Future of Software Engineering (FOSE 2007), pp. 342–357. IEEE (2007)
5. McMinn, P.: Search-based software test data generation: a survey. Software Testing, Verification and Reliability 14(2), 105–156 (2004)
6. Meyer, B.: Object-Oriented Software Construction, 2nd edn. Prentice Hall (1997)
7. Meyer, B., Fiva, A., Ciupa, I., Leitner, A., Wei, Y., Stapf, E.: Programs that test themselves. IEEE Computer 42(9), 46–55 (2009)
8. Pacheco, C., Lahiri, S.K., Ball, T.: Finding errors in. NET with feedback-directed random testing. In: Proc. International Symposium on Software Testing and Analysis (ISSTA 2008), pp. 87–96. ACM (2008)
9. Ryoo, S., Rodrigues, C.I., Baghsorkhi, S.S., Stone, S.S., Kirk, D.B., Hwu, W.W.: Optimization principles and application performance evaluation of a multithreaded GPU using CUDA. In: Proc. Symposium on Principles and Practice of Parallel Programming (PPOPP 2008), pp. 73–82. ACM (2008)
10. Silva, L.S., Wei, Y., Meyer, B., Oriol, M.: Evotec: Evolving the best testing strategy for contract-equipped programs. In: Proc. Asia Pacific Software Engineering Conference (APSEC 2011), pp. 290–297 (2011)
11. Tracey, N.J.: A Search-Based Automated Test-Data Generation Framework for Safety-Critical Software. PhD thesis, The University of York (2000)
12. Wei, Y., Gebhardt, S., Oriol, M., Meyer, B.: Satisfying test preconditions through guided object selection. In: Proc. International Conference on Software Testing, Verification and Validation (ICST 2010), pp. 303–312. IEEE (2010)
13. Yoo, S., Harman, M., Ur, S.: Highly scalable multi objective test suite minimisation using graphics cards. In: Cohen, M.B., Ó Cinnéide, M. (eds.) SSBSE 2011. LNCS, vol. 6956, pp. 219–236. Springer, Heidelberg (2011)

Author Index

Alexander, Rob 251
Andrade, Aline Santos 188
Arora, Vikhyat 294
Asoudeh, Nesa 288
Assunção, Wesley Klewerton Guez 19
Atkinson, Colin 239

Bansal, Priti 294
Barrett, Stephen 306
Barros, Márcio de Oliveira 34, 188, 275
Bechikh, Slim 50, 245
Ben Chikha, Soukeina 50
Ben Said, Lamjed 245
Bian, Yi 111
Bourcier, Johann 312
Boussaa, Mohamed 50
Briand, Lionel 66, 141
Bruckmann, Thomas 141
Buzdalov, Maxim 300
Buzdalova, Arina 300

Chen, Kathy 66
Chen, Tsong Yueh 224
Cheng, Betty H.C. 81
Cheng, Jun 111
Cinnéide, Mel Ó 126
Clark, John A. 251
Cody-Kenny, Brendan 306
Colanzi, Thelma Elita 19

de Souza, Jerffeson Teixeira 172
de Vega, Francisco Fernández 282

Efstathiou, Dionysios 312
El Boussaidi, Ghizlane 96

Farzat, Fábio de Almeida 275
Fredericks, Erik M. 81

Ghannem, Adnane 96

Harman, Mark 224, 257

Kalboussi, Sabrine 245
Kessel, Marcus 239

Kessentini, Marouane 50, 96, 126, 209, 245
Kessentini, Wael 50
Kolesnichenko, Alexey 318
Koskimies, Kai 269
Kumar, Vineet 294
Kuo, Fei-Ching 224

Labiche, Yvan 66, 288
Langdon, William B. 257
Li, Zheng 111

Maciel, Rita Suzana P. 188
Mahouachi, Rim 126
Malik, Shreya 294
Matinnejad, Reza 141
Mayo, Michael 158
McBurney, Peter 312
Meyer, Bertrand 318

Nejati, Shiva 141
Nogueira, Ana Filipa 282

Oriol, Manuel 251

Paixão, Matheus Henrique Esteves 172
Parfenov, Vladimir 300
Patrick, Matthew 251
Petke, Justyna 257
Pitangueira, Antônio Mauricio 188
Poskitt, Christopher M. 263, 318
Poulding, Simon 263
Poull, Claude 141
Pozo, Aurora 19

Ramirez, Andres J. 81
Ribeiro, José Carlos Bregieiro 282

Sabharwal, Sangeeta 294
Schumacher, Marcus 239
Shelburg, Jeffery 209
Sievi-Korte, Outi 269
Spacey, Simon 158
Systä, Kari 269

Tauritz, Daniel R.   209

Vathsavayi, Sriharsha   269
Vergilio, Silvia Regina   19

Weimer, Westley   1
White, David R.   16

Xie, Xiaoyuan   224

Yao, Xin   4
Yoo, Shin   224

Zenha-Rela, Mário Alberto   282
Zhao, Ruilian   111
Zschaler, Steffen   312